FREEDOM OVER FEAR

The Business Owner's Guide to Achieving Financial Freedom

Shanine Alessia Young
Fenisha Walters
Jordan Young
Eric Jackson
Brittny Ortiz-Jackson
Monique Singleton
Nishia Slater
Latoya Whitfield

Filled with Inspirational Stories, Practical
Tips & Strategies from Business Owners.

Freedom Over Fear: The Business Owner's Guide to Achieving Financial Freedom.

Scripture quotations marked NLT are taken from the New Living Translation Version.

Printed in the United States of America.

ISBN: 978-1-7379081-3-5

Imprint: Independently Published.

Books may be purchased in bulk quantity and/or special sales by contacting the publisher at info@reachingwhileteaching.com

Book Cover Designed by Katarina
Edited by Camile Jené and Crystal Clear Editing

To book any of the co-authors for speaking engagements, contact them directly or email Shanine Young at info@reachingwhileteaching.com for more information.

Table of Contents

This is a collection of stories and advice shared by eight business owners who decided to choose Freedom instead of Fear.

Caution: You might notice a loss of fear while reading this book and a greater desire to go after your goals and dreams.

Pre-face

Matthew 7:17-20 says:
Likewise, every good tree bears good fruit, but a bad tree bears bad fruit. A good tree cannot bear bad fruit, and a bad tree cannot bear good fruit. Every tree that does not bear good fruit is cut down and thrown into the fire. Thus, by their fruit you will recognize them. NLT

I lead with this verse, so as the reader, you can understand that the author of this book Shanine Young, my sister in Christ, is rooted in good soil and her book is evidence that she is bearing good fruit. She has helped several entrepreneurs fulfill their dream of becoming self-published authors. To further illustrate this point, she also allowed several inspiring people to be co-authors of this book. When you know that the gift God has honored you with is just for you, you gain the freedom to genuinely collaborate and help others receive the same success as you.

Freedom Over Fear is an extension of all the gifts, talents, and abilities God has blessed Shanine with, packaged so eloquently to bless others to achieve the very same things she has accomplished. It is a transparent, candid, and captivating book written to address how the mind can keep you from being free. It is written from a place of wisdom with tangible solutions to help YOU overcome fear and walk with the confidence God already gave you to receive an overflow of financial blessings and opportunities.

Here's something to ponder on: can you recall a time when God placed someone in your life and used them as a vessel to fulfill your God-given purpose? I know without a doubt God placed this amazing woman of God in my life to complete an assignment that I put off for far too long. I met Shanine through a few mutual business partners who turned into my family, The 9-5 CEO's. As a mindset and business coach, I am elated to see my sister incorporate mindset in her pursuit to bring other entrepreneurs up with her. Mindset is a crucial topic for all my clients because no matter how many courses, money invested, or cute social media posts, you won't see the growth you want and deserve if you don't have a mindset shift. I was given the honor to write this preface because God knew that this was the push and motivation that I needed to publish my first book. I allowed fear and imposter syndrome to prolong writing the book God gave me a name for years ago. Thank you to Shanine and all the co-authors who wrote this book for people like you and me that just need a genuine push. I am no longer afraid, and I can't wait for you to read and feel the same way.

Wilda Jean
Mindset and Business Strategist
The CEO Transformation

Introduction

Last time I checked, there were over 143,000,000 people around the world entering these five words in the Google search bar every few seconds, "how to become financially free". This question keeps many people up at night and causes them to seek answers. Many people are not okay with just getting by, they want to be in control of their finances and life choices. It would not be very reasonable to think that none of these people are business owners or entrepreneurs. However, many of these searches are from millions of people who started or are too scared to start a business or are in the process of creating a business plan. Therefore, financial literacy is critical; whether you are a current or aspiring business owner or enjoy your 9-5 employment, I urge you to take some time every day to educate yourself on this topic. Financial stress can contribute to headaches, absences from work, sleep problems, depression, relationship issues, and much more.

As the visionary author of this book, I remember googling those five words and desperately searching for options to increase my income. I might not have been poor to the point where I didn't know where my next meal was coming from, but I was unhappy with my financial situation. I desired more freedom and did not like having to stress about money. I realized something had to change, and that change had to start with me. So, I began to switch up my morning routine, changed my environment, invested in myself and my business, and began to see things change for me. I began to seek out ways I could become mentally, physically, and spiritually stronger. From creating positive daily habits to taking courses on various topics, I have seen so many benefits from investing in the things that matter most. I believe that mindset is everything so I decided to no longer operate with a broken and doubtful mindset.

My husband Jordan and I decided it was time for us to share with the world our viewpoint regarding Financial Freedom and how money or the lack thereof can impact so many areas of our lives. We came together, brainstormed and came up with the topic for this life changing book. *Freedom Over Fear: The Business Owner's Guide to Achieving Financial Freedom* provides you with practical strategies and tips from several successful business owners to help you improve your mindset and finances. This book sheds light on some of the reasons we operate in lack and may be struggling financially, it touches on the possibilities that come from releasing fear and embracing freedom.

While you are reading, I urge you to take notes and start applying some of the strategies shared in each chapter so that you can begin walking in financial, emotional, and spiritual freedom. The common theme throughout this book is that financial freedom looks different for everyone and you shouldn't allow fear to hold you back from experiencing true freedom.

Building My Legacy One Day at a Time

Shanine Alessia Young

Self-Publishing Coach and CEO of Reaching
While Teaching
www.reachingwhileteaching.com
Instagram.com/reachingwhileteaching
Facebook.com/reachingwhileteaching

Shanine Alessia Young is a full-time entrepreneur who is passionate about helping entrepreneurs publish and market the Right book that will grow their business and help them make an impact. She is a wife, mother of one and devoted believer. She believes everyone is gifted with unique abilities and skills that they can use to impact the world and make a difference. Her love for and expertise in content marketing allows her to assist her clients with strategies that help their business/brand increase visibility and profitability.

Working in the educational sector as a Certified English teacher for over seven years has allowed her to develop skills to not only reach but teach her clients how to be confident and strategic about the goals they have for their book and business. Shanine has helped numerous entrepreneurs turn their idea into reality by coaching them through the process of getting their book published and has coached over 100 entrepreneurs on content marketing. It brings her great joy when she sees her clients shift their mindset and start to see Results!

Building My Legacy One Day at a Time

1. Share what you do and how you got into this business.

I am a teacher at heart. I taught in the education system for the past eight years as a certified English Teacher before I decided it was time to use my passion for teaching and empowering entrepreneurs. I help entrepreneurs grow their businesses by teaching them how to publish and market the right book. I strongly believe that every business owner should be a published author for several reasons. It is a way for you to show that you are an expert in your field, it can help you land speaking opportunities, and can create several different streams of income for your business.

I got into this business shortly after I published my first book. I thoroughly enjoyed the process of being in control of the creative process and being my own publisher. Don't get me wrong, it was a lot of long and restless nights, endless google searches, and countless calls to mentors and coaches where I tried to pick their brain. The process was not easy and it took longer than I expected. God gave me the vision and the name of my book in the summer of 2017 and I started writing, but I was unsure how to take this from the idea phase to the published stage. I took a pause in writing for about a year, then went on to continue writing in 2018. While writing, I began to research to try and figure out the next steps to take in order to get my book published correctly. Working full time as an educator is very time consuming and it was difficult juggling the two but I found a way to make it work.

Once I became a published author, and got recognition and features in different press releases and podcasts, several individuals became curious about what it took to reach this accomplishment. They wanted to know how long the process took and the requirements to get their book published. I mentored a few people and grew a passion for assisting in getting their book from the idea phase to the published phase. Two months after publishing my book I created a course that walked authors through the process of getting published and unique ways to market their book. That led to the Reaching While Teaching coaching program for authors which transformed into my exclusive Books 2 Impact coaching program. This is a very detailed and structured coaching program where I get to work closely with entrepreneurs and show them how to write, publish, and market the right book that will grow their business. There is a self-paced course attached, a plethora of resources, and services that are infused into the program to ensure it is a smooth publishing process. Weekly one-on-one or group coaching sessions are also available. The program is constantly evolving and my clients are killing it. Every week, they are checking off the goals we set in our weekly coaching sessions, constantly increasing sales, and most importantly, increasing their confidence.

I am a Coach; therefore, I help push my clients past the finish line. I treat them all like family and it's crazy to see how one act of obedience in writing my first book led me to this point.

2. What were some of the fears you experienced before venturing out and starting your business?

Before starting my business, I feared the opinions of others. I used to wonder and worry about what this person might say if I announce this new book or program. It crippled me at my core because growing up I was known as a people pleaser. My motive was always to make others happy but it became unhealthy because I remember several times going out of my way to do so even if that meant putting myself in a worse position. People pleasers tend to act out of insecurity and in the back of my head I feared disappointing others and what they would think of me. I went back and forth a few times before announcing my business and registering it with the state of Florida.

Before venturing out and taking that leap of faith to become a full-time entrepreneur while homeschooling my daughter, the list of fears just kept getting longer and longer. Would I make enough to assist my husband with the bills? Would people look at me differently? Would I be able to juggle all of this and my other responsibilities?

3. How did you overcome those fears/obstacles? Was it worth it?

Fear starts in the mind but so does freedom. I overcame these fears by shifting my mindset. I had to start speaking what I wanted to see happen and refusing to let these fears discourage me or cripple me. I became more intentional about writing down affirmations, writing down my goals, and going after them one by one. I had to fill my mind with more scriptures that challenged any limiting beliefs I had.

Even after I started my business, some of these fears of feeling inadequate and doubting my earning potential and whether I deserved to be making 5 and 6 figures in my business continued to linger. I remember several mornings, waking up earlier than usual and going to my physical prayer closet and sitting on the floor and looking over my goals and checking my progress. Each month God would exceed my expectations.

One of the biggest fears for me to overcome was fearing what people would think of me and what they might say about me once they started to see me pursue my dreams and grow my business. My family is one of the reasons I kept going despite the opposition and questioning I received from a few people who could not understand the vision God gave me and my family. Putting them first and visualizing what I wanted is what helped me to stop fearing or worrying about other people's opinion. At the end of the day, I have to answer to God and be accountable for my actions. If He told me to go left but I think everyone else thinks I should go right and I disobey Him because I fear what people may think, then essentially, I fear people more than God. I must constantly remind myself that God's approval is all I need.

Earlier this year, my husband and I decided to take a leap of faith. We sold our home in Florida, made a good profit from it, and then moved to Georgia to pursue our business dreams. It was quite difficult leaving my job as an educator and the majority of my family behind in Florida and having to homeschool my daughter while running my business full time. At first, I had no idea what I was doing. And my almost two-year-old daughter was dealing with severe allergies. That was my biggest concern. We had to get tests done, change her diet several times, and simply be there for her. Once we started to see progress, I realized I had to get a system in place and get my daughter on a schedule to be able to effectively run my business, hold coaching sessions with my clients, and teach courses.

Taking action and setting goals helped me to start making progress and reach my monthly income expectations. Strategy is key, and once I started setting SMART (Specific, Measurable, Attainable, Realistic and Time-Bound) goals for my business and stopped stressing about whether I would make enough to help support my family, that's when I started to make the impact and income I desired.

4. When did you realize it was time for you to start working towards your own financial freedom? What difficulties did you face?

Once I realized that there is nothing wrong with being wealthy, I started taking the necessary steps to become financially free. Growing up I heard so many parables & Bible verses about how it's harder for a rich person to get into heaven and how the love of money is the root of all evil. Subconsciously I don't think I had the right attitude towards money. I knew I needed it but I always would say that I want to be comfortable and don't ever want to be rich. Maybe I believed I would become evil. From experience, I've noticed people tend to do a lot of evil because they don't have money. They steal, become so desperate that they even kill just to make ends meet and rich people tend to cut many corners and scam people as well.

My mindset towards money was my biggest challenge; since a teen I've always been a hustler. I was nicknamed "go getter" because I always found creative ways to increase my income from selling candy bars to washing cars. I knew money was attainable but I just feared what would happen if I obtained too much of it. There were moments in my childhood where it seemed my family were balling in cash and then moments where we had to be a little conservative with our money. Those times probably encouraged me to continue to hustle and save my money and that drive carried into my adulthood. From the age of 18 to 30, I would work every summer and put money aside for a rainy day. Making money wasn't too much of a problem for me since I've always been resourceful but understanding that it's okay to be wealthy and knowing all the ways to make my money work for me was a little challenging and difficult to understand while growing up.

In addition, knowing that I wanted nice things in life and did not want to have to ask my parents for everything helped me see it was time to become financially free or at least try my best to not be broke. My parents instilled principles in me and helped me see the importance of managing my money and how I needed to set money aside every paycheck for my savings. It was difficult trying not to keep up with the Joneses and being as responsible as I could be with my money but I had a goal in mind so I remained motivated. I might not know all the tips and tricks on how to make my money work for me but I do know a few and those few tricks worked for me.

5. Financial freedom does not happen overnight and takes work. Share three actionable steps that show you are serious about achieving financial freedom.

1. Shift your mindset (Money Mindset)

If you are serious about achieving financial freedom then you need to make sure you have the right mindset. Start changing the voices you let in your head. Reevaluate the shows you are constantly watching. Be intentional about reading books, listening to podcasts, and watching videos and shows that will help you become more financially literate. This book is definitely a good start. Doing these things can help you improve your set of beliefs and attitudes towards money. You want to have a positive and healthy mindset towards money because someone with the right mindset and actions can make anything happen.

Sometimes we struggle to even dream about a hopeful turnaround for our future financial situation, because our mind is stuck on what we are lacking and how things are not working out in our favor right now. You might feel you don't deserve any better.

Try to understand the limiting beliefs that you currently have; write them down and be honest with yourself, then next to them write down new beliefs you want to have towards money. Maybe you think you will always be broke or you will never be able to retire. Let's cancel those negative mindsets and swap them out with some of these positive ones:

Positive mindsets to have:

- It's possible to achieve my financial goals
- I can be wealthy and emotionally healthy
- I will be able to retire when I want
- I don't have to live paycheck to paycheck
- I am a giver
- I am ending the cycle of being broke
- I am financially FREE

2. Start a side hustle

I recommend using some of your gifts or skills to help you establish a side hustle in order to get one step closer to becoming financially free. Of course, you can earn a couple more bucks a month, and you might even grow a passion for your side hustle and want to turn it into a legitimate business. A side hustle can help you reach your financial goals faster, build your emergency fund, have extra spending money, pay for travel, and have more flexibility.

If you are good with writing then here are some ideas below on what you can do to start earning some extra income.

Writing side hustles:
- Write resumes and cover letters for people looking for jobs
- Create an eBook and sell it on Amazon
- Write articles or blogs online for sites like textbroker.com or medium.com
- Become a ghostwriter for people interested in writing a book

If you are great with designing and are creative, then you might want to explore these design options.

Design side hustles:
- Create logos for businesses and websites
- Create social media graphics for businesses
- Design book covers for authors
- Design websites for people and businesses

If you are good at organizing, these might be the best options for you to consider.

Organizing side hustles:

- Declutter and organize homes and office spaces
- Organize and plan events or parties for people
- Set up and organize a sales funnel for businesses (slight learning curve)

If interested in learning more about decluttering and organizing homes, check out https://www.itsordered.com for inspiration.

If you are a teacher or great with kids and enjoy spending time with them, you might want to explore these options.

Teacher/kid involved side hustles:

- Babysit your neighbor's or family member's children
- Tutor online or in person (inceducationllc.com is a great company)
- Provide Test Prep for exams or score test items
- Become a curriculum developer

- Become a part-time instructor at community centers or after school programs

If you are artistic or musically inclined then these side hustles might work for you.

Artistic/Music related side hustles:

- Create instrumentals for artists
- Become a live DJ
- Become a make-up artist
- Create a podcast
- Perform at concerts or events

These are only a few ideas. There are so many ways to make money online and offline. If you love animals then consider dog walking or pet sitting jobs. Below are some of the recommended websites and resources for you to check out to find opportunities and announce opportunities if you are ready to start a side hustle and start making more money:
1. Fiverr
2. Upwork
3. Freelancer.com
4. LinkedIn
5. Inceducationllc.com
6. Local Newspaper
7. Facebook Groups
8. NextDoor app
9. Shopify, Etsy, Wix.com (ecommerce)
10. Uber eats and DoorDash
11. OfferUp (sell items)
12. Amazon KDP
13. Anchor.fm (podcast sponsorships available)
14. Clubhouse app (networking, donation opportunities)

15. Contena for Freelance and Remote Writing

3.   Use your credit card wisely

Our actions can sabotage our financial future and that's why so many people stay broke forever. Credit cards are a tool and should be used correctly and effectively. Do not use your credit cards like you don't have to pay back the money you charge.

"Our actions can sabotage our financial future and that's why so many people stay broke forever."

Only use what you have in your bank account or money that you actually have available. I always try to pay the statement balance when my credit card bill is due instead of the minimum balance due to the fact that I do not like to pay interest on my money. It is wise to pay off your full balance every month to avoid paying the interest. This is not possible if you spend more than you can pay for any given month.

Here are 5 more tips to help you use your credit card wisely:
- Try to use a credit card that offers rewards
- Remain under 30% of your total credit limit (Be mindful of your utilization)

- Only use your credit card for necessities and not wants
- Set up balance alerts (for example you can set an alert for when your card approaches 30% of your credit limit)
- If possible, go online and pay your balance early before the balance is due, preferably in the middle of the billing cycle.

Credit cards are tools and to reiterate, it is important to remember when you pay for something with a credit card, you are obligated to pay that money back later so you must be wise.

6. Based on your expertise, share three practical tips/steps other entrepreneurs can take to continue to grow their business.

1. Slowly remove yourself from your business

I read this tweet on Twitter not too long ago that stated, "You don't really have a successful business until you're able to step away from it and verify that it can continue to thrive and grow on its own." If you are wondering how this is possible, I will give you a few pointers on how you can get closer to this goal.

First things first, start *delegating.* Build a team of professionals who are stronger in areas that you are either weak in or don't care to work in. Assign them certain tasks. For example, get someone that is skilled in graphic design to create your logo or social media posts for the next month. These could be paid jobs, you can hire contractors or you can get a family member to intern with you and provide them with experience to add to their resume. Forming partnerships and collaborations also help you to be able to delegate tasks and step away from the business a bit.

It is not very wise to get too attached to your business to the point where you are willing to see it crumble because you don't want to get anyone else involved with tasks that you need help with. Certain areas such as accounting, administration, and email marketing should not be the business owners' responsibility anymore after a certain point. The goal is to run the business without having to be all in it. The goal as a CEO is to be able to do the tasks in your business that brings you joy. For me, connecting with people and coaching them brings me joy so I want that to take 90% of my time.

2. Automate your business

Putting the right automations in place makes life so much easier for a business owner. According to kissflow.com, automation is the use of technology to execute recurring tasks or processes in a business where manual effort can be replaced. Setting up the right systems for automation can help your business run more efficiently and increase your profit. Certain automations can also help you acquire more leads, increase your engagement, provide customer service, and eliminate human error.

Responding immediately to certain emails are crucial; responding a day too late might decrease your chances of qualifying a lead. There are website hosting platforms like Wix.com that allows you to create forms on your website and set up an automatic response once someone fills it out. This response can also be in the form of a free piece of content. For example, you can offer a free eBook, video, or another type of resource to individuals who sign up for your email newsletter.

Depending on what you need in your business, there are a few ways to automate the process. Here are some helpful apps and tools that I love to use and some of these have been recommended by a few of my business partners who were able to scale their business to over 6 figures.

Content scheduling apps/tools:
1. Planoly
2. Zoho Social
3. Later
4. Coschedule
5. Buffer
6. Tweetdeck
7. Sendible
8. Hootsuite

Content Creation/Publishing Automation

1. Elink.io – this site allows you to choose sources and add filters to make your content relevant. You can convert weblinks into beautiful visual content that you can share as HTML email newsletters. This saves you so much time.
2. Coschedule – this site allows you to automate social media campaigns and other tasks because it integrates with your social media platforms, blog, and email while allowing you to manage your entire content all in one place.
3. Tailwind – this site also allows you to automate the process of publishing and sharing content along with other activities related to the creation, distribution, and promotion of your content. It even generates hashtag suggestions for Instagram posts.

Automatic Social Media Message Replies:
1. IM Auto Reply (Best for Facebook Messenger, WhatsApp
2. Mobile Monkey (Best for Instagram)
3. Crisp.chat (Best for Twitter, Facebook, Whatsapp and more)

Schedule emails:
1. Vacation Responder for emails
2. Mailchimp (suite of tools to help you create beautifully designed emails and allows you to schedule and send emails and check your stats.)
3. HubSpot (allows you to schedule sales emails directly in Gmail.)

While you have automations in place, you want to make sure you are setting boundaries in business as well so that you do not have clients and customers having access to you after hours. Have email/message responses that can assist them or remind them of your office hours or hours of operation.

3. Charge your worth

As business owners, we must consider the value, time and effort we are bringing to the table when it comes to the prices of our products and services. Do not worry about the few people who might have an issue if you decide to raise your prices and start to focus on making a profit for the services and products you provide. People are either going to be okay with your prices or they are not going to be okay with them. Your ideal customer will gladly pay for your product or service because they see the value in it.

All of the investments I have made into myself and my business is one of the main reasons why I realized I needed to increase my prices and start charging my worth. When I first started coaching entrepreneurs and helping them become published authors, I was not as confident as I am today and due to my lack of confidence, my prices were dirt cheap. I was overworked and underpaid and although it felt good making an impact in their lives, I was also extremely drained. My workload kept increasing as my client load increased and at times I found myself doing more than coaching. Since I was destined to see my clients succeed, I would go above and beyond and do extra tasks that they probably should have been doing themselves. As months went by and I saw that each client kept getting results and I kept bringing them past the finish line in helping them become published authors, that's when things clicked for me even more.

Knowing the difference between what you are getting and what you deserve are two different things. In life, sometimes we settle, and as a business owner, I am no longer settling and charging less than what I am worth. Once you accept this realization and know your worth then you can confidently state your price and charge your worth. You will notice you will start to attract a certain clientele because you exude the confidence and expertise they can spot from a mile away.

This book is very personal for me because it feels so liberating being able to pursue my dreams of being a full-time entrepreneur. This vision of creating and orchestrating this collaboration project has been on my heart for a while now and I needed to make sure that I reached out to people who shared the same vision as me. Every single co-author was brought to my attention in my quiet time with God and I reached out to them and it was so divine how they were all onboard and ready to share their stories of freedom.

If I could provide you with some more words of advice, I would encourage you to put aside any pride you might have because you might need to network and lean on others in order to be successful. We can't do everything on our own. Asking for help takes strength and humility. And it shows you care about your business more than your ego. Sometimes it's not easy to trust people. It is definitely a process, but every day I'm stretching and growing so that my business can do the same. I will encourage you with this; trust that you did your research on that business partner or assistant of yours and they are capable of fulfilling their role. Team up with the right people that can help take your business to the next level and make sure your visions are aligned.

How to Connect with Me:

If you want to make an impact and write that book that God has been telling you to write then watch this brief video to learn a little more about the Books 2 Impact Coaching Program by scanning the QR Code with the camera on your mobile device.

Acknowledgements

Thank You To My Pre-Order Supporters

1. Tiasha Jones
2. Terrence Isom, Creative Floor Design, LLC
3. Sherine Isom
4. Gabriella Gabbidon, IG: @thedaillylifeplanner, https://msha.ke/thedailylifeplanner/
5. Jordan, @jyoungsfl, Jyoungsfl.com
6. Phillip Bryant, Phillip Bryant LLC, Maximize your Moment Purpose Coaching, IG: Imphillipbryant, www.phillipbryant.com
7. Gavin Duff, Orda 66 Paintball, orda66paintball.com
8. Annalesia, Stylish Empress, FB, Annalesia Bennett www.stylishempress.com
9. Vivian Gamble
10. Charnele Coley, Charnele Coley's Tutoring Services, FB: Charnele ichooseu Coley
11. Stephanie Williams, Stephanie Speaks LLC, IG: Steph.Speaks, www.destinedtoconquer.com
12. Chelsie Purcell
13. Marcia Young, Valencia's Caribbean Fusion, valenciasrestaurant.com
14. Tyahna Campbell, Future Attorney
15. Nicolene Smiley
16. Tameka Harty, T. Harty Designs
17. Nicolene Smiley
18. Garth Campbell
19. Monica Tookes, Tookes Time, LLC,
20. Terry-ann Porter, Nurse Terry, msha.ke/nurseterry
21. Joni Fletcher
22. Glenesha Webster, Amazin Tax & Financial, Amazin_Financial, Amazincredit.com
23. Bee-yonce (Bee Gallimor)

24. Christiana Smith, Christo's Closet, FB: christocloset, www.christocloset.com
25. Philip Akinsulire, Philip AK, Social media: @philipak418, www.Lyfeaktivation.com
26. Jennifer Brown, FB: Jennifer Brown, Realtor
27. Patricia Rollé
28. Rebecca Campbell
29. Patrice Duncan, Social media: @PatriceCetrine
30. Jason Smiley
31. Georgia Thomas
32. Imani K Brown, Little Inkplay shop, @lipsbrand.online, littleinkplayshop.com
33. Tricia Lewis, Vintage Glam Events & Design consulting, IG: @vintage_glam_events, https://www.vglamevent.org/
34. Jillean McEwan, QEJEWELRY , IG: qejewelers, www.qejewelry.com
35. Maxine Polanco-Duff, Protocol, IG: protocol585, FB:protocol, www.maxprotocol.net
36. Ashley Anglade
37. Jasmine Ramsey, Elevated Expression, IG: elevatedexpression, www.elevated-expression.com
38. Patricia Semiens, IG: itsmommietyme, www.itsmommietyme.com
39. Valary Campbell, Glory House USA, Inc.
40. Daphne Beard, Agape Support Services, IG:drbeard_7, www.drbeard7.com

God's Plan: My Winning Season

Fenisha Walters

Pharmacy Student and Product Developer
www.julietshealing.com
Instagram.com/julietshealing
Facebook.com/julietshealing

Juliet's Healing was founded by Fenisha Walters, a pharmacy student, who witnessed her mom, who's middle name is Juliet, having medical complications. She would see her mom using essential oils and smelling salts to soothe her conditions. With this background, along with her own skin sensitivities, she wanted to create solutions that would cater to all skin types and conditions thus establishing her skin care business, Juliet's healing.

"Let your conversation be always full of grace, seasoned with salt, so that you may know how to answer everyone."Colossians 4:6 NLT

God's Plan: My Winning Season

1. Share what you do and how you got into this business.

How I stepped into Juliet's Healing is a journey. I miraculously got accepted into pharmacy school at the peak of the COVID 2020 season. With that being said, the loans are about 32k per year. I told the Lord, "I am not graduating with a six-figure debt!" I began to brainstorm many ideas, I read numerous books on mindset, I watched many videos on having multiple streams of income, and I researched numerous investments. I took it a bit further to read books about how to make money while in school. I started with making a few investments in the stock market and then left it at that. At this point, I was still working my 9-5 job; I wasn't completely worried. Things took a turn as my skin sensitivities increased due to being indoors during COVID.

One night, I decided to make my own soap and to give it a try. That night, I made a honey turmeric soap. It was the hardest and gooiest bar I have ever made. The honey was oozing out of the bar, and I sprinkled the turmeric throughout. I dashed turmeric on top of the soap as well. Measurements were out the door with the additives! However, it worked! My skin cleared up and I felt amazing.

I told my friends about the soap and asked them if they wanted to try it. They did, and they gave me good reviews as well. They loved how the bar lasted longer than the typical two weeks, the smell, and how it made their face feel smooth. Once I got these reviews, I spoke to my father about starting a business. He gave me advice and said, "Go for it." From there, with the leftover I received from financial aid, I invested into the soap making business. I started by buying a book about soap making, skincare, and essential oils. My aunt shared with me her essential oils and books to be used for certain health conditions. I then invested about 3k on equipment, carrier oils, butters, and essential oils. At first, I was using water as a part of my base. Then I switched to goat's milk due to the additional benefits. Next, I decreased the number of scents used in the bars because some individuals' skin health was deteriorating due to being on lockdown.

Initially, the process was exhausting. Soap making takes about 4-5 hours total if you're doing it in one sitting. First, the initial calculations of butters, oils, lye, and the liquids. Followed by mixing the lye and water or goat's milk to form a solution. Then, the butters and oils must be weighed and melted down. After, the oils and the lye solution have to be cooled to a certain temperature, or the finished product will have cracks, or a gel phase, which doesn't look aesthetically pleasing. In addition, if too much lye or too much liquid is used in the solution, the soap may not form as it should. Too much lye leads to lye-heavy soap which has lye seeping through the soap once cut and it can burn the consumer's skin. This has happened to me, twice! Loss of profit, twice! Finally, the solution is poured into the oils, blended, and poured into the mold once the consistency is to my liking. In the end, the exhaustion you received while reading this process, is the exact exhaustion I experience while doing the process but about 5x greater. Not to mention, once the soaps are cut, they must dry for 4-6 weeks before use. In the end, low turnover time and small return on investment. Unless larger batches are made consistently to have stock for each week and/or month, this process will need to be done quite often to make a greater profit. Or higher prices, in which many did not want to pay. I started with $9-13 a bar; it didn't last long. The prices steadily started declining and the number of bars I made did, as well.

Upon my initial review of the soap making business, I realized this wasn't the best move to only sell soaps. The soap making took up too much time, and I was taking 19 credits that semester (Yes, Pharmacy school and soap making can work but the scale tips towards studying over making soaps). With that being said, God and I had a conversation about branching out and products that can be readily accessible. Then BOOM! BODY ODY ODY BUTTER!

Body Ody Ody Butter was an instant success. Every time I made them; they would sell out quickly. The quality and longevity of the body butter made customers want more. From the body butter, I started making body butter tubes, lip balms, and more.

Rewind to the soap making, I had a hiatus and completely started making body butters and other products. I allowed the soaps I made to sell out and I honestly did not know what God had in store for that section of Juliet's Healing. Until… Jamaica happened. I met this amazing woman and I connected with her. She has inspired the JamRock collection, and she and her family are the ones who make all the JamRock soaps. This was when I truly understood, "Be still and know that I am God." God knew I had no intentions of making soaps anymore, He decided on opening the door for me. Today, I still make specialty soaps that consumers tell me to make in abundance. However, the majority of the soaps are made in Jamaica, and it motivates me to keep going, knowing that I am helping a family simultaneously.

2. What were some of the fears you experienced before venturing out and starting your business?

My definition of fear is an entity or state of emotion or being that is inflicted on oneself that creates emotions of anxiety, discouragement, and in the end – failure. Truth be told, I am a major risk taker. I enjoy making decisions that may not be completely "safe." With that being said, I didn't have any fears of losing money or anything of that nature. Money comes and goes; I've been with and without. My major "fears" were within myself.

Some emotions I battled with were not being good enough, what if it doesn't succeed, and how can a perfectionist create an imperfect business.

Not being good enough – number one silent killer. Insecurities have a way of seeping in every now and again. There are times when I reflect on past decisions and circumstances, and it creates a whirlwind of self-doubt. This self-doubt manifests itself in many areas whether it's making the right decisions or saying the right things. In addition, I'm a PK (pastor's kid) and all eyes are on you consistently. We must uphold an image and remain on a pedestal that we never asked for. It creates a battle of trying to be a human and trying to maintain that perfect picture. The reality is that while the perfect picture is being held up, behind the picture is what matters. When a façade is being portrayed for an extended amount of time, you tend to forget your identity, value, worth, standards, and yourself. This results in the feeling of not being good enough because you don't know who you are or what you are capable of.

What if it doesn't succeed – Let's create a perspective. I have been an A/B student since I started school. The reason I was able to be this student is because I study for hours and hours. It is easier to become prepared for a subject that you are being taught and what you have knowledge in. However, there are no blueprints for an entrepreneur because everyone has their own story. There are times when I tend to create and present excess pressure on myself. In the end, you can only exert so much. I've witnessed many things in my family. I felt as if I needed to succeed in everything that I did to create a smooth pathway for myself and to please my parents. This mentality was good up to a point. When I ended up in urgent care trying to do everything and be the best at everything, I had to ask myself, "Is it worth it?"

The perfectionist creating an imperfect business – I tend to be a perfectionist. YES, I do. I analyze situations before I step into them. They must have order and it must make sense. I have sat for hours to get the situation perfect. Again, it's easier to perfect a craft that has been established for you. Perfecting an idea that you yourself are creating can be terrifying. This perfectionist is trying to create a perfect business. However, the perfect business doesn't exist.

3. How did you overcome those fears/obstacles? Was it worth it?

Before I could start a business or move forward in life, I had to face myself and those limitations I placed on myself. I had to tell myself, the horizon is there, but I will go beyond it. For, the horizon in itself is a limit because that is as far as our eyes can see. I had to remove people, situations, and habits to get to this place of saying "Girl, you are more than enough." I went through a period of re-evaluation of myself. I went through my fears, traumas, and bad habits. I had to face each of them and put them all behind me. Once they were behind me, I stepped into the improved version of myself.

The pressure became my friend. At the end of the day, a little pressure is healthy. I had to learn how to not be in opposition to pressure, but to rearrange it. For instance, it takes less energy and force to go down a hill, but to go up the hill, you expedite more energy. I gained the ability to cope with pressure and manipulate it to only come forth in certain situations and circumstances. How? First, I stopped giving my attention to negative aspects and situations. I looked for positivity and peace in every activity. I removed certain people that weren't contributing to my well-being. I told myself, "I will walk alone if I must." I try not to compare myself to others or look at them and want to be like them. I look in my lane and stay in it. The reason is due to the creation of anxiety.

Next, I changed my schedule to better fit my vision and the career path I wanted to be on. I stopped doing activities for a "just because" reason. Every activity must have a reason and/or purpose or, time has been wasted. Peace is always worth it!

Perfectionist was thrown out the door quickly. I have made soaps that came out perfect and others that had to be thrown out. My dad has this motto, "Once excellence becomes a tradition, there is no end to greatness." I turned from the perspective of perfection to finding excellence and how I can bring excellence to the table. Excellence meaning, I have put my best foot forward and did it to the best of my ability. It may not be perfect, but it portrays and exemplifies the work that has been put into it. That is what matters, finding the beauty in everything you do. The beauty motivates the dream and the vision.

4. When did you realize it was time for you to start working towards your own financial freedom? What difficulties did you face?

Six figure debt: Debt is like carrying a burden on your shoulders. It amazes me how many are content with having to pay off a student loan for the next 30-50 years, if not, for the rest of their lives. They think they are making dents in their student loans, until they see the amount of interest they have been paying and the balance that remains. Graduate students don't get the option of having a subsidized loan on a regular basis, unfortunately.

Dependency: One of the worst feelings is to have someone hold something over your head. The feeling as if you need them to survive. The majority of the activities I partake in and the decisions I make, are based on my desire to live a certain lifestyle and to be independent. Not only for myself, but for the generations that come after me. They can see the blueprint laid for them and not have to live a life of bondage to anyone or anything.

Working for someone else: One of my biggest pet peeves is working for someone else. Let me clarify, working with someone and working for someone are two completely different things. I personally do not enjoy working for someone else while I sit at a desk with aches and pains. Being told when you can take a break, come in, clock out, how many days you can take off, etc. However, I understood that to be a leader, you must learn how to follow first. I had a few jobs, up until February 2021. February 2021, I made the decision to walk on my journey.

Unhappiness: I was unhappy with certain situations, living arrangements, many aspects of my life. I decided that I needed to make changes. In addition, I know how it feels to be checking your account and get a bit depressed. It happens, but we all start somewhere.

Something that I have built: Having something to my name is a motivation factor. I created this business not only for myself, but for those who look up to me. Most of the decisions I make and do are for my nieces and nephews to feel as if they can accomplish anything, like their aunt.

The main difficulty I faced was prioritizing business and school. At the start of my business, I was mainly focused on school and a couple hours would go towards the business. Now, I set out hours throughout each day to accomplish a specific goal for both the business and school. For instance, one day the goal would be to read and study Heart Failure and take product pictures to upload on the website. Every day, I work on both priorities.

5. Financial freedom does not happen overnight, it takes work. Share three actionable steps that show you are serious about achieving financial freedom.

Who/what/where/when/why/how:
     The first step to achieving financial freedom is to answer some preliminary questions. Here are a few:

What is your definition of financial freedom?
What are you going to do?
What are your goals?
What is your purpose?
Who do you need to help make it happen?
Where do you see yourself in the next 5 years?
Where are you going to place this product or vision?
When are you going to achieve financial freedom?
When is the best time for you to start working toward financial freedom?
Why do you want to achieve financial freedom?
How are you going to implement strengths and weaknesses within the plan?
How are you going to reach others?
Use these answers and analyze your current situation and position.

Strength VS weaknesses:
     Second Step: Analyze your strengths and weaknesses. Once you analyze both, write down your vision. How will your strengths enforce the vision? How can you maximize your weaknesses to become strengths? A weakness isn't an error or a fault. Look at your weaknesses as a character trait to work on. Every weakness, do an activity that can test it. For instance, I had a weakness in public speaking. I

decided to do more public speaking. Now, I can stand in front of a crowd and feel comfortable and in the end, it is no longer a weakness.

R&D:

This is the most important step – research and development. Once you have an idea, have your goals written down, etc., begin your research. Reading is fundamental! Buy a kindle edition or a physical book. I started with buying wealth mindset books to begin my journey. Why? Your mind is one of your greatest assets. The more you invest in it, the more your mind will come into alignment with your ideas and decisions. YouTube is everyone's friend. Utilize all resources possible.

Networking is your best friend. Talk to people in the area you want to grow in. Connect with those who will instill "gems." A wise man told me, have a couple people above you, on the same level as you, and below you. Look up to those above you, relate to those on your level, help those below you. Balance is key.

Keeping a financial journal can be a part of development if this is your forte. Chase has a free financial journal you can use to track your finances, write down your financial goals, and more. Use these tools to develop your financial success and progress.

6. Based on your expertise, share three or more practical tips/steps other business owners can take to continue to grow their business.

Set a foundation and build on it – Building a strong foundation is critical. Plan your budget, pay yourself first, build business credit, keep your personal and business finances separate, and define your meaning of financial freedom. Most importantly, ask yourself, how do you contribute to your foundation?

Be honest with yourself and your business – Everyday will not be a great day in the beginning. Stay encouraged and positive, for it is only the beginning. Don't be discouraged; everyone has a story. Use your low days to make a Reel for Instagram or an email campaign. The more you put in, the more you will get out.

Watch your circle like a lion watches its prey – On your journey, people will come and go. It is essential for growth to experience change. If people are not benefiting or encouraging you, reconsider those types of people.

Pray 1000x – Pray about everything. The Lord will not lead you astray.

Envision it, write it down, make it happen – Habakkuk 2:2 (KJV) says, "And the Lord answered me, and said, Write the vision, and make it plain upon tables, that he may run that readeth it." Write where you want to be for the next 5, 10, 15, and 20 years.

Every change begins with you – Believe it or not, nothing can happen in your business until you decide to make the first step. The first step being in your mind, translates to your vision, then transfers to your actions. The business will not be known until you say something or do something.

I decided to be a part of this book mainly because I thought my story wasn't worth it. That feeling of doubt makes me want to do more. I turn those doubts into gold. In addition, for those who are juggling school and business, you can do it! It is a challenge, but you will overcome it.

Some words of advice: Many times, we create our own weaknesses or fears. If you are called for a reason and a season, you have already been prepared for it. Many doors will open, but wisdom will lead you to the door and carry you behind the door.

Always ask questions, the more you ask, the more you will know.

Read! Knowledge isn't power unless it is used and applied and translated for generations to come.

Run after the dreams that aren't as tangible and ~~Foundation~~ easy to obtain. The hard dreams are where you build your perseverance, persistence, endurance, and longevity. This foundation will allow you to stand during the storm because they will come to test the land on which you stand.

Always have a back-up plan. Finally, always remember to give thanks.

I leave you with these final words, "do it despite your fear." – Dr. Adwoa Nornoo

How to Connect with Me:

If you want to purchase any of our handmade luxury soaps filled with organic, quality ingredients then visit julietshealing.com

Acknowledgements

Thank You To My Pre-Order Supporters

1. Bivions Gamble, (FB) Vivian Gamble
2. Ronnie Gumbs
3. Odette Dixon
4. Renneil Sherman, Sherman Chiropractic Center, (IG) shermanchiropracticcenter, www.shermanchiropracticcenter.com
5. Sue-Ann English-King, FB: C&S Catering and Decors
6. Niesha Mack, Party rental service Bounce-up Entertainment, PYQ Hair (Pretty Young Queens Hair)
7. Desrene Stewart, Author of "Birthing Praise Out of Your Pain" and host of "Transformation Egg to Butterfly", www.desrenestewart.com
8. Cashus Clay, Sun and Moon Essentials, IG: sunandmoonseamoss, sunandmoonessentials.com
9. Lorna Dunn, Spry Recovery Room- *Toni Dunn, Physical Therapist*, Instagram: spryrecoveryroom
10. Ayanna Walls
11. Doreen Wright
12. Faith Lanuzo
13. Aliceson Swaby-Smith
14. Leo-Paul Brown
15. Maxine Coley
16. Alex Scarlett
17. Omar Henry, GR8NESS ENT, IG: @gr8nessent, Fb: Gr8ness Ent. www.GR8NESSENT.com
18. Taylor Alexander, Flawless Damsels Boutique,Ig: flawlessdamsels FB: Flawless Damsel Boutique www.flawlessdamsels.com
19. Living Word Christian Center International Ministries, IG: livingwordccim, Churchofchoice.com

Faithing It 'Til You Make It

Jordan " Jyoungsfl " Young

Musician & Logistics CEO
www.jyoungsfl.com
Instagram.com/jyoungsfl
Facebook.com/jyoungsfl

Jordan Young is commonly known as Jyoungsfl. He is an independent recording artist, vocal producer, songwriter, and musician. Young is also an entrepreneur whose eyes are set on providing opportunities for people to advance and become their own boss. He is the co-founder of Valencia's Transportation Services, a logistics corporation based in South Florida.

"When preparation meets opportunity, that's where you will find success."

Faithing It 'Til You Make It

1. Share what you do and how you got into this business.

I am a musician, artist, and songwriter from Sunny South Florida. A husband and father of one, and a proud owner of three businesses. These businesses include; an entertainment business, a print shop, and a logistics business.

I have spent most of my years being involved in music in some way, shape, or form. At the age of five, I gave piano a shot. Watching my older brother play had a big influence on me. He taught me how to play my first song on the piano and was amazed at how fast I learned to play. I immediately fell in love. With my mother being a choir director and so active in church, I quickly became fascinated with the performing arts at a young age. As I grew older, I drew inspiration from artists and producers like Michael Jackson, Chris Brown, Ryan Leslie, and Kanye West which led me to become an artist and songwriter. Now at 28 years old, I produce, song-write, and create music that is enjoyed all across the globe. Music is a passion of mine and I have always felt called to it.

My story is quite unique. I went to school to study electrical engineering while working in the field as a cable technician. Being raised by Jamaican parents inspired me to indulge in entrepreneurial endeavors, so on weekends I would perform at different venues. In no time, I became an engineer and held a position at one of the leading companies in the aviation industry. I was thrilled; making a salary that far surpassed my parents when they were my age, and doing something that I really enjoyed. I was a top performer. I drove 120 miles daily to commute to work and frequently worked overtime, without a problem, in order to meet and exceed company goals and expectations. Our team of engineers started at about 6 people. Eventually some of these individuals took on different roles or other jobs and our team soon became minimized to 2 people. With the team being so small, our workload pretty much tripled. Of course, I rose to the challenge. The two of us held things down for about 2 months before the company hired new engineers. I trained these new hires to also be the best at their game, and they excelled.

March 2019, my wife Shanine and I were anticipating the birth of our daughter. At this time the company was experiencing some slowdowns and was on the verge of laying off one of the new hires. In order to take these individuals off the chopping block, they approached me. They asked if I could temporarily take a demotion, retain full pay, and upon returning from Paternal leave, I would reclaim my position. They expressed that because I was the only one with technician experience, I was also the only one capable of making a move like this. To be honest, I was a bit hesitant. I was hesitant because I'd heard of the company giving people the "short-end" of the stick, but never experienced it myself. I was trusting and it felt like the Christian thing to do, so I agreed.

April 25, 2021 our daughter was born, and we were so overjoyed. After a month of being home with my family, I showed up to work expecting to go back to my original position. They claimed they needed me to stay at this position a while longer, because things had not "ramped up" the way they had hoped. Six months later, I had enough and wanted my position. They promised to give me back. They refused to restore my role, and claimed the terms of our verbal agreement never happened. After all I had given this company, I could not believe they would renege on their promises and ignore all the sacrifices I'd made. After this experience, I made a vow to myself to never be dependent on a company again. I continued to work for this company, while building up a nest-egg for business investing. By June 2020, COVID was affecting businesses worldwide, and as a result, I was furloughed. This gave me the push I needed to start and legally establish my second business, Thunder Printshop. Thunder Printshop is focused on providing small businesses with graphic design and custom apparel. This business really thrived throughout the peak of the 2020 COVID pandemic and served several local businesses and other companies throughout the United States.

Fast forward to 2021, Shanine and I decided to move to Georgia. This was a huge sacrifice; however, we took the leap of faith in hopes of expanding our network and net-worth. After selling our Florida home, we walked away with a great deal of equity. Eager to invest, we sought out lucrative business opportunities that would serve as an asset to provide residual income and allow us to make money in our sleep. After speaking with a friend about his business venture in logistics, I became intrigued and decided to do my own research about this line of work. For those of you who are unaware, logistics is the commercial activity of transporting goods to customers. The most captivating part of my introduction to this industry was how lucrative it could be versus how much work is actually involved. Once I did all the necessary research and formulated a plan, I quit my job and bought my first vehicle. After three months of being in business, I now have two vehicles and two drivers to transport goods.

2. What were some of the fears you experienced before venturing out and starting your business?

Before stepping into full-time entrepreneurship, we developed a lifestyle that made leaving the security of our 9 to 5 jobs extremely scary. We feared not having enough to make payments on time, losing our home, savings, and livelihood. The fear of being uncomfortable without the security of a steady income outweighed my desire for freedom. Uncertainty made taking that leap of faith impossible for us. Outside of the financial fears of not being able to provide for my family, there were a plethora of psychological fears that kept me bound.

Initially, I started recording music out of my house with a very minimalist set up that consisted of a headset, microphone, and some desktop speakers. Professional studios have equipment which are valued at tens of thousands of dollars, and in some cases much more. In my efforts to create high quality music, I believed in the notion that the products that you create have to be perfect before releasing them in the marketplace. This belief coupled with the lack of resources caused me to become fearful and doubt whether I should be pursuing a career in the music industry.

One of the biggest fears regarding music was not feeling adequate enough or able to measure up to a certain standard. While I was confident in my talent, I found myself falling prey to the comparison trap and seeing where others were in their careers and I started to measure my level of success up against the achievements of others. One of my biggest desires in my pursuit of a successful music career is making timeless music. I want to make music that not only touches the soul but inspires people and impacts their lives. I was fearful that with all my efforts, because of poor sound quality, everything I was doing was in vain. I was afraid that I would fail because I just didn't know how to make the transition from hobby to business.

When I was furloughed in 2020, my fear was that with running my own business I wouldn't be able to bring in enough money to provide for my family. With this doubt I questioned whether or not I should pursue the print shop business venture or start applying for other means of work. The print shop business was uncharted territory and something new that I did not know much about so I doubted the income potential. All I knew was there was a need and I would be able to fill that need. I shared similar fears before starting my logistics business. At this time in my life, being a husband and father fueled my determination for success but there was always that fear of failing.

3. How did you overcome those fears/obstacles? Was it worth it?

The way I overcame my fears is simple. I was sick and tired of being sick and tired. I felt extremely betrayed by the company I worked for and was later furloughed from. A lightbulb went off from the moment I decided I was fed up and had had enough. My company did not care about my work ethic, contribution, sacrifices I'd made for them, if I had problems going on at home, or anything else pertaining to my personal life. To them I was just a "number" that affected their bottom line. As long as I worked for them, they had no reason to treat me differently because of one reason. I needed them. I needed the money. I needed financial security. I realized that I was a slave to my own fear. The fear was so great, I became a slave to my 9 to 5. When I came to this realization, I didn't want fear, a company, or anyone else to ever have so much power over me again. My desire for freedom became greater than the overwhelming fears I had. My desire to focus on fulfilling my dreams became greater than the desire to fulfill someone else's.

Becoming my own boss was extremely worth it. I gained a lot more time to spend with my family, and the extra hours I was putting in were rewarding and fulfilling. I was able to focus on expanding my music career, and help others achieve their branding initiatives. I found that by helping others, I was able to help myself and that was the most exciting part for me.

4. When did you realize it was time for you to start working towards your own financial freedom? What difficulties did you face?

I realized it was time to start working towards my own financial freedom when I found myself "owning a job." What do I mean by that? As an employee, I worked a mandatory 40 hours a week and about 10-15 hours of voluntary overtime. When I left work, my job for the day was done. I didn't have to worry about answering phones, sending emails, or completing an assignment. Once I left for the day, I was free to do as I pleased. There isn't really a clock in/clock out set up as an entrepreneur or small business owner. If you don't get the job done, you don't make any money.

Eventually, my business started to really pick up some momentum and the work became overwhelming. It was easy for me to do 70+ hours weekly. It became exhausting and I started to see it as a chore rather than a business. With all the uncertainty surrounding COVID, I did not feel comfortable inviting anyone into my house to work for me, so I had to do what many of our South Florida natives understand as "thug it out," the term which means to press on. For some time, my wife helped me fulfill many of the orders, but without an end date to the pandemic, I knew I needed to pivot. That's when I decided to get into logistics.

Logistics is the overall process of managing how resources are acquired, stored, and transported to their final destination. As mentioned earlier, I was informed by a friend about this industry. He built his business to the point where he was hands-off and he was making money in his sleep. This is a common goal for anyone seeking financial freedom. I had no previous experience, other than my colleague's recommendation. At this point, I had already lost my security of a 9 to 5, and was being overwhelmed with the workload from the print shop. So, I approached this opportunity with an "all or nothing" attitude. In my research, I found out that Atlanta, Georgia is considered the transportation hub. It serves as the center for logistics and supply chain. At the time, I found this so intriguing because there are so many opportunities for expanding my music career as well. My production team had already been considering making the move for some time, so this felt like the perfect timing. The cost of living in Atlanta compared to South Florida was also very attractive. When I presented the idea to Shanine, the idea of relocating was unthinkable. Both our lives had been built in South Florida. Our families, friends, church family, and overall support were there and by moving we'd be sacrificing that close proximity with our loved ones. We both had a lot to lose but so much to gain. After showing her my plans, we prayed about our decision, and let God do the rest. Eventually we got the confirmation we were seeking and we decided to make the move.

The difficulty came when trying to acquire property. In order to obtain a loan for the property we wanted, at least one of us needed an income with a W2 to make it work. I started looking for jobs in the area immediately. Within a week, I had two job offers and we were officially Georgia bound. Due to the housing shortage and low interest rates caused by the pandemic, our house was listed on the market. Within 4 hours we started receiving cash offers for more than the house was worth and even higher than our list price. Our house was sold in less than 24-hours and we literally had to move like lightning to get going.

Fast forward, we made the move to Georgia, where we stayed with a relative for a few months while we waited for our house to finish building. For 2 months, I worked at my new job as a maintenance technician and it was a lot of pressure. It was a high humidity, high heat, hazardous, warehouse environment that made 2 months feel like an eternity. I was doing 65+ hour weeks and the labor was extremely taxing on my body, but I refused to give up because I knew that this was a means to an end. After closing on our new home, I closed that chapter of working for someone else and began something new. I started my logistics business and the rest is history.

5. Financial freedom does not happen overnight, it takes work. Share three actionable steps that show you are serious about achieving financial freedom.

1. Stop delaying, stop making excuses, and start today. Some people find every excuse in the world to explain why they haven't started their business yet. For those individuals, it will never be the right time to start. Unfortunately, their dreams and aspirations go to the grave with them. Meanwhile, somebody with way more on their plate and much more to lose allows their hunger for success to drive them to push and start.

2. Increase your Financial IQ
This is the most important information I have ever received and I find that it is only fair to share. People go to school and take out six figure school loans in order to get into the profession they desire. Many people never finish paying these loans back, but have no problem investing it

in the beginning. Why is it we can pay $10K for a semester of prerequisite courses that have nothing to do with our field, but struggle to pay significantly less for a course from a private coach or entrepreneur in the same field as us?

3. Reading is Essential
Read books and invest in your most powerful asset, your mind. Once we learn to operate like this, we will truly learn to work smarter, not harder. I recommend Robert Kiyosaki's book "Increase Your Financial IQ." It is a great read that will change your mindset on money, and go into detail on how Robert created a $80K asset, without investing a dime of his own money.

6. Based on your expertise, share three practical tips/steps other business owners can take to continue to grow their business.

1. Own a system, not a job.
Create a system that allows you to delegate your work load, so that you can obtain more time to do the things you want to while maintaining a passive stream of income. Once you've built a great system, the money will come. Then, you can focus on expansion.

2. Utilize OPM
OPM is an acronym for Other People's Money. When creating a business, a lot of people misunderstand the saying, "It takes money to make money." This is true in a sense that if you don't plant you can't harvest, but many do not know that the money you use to start a business is accessible through grants, loans, and even private investors. If you have a great plan, people or banks will

invest in you because they trust they will get a return on their investment.

3. Celebrate your wins, and embrace your losses.

Every win, big or small, deserves to be celebrated. I believe that "encouragement sweetens labor."

Change your perspective on losses. A loss can be disheartening, especially when they seem to all come at once. In fact, I've had my share of losses that were quite costly. These losses helped me frame my business with policies and proper paperwork to avoid costly mistakes. You can plan as much as you want, but there will always be something that comes up that you weren't prepared to handle. When making decisions on the fly, sometimes the repercussions result in a loss. Your losses are building blocks to increasing your financial IQ.

I decided to be a part of this book because I felt like I had an obligation to talk about my experiences in hopes to provide the inspiration you need to start. We take risks every day. We jump in a car and drive a highway to get to work daily with no fear that we'll get into an accident. We might experience heavy traffic, and see a huge accident on the way there. The vehicles involved may be completely totaled and on fire. There might even be loss of lives on the road. Being able to see that, doesn't seem to stop us from driving though. We keep on driving, and don't let the demise of others instill fear in us. We keep on driving.

I encourage you today to keep on driving towards success and keep chasing financial freedom. You already hold the keys. Once you unlock your mind from the fear you are experiencing, you can truly walk in freedom.

How to Connect with Me:

You can connect with me via Instagram (@jyoungsfl), email (info@jyoungsfl.com) or by scanning the code below.

Acknowledgments

Thank You To My Pre-Order Supporters

1. Tyree Thiena
2. Pastor Alexander Scott
3. Richard Young
4. Norman Suer
5. Sherine Isom, Crystal Clear Editing
6. Emily Bolhuis, Eminflow
7. Ricardo Sanchez
8. Kasheem Herbert
9. Christopher Young
10. Nakeita Mcneil, ND and Consulting, Facebook: NDAC Instagram: ndac_company

Creating For A Higher Purpose

Eric Jackson & Brittny Ortiz-Jackson

Creatives
www.sofloinspire.com
Instagram.com/sofloinspire
Facebook.com/sofloinspire

Soflo Inspire came about in the summer of 2019 by a young couple, Brittny and Eric. Both creatives combine their long time passion for the art of photography & cinematography with their love for others.

"Whatever you do, work at it with all of your heart, as working for the Lord, not for men."
Colossians 3:23

Creating For A Higher Purpose

1. Share what you do and how you got into this business.

Brittny:
Eric and I help entrepreneurs and small businesses transform their brands through consistent, high-quality, and strategic content. Before we created Soflo Inspire (and before we got married), we had our own separate businesses. Eric worked with fashion models and brands, and I worked with creatives and weddings. In 2019, Eric and I decided to go to a local Starbucks. There, we each officially registered our companies under their own LLCs. Over time I began to edit videos for Eric, and he began to assist me at photography gigs. The more we worked with each other and started meeting more people, we eventually realized there was an overwhelming need for consistent, quality content amongst business owners and entrepreneurs alike. We realized that together, we could undoubtedly help. We absolutely love creating lifestyle photography and videography, we love the unique stories of business owners and entrepreneurs, and we love bridging the gap between creativity and business!

Since then, Eric and I have joined forces to help hundreds of entrepreneurs and small businesses with their content, so we decided to merge into one company instead of two separate LLCs. Soflo Inspire was officially registered on November 18th, 2020. Eric and I tied the knot shortly after.

We have received so many testimonies from our clients, and nothing brings us more joy than when they light up with excitement and great news! One of our amazing clients recently moved from Suriname, South America to Northern America, and she shared that she was in tears watching the video we created because it was a vision she had for a long time. The content we created for her played a huge part in bringing her vision to life. She can use the content for her website and run ads on it as well. Another client of ours was preparing for a soft launch for her products, and she needed photography and videography content. Once she launched, she reported to us that after three days of running ads on the content we created, she received over 100,000 views. As a result of each testimony, we continue to help entrepreneurs and small business owners take their content, brand, and business to the next level.

2. What were some of the fears you experienced before venturing out and starting your business?

Brittny:
Back in February 2020, right before the lockdown, I was driving out of Miami from what would be the last wedding I would photograph for the company I worked for at the time. It was very late, I was drained, and I remember staring lifelessly at the road ahead. A very deep conviction

to leave my job washed over me as I was driving, and it was the hardest decision I had to make. That job paid fairly well, and I had been with the company for almost three years. However, no matter what I did, I couldn't shake away the feeling that it was my time to go. As I drove back to Fort Lauderdale, I cried, and I asked God to help me. I was so scared. I was scared of what would happen next. I was scared of not doing things right, I was scared of not getting more clients to sustain myself, I was scared of the legal aspects of a business, and I was uncertain of what the future would hold for me if I did leave. I couldn't help but ask myself, "Am I doing the right thing? What if I fail? What will my life look like once I leave this job? Can I even do this?" A few moments later, God reminded me that HE is my ultimate provider and that I am not alone.

Eric:
Starting out, I had some fears: not being good enough and the fear of failing. When I first picked up a camera four years ago, I remember it being the first big purchase I ever made. I was 20 years old and in my second year of college. I had my first start-up business; a clothing line known as Agapi Supply. I remember opening up a credit card at Best Buy to purchase my first camera, the Canon T6i, my favorite starter camera. At the time, I was extremely nervous, debating should I get this? What if I can't pay the camera off in time? Where am I going to get the money from? What if this doesn't work? Well, I can tell you that none of those concerns mattered four years later because sometimes you can have your plan all laid out, but God will have you going in another direction. A better direction. My initial intention when I bought my first camera wasn't even to become a photographer. I bought it to have quality images and videos for my clothing brand

because I knew the importance of having quality content. Personal branding was something that was always so fascinating to me, even before I got into business. That's what really compelled me to step out and invest in buying a camera. Once I got over the first hump of thinking of the "what ifs," the road took a slight turn for the better. I started off taking photos of my friends and used them to model my clothes. Then I started taking photos of aspiring models, which then transitioned into professional models and authentic brands. I remember shooting my first paid event; it was a sweet 16 party for a lady at my church. She paid me $60 to shoot photos and videos, and until this day, I couldn't be any more grateful because even though she loved everything, I look back at my work then, and I think – if it were my daughter's sweet 16, I would never have hired this rookie. But I had to start somewhere, and that was the kick start to my photography journey.

After that, I was getting hired back-to-back for more events and photo sessions. When it came to photography, I covered pretty much everything. Birthday parties, weddings, studio sessions, boxing, basketball, clubs, to only name a few. I took photos of literally everything at one point and had a gig almost every other day and every week. I fell so in love with the art of photography, and I wanted to succeed so badly that I eventually hit an unexpected wall--I experienced burnout for the first time. Not only was I burnt out physically, but I was also burnt out mentally. In fact, I believe the mental aspect was even more dreadful. I was stuck. My self-confidence in my work was at an all-time low, and I felt like throwing in the towel. I thought, "Maybe photography isn't for me?"
Then the "maybes" became feelings of regret.
"I shouldn't have dropped out of college."
"Would I even make it to be full-time?"

These thoughts raced through my mind for weeks.

3. How did you overcome those fears/obstacles? Was it worth it?

Eric:
I remember praying to God that I didn't want to do this alone anymore. I asked him to surround me with mentors that could help me along the journey. I also prayed for guidance and strength to get through that flunk.
God didn't waste any time. A few days later, a very unique guy named Icon that I met at a photo session called me up and said, "Hey, I love your work and would love for you to help me shoot this major event in Naples, Florida, for three days."
I'm usually more skeptical when meeting someone for the first time, but it was like God was telling me, "Son, go. I got you."

So, I packed my bags and took a road trip with a stranger I had met only once. From that day, Icon and I became good buddies. He taught me so much when it came to strategies in business. That made me feel like everything I did to that point was worth it. The long nights of editing, the back-to-back shoots, and the low and high moments all led to that opportunity. Sometimes it only takes that one person, that one opportunity, that one post, to change the trajectory of your life.

Brittny:
Remembering that God is my ultimate provider propelled me to take action that night and put in my two weeks' notice the next day. Just a few weeks after that, the entire world went into lockdown. However, I still had to figure out a plan for my life, and I had to figure out how to pay

rent. I used that time during the lockdown as an opportunity to self-reflect, get clear on my vision, and meditate on some of the information I learned at a previous mastermind I attended alongside Eric.

The mastermind Eric and I had the honor of attending called "Prospecting on Demand," was created by Alex and Shira Schlinsky, Brian Downard, Iconic Becker, and their amazing P.O.D. Team. The only way I overcame a majority of my fears and obstacles was through God and His word, creating Soflo Inspire with Eric, community and mentorship with P.O.D., and changing any self-limiting beliefs that were holding me back from growing. A lot of my fears were rooted in a lack of confidence and a lack of knowledge. But the more Eric and I took the time to learn about the very things that scared us, the more we grew and the easier it became to take risks.

While Eric and I continued to brainstorm on generating income, God blessed us with a few clients every month to hold us down. We continued to post on social media during that time, and we continued to learn about building systems for a business. Initially, I was scared of not doing things "right," but I simply had to ask questions, learn, and make mistakes to get better.
I was scared of not getting more clients, but I had to seek God for guidance, have faith that He would come through, and be obedient to the steps He needed me to take. I was scared of what the future would look like when I left the comfort of my primary job, but when I left, my entire life changed in ways I would have never even imagined.

As I write this chapter and reflect on where I am now, I know God collected all of my tears that night and showed me that it was all worth it.

4. When did you realize it was time for you to start working towards your own financial freedom? What difficulties did you face?

Brittny:
There was not a single defining moment when Eric and I realized it was time for us to start working towards our financial freedom – there were a series of moments. When in our late teens/early twenties, I began to feel the pull of something greater. In the back of my head, I always felt like something was missing, but I couldn't quite tell what it was. I always wondered if there was more to life than what I was experiencing. Deep down, Eric and I always wanted to be a part of something bigger than ourselves. We just didn't know what, why, or how. Eric also grew up in a single-parent household, which motivated him to have a different mindset and outlook on money and freedom.

Once or twice a month, Eric and I would go to the beach and check-in with each other. During one of these chats, we talked about our goals, dreams, and concerns. We want to be in a position to take care of our parents as they get older. We also knew we were heading into marriage, and we didn't want finances to be a burden. We want to be financially secure and help the people around us.

On this road to financial freedom, there have been difficulties Eric and I have faced together. We had to figure out how we could use our gifts and talents to help others, who we could serve, what to offer, pricing, how to generate consistent leads, social media strategy, how to balance creating and posting our own content, how to file taxes the right way, and hire editors for our team. We had to figure all this out while juggling premarital counseling, health concerns, and waves of uncertainty.

5. Financial freedom does not happen overnight; it takes work. Share three actionable steps that show you are serious about achieving financial freedom.

Eric:
The road to entrepreneurship isn't easy, especially when starting out. But what fuels us to keep going and pursue financial freedom is the ability to have more time with our loved ones, build a legacy for the generation after us, and make an impact beyond the lens. One of my driving factors? My 10-year-old niece and nephew, Travis and Trinity, because they're the generation of the future. But, to achieve financial freedom, we know it is essential to start with our mindset.

Brittny:
On this journey to financial freedom, we have to be honest with ourselves and be humble enough to go before the Lord and ask Him to reveal what's in our hearts and minds. Eric and I are committing to improve our mindset by seeking and understanding what could hold us back from walking in the purpose God has for us.
Our second commitment on this journey to financial freedom is establishing the proper systems within our business to generate consistent revenue and improve the customer experience for each of our clients. Proper systems are the key to a consistent flow of income.
Our third commitment to financial freedom is hiring and collaborating with people who are skilled at what they do!

Having the right team in place will allow the business to scale and flow smoothly.

6. Based on your expertise, share three practical tips/steps other business owners can take to continue to grow their business.

Eric:
Working behind the scenes with a guy like Icon gave me the boost I needed to gain a little more clarity on what I really wanted to do as a photographer and as a business owner. Facing burnout by juggling my part-time job, my passion, family, and college, really led me to want more. It led me to focus only on what really mattered and would bring the highest return for my future. It led me to go all in. I felt like I was playing small for too long.
My first piece of advice to anyone when starting this entrepreneur journey is finding a mentor or, better yet, a community of like-minded and non-like-minded individuals with goals aligned with yours. It's the best way to get to where you want to go faster while enjoying the process more.

I would also share, do not compare yourself to others. One thing that led me to mental burnout was constantly trying to keep up with everyone and follow what was most popular. That only leads to a dead end. Once I realized and truly believed that I had something unique to bring to the table, I stopped watching everyone else. I started to focus on what I could do to make the most impact. Focusing on how I could make the most impact with my God-given gifts led to amazing financial breakthroughs and opportunities. I went from $60 sessions to working with entrepreneurs like Daymond John and realtors all over South Florida and brands like Bacardi, and most importantly, I met the love of my life. None of this would've happened if I had stayed in my comfort zone or let the fear of not being good enough hold me down.

My last piece of advice would be throughout all the challenges and adversity life throws at you, if your "why" is strong enough, you'll most likely figure out the "how" and, ultimately, your "way" towards your purpose.

Brittny:
If you are looking to grow your business, my recommendation is to:
   1. Evaluate your self-limiting beliefs.
   2. Narrow your business idea down to a specific niche.
   3. Write out a business plan.

One of the biggest game-changers for my journey was making the time to sit down and evaluate what I believed about myself, what I believed about the world, and what I believed about God. We have to acknowledge and face strongholds and bring them to Him if we want to grow and move forward. This was especially important to my growth because I had to undo some of the damage I experienced in my life before I could take on the responsibility of being a business owner. I knew that I couldn't pour from an empty cup or expect to serve others if I was broken inside.

I was led to search for free self-limiting belief templates, and I went to work on myself. Once I was able to sit down, challenge my negative beliefs, and stand on the word of God, my life began to transform gradually.
After I worked through what was holding me back, I had to figure out what niche I wanted to create my business around. I went through a few different niches before

choosing the one I really enjoyed, and I had to tweak my offer, systems, and content as a result. You may not know what specific niche you want at first, but dedicate some time to explore a few options. Your niche is important because you will build your offers, systems, and content around it.

Another step that helped us grow our business was writing out and revisiting our short-term and long-term goals. Since Eric and I know what our short-term and long-term financial and business goals are, this plays a huge role in the steps we take daily. We always plan each month, week, and day according to what we need to accomplish. Please note that you do not have to have the perfect website, offer, or equipment to start – you just have to start!

Although we're still on this journey to financial freedom, once we heard we had the opportunity to share our story through this book, We felt it was a no-brainer. We understand the impact people's stories and testimonies can have on someone going through a similar situation or just starting. A part of our mission & goals is to truly inspire others along our journey and help others walk in their God-given purpose.

How to Connect with Us:

You can connect with us via Instagram (@sofloinspire) or email (sofloinspire@gmail.com)

Acknowledgements

Thank You To My Pre-Order Supporters

1. Cherilyn Kitson
2. Dania Previl
3. Tiasha Jones
4. Lizmarie Santiago
5. William Barr, Godspeed Clothing, @godspeed_clothing,thegodspeedclothing.com
6. Ashleigh Puranda
7. Sofia Kellman, IG: sofiakellman
8. Abby Jerome, Ceotribe- Create Every Opportunity Together, IG: _ceoabby, theceotribe.com
9. Andre Moise, AndreMoiseStudios, @AndreMoiseStudios, tave.com/AndreMoiseStudios
10. Ashleigh Puranda
11. Abby Jerome, Ceotribe- Create Every Opportunity Together, IG: _ceoabby, theceotribe.com
12. Andre Moise, AndreMoiseStudios, social media: @AndreMoiseStudios, tave.com/AndreMoiseStudios
13. Brandon Iconic Becker Klevr Solutions
14. Eva Floreus, EFPHOTOGRAPHY,social media: @Efphotography_
15. Mischa Beth, Braveheart, LLC, FB: mischabethludwig
16. Dwayne and Tao Howard | Awake The Flame Ministries
17. Susan Becker (Iconic's Mom)

Reaching Goals Through Mental Health

Monique Singleton

Bookkeeper & Party Rentals Owner
Instagram.com/thembsenterprise
Facebook.com- Monique Brown-Singleton

Monique Singleton, Owner of The MBS Enterprise & MJS Event and Party Rentals has worked in the social services field for 5+ years and has now been in Bookkeeping & Payroll Management for 3+ years. She is a living witness that a mental illness will not predict your future ahead! You are capable!

"Trust in the LORD with all your heart; do not depend on your own understanding.Seek his will in all you do,and he will show you which path to take." Proverbs 3:5-6 NLT

Reaching Goals Through Mental Health

1. Share what you do and how you got into this business.

Hello! I'm Monique. I'm a full-time employee by day and a virtual bookkeeper and payroll manager by night. I help small service-based business owners manage their money so they can make more money and reach their goals. I'm also the owner of an event and party rental business. You can just call me GIRL BOSS!

First things first, I never understood the importance of finances until adulthood which is common where I'm from. I learned the importance of paying your bills on time, which was very fundamental to me. However, the concept of saving money was never talked about much. Would you believe that I was spending money as soon as it touched my hands? It was sad but true. I have seen thousands of dollars come across and handled it so poorly due to the immaturity of understanding how to handle money. It's all about transparency here. When you know better, you do better. I didn't truly understand the concept of saving money until I met my husband, Jewon. I visually saw him strategize and set goals on saving money. I felt like if he could do it, I could too. He has been the major influence behind my hustle. I've learned throughout the years that it is not about how much money you make, but it is about how you budget the money that you have.

My introduction to entrepreneurship started back in 2013 when I became a Mary Kay Beauty Consultant. I did that for about two years. I really enjoyed the experience of impacting lives through beauty, but I did not understand the concept of running a successful business.

The vision for my first business came to me at a wedding I was attending. I saw how Chiavari chairs could upscale formal events. I initially felt like the idea was crazy, but I consulted with a successful decorator, and she encouraged me to go into the rental business. I'm glad I followed her advice because as of today, I'm happy to say I have a successful business. She remains a consistent customer and I'm grateful for all the referrals she has sent my way. I've been able to network with awesome decorators in the industry. I'm extremely grateful for the mindset shift I experienced and the success. Since starting, I have made multiple investments in my business and plan to do more in the future. I have been able to turn MJS Event & Party Rentals into a business that will fund our children's future.

How I started my 2nd venture was quite interesting. I graduated from the University of West Alabama in 2013 with a Bachelor of Science Degree in Sociology and a minor in Computer Information Systems. I worked in the social services field for 5+ years and then shifted into bookkeeping and payroll management in 2018. I really couldn't believe that I decided to take this route with zero experience, but I'm here to tell you that God can qualify you for any position if it is in his will. And I had no idea this decision would serve my future.

As 2020 rolled in, I was ready for another shift. I wanted to become a Nursing Home Administrator, but little did I know, God had a different plan for my life. In March 2020, I attended a virtual women's conference hosted by the Epic Fab Girl Community. It changed my perspective on life forever. The conference helped me to evaluate myself and realize my worth as a woman of faith. God revealed his purpose for my life while attending this virtual conference, and I decided to turn my skill set of bookkeeping into an actual business. I started The M.B.S. Enterprise Bookkeeping & Payroll Services in May of 2021.

I'm often asked how I maintain a full-time job along with my two businesses. If you keep on reading, I'll show you how.

2. What were some of the fears you experienced before venturing out and starting your business?

The biggest fears I experienced before venturing out were feelings of being incapable, feelings of failure, and the fear of not finding balance through marriage and motherhood.

In 2016 I started experiencing chronic hives. The doctors could not figure out the leading cause. I was later diagnosed with Anxiety Disorder and Depression in 2018.

I had to get used to a new norm. The happiest moments of my life were mixed in with the worst moments of my life. I no longer recognized the confident go-getter and motivated version of Monique I once knew. I lost all hope. I felt that my condition would hinder my growth as a business owner and could not function under those conditions. I also felt incapable of running a virtual bookkeeping firm because I had minimal knowledge of the bookkeeping industry. Comparison also knocked on my door, and I began to fear someone being better than me or being ahead of me in the industry.

Allow me to be honest for a moment because I know you've probably had these similar feelings too. It happens to everyone. I constantly wrestled with the fear of failure because I still worked a full-time job, cared for my family, and ran a business. Let me tell you, fear is a major disabler. Fear paralyzed my mindset tremendously to the point where I became angry and frustrated with myself. The devil had me making every excuse. I had to make a conscious effort not to feed into it. I had to go to war with fear! It was not until then that I experienced the freedom that I truly desired.

3. How did you overcome those fears/obstacles? Was it worth it?

I honestly thought that being a business owner was impossible for me until I placed a plan into action with the help of a great support system. Let me take a moment to show special recognition to my dear family and close friends for helping me throughout my journey of motherhood with my angels Madisen and Makenzie while battling my stages of anxiety and depression. This was a very difficult stage in my life that a lot of people did not know about. To the public, I was well put together, but behind the scenes, I was a complete wreck. I came to a point where I wanted to end my life due to the misery of my health condition, but I'm here today to tell you that the devil did not win!

It is so easy to make excuses! I had to understand that what I experienced was no mistake. I, Monique, had to adjust to my new normal in order to re-discover the sweet treasures of life. There is a saying, "Get comfortable with being uncomfortable." Repeat that, and then you will have that "Ah-ha moment"! I had to understand that being uncomfortable meant that I was changing and evolving into the person that God had destined me to be.

I overcame my obstacles by investing in a business coach. Since entering entrepreneurship, I've had a total of 3 coaches. You must spend money to make money, right? Investing can be scary, so it is very important to be strategic when choosing a business coach. Maybe you think investing in a business coach is expensive. Most business coaches provide payment arrangements to make it easier and convenient for their clients.

You can invest in yourself through purchasing a masterclass or eBook as well. Never be afraid to invest in yourself because I promise you will see a return on that investment if you apply what you have learned to your business. If you're serious about your business, please consider investing.

I also enrolled in legit courses to help deepen my understanding of bookkeeping fundamentals. I joined bookkeeping Facebook communities which have been so beneficial when I get stuck on something that I may not understand and receive tips that I can apply to my own business. I also joined a community of faith-based women entrepreneurs. I purposely surrounded myself with like-minded individuals virtually and in person. Have you ever heard that you are the company that you keep? You must surround yourself with positivity to stay motivated in your business.

I also overcame obstacles by knowing that sometimes you must sacrifice in order to reach new heights in your business. Entrepreneurship can be a lonely place at times. There will be people that will not understand the reasoning behind your hustle, and I am sorry to inform you, it just might be the people that you did not expect at all. You will even get questioned on why you work so hard, but IT'S THE FINANCIAL FREEDOM FOR ME!

Another tool I introduced is Meditation. Each morning, Monday through Friday, I rise at 5:00. Meditation sets the mood for the day, and it is also a sacred moment with God. I surround myself with positive affirmations, journal my thoughts, and what a difference I saw. As an entrepreneur living with a mental illness, I must take care of myself so that I can serve my clients most efficiently. I decided to go face-to-face with my fears and figure out alternative ways to combat my fears, and opportunities continue to come my way, and blessings continue to flow in my business.

Looking back, I can say that it was worth it. I didn't realize just how strong I was until I went through this season of my life. When I think about fear, these two bible verses come to mind:

"So do not fear, for I am with you; do not be dismayed, for I am your God. I will strengthen you and help you; I will uphold you with my righteous right hand." – Isaiah 41:10 NIV.

"Trust in the Lord with all your heart and lean not on your own understanding; in all your ways submit to him, and he will make your paths straight."– Proverbs 3: 5-6 NIV.

4. When did you realize it was time for you to start working towards your own financial freedom? What difficulties did you face?

I realized that it was time to start working toward my financial freedom when I began to hunger for something greater than what my profession could give me financially. That is my definition of financial freedom. It may look different for you. I had to keep it real with myself and understand that I could not achieve my financial goals just by working my full-time job. I wanted more for myself and my family. I also started to think about my legacy. How could I create that? I can vividly remember crying out to God for direction because nothing felt fulfilling anymore. I got tired of trying to do things my way because each time, it failed. I started researching ways to make multiple streams of income, and there were a lot of options out there. I became determined to create a better avenue for my family and me.

5. Financial freedom does not happen overnight, it takes work. Share three actionable steps that show you are serious about achieving financial freedom.

The first actionable step is changing your mindset. Everything starts where you believe it. You must speak things that are not as though they are. I think of dieting when it comes to mindset. The key to a successful diet is consistency. It starts with the mindset. You must train your brain, and the body will follow. The same applies to your business. You must shift your mindset to believe that you can achieve financial freedom in your life. If you don't believe you can do it, you can't. Understand your worth and what you can bring to the table.

The second actionable step is enhancing your skills as an entrepreneur. Did you know another word for an entrepreneur is lifetime learner? This world is ever-changing, and my friend, you will have to adapt to it.

For example, the pandemic caused several entrepreneurs to become very creative with their businesses. Entrepreneurs had to learn new ways to interact with their clients and customers. The solid fact is you will never stop learning.

To aspiring business owners, never count yourself out just because you don't have a skill set. You can teach yourself to be an expert. The best lessons come from experience. The third actionable step is to stop treating your business like a hobby. If you want to be taken seriously, you must treat your business as such. It requires commitment, sacrifice, and hard work to be a successful business owner. It is important to understand your value and know your worth in the world of entrepreneurship. Run your business like you have a legacy depending on it. If you are a full-time employee like me, where time is of the essence, automate as much as possible. You will show up like a boss even when you are not there. You owe it to yourself to win by achieving the financial freedom that you desire.

6. Based on your expertise, share three practical tips/steps other business owners can take to continue to grow their business.

Understand that quality over quantity in your business is essential for continued growth. It is so vital to engage and nurture the clients and customers that you have. It is easy to look at numbers and think you are doing good, but that is not always the case. It's all about the value that you bring, and creating a lasting relationship with the community you have created. Let me give you an example. When I first started with marketing my business on Instagram, I had less than 500 followers. Guess what? I landed amazing clients based on my consistency of showing up and the value that I provided, not by the quantity of my followers.

Never stop exploring ways to expand. Always set attainable goals but never stay complacent. Once you reach one goal, will you stay comfortable there? There is always room for growth. What is your next move? How would you like to see your business grow? What steps will you take to see that growth?

Take advantage of the power of networking. It opens the door to long-lasting relationships that bring about opportunities to grow your business. Networking is great for any business owner, both within and outside your industry. Networking gives you so much exposure and builds your confidence as being an expert in your industry.

I decided to be a part of this book to share my entrepreneurship journey with fellow business owners that may be afraid to take that leap to advance themselves to a new level. I also wanted to encourage someone that is on the fence about starting a business. I get excited thinking about being a part of a generational gem that will touch so many lives now and in the future. I will end by saying that entrepreneurship is not easy but so worth it.

My prayer is that this book serves as the answer that you've been seeking. My prayer is that this book gives you the confidence to walk in your God-Given Purpose. My prayer is that you understand that you can run a successful business, regardless of unforeseen circumstances.

Which will you choose? Freedom or Fear.

I want you to revisit this question. What does financial freedom look like to you? If you don't know what it looks like, take a moment to write it down. Sometimes we must write things down to make them plain, and it doesn't have to be all fancy.

My advice to the entrepreneurs going through a season of fear and unhappiness in their business is to remain consistent even when you feel like no one is watching. Take a moment to evaluate your business. What's not working? What could you do better? Are you consulting God with your plans? It's only through him that we can be guided in the right direction in our businesses.

Don't count yourself out. It may be time to go back to the drawing board to try a different tactic to make money in your business. Accept this moment as a season of discovery. You cannot fight this battle alone. Once you place God as the C.E.O. of your business, you will see the difference.

Remember, F.E.A.R. is False-Evidence-Appearing-Real. Acknowledge your fear, face your fear, and combat your fear! Ready to shift gears? Ready, set, go!!! Walk into your purpose!

How to Connect with Me:

If you want to learn more about me and my bookkeeping and payroll services then scan the code below.

Acknowledgements

Thank You To My Pre-Order Supporters

1. NaToya Sanders, Sweethoney's Designs,LLC (IG) _sweethoneys ; (FB) Dweethoney's LLC, sweethoneysdesigns.com
2. Kimberly Bowens, Reality Check Counseling Services, (FB) Kimberly Bowens, NCC (counselingisheartwork) https://www.psychologytoday.com/us/therapists/kimberly-bowens-pensacola-fl/369110
3. Doristine Norris, MK's Bookkeeping Services, LLC, (IG) mksbookkeeping
4. Kennesha Powell, The Kees to Real Estate, IG: keekeesellshomes
5. VaShard Chandler, Royal Express LLC, IG: kuntry_boi, http://getroyalexpress.wix.com/royalexpresskuntry
6. Laquanda Irby, Chef Lala's Catering & Personal Chef Services, IG: Cheffinwithlala
7. Leshia Smith, MDCT Credit Solutions, IG: MDCTcreditsolutions, FB: MDCT Credit Solutions, LLC, www.mdctcreditsolutions.com
8. Felecia Brown , So F.A.B. Events LLC, IG: sof.a.b.events
9. LaShay Ormond, Littles Toybox, www.littlestoybox.com
10. Creola Moorer, Cre'Amora's Cove LLC
11. Dorcas Pittman, Drkness 2 Hope, LLC, darkness_2_hope, www.fromdarkness2hope.com
12. Kiara Milner, ORRganized Books, LLC, @ORRganizedBooks, www.orrganizedbooks.com

13.Synauri Boykin, Sashay's Sugar Scrubs: Healthy skin and hair begins with a simple rub of Sashay's Sugar Scrubs

14. Shamaria Woods, M&M Tax Service, LLC, Facebook: MMtaxservicellc

15. Kelnecia Witherspoon, Yoni Cartel LLC, Facebook: Yoni Cartel Facebook Group, https://yonicartel.square.site/

16. Nameica Turk-Craig, Nameica Speaks & Co, Social media: @nameicaspeaks, www.NameicaSpeaks.com

17. Linda Jones, Touched By Faye Designs, Facebook: Touched By Faye Designs

18. Karkeyetta Wolfe, Di Vine Makeovers LLC, social media: TyerraReign

19. Dequisha Key-Epps, Amara Nicor Fashions, www.amaranicorfashions.com

20. Shemeka Robinson, Shemeka Robinson, Realtor with Residential Movement Real Estate Montgomery, website: Rmre.group

21. Quanda Pugh, Quanda Pugh Styles, Instagram: QuandaPugh

22. Lakaren Pettway-Pernell, Tip Top Shape Hair Salon/ Gifted Hands

23. Stephanie Williams, Bella's Dream Creations and Décor, Facebook: Dee Dee Williams

24. Ardeana Thompson, The All Things Apple Foundation

My Strength Through Freedom Over Fear

Nishia Slater

Self-Empowerment Coach & Mentor
Instagram.com/ladynishia
Facebook.com- Nishia Slater

Nishia Slater is a Self-Empowerment coach, author,
speaker, and mentor. She loves to encourage, uplift,
and inspire women to discover their true identity
through a series of questions and activities that will
help them to identify their skillsets, talents, all while
shifting their mindset.

"Keep smiling because life is a beautiful thing
and there's so much to smile for."

My Strength Through Freedom Over Fear

1. Share what you do and how you got into this business.

I am a Self-empowerment coach, author, public speaker, and mentor. My passion is encouraging women to overcome their adversities by uplifting and empowering them to identify their skill sets, goals and talents, all while shifting their mindset. I was raised by a single mother and grew up in a traumatic environment that resulted in an identity crisis I didn't realize I needed to heal from until I became an adult. My adversities pushed me into this field to support women and create a safe space for them. Often, when I did not know where or how to get help, I would give up and give in. I believed that nobody cared about me, and I felt alone. I went in circles for years, trying and crying out for help, but nobody seemed to pay me any mind. I taught myself how to hide my way through life, so if anyone looked at me, they would not be able to tell something was going on with me. Even though I was always tall, I found ways to hide, especially in photos. Honestly, I always felt that nobody cared enough to help me because it always seemed like I had my life together. That was not a good look for me. Here I was screaming for help, but hiding in plain sight.

In 2017, I finally said enough is enough, I was done playing small with myself. I wanted to be in the big leagues. My main focus was to live a healthy lifestyle and implement some changes as I went along. Later that year, my mindset began to shift, and I did not know or understand what to do next with the power within me. As I implemented change and embraced all the newness in my life, my new mindset took over, and I began to do the seemingly impossible.

Eating healthy was not a part of my plan. I just wanted to get healthy! But then I saw and felt myself losing weight. When I was invited to events that required me to exercise, I went from saying "no" to saying "yes". The more that I said yes to things, I felt my mindset shifting in positive ways. As this journey became real to me, I thought it would be a great opportunity to share my journey with other women and help them along their journey.

One day I sat quietly and started reflecting on my life. I no longer saw the hurt, quiet, and shy girl. There was a glow over my head. The healing taking place was unstoppable, and I could not do anything if I tried. When I picked up the pen and paper and started to journal, I decided enough was enough. This journey should not be kept a secret, and I need to do what I love, which is to help people. I wrote down my plan to help women and the benefits they would get from it, based on my results from an unhealthy lifestyle into a changed woman. I just knew what I had to offer women would be life-changing. I had no idea how to properly structure my business, I just knew women would benefit from me, so I started my Coaching business in 2020.

2. What are some of your fears you experienced before reaching out and starting your business?

I had a fear of feeling exposed. I did not believe people wanted to hear what I had to say, so I kept quiet about my business for a while. Growing up, I was a mute and a people watcher, I kept to myself and did not talk or interact with too many people unless I was teaching them outdoor games. I felt like nobody wanted to listen to me or hear the things I had on my mind. That mindset followed me into my adulthood.

That all changed five years ago! I slowly started to speak up for myself. I was passive at first but became more comfortable voicing my opinions on things to people. I did not want to be argumentative, so I never said too much. I only gave my opinion when asked. My goal was to never make people mad.

I also feared that I would not be able to reach people, especially since I launched right before the pandemic. Launching my business right before the pandemic was so dreadful. I thought no one would support me because there was so much going on in this world. I knew people needed a support system, an accountability partner, and a coach, but that is not how society made me feel. So, I delayed starting my business. The more people started asking me about what a Life Coach is, the less I talked because I did not want to be lumped with other coaches and I knew I was not a licensed therapist.

My family history scared me as well. There are not too many successful people in my family. Growing up in poverty, I did not see successful people around me, so I thought it was normal to struggle. There were not too many people speaking positive things into my life, which made me feel like struggling was the way to live. Complaining was not an option for me because I did not have anyone that would listen to me, anyway, so I kept it to myself. It felt like everyone was comfortable with where they were, so why would I do something or become someone different? The adults around me did not tell me they believed in me. No one even asked what I wanted to be when I grew. This led me to believe there was no hope. I thought there was no way I could beat the odds stacked against me. Having no idea where to start is scary too. Over the years, I have watched companies succeed, but I did not have a blueprint for my business. I allowed that to hinder me from stepping out on faith, and I used that as an excuse. I spent countless hours researching and asking others for help to get me on the right path. It took a lot out of me because I had a hard time asking others for help.

3. How did you overcome those fears and obstacles? Was it worth it?

I overcame my fears by building my confidence. I told myself not to compare myself to anyone else, and they definitely couldn't compare to me. I learned how to be unique and transparent, all while being my authentic self. For 30 days straight at the same time, no matter where I was, I recorded myself for at least 1 minute so I could get in the habit of talking while others listened. It worked. I was able to come out of my comfort zone.

I studied and followed other successful coaches/therapists. I knew I had the words; I just needed to work on the delivery and engagement. Once I became confident, I started going live on social media. I received compliments left and right. This let me know I had arrived. I knew what I had was valuable and would help people. I used the pandemic as the reason people needed my services, and I stopped counting myself out. I knew there was hope for others, and I wanted to be the person to help. Instead of concentrating on current events, I practiced speaking positive things about myself to increase my self-confidence. The more I spoke, my plan to bring attention to my Coaching business became clear. I wrote down what I wanted to say to others to draw clientele.

The more I thought about failing, the more I wrote down goals and dreams I wanted to create for my life. At first it was scary, because I had to tackle my faulty belief system, but I fought myself through it. Tears of growth became my best friend because I was able to actually write out my goals and accomplish them as I went about my day. Success was in my near future, especially when I started believing in myself. I no longer thought about my past struggles with sadness. I started reflecting and seeing the growth in such a short time. Growth became familiar to me.

Once I learned how to research, things started clicking. It took time, but I learned how to start my business and where to start. I have clarity on what I offer as a Coach and the transformation I can help women have. Within a few months, the structure of my business came together, which helped me have more confidence in my skills. This showed me I was on the right track and encouraged me to keep going.

4. When did you realize it was time for you to start working towards your own financial freedom? What difficulties did you face?

I realized my financial freedom was calling me when I kept checking my bank account, and I did not have any savings or a financial future for my children. The fact that money was not discussed in my childhood, forced me to ignore it, even with my children. It seemed so difficult to save and invest in my future.

I faced the difficulty of having to figure out how to pay for college. Growing up in the '80s college was not discussed. My family could not afford college. I always wanted to be a lawyer, to change the injustice in this world. That was short-lived, when I found out the cost. When I decided to go to college for accounting, an advisor showed me how to get grants, scholarships, and loans. This changed my life forever. If I knew those options were available to me, I would have pursued my dream of becoming a lawyer.

Finding financial stability for my family was not easy. In my early 20's, saving for a rainy day was a joke! I had no plan for the future. I would stash a couple of hundred dollars here or there, and if something came up, I would use those funds. I had no idea what an emergency fund was, even though it felt like I always had an emergency. After I got married at 25 and became pregnant with my 3rd child, I knew I needed to establish a better way to help secure our future by learning how to properly invest.

5. Financial freedom does not happen overnight. It takes work. Share three actionable steps that show you are serious about achieving financial freedom.

I have taken several steps to obtain financial freedom. These steps have helped me to gain confidence as a business owner.

1. Create a budget - Creating a budget for the month is key. I can monitor exactly what comes in and determine fund distribution.

2. Track business activity-The spreadsheet allows me to keep track, monitor activity, spending habits, and areas of overspending that I no longer need for my business. The spreadsheet covers daily, weekly, and monthly spending tasks. This gives me an idea of what I need to work on and where I am at the moment. It also highlights areas that need my attention the most and the things I can outsource. Even with a single-member LLC, I must learn to delegate, and this spreadsheet assists me.

3. Increase education - I invest in myself properly and consistently. When I first started my business, I was clueless about the ins and outs of being a CEO. Educating myself on services and investing in my business financially has helped me to grow. I took classes, received certifications, attended training and studied the requirements to operate my business in my state.

6. Based on your expertise, share three practical tips/steps other business owners can take to continue to grow their business.

1. Delegating - As I mentioned previously, a budget is important. Once you have created that budget, create sub-lines to see where you have room to hire out. Just remember, even though you might be a single-member LLC, that does not mean you have to do everything.
2. Establish a team - Get a team of people to work with you. You need people to bounce ideas off of and help you brainstorm. Keeping everything inside does not help you in the long run. When thinking about expanding your business, consider all options. When I started my business, I did not have a budget, and I did not want any help. You could not tell me anything about expanding, let alone to hire a coach. I knew I was headed for destruction if I stayed on that path. Instead of keeping things in and relying on myself, I hired a coach. It might be wise for you to hire a Coach who has longevity in your field and will assist you in taking your business to another level. Hiring a coach for me was an amazing decision. My coach was able to step in when I felt like I was stuck and going in circles. We brainstormed ideas together, and she gave me honest feedback.
3. Take the leap - Honestly, I had no clue about coaching when I first started. I was told to "just start" and that everything else would come. Even though I do not recommend this, I can say it was the best decision I have ever made. Sitting in my comfort zone, I was able to play it safe and I definitely did not take any losses. A good rule of thumb is to start scared and get as

much help as you can because your goals and dreams are calling you, and if you want to build that legacy, there is no greater time such as this.

I chose to be a part of this book because financial freedom is important to me. This collaboration shows me that I am not alone in either business or life because I am surrounded by inspiring, uplifting, and encouraging individuals.

After sitting in my comfort zone for over 30 years, I knew change had to come. Those goals written down were just on paper. I was not living my dreams; I was just surviving. Being a part of this book affords me the opportunity to build a solid foundation for my children, while creating a legacy for my family. My children are watching me, so I decided to step out of my comfort zone and live out my dreams on purpose

How to Connect with Me:

If you want to connect with me and need help while you are on this path to self discovery then email me at starlifewellness@gmail.com

Acknowledgements

Thank You To My Pre-Order Supporters

1. Charon King-Willis, Second Chance Division, Second Chance Div.
2. Cheney Norville
3. Sylvia Borup , My Scented Life with Sylvia B, Facebook: Sylvia Borup Independent Scentsy Consultant, https://sylviaborup.scentsy.us
4. Shakera Seward, Sisterhood of Healing Inc., Facebook, and Instagram: Sisterhood of Healing Inc, Clubhouse: Keke Seward, www.sisterhoodofhealinginc.com
5. Janis Long
6. Anjanette Foster-Miles, IG: https://instagram.com/sistaluv_1
7. Angela Rambaillie, www.facebook.com/ang.lotus.39
8. Michelle Ketelhut
9. Heidi Hess, http://heidijo.lifeinfoapp.com
10. DaJuanNa Hargrow-McGee, Twitter: SmokieDaFunsize
11. Victoria Wilson
12. Syri Gester

Purpose Overcomes Fear

Latoya Whitfield

Money Mindset Coach
latoyawhitfield.com
Instagram.com/financialcoachwhit
Facebook.com- Financial Coach Whit

Latoya Whitfield is an impactful coach, mentor, and speaker. She loves to empower Queenpreneurs to tap into their greatest potential through teaching generational wealth methods in the form of money mindset and faith based coaching. Her financial planning is purpose filled to accomplish goals created in faith and carried out in action.

"For I know the thoughts that I think toward you, saith the LORD, thoughts of peace, and not of evil, to give you an expected end." Jeremiah 29:11

Purpose Overcomes Fear

1. Share what you do and how you got into this business.

My name is Latoya Whitfield, and I am a money mindset and empowerment coach. Women come to me when they are ready to transition from corporate to queenpreneurship. I help them to reach their full potential by using three main principles. Prayer, planning, and preparation! I know what it's like to pursue a purpose-filled life and monetize it. My six-week faith-based coaching program consists of money mindset, purpose, personal and business finances, and strategic planning. My goal is to help them see what they can't see in themselves so that their desired purpose creates abundance and leads to a financially free life.

I worked in banking for about five years and public service for about four years, so my desire to educate came quite naturally. Banking can be a fast-paced industry. Usually, people come in for only one purpose, and that is to get money. They are not expecting to have a learning session. The goal was to get the customer to sit down in front of a banker to do a needs assessment. Usually, we would uncover some ugly truths that the clients did not want to face.

It can be embarrassing to discuss your finances, especially if it involves bankruptcy, overdrafted accounts, or late payments. However, I found that I could always put clients at ease. I would often share the story of my mismanagement of finances and how I overcame it. This transparency allowed them to be more open and honest about their situation.

At that moment, I realized that I was meant to provide a deeper transformation. That is when I decided that it was time to start my own business. I knew that I had something special, and that was "Me." My experience was life-changing for so many. I was a single parent for eight years, so I was aware of the many challenges that came with that. Many mothers gravitated towards me for that reason. They knew that I could help them through their financial journey because I had been through it. The thing that pushed this business the most was generational wealth. I knew that I never wanted my daughter to continue a life in poverty and I wanted to show other women that they could break the generational curses too. As you continue reading, you will see how my business evolved over time. It involved some risk-taking that helped me to overcome my fears of becoming an entrepreneur.

2. What were some of the fears you experienced before venturing out and starting your business?

Honestly, I feared that I would not receive any support. In 2016, I started my business, and I had no clue how to run a business. However, after working in banking and experiencing my financial struggles, I knew I had the knowledge and the passion for getting people to their next level financially.

Upon starting my business, most of the people that supported me were people that I didn't know. This is great, right? Not so much for me! I thought that your supporters would be people that you knew, but after I shut that business down after only six months, I knew that I needed to find out how to truly run a business. I started to realize that I should be embracing strangers. These people wanted my services, and I needed to appreciate them. It is sometimes hard for people that are familiar with you to accept that you are elevating. They won't necessarily view you as an expert in your field.

I was a perfectionist. So, when I decided to pursue my business again, I felt that it had to be perfect. However, I quickly learned that perfectionism did not equal success. At the start of the pandemic, my purpose called for me. I was moved to start a Facebook group, which addressed financial pain points—credit, budgeting, savings strategies, and debt elimination. I became a resource, and people were achieving the results from my teachings. I had numerous inquiries, and before I knew it, I witnessed the re-birth of my business. I can't describe the feeling. It was impeccable to know that my gift was making room for me effortlessly. You will find out that your purpose is not hard; it is easy if you believe in yourself! What a gift!

3. How did you overcome those fears/obstacles? Was it worth it?

This may sound simple, but I just did it. I was so tired of living check to check. I was so tired of not living my purpose. Do you know that feeling? A feeling of emptiness. See, I had my family, my children, a house, and a "decent job." Was that enough? Grateful, yes, but there was more to life. There was generational wealth that I needed to create for my children. I needed the freedom to take off work when my family needed me. I wanted to travel freely. I wanted to maximize my income.

So, I did it! I once heard that if you do not understand your purpose, start serving. In this Facebook group, I was able to give my time, resources, and knowledge. While doing so, my name became well known.

You see, sometimes you are a hidden gem waiting to be found, but what if you allowed yourself to **be found.** Everyone around me said I was great and destined for great things. But did I? Somewhere along the line, my subconscious thoughts got the best of me. It was not until I decided that I would no longer stay in that box!

I found my happy! So, was it worth it? Absolutely. You deserve to find your happy. It makes no sense to live in a world full of regrets when everything is possible. EVERYTHING! My only regret is not believing in myself sooner. I wish I had viewed my failures as lessons. It was never an opportunity to give up; it was merely a sign to keep going.

I am often intrigued by success stories of millionaires or celebrities that had a challenging life. I have always wanted to know what kept them going. It's not luck but it takes persistence to reach purpose no matter how many hurdles you must take.

I remember reading Tyler Perry's story. He had a vision that took him far beyond his circumstances. He was in an abusive household and experienced sexual abuse by adults outside of the home. He had a GED education and worked odd jobs that were unfulfilling. His passion was writing plays. He worked diligently and saved $12,000 for his first musical, *I Know I've Been Changed.* Perry expected that he would have 1,200 guests. To his surprise, only thirty people showed up, which led to his homelessness when he was unable to pay rent and car payments. Did Tyler give up? No, but he could have. That feels like a slap in the face to use all your hard-earned money, and no one shows up. But guess what, it was only an opportunity to get better because this was still purpose-driven. In 1998, he rented out Atlanta's House of Blues to showcase his play, "I Know I've Been Changed," one more time. His tickets started to sell out this time, and he eventually had to move to larger theatres.

What if he had given up? The moment you use your adversity as a motivator, you will experience success. When you find your purpose, failure does not exist. Every obstacle in life pushes you into purpose. You have something that the world needs. They are waiting on YOU to be found.

4.When did you realize it was time for you to start working towards your own financial freedom? What difficulties did you face?

Just like yesterday, I remember the discrimination for using FMLA (Family Medical Leave Act) at my previous job. Yes, policies were in place, but if you dared to take off for being sick, you would be secretly punished. The punishment was to make sure that no one would help you. As I arrived back at work, I had a tremendous load of paperwork. Their attitude said, "we do not care" and "just deal with it."

I decided that I would change things for my family. I no longer wanted to continue working in a place that did not value my family or me. I wanted freedom. I remember the feeling of unfulfillment. I stated, "Is this all life has for me? To sit at a desk and repeat the same tasks daily?" That same day I printed positive quotes and placed them all over my office.

"It's never too late to be what you might have been." – George Elliot
"Stop thinking, Start doing."
"Great things take time."
"Don't stop when you're tired, stop when you're done."
"The more you learn, the more you earn."

I said these daily. It helped me to think beyond the office. I realized that it was not about my degrees. I had a bachelor's and a Master's, yet I was only making 45K per year. There is something very wrong with this picture. It hit me, and I realized that my skills could be taken outside of these four walls.

I had prepared myself for two years. As I started to transition from corporate to queenpreneurship, it was not easy. Now that I had to combat my fear of starting a business again, I had to believe that I would keep going no matter how challenging it was. My motto is to always pray, plan, and prepare. I did all those things, and I was ready to make a smooth transition. I had six to eight months in savings and not many bills. Then boom, my brother, who has mental health issues, got in a situation that involved a high financial cost. This was devastating. I am the financial breadwinner in my family, so I knew that the majority of this would fall on me. So, it did! I had to wipe out my savings to get him the care that he needed. What I experienced was much deeper than money management. It was "money mindset". Money mindset is what kept my business open, and it just may save yours. In fact, I'm sure of it.

After feeling discouraged, I knew that I could not allow myself to stay in that place. I had to remember that there were people out there depending on me. I had to move! I now knew that this journey was necessary if I wanted to teach this method to others.

Money mindset is thinking beyond what's in your wallet or your account. It is the idea that your God-given gifts will make room for you. So, I allowed those gifts to work. I am well known for being an expert in finances, but people really didn't understand the concept of a money mindset coach. God gave me the vision to host an event. He told me that I would teach business credit at this event. However, it presented the opportunity also to teach money mindset.My relationship with God is so strong, and I can hear Him when he speaks to me. He told me that this event would sell out. So, I booked the venue, and the next day, I made my money back. Within only seven days, the event was sold out. I had over twenty sponsors that contributed to this event.

This, my friend, is what money mindset looks like. It's so divine that even people that don't know you will fund your dreams.

5. Financial freedom does not happen overnight, it takes work. Share three actionable steps that show you are serious about achieving financial freedom.

1. Know your Purpose
    Always chase your purpose, not the money. But how do I find my purpose? It can only be found in your creator. Once you find your purpose, this will increase your confidence to stay on your path and not someone else's. Purpose is your drive when things slow down. Purpose is your reason for waking up daily. Purpose pushes you when life kicks you down. Purpose provides a fulfillment that goes beyond money. Have you ever heard the stories about millionaires that are completely unhappy? Now, this may not make sense to you, but if that person is focused on a career to please others, how can they experience financial freedom? Financial freedom happens when all areas of your life are free. When you are genuinely happy, money is just the icing on the cake.

2. Write down your goals
    You should always write down goals. This serves as your blueprint. I usually like to refer to Habakkuk 2:2. "Write the vision, make it plain." By writing things down, you create a visual. You have something to work towards. It is also a reminder of your "Big Dreams." One method that works is to write down all your huge goals and break them down into smaller goals. For example, you may put down your five to ten-year goals on your vision board. It only seems unattainable until you break it down. For example, if you wanted to make $100,000 per year, that is only $274 per day.

Now when you look at it like that, it seems pretty possible. Therefore it is so crucial to write down your goals and focus on them daily.

3. Create a spending plan
    Have you ever heard the saying, " It's not how much you make, but how much you can keep." This has to be the best statement ever! I often hear people saying that If they could make more money, they would have a better life. However, if you are not managing what you have, this will not help you. Whatever you do not manage, you will lose. This applies to time, talent, and treasures.

6. Based on your expertise, share three practical tips/steps other business owners can take to continue to grow their business.

1. *Stay consistent*
    One of my favorite scriptures that I use for encouragement is Ecclesiastes 9:11 "The fastest runner doesn't always win the race, and the strongest warrior doesn't always win the battle." The race is a marathon, not a sprint. Many times, we can start comparing ourselves to others that are in our industries, especially new entrepreneurs. For example, if you have been in business for one year and someone else has been in business for three years, that will look different. That means that business owner had some lessons that contributed to their success. As you continue to learn, you will start to see the growth of your business as well.

What can you do to ensure that you are consistent?

- Always review your previous day to see what worked or did not work. If it's not broken, don't fix it. For example, if you are making posts on social media, it is important to review the insights. The time of day that you post, as well as the language that you are using, may be key.
- Plan out your months. You should always have a strategy in place that will continue to grow your business. It may be email marketing, organic marketing, or social media marketing. It is more challenging to sell to a cold audience than a warm audience.
- Get an accountability partner. This may simply be another entrepreneur in business. This is someone that can push you when you are feeling discouraged. When like-minded individuals surround you, you are more likely to be creative. This type of relationship is a great asset to your business, so don't ever take it for granted.

2. *Invest in your business*

Outsource
As much as you think that you can do everything in your business, it is not possible. If you want to see growth, you must expand and outsource to other experts that can help you strengthen your business. There will be people that are smarter than you; you might as well hire them so that they can become a key asset to your company.

Hire a coach
Hiring a coach was a pivotal point in my business. I had no idea how to become a profitable coach. It took

research and social proof before choosing my coach, but after six months, I hired her. As a result, I made three times back what I had invested. Talk about ROI (Return on Investment)!

Attend networking events

I know many people don't attend networking events due to their introverted personalities. However, did you know that Barack Obama, Bill Gates, Michael Jordan, Albert Einstein, Mark Zuckerberg were all introverts? At some point, these people had to interview or even talk in front of the entire world. Networking events will help you develop your personable skills and increase your business growth.

Market research

Things are always changing. It is important to know the pain points of your audience. Once you know it, you can constantly learn how to solve their problems. Problem-solving is equivalent to a profitable business. Take for instance, your phone! Ask yourself, what problem does it solve? Now ask yourself, what problem does your product or service solve? If you don't know the answer to that question, I suggest you start to do some more digging to find it.

Take risks

This may sound cliché, but it is certainly a method that works. Starting your business was a risk. It could have succeeded, or it could have failed, but your purpose said I would succeed. That is defined as faith, the evidence of things unseen. While I encourage you to plan and prepare for your risks, I also believe some things are out of your control. I left corporate with the expectation that my savings would not deplete. But somehow, God allowed it to be a teachable moment that I can now teach to others. The power of Money Mindset!

After coaching several clients that were struggling in business, I came to one conclusion. The answer was simply fear that was connected to the lack of money and knowledge. Until you can form a spirit of abundance, you will always lack something. If you play small, you will reap small. The one thing that is guaranteed to grow your business is big dreams and crazy faith. You will never know how far you can go until you really start to believe it. Money Mindset can change your life, **ONLY** if you allow it to.

Remember that only you can set the limitation on how far you can go! I dare you to choose ***FREEDOM!***

How to Connect with Me:

If you want to connect with me and learn how to confidently transition from corporate to queenpreneurship with a golden financial plan then visit latoyawhitfield.com

Acknowledgements

Thank You To My Pre-Order Supporters

1. Brienna Hamlet, Virtually at Best LLC, (IG) virtuallyatbest, (FB)Virtually at Best, bit.ly/virtuallyatbest
2. Tiffany LaMeia, Tiffany LaMeia & Co. Facebook, www.tiffanylameia.com
3. Caelen Love, Raising the Bar Consulting, IG: Rtbarconsulting, www.rtbarconsulting.com
4. Latriece Benson, She Pressed, spdesigns.shop
5. James Carter, Coach Carter LLC, @coachcarterllc, https://linktr.ee/coachcarterllc
6. Arkesha Hampton, Devoted Holistics, Facebook and Instagram,devotedholistics.com
7. Courtney Green, This Is It by CG, LLC, FB: This Is It, www.thisisitbycg.com
8. Beverly Johnson, Genesys Fitness, FB: Genesys Fitness, www.beverlykjohnson.com
9. Christy Baker, Baker's Paradise, LLC, Facebook
10. Sarita Timmons, Facebook: In Good Hands HomeHealth Care, Ingoodhandshhc.com
11. Rachanda Smith, Chanda's Consulting, LLC & Love Beyond, http://linktr.ee/rachanda1
12. Selena Carter, Step N2 Success, Fb: stepn2sucessnow, IG: step_n2_success
13. Erika Curry, Love Street Boutique, LLC, FB:The Love Street Boutique,Ig:TheLoveStreetBoutique www.thelovestreetboutique.com
14. Tobea Cook, FB: Inner Healing Counseling LLC, www.Innerhealing-counseling.com
15. Tyesha Draper, Captured by T&J LLC, @capturedbytj

16. Patricia Edwards, Flawless Belle, IG:flawlessbelle11
17. Tiffany Draper, Studio 53, LLC, @TiffanyDraper, www.studio53huntsville.com
18. Brenda Ingram, Heavenly Hands Bakery
19. Rosalyn Riggins, House of Glam Beauty Spa, FB: House of Glam Beauty Spa https://houseofglambeautyspa.as.me/
20. Ashley Brown, Falyssa B. LLC, IG: @falyssabllc
21. Sunny Garcia, Sunny Lashes LLC, IG:mysunny_lashes, www.sunnylashesme.com
22. Monretta Vega-Pair, Envisionary Counseling LLC, FB:@envisionarycounselingllc IG: @envisionary_counseling, www.envisionarycounseling.com
23. Denise Grant, Destiny Estates LLC, denisegrantrealtor@gmail.com
24. Alexis Ingram Smith IG/Tik Tok: @vibrantprestige, www.vibrantprestige.com
25. Tushundra Owens, Co-Owner of Kloset Vanity, IG: @Klosetvanity
26. Audrey Armstrong, The Beauty Mark, @thebeautymarkesthetics
27. Demberia Grandy, Chanda Davis Real Estate , dembisellshomes.com
28. Wendy M. Nicholson, Wanderer Shirts & Creations, IG: wanderer_tees
29. Amber Black, Amber Black & CO, IG: @amberblack.co
30. Evelyn Euphoria, Euphoria Boutique, IG: @euphoria_boutique0306
31. Audrey Armstrong, The Beauty Mark Esthetics, IG: @thebeautymarkesthetics

Reflection Questions

1. What is one fear you overcame recently?
2. What are some ways you plan to shift your mindset to knock down any limiting beliefs you might have?
3. What do you believe about debt? How do you feel about paying your debts?
4. What were you taught about money growing up? (savings, investment, debt, etc.)
5. What's one thing you learned in this book that you will apply to your life and business?
6. What is a financial goal that you accomplished this year? How did it feel?
7. In what areas of your life are you lacking freedom?
8. What is your motivation for becoming financially free?
9. What is one actionable step you can take that shows you are serious about becoming financially free?
10. How will you continue to choose freedom over fear?

Final Words

Thank you so much for taking the time out to read our book. I sincerely hope this encourages you, empowers you, and challenges you to overcome any fears that are preventing you from accomplishing your goals. I would love to hear your thoughts, and if anything written resonated with you, feel free to email me at info@reachingwhileteaching@gmail.com.

Inspired to take that leap of faith and write that book you keep putting off? Get started by downloading my FREE Self-Publishing Checklist or FREE Book Outline on reachingwhileteaching.com.

If this book was a blessing or an encouragement to you, please share it with your friends and family and even your online friends by using the hashtag #freedomoverfearbook

Visionary Author and Coach, Shanine Alessia Young

Business Listing Section

Brittany Williams
BW Financial Consulting Services LLC
www.bwfinancialconsultingservice.com
Email: info@bwfinancialconsultingservice.com
Located in Huntsville, Alabama

Brittany is a financial coach that teaches people the importance of changing their mindset about wealth and money management. She coaches men and women on the importance of building generational wealth in order to have long-term financial success.

Business Tip:
Never lose faith as a result of being fearful of the unknown! Faith will open doors that fear could never!

William Winfield
William Winfield LLC
www.willgotthesauce.karta.com/page/Hlw21
Email: williamwinfield38@gmail.com
Social media: www.instagram.com/willisblessed
Located in Tacoma, Washington

Coach Will helps 9-5 coaches, authors, and speakers to package their expertise and book more business.

Business Tip:
Your job isn't to sell, but to attract people who want to purchase from you!

Beverly Johnson
Genesys Fitness, www.beverlykjohnson.com
Email: info@beverlykjohnson.com
Social media: www.facebook.com/genesysfitness
Located in Huntsville, Alabama

Genesys Fitness develops strategies to demolish old habits and embrace a healthy, whole lifestyle. It's about letting go of the old habits and embracing the new ones. Through coaching, the foundation and a roadmap is created to reclaim your identity through customized coaching, fitness training, and strategies to build sustainable changes. We believe that by helping women rediscover who they are after suffering a loss, she will be empowered to become her ideal self – physically, mentally, and emotionally.

Business Tip:
Never fear asking for help. Building relationships and collaborations are essential for growth.

Ashley Brown
Falyssa B LLC, https://www.falyssab.com/
Email: fabshopping@falyssab.com
Social media: https://www.instagram.com/falyssabllc
Located in Madison, AL

Falyssa B LLC specializes in custom chocolate dipped treats and cold pressed juices.

Business Tip:
When it comes to your business, be audacious! You absolutely have to become comfortable with taking calculated, yet bold risks.

Brenda Ingram
Heavenly Hands Bakery
Email: ingramb17@yahoo.com
Located in Coffeeville, MS

All cakes, pies and treats are homemade with love.
Customers are always treated with respect.

Business Tip:
Always be nice to people.

Chavon Thomas
Power and Grace Leaders, Inc
chavonanette.com
Email: chavonanette@gmail.com
Social media: www.instagram.com/chavonanette
Located in Virginia Beach, Virginia

Chavon serves by helping people break fear, build faith, and lead confidently online and beyond to make an impact in the world and fulfill purpose.

Chavon is an Amazon #1 International Bestselling Author, Transformational Speaker, Leadership and Life Coach, and Talk Show Host. She is the CEO of Purpose Unwrapped, LLC and non-profit Power and Grace Leaders, Inc. Also a board member- COO- of an Accreditation organization- Governing Council.

Chavon is affectionately known as the Fire Leadership Coach. She marries practical and spiritual tools to empower and equip kingdom people to lead in the world.

Business Tip:
Be Courageous, Confident, and Build with Community.

Stephanie Williams
Stephanie Speaks, LLC
www.destinedtoconquer.com
Email: Stephaniespeaks@destinedtoconquer.com
Social media: www.instagram.com/Steph.speaks
Located in San Antonio, Texas

Stephanie Speaks, LLC is an organization serving, reaffirming, and championing women seeking to Survive and Thrive. I am a Transformation Coach, Motivational Speaker, and Best-Selling Author. I help women define their purpose, awaken the power within and maximize their true potential. By providing compassion-centered life and business coaching to help cultivate freedom and abundance in their life

Business Tip:
You have to step out in faith and obedience, completely let go and surrender and allow your purpose (gifts and talents) to serve you as you help others. Everything you need is already within you; you need to make the forward movement, and the resources and tools you need to carry out the vision will just be waiting on you to make the first step. As Nike says, "Just do it" create and build the life you desire while building generational wealth and a legacy of impact. Your purpose is not for you; it's for those whose lives you are transforming through your story.
Keep doing and being GREAT!

Ashley Dumas
Scentsible Sista, LLC
https://www.scentsiblesista.com
Email: scentsiblesista@gmail.com
Social media:
https://www.facebook.com/scentsiblesista/
Located in Columbus, MS

Scentsible sista is an online candle store that strives to bring calm, therapeutic fragrance to your home or office. We offer many scents from fruity, fall, to warm summer fragrances. Our mission is to bring about peace in everyone's home one candle at a time

Business Tip:

Start with a narrow focus and expand as you scale.

Celia Thompson
Lia Divine Fitness
http://www.liadivinefitness.com
Email: celia.cthompson@gmail.com
Social media: http://instagram/liadivinefitness
Located in Plantation, Florida

Lia Divine Fitness is a black woman owned business that specializes in helping each individual to achieve their body goals all while staying motivated and confident rocking our athleisure and shapewear.

Marcia Young
Valencia's Caribbean Fusion
https://valenciasrestaurant.com/
Phone: 954-653-2165
Social media:
www.instagram.com/valenciascaribbeancuisine
Located in Margate, FL

Valencia's Caribbean Fusion Restaurant has delicious Caribbean food in the heart of Margate, Florida. Enjoy tasty Caribbean style dishes for an affordable price.

Special Thanks to These Businesses

Valary Campbell, Glory House USA, Inc.
Terrence Isom, Creative Floor Design Inc.
Tricia Lewis, Vintage Glam Events & Design
Consulting, https://www.vglamevent.org/

FREEDOM OVER FEAR

The Business Owner's Guide to Achieving Financial Freedom

Shanine Alessia Young
Fenisha Walters
Jordan Young
Eric Jackson
Brittny Ortiz-Jackson
Monique Singleton
Nishia Slater
Latoya Whitfield

…iel G. Dorner, G. E. Gorman and Philip J. Calvert 2015

…hed by Facet Publishing
…gmount Street, London WC1E 7AE
…facetpublishing.co.uk

…Publishing is wholly owned by CILIP: the Chartered Institute of
…y and Information Professionals.

…l G. Dorner, G. E. Gorman and Philip J. Calvert have asserted their
…under the Copyright, Designs and Patents Act 1988 to be identified
…hors of this work.

…h Library Cataloguing in Publication Data
…alogue record for this book is available from the British Library.

…I 978-1-85604-484-4

…published 2015

…printed on FSC accredited material.

…eset from author's files in 11/14 pt Garamond and Myriad Pro by
…et Publishing Production.
…ted and made in Great Britain by CPI Group (UK) Ltd, Croydon,
…0 4YY.

Information Needs

Principles and practice in information

Daniel G. Dorner, G. E. Gorman and Philip J. Calver

© D

Pub
7 Ri
www

Face
Libr

Dar
righ
as a

Exc
Act
in a
or, i
of a
con
Pub

Brit
A c

ISB

Firs

Tex

Ty
Fa
Pr
Cl

Contents

List of figures and tables

Figures

Tables

List of scenarios

Dr Philip Calvert is Senior Lecturer in the School of Information Management at Victoria University of Wellington (New Zealand). He has also taught at Nanyang Technical University (Singapore) and worked as a librarian in the UK and other countries. His research interests focus on the management of information organizations, especially the cost effective provision of quality services. He has published extensively on service quality and performance measurement. His last book was *Improving the Quality of Library Services for Students with Disabilities* (Libraries Unlimited, 2006).

Dr Daniel Dorner FLIANZA is Senior Lecturer and PhD Programme Director in the School of Information Management at Victoria University of Wellington (New Zealand). He is also Joint Director of Asia-New Zealand Informatics Associates (providing consulting and training for informatics in Asia). He has worked as a librarian in both New Zealand and Canada, and has been involved in a variety of professional training programmes in Vietnam, Thailand, Laos, Cambodia, Singapore, Sri Lanka and Bangladesh. His research interests include information policy, digital preservation management and information literacy education in developing countries. He has had long-term involvement with IFLA, currently as Chair of Division V and a member of the IFLA Governing Board. He was also co-editor of *Metadata Applications and Management* (Facet Publishing, 2004).

Professor G. E. Gorman FCLIP, FRSA recently retired as Professor of Information Science at the University of Malaya (Kuala Lumpur); prior to that he was Professor of Information Management at Victoria University of Wellington (New Zealand) and Senior Lecturer in Information Studies at Charles

Sturt University (Australia). He is currently Joint Director of Asia-New Zealand Informatics Associates (providing consulting and training for informatics in Asia). He has been involved in a number of professional training programmes in South Africa, SE Asia, Bangladesh, Lebanon and elsewhere. His research interests are in the areas of professional education in SE Asia and cultural impacts on informatics-related topics, especially information literacy and knowledge management. He is Editor-in-Chief of *Online Information Review* (Emerald) and the author of a dozen books and some 400 articles. His most recent book, co-edited with Dr David Pauleen, is *Personal Knowledge Management: individual, organisational and social aspects* (Gower, 2011), and he is currently working on a third edition of *Qualitative Research for the Information Professional* (Facet Publishing) with Dr Gillian Oliver (Victoria University of Wellington).

Preface

What can be uttered in a word but contemplated forever? What do fools ignore and pragmatists suffer? What is evaluation's greatest challenge? These questions present no riddle, no mystery, and no conundrum. The answers are: complexity, complexity and complexity. Every attempt to conduct an evaluation is beset with the impossibility of covering every angle; every attempt to conduct a review is faced with the impracticability of chasing down every single issue.

(Pawson, 2013, 29)

Pawson wails, 'complexity, complexity, complexity', in relation to evaluation, but he could just as well be speaking of information needs analysis (INA). For some reason the common view among information professionals is that INA is a mysteriously complex undertaking. Perhaps this is because they lack experience in this type of applied investigation; as in almost any endeavour, lack of experience makes something seem more daunting than it actually is. If in contrast information workers see INA as simple and straightforward, they lack INA experience, or perhaps see it as something related just to information literacy. In reality INA is neither more complex nor simpler than any other kind of investigation in the social sciences. But the aura of complexity remains the standard view of INA, and this has been a key motivation for writing this book. In the book we seek to show that, with a step-by-step approach to the theory, process and procedures of INA, readers will understand that it is a straightforward type of applied research with information in a variety of information contexts as its focus. In other words INA is not necessarily the complex beast that many assume it to be.

A second motivation for this book is a desire to help our readers better realize that INA is ubiquitous in society and that it is not the preserve of information professionals or information organizations. In the information-rich developed world, where the majority enjoy ready and rapid access to information, it is essential to understand that we are all engaged in INA at some level, and that if we are not, then we are the poorer for it in our professional, social and private lives. With regard to this second motivating factor a scan of the literature shows that physicians do it, motorists do it, parliamentarians do it, even members of the aerospace industry do it.... Just a quick browse of a blog like https://twitter.com/search?q=information%20needs%20analysis&src=typd surprises with the range of professions, interest groups and others concerned about information needs in various contexts. Interestingly, those in health care have a relatively long history of involvement in information needs and INA, perhaps spurred on by the growth of evidence-based medicine in recent decades. Looking just at primary care physicians and nurses, for example, a very interesting literature review by Clarke (2013) indicates just how intensive has been medical interest in INA. One suspects that other professions may have similar interest in the field, albeit perhaps not as detailed.

So INA is supposedly complex, and it is clearly ubiquitous in society, rather than the preserve of information professionals. If there is a third key characteristic of INA, and this relates to the second point, then it is context. Context is critical to any kind of real grasp of information needs and INA; we must understand that a barrister's chambers is contextually unique compared with an aeroplane cockpit, which in turn differs from an automobile assembly line or an employment agency. Each context has specific and unique information needs, which means that an INA must be undertaken in full understanding of the uniqueness of each context. Having a full working knowledge of this reality, we might then feel moved to cry robustly, along with Pawson, 'context, context, context'!

Structure and content

Our practical intentions in writing this book are twofold: (1) to present a broad overview of INA so that it is understood in relation to needs analysis in general and as a key component of the decision-making processes that occur within specific information management contexts, and (2) to provide a professionally focused, hands-on tool for individuals (whom we refer to as investigators) in conducting INAs in those various contexts.

To achieve these intentions we present the results of our thinking and research in ten chapters, divided into three parts (Chapters 1–4, 5–8 and 9–10). Chapters 1–4 present an extensive overview of INA and the theoretical underpinnings of needs analysis. Chapters 5–8 discuss the most common methods used in gathering data for an INA. Finally, Chapters 9–10 bring the INA process to a conclusion by presenting the main data analysis methods used in INA, and offering suggestions about how to present the findings that arise from the analysis.

While readers may be tempted to cut directly to the nuts and bolts of conducting an INA by beginning with Chapter 4, we strongly argue that this is like stepping into a chess match halfway through play and trying to understand the moves without knowing either the principles or strategies of the game. We strongly advise that Chapters 1–4 be read so that a potential investigator understands fundamental aspects, theoretical underpinnings and models of INA in order to avoid the pitfalls of complexity and context.

In Chapter 1 we define our terms and also discuss how needs analysis differs from needs assessment. In this chapter we further address the various types and levels of information needs and the reasons for conducting INAs. We offer this definition of INA, which guides our thinking throughout the volume:

> Information needs analysis is the process of making value judgements regarding solutions to an information-related problem faced by a client group, service provider or facility in order to facilitate fulfilment of a necessary, useful and defensible purpose.

In Chapter 2 we discuss the contextual nature of information needs, examining them in relation to culture, purpose and perceived importance, as well as to communities. In Chapter 3 we turn to differentiating the levels, models and types of needs analysis in general as found in the literature. We then delve deeper by examining the application of some of these models and types in information management contexts, and then draw upon their key elements to develop our own models of INA. In Chapter 4 we focus on practical aspects of INAs: the four principal stages that occur in an INA, the main activities in those stages and the interrelated nature of the activities.

Then, with some understanding of these issues in needs analysis and INA, the reader is better prepared to understand the basics and nuances of data gathering for an INA – here we seek to put the lie to the assumption that INA is unbelievably complex. By breaking down processes and procedures into their simple components, INA data gathering is seen for what it is: just another type of applied research with a very particular focus. This is the purpose of the second group of chapters (5–8)

Thus Chapter 5 provides an overview of data-gathering methods, offering practical advice to assist with the choice of these methods, which means taking into consideration such matters as the ease, speed and cost of data collection.

Such key concepts as validity, reliability and ethics are also discussed.

It is not always necessary to collect new data for an INA, and this we explain in Chapter 6. All organizations will have existing (or historical) data that can be analysed to understand contextual aspects of information needs. These internal data may be found in hard copy or electronic documents, and they may be retrieved from electronic systems and archives. There are also many sources of data external to an organization, and these are also addressed in this chapter.

Since it is usual in an INA to collect new data, Chapters 7 and 8 describe the most common forms of data collection: the survey and the interview. In Chapter 7 we look at the strengths and weaknesses of surveys and offer guidance on all aspects of the method, from planning through data collection and data analysis. The discussion in Chapter 8 then focuses on the characteristics of data gathering through interviews and focus groups. We make clear the distinction between qualitative approaches here and how they differ from the quantitative approach in surveys. Chapter 8 also discusses observation, diaries and usability testing.

The third group of chapters (9 and 10) covers what needs to happen after the data are gathered. In Chapter 9 we provide readers with the essentials required to analyse and integrate the data gathered in INAs, both in respect of preliminary data gathered for INA planning purposes and the types of data obtained through the processes detailed in Chapters 6–8. And, while Chapter 9 provides guidance on the application of the main data analysis methods likely to be used in INAs, we keep the discussion at a practicable level rather than attempting to provide the type of highly detailed instruction found in textbooks (to which we refer readers in some detail).

We bring the book to its conclusion in Chapter 10, explaining the writing and presentation of the INA report in whatever format required. This chapter addresses the importance of an INA's audience, issues related to validity and reliability, style and level of detail in the report, as well as the report's structure.

Throughout the book we have sought to keep in mind our audience, which consists of students, practitioners and researchers in information needs analysis, whatever their specific frames of reference might be. To help make the work user friendly for this audience, we state the focal questions of each chapter at the beginning, include scenarios in most chapters to help give a sense of practicality to the discussions, summarize each chapter at the end and include suggestions for further reading.

While any errors and infelicities remain the authors' responsibility, we trust that the intent of this work has come to fruition in a manner and form that will interest and instruct anyone curious about information needs, and especially information needs analysis.

Acknowledgements

We wish to give our sincere thanks to Ms Lynley Stone of the Information Workshop, Auckland, New Zealand for her significant contribution to Chapter 7, which provided a baseline for making this an understandable guide to surveys and survey data analysis. We hope that our iteration of her ideas is a credit to her input.

G. E. Gorman adds:

I wish to thank my former students and colleagues in the Faculty of Computer Science and Information Technology at the University of Malaya for their kindness and patience while parts of this book were being created. I further wish to thank those postgraduate students who, in a series of research seminars, contributed significantly to my thinking on INA and why it has been so misunderstood for so long. But most especially I offer my warmest thanks and deepest gratitude to Helen Carley, Publishing Director of Facet Publishing, for never quite losing faith in this enterprise over many years. A special thanks goes to the unflappable Lin Franklin and the anonymous copy editor and proofreaders for their unerring eye for detail and fearless attacks on the many infelicitous turns of phrase.

References

Clarke, M.A. (2013) Information Needs and Information-seeking Behaviour Analysis of Primary Care Physicians and Nurses: a literature review, *Health Information and Libraries Journal*, **3**, 178-90.

Pawson, R. (2013) *The Science of Evaluation: a realist manifesto*, SAGE Publications, London.

CHAPTER 1

Background to needs analysis for information managers

Introduction

Needs analysis, or information needs analysis (INA), is a practice-based activity conducted mostly, but not exclusively, by an information manager, usually in relation to user and community needs. Typically, such a person, or team of people, simply roll up their sleeves and get 'stuck in'. Perhaps there has been a flurry of e-mail exchanges with others who have done a needs analysis, and some anecdotal evidence has been gathered about how to approach this activity. Unfortunately, needs analysis is, like any research, an activity that requires careful planning, including an understanding of precisely what needs analysis is.

In this opening chapter we address a number of preliminary questions which must be understood in order to have a good grasp of INA and the INA process. Specifically,

◆ What is 'needs analysis' and how does it differ from 'needs assessment'?
◆ What are 'needs', and what is the difference between 'wants' and 'needs'?
◆ How important are value judgements in identifying needs and solutions?
◆ What are the various kinds of needs that might emerge in an information setting?
◆ How do we identify needs in an information setting?

To use this book effectively, and hence to undertake effective INA, it is necessary for readers to understand the meaning of certain key concepts. The concept of 'need' and the distinction between 'need' and 'want', for example, are central to this book, as is the distinction between information needs analysis and information needs assessment. How, indeed, do we define 'need' and 'needs analysis' in the context of information work? What types of INA might one undertake, and why do so in the first place? These are all questions and issues that should be addressed by anyone prior to conducting an information needs analysis.

Information needs analysis rather than information needs assessment

At the most basic level we can view INA as an investigative process that allows us to identify and analyse the information-related needs of a particular group in a specific context and the use of that data to inform a decision. Information needs analysis includes the identification of information needs, the analysis of the needs so that they are understood and the assessment of the needs with respect to the impending decision.

As distinct from 'needs analysis', the term 'needs assessment' refers to a process employed largely within social, health and education services to evaluate the needs of particular groups 'as the basis for the distribution of social goods' (Percy-Smith, 1996, 8). The social goods in these contexts are public services such as legal aid for the poor, health care for people with diabetes, and reading recovery programmes for young people with learning difficulties. Reviere et al. (1996, xi) state that 'as a type of applied social research, needs assessment is meant to foster program development and policy-making'.

We use the term 'information needs analysis' to focus our discussion on information-related contexts and to demonstrate to readers that the research-based core of INA can be used in a much broader range of situations than those to which needs assessments traditionally have been applied.

A look at definitions from the *Oxford English Dictionary 3rd edn Online* (2010) helps to clarify our reasons for using the term 'information needs *analysis*' rather than 'information needs *assessment*'. According to the *OED Online*, the noun 'analysis' means 'the methodical or systematic investigation of something complex in order to explain or understand it'. Thus needs analysis refers to examining needs methodically to explain or understand them for the purpose of interpretation (with respect to a specific context). On the other hand, in the *OED Online* the noun 'assessment' means 'estimation, evaluation'. Needs assessment, therefore, because of its association with social, health and education services, implies evaluation of people's needs for the purpose of distributing resources (such as the previously mentioned social goods), or determining the policies upon which the decisions about distribution of resources will be based.

We argue that in managing libraries and information services there are at times decisions that require relatively straightforward INAs to be undertaken but which do not necessitate more complex needs assessments such as those described in the social, health and educational services and policy literatures. For example, the digital services area of an academic library might have to conduct an analysis of client needs in a very short time frame to decide which features should be implemented on the user interface for a new full-text journal service to which the library has just subscribed. In this situation it is necessary to identify and understand the needs of the client groups in a very specific context, but a full assessment of needs is not required. However, in contexts in which more complex information needs assessments are required to distribute resources (such as in deciding whether to build a new library) or to determine policy (for example, a policy to establish priorities for digitization projects), needs analyses must always be conducted to provide the data upon which the assessments will proceed. As a result, INAs are essential to information needs assessments; but in many information-related contexts the highly complex needs assessments (of the type discussed in the social, health and education literatures) are not appropriate, and simpler analyses can be conducted to support the decision processes.

At this point we also wish to emphasize that INA in the information sector is not limited to the information needs of clients, but rather extends from clients to staff to whole-of-institution analyses of information needs. As Bishop indicates (specifically in the context of collection management in schools), needs analysis is not only about the community or context but also about the institution itself: 'your community analysis should also include a detailed description of the school itself. It is extremely important to have knowledge about the students, teachers and administrators who utilize the media center' (Bishop, 2007, 21).

Before proceeding further, we wish to emphasize that, irrespective of whether undertaking a straightforward INA or one which is part of an intricate information needs assessment project, understanding what a need is lies at the heart of understanding what needs analysis is all about.

Understanding the concept of need

Many writers on the topic of needs analysis and needs assessment simplify the concept of need to the point where important elements of its meaning are lost. Gupta, Sleezer and Russ-Eft (2007, 15), for example, state that the 'gap between the current condition and a desired condition is called a need'. We believe this conceptualization on its own is too simple and wish to emphasize that the concept of need is complex, as any dictionary will confirm. Therefore, we focus our discussion of the meaning of need within the present context of INA. In the needs analysis/assessment literature we find diverse approaches taken by different writers, which is a clear indication that the concept is not easily explained or understood. By drawing on the strengths of different approaches and by adding our own perspectives we are able to clarify the essential aspects of this complex concept.

The approach taken by Witkin and Altschuld (1995, 9) helps to clarify a major problem in understanding the concept of need. They point out that the term is ambiguous, because 'need' as a noun has quite a different meaning from 'need' as a verb, and often the two meanings become confounded to the detriment of the outcomes of many needs assessments. They state that, as a noun, need 'refers to the gap or discrepancy between a present state (what is) and a desired end state (what should be)'. In other words a need is not a tangible entity; it is an inference that there is discrepancy between what is now and what should be in the future. Witkin and Altschuld further suggest that 'in a sense, a need is like a problem or concern'. Their explanation of need up to this point is similar to that of Gupta, Sleezer and Russ-Eft (2007); however, Witkin and Altschuld then explain that there is a problem with how we generally use the term as a verb. They say that, as a verb, need 'points to what is required or desired to fill the discrepancy – solutions, means to an end'. They then state:

> There is an important difference between needs and solutions. If you find yourself saying, 'I (we, they) need child care, hot lunches, a phonics program, money to hire recreation directors in our parks program, stiffer penalties for drunk driving,' you can be sure you are discussing solutions, not needs. [They] … are means to achieve some desired end – in effect, they are solutions to the underlying problem or concern.
>
> Witkin and Altschuld, 1995, 9

Thus when we conduct an INA, we must first identify the gap or problem before we point to possible solutions. In failing to do so we would be providing solutions before we knew what the real problem was and thus could be expending resources ineffectively. This is articulated clearly by Deep Thought in *The Hitchhiker's Guide to the Galaxy* (Adams, 1984, 28): having given '42' as the answer, he then opines, 'once you do know what the question actually is, you'll know what the answer means'. This is highlighted in Scenario 1.1.

Scenario 1.1 Computer access in Milhauser Public Library

Staff in Milhauser Public Library notice there are long queues of people waiting for access to the computers provided for online searching, and many users have lodged complaints about this problem.

The public service staff meet to discuss the situation and conclude that the problem can be resolved by adding 10 new computers and initiating Wi-Fi access in public areas of the library. They obtain permission from the library director, and the IT team quickly installs 10 more public access computers and implements a high quality Wi-Fi system. Problem solved – but in reality a solution to the need has been identified without understanding what the problem actually is.

There may in fact be several other reasons for the long queues, and none of these has been considered. If most of the people who are dependent on the public access computers need to spend lengthy periods of time at them, the context requires that the library staff determine why this is occurring. Providing more computers and Wi-Fi access might not reduce demand and waiting times at the public access computers. By conducting an appropriate INA the library might learn that the people who rely on the public access computers are either individuals in older age brackets who do not use mobile devices such as smartphones, tablets or laptops, or they are from across different age groups who cannot afford these devices. Therefore, there are still many library users who will remain dependent on the public access computers. And, even more important, the public service staff might find out that most of these computer users simply do not know how to search efficiently for information and therefore are taking longer than they wish to find the information for which they are searching. Therefore the problem could be resolved simply by placing tips for better searching beside each computer.

To determine an appropriate solution to the problem the library must understand what its clients' needs are, as well as what its own needs are. By focusing simply on the number of computers and Wi-Fi access rather than on what people's needs are and what the library's needs are, the library might expend resources when they are not needed; and the clients' needs for simple tips to improve online searching or for simple solutions other than Wi-Fi access might not be addressed.

Another important point raised in the needs assessment literature is that the conceptualization of a need involves values and judgements, often combined into what we call value judgements. Reviere et al. (1996, 5) offer a simple definition of values as 'ideas about what is good, right, and desirable', adding that values 'are generally thought to be a central basis for judgment and behavior'. They contend that the diversity of interpretations of need points to the variety of values and assumptions that may occur, and that it is therefore important at the planning stage 'to recognize and be prepared to work with this variety of values and assumptions'. An example to illustrate their point is that well educated, middle-class parents who are themselves library users are better placed to express their needs for public library services for pre-school children than are poorly educated parents who have never been library users. Therefore, addressing the needs of parents for services to pre-school children requires an INA that incorporates the values and assumptions of library users as well as those of non-library users, a group less likely to be able to articulate needs.

The tension between the welfare state view of needs and the market-based view is addressed by Percy-Smith (1996, 5). The welfare state view holds that needs can be identified objectively by professionals, measured and then used as the basis for determining access to resources. The market-based view contends that needs are better described as subjective preferences that people will act upon based on their own personal priorities. Leaving aside political opinion, we would suggest that both views point to the reality that needs must be identified by someone. Whether this someone is a purportedly objective observer or an intimately-involved individual is neither here nor there. Put most basically, a need is identified, and a competent INA investigator will want to ensure that an investigation takes account of both those who identify the need and those who have not done so but are part of the same cohort. According to Charles and Webb, as cited in Percy-Smith (1996, 6):

> Even to describe social need . . . we require some standards or criteria: needs do not exist in the real world already labelled. To call a condition such as poverty a social need implies an idea of what is not or ought not to be acceptable.
>
> Charles and Webb, 1986, 11

Thus information professionals who are analysing information needs are making value judgements at the outset, because the process commences by acknowledging that a problem or concern exists. The purpose of an INA is to obtain data about information needs in order to determine how best to resolve a problem, which is a values-based exercise. Resolving a problem requires value judgements, and traditionally library and information professionals are loath to make value judgements.

The bottom line in INA is that someone must make these value judgements, based on the best available evidence, about a particular direction to take. At times these value judgements can be relatively inconsequential, whereas at other times they can bear upon decisions with significant impact both in terms of the outcomes for the people whose needs are being assessed and the resources being allocated. Therefore, INA that leads to productive action is not for the faint-hearted, but rather for the reflective professional who is willing to put his or her opinions out for public scrutiny.

Defining 'needs' in relation to 'wants' and 'demands'

It is important at this point to remind readers that 'needs' are distinctly different from 'wants' – a continuation of the age-old debate within the information professions about whether one should 'give 'em what they want' (demand-driven services), or 'give 'em what they need' (value-driven services). The *OED Online* provides a range of definitions of 'want', implying that 'want' and a 'need' are the same; however, one of the *OED Online* definitions gives a clear indication that 'want' and 'need' may well be different. A 'want' is defined as 'something that one wishes to have (as opposed to what one needs or requires)'. McKillip (1987, 16) simplifies this for us when he says a want is 'something people are willing to pay for'.

The distinction between needs and wants was made most succinctly many years ago by Robert Broadus, when he said, in relation to the selection of materials for collections, 'selection by demand (wants) in its extreme form may overlook vital differences among materials, and extreme emphasis on value (needs) may treat materials as ends in themselves' (Broadus, 1981, 35). 'Value' in this sense implies a value judgement by the selector, just as needs analysis implies a value judgement by the INA investigator. Conversely, simply fulfilling clients' wants without consideration of their needs is merely a reactive, 'knee-jerk' way of dealing with service requirements and is inappropriate in an era dominated by strategic planning, accountability and transparency, for good or ill.

Note that Broadus equates demands with wants; in our view it is important to distinguish between them, as in some circles a 'demand' is seen as a 'need'. McKillip, having stated that a want is something people are willing to pay for, then goes on to say that 'demands differ from wants because the target population, rather than a service provider, usually originates and presents a demand' (McKillip, 1987, 17). There is, in neither 'want' nor 'demand', a recognition that dispassionate observation is in play – as indeed it is not; yet this is what characterizes a need, and what makes it different from either want or demand.

Given the distinction we make between 'needs', 'wants' and 'demands', we find unacceptable a definition of 'need' proffered by the *OED Online* as 'a particular point or respect in which some necessity or want is present or felt; a thing lacking or wanted; a requirement'. Note here the conflation of 'want' and 'requirement' and 'necessity'. In our view this muddies the waters and is quite unhelpful in a work devoted to INAs rather than demand fulfilment.

More to our liking is the definition offered by the American *Webster's Dictionary*: 'a need is something that is necessary or useful for the fulfillment of a defensible purpose' (*Webster's Third International Dictionary*, 1976). Necessity and usefulness seem to us to be key components in needs and needs analysis in an information setting, where we see the purpose of needs analysis as determining what is necessary and useful for decision making, and then making those decisions, whether for physical facilities, services or systems. We then add to this context-free dictionary definition the view of someone intimately involved with needs analysis, Jack McKillip: 'a need is the value judgement that some group has a problem that can be solved' (McKillip, 1987, 10). Note here the emphasis on value judgements and context, i.e. a group with a solvable problem.

For our purposes, then, we combine these two definitions to produce the following definition of 'information need', which guides our thinking throughout this book:

> An information need is a value judgement that a particular client group, service provider or facility has an information-related problem requiring a solution in order to fulfil a necessary, useful and defensible purpose.

Note that in some contexts an information need may be experienced by non-users of libraries or information services as well as by the users. Therefore, the term 'client group' in our definition always needs to be considered in relation to the specific context in which the information needs are being analysed, and it is used in this book as an inclusive rather than exclusive concept.

What does this definition mean in practice? First, by emphasizing value judgements, even in the simplest of INAs, we are indicating the ultimate relativity of the perceived need. 'The person seeing the need and the person experiencing the need may differ' (McKillip, 1987, 10). In the final analysis it is the need articulated by a particular client group in a specific context that wins the day, and it is the role of the information professional to understand the need in relation to these variables – client group and context – which will differ from circumstance to circumstance.

Second, use of the word 'problem' immediately implies the likelihood of a 'solution' – nearly all problems have solutions, however simple or complex they may turn out to be. 'A problem may have many potential solutions, solutions that vary in the probability of alleviating the problem, and in the cost and the feasibility of implementation' (McKillip, 1987, 10). The purpose of INA is to provide information professionals with carefully analysed data so that they may offer the best possible solution to the particular problem besetting a specific group in a specific context.

Stufflebeam et al. (1985) add considerably to the discussion through their analysis of the *Webster's* definition, which we have largely incorporated into our definition. In particular their emphasis on 'defensible purpose' we find most convincing. A defensible purpose must meet specified evaluative criteria, and these criteria are invariably situational. As a result, 'any needs assessment information must be judged and interpreted within the context of purposes, values, knowledge, cause-effect relationships and so on in order to reach a decision about what constitutes a need' (Stufflebeam et al., 1985, 12).

It is through the defensible purpose that these values and relationships (the basis of needs) become operational. But defensible purpose is never carved in stone; rather, it is something of a moveable feast involving social, philosophical and political considerations that change as situations evolve. Therefore,

> the question of defensible purpose is seldom permanently resolved. We must continually assess and reassess our philosophies, purposes and actions. This is a difficult and dynamic problem and not one to be ignored. It must, therefore, be a critical ongoing concern for the needs assessor.
>
> Stufflebeam et al., 1985, 15

This requirement for flexibility makes INA both frustrating and perhaps the most exciting aspect of an information professional's job. Here, though, we have made a leap from 'information needs' to 'information needs analysis', which itself requires defining.

Defining information needs analysis

Information needs analysis is a key component of the decision-making processes used for planning, implementing and evaluating systems and services in libraries and information centres. The scope of an INA ranges from determining the features of a book delivery scheme for elderly rural residents of a public library system, to deciding whether the metadata for managing newly acquired datasets in a research library's open-access repository is meeting the needs of both researchers and staff, to deciding on the type of meeting rooms required for the building design for a new suburban library.

In each of these examples INA is the solution-seeking process that follows identification of the need. In our terms it is defined thus:

> Information needs analysis is the process of making value judgements regarding solutions to an information-related problem faced by a client group, service provider or facility in order to facilitate fulfilment of a necessary, useful and defensible purpose.

In simpler terms INA is the process by which we delineate, obtain and apply information to determine the solutions that are useful or necessary in serving that defensible purpose for a particular client group, information service, system or facility. Delineating and obtaining information falls well within standard approaches to data gathering and processing; application is the provenance of value judgements, which, as we have indicated, form the core of needs analysis. According to Stufflebeam et al. (1985, 17), 'a need is a resulting decision coming out of a process that should include the compilation and review of several bits of information that culminates in a judgement of what constitutes need'.

From another vantage point we can view INA as an investigative process in an information-related context that involves the following steps:

◆ identifying that a client group has an information need
◆ determining the most appropriate method to gather data in order to determine what the information need is
◆ gathering the required data
◆ analysing the data to determine the essential constitution, nature or form of the need to inform the decision-making process used to resolve the problem.

Thus when we peel away the theoretical layers and look at INA from a purely practical perspective, we can see that in essence it is applied research – that is, it is research applied to identifying and resolving a problem experienced by a client group in an information-related context.

Types of information needs

Information needs can be viewed in relation to other types of needs. Here we present three perspectives that help us establish the varieties of information needs that INAs must address.

Abraham Maslow's theory of a hierarchy of needs is perhaps the most famous of all categorizations of needs. Maslow (1954) theorized that human beings are motivated by their needs. Individuals must satisfy their basic physical and emotional needs before they move up the hierarchy to satisfy such higher-level needs as esteem and self-fulfilment. Maslow's original hierarchy of needs listed five levels:

1 Biological and physiological needs: the very basic physical needs for air, food, drink, shelter, warmth, sex, sleep, etc. When not met, we feel hungry, thirsty, sick, tired, in pain, etc.
2 Safety needs: the needs for security, order, law, limits, safety and stability. These are psychological needs for protection from chaos and dysfunction.
3 Love and belongingness needs: the needs for belonging to a work group, family, etc. and for feeling affection, being in relationships, etc.
4 Esteem needs: the needs for self-esteem based on achievement, mastery, independence, etc. and for status based on recognition from others.
5 Self-actualization needs: the needs for maximizing one's personal potential, realizing self-fulfilment, seeking personal growth and peak experiences.

Maslow's hierarchy provides a structure that can be used by information professionals to conceptualize the varieties of information needs that client groups may have as a result of their needs as human beings. For example, Nicholas and Herman point out that it is unusual for people to have information needs *per se*:

> rather when they experience a problem or difficulty or are under some pressure, these cognitive and emotional needs of theirs may be met, or at least partially met, by obtaining and then applying some appropriate information.
>
> Nicholas and Herman, 2009, 18

Nicholas and Herman go on to say that information needs arise from a desire to meet one of three basic human needs: 'physiological needs (need for food, shelter etc.); psychological needs (need for domination, security etc.); and cognitive needs (need to plan, learn a skill, etc.)'. These authors then refer to

Norwood (1999, rev. 2014, cited in Huitt, 2007), who identifies five types of information that are directly related to Maslow's hierarchy of needs:

1 For *coping information* to resolve basic physiological needs (e.g., hunger, thirst, bodily comforts).
2 For *helping information* to resolve needs related to the personal safety level.
3 For *enlightening information* to resolve higher-level needs such as those related to personal relationship development.
4 For *empowering information* for resolving needs related to personal esteem, for example to gain approval and recognition.
5 For *edifying information* for resolving needs related to self-fulfilment and realizing one's potential.

It is important to realize, as Nicholas and Herman point out, that the success of individuals in meeting their primary need is dependent on them meeting their information need, which means that satisfying information needs is critical for people to satisfy their basic human needs.

In practice we find that the missions of different libraries and information services help to identify the client group(s) and the broad area(s) of information need that the agencies are meant to address. For example, a public library's mission in most instances will require the library to provide information resources and services to meet all levels of human need at a general level, whereas the mission of a specialized health information service might require it to focus specifically on meeting the information needs of its client group, say oncology specialists. In the latter example the physiological needs of people suffering from cancer are part of the information service's focus, but the service is not aimed at their information needs; rather it is aimed at the information needs of its clients, the oncology experts – an information need that helps the client group master an area of specialization, thus meeting the group members' need for esteem. Maslow's hierarchy of needs might assist libraries and information managers in understanding information needs at a general level, but it cannot be used without reference to the specific contexts in which the information needs occur.

Nicholas identifies what he describes as

eleven major characteristics of information need: subject, function, nature, intellectual level, viewpoint, quantity, quality/authority, date/currency, speed of delivery, place of publication/origin, and processing and packaging.

Nicholas, 2000, 38

Somewhat disappointingly, Nicholas focuses on the characteristics of information rather than on people's needs for the information to support their basic human needs, which suggests that his interest lies in the resources to resolve problems rather than in discovering what the needs or problems actually are.

Another highly cited taxonomy of needs was devised by Bradshaw (1972). His taxonomy is based on how *social* needs are defined, and he argues that the way we define needs may reflect the values or perspectives of particular groups (Percy-Smith, 1996, 7). Bradshaw's taxonomy has four categories:

1 Normative need is defined according to a norm or standard generally set by experts or professionals. Any person or group that falls below the standard is in need; for example, people whose income falls below a threshold will qualify for supplementary income.
2 Felt need is need which people feel; that is, it is a need from the perspective of the people who have it, though for a variety of reasons these needs are not expressed.
3 Expressed need is the need that a person or group perceives to exist, which might in fact differ from what the experts or professionals have defined as a need based on a norm or standard. (People can feel need which they do not express, and they can express needs they do not feel.)
4 Comparative need is a need identified when an individual or group is compared with others who are not in need.

Reviere et al. (1996, 5) comment that normative needs are likely to be paternalistic; felt needs are equated with wants and therefore might not be needs at all; expressed needs are felt needs that are expressed, that is, they reflect demand; and comparative needs are the gap between what is available to similar groups. Because of their weaknesses, Bradshaw believes that, to identify real need, it is necessary for these four perspectives to coincide (Percy-Smith, 1996, 7). In other words it is imperative that INA investigators tap into each perspective to improve the likelihood of identifying the real need.

The most useful categorization to assist information professionals in conceptualizing information needs is the one provided by Witkin and Altschuld. They divide needs into three levels and provide examples at each level, including examples relevant to information professionals:

• Level 1 (primary). *Service receivers*: students, clients, patients, information users, commuters, potential customers

- Level 2 (secondary). *Service providers and policymakers*: teachers, parents, social workers, caretakers, health care professionals, plant workers, postal employees, librarians, administrators, supervisors, managers
- Level 3 (tertiary). *Resources or solutions*: buildings, facilities, equipment, supplies, technology, programmes, class size, surgical procedures, information retrieval systems, transport, salaries and benefits, programme delivery systems, time allocations, working conditions.

Witkin and Altschuld, 1995, 10

We believe that the model provided by Witkin and Altschuld provides an ideal framework for conceptualizing the major types of needs that occur in information-related contexts and form the focal points for INA activities in library and information services. These levels are referred to throughout the remainder of this book and so should be well understood from this point forward.

In our information context the people at Level 1, the service receivers, are the information users who are the prime target for an INA. Witkin and Altschuld also note that service receivers include those within the system (for example, library users) and those outside the system (the non-users). The former are readily identifiable, and their characteristics are generally known, whereas the opposite is true for those outside the system. At Level 2 the service providers and policymakers are the librarians and other information professionals who plan, implement, provide, evaluate, offer training and so on for services aimed at meeting the needs of the information users in Level 1.

According to Witkin and Altschuld (1995, 11–12), the people in Level 2 'may also have unmet needs related to the functions they perform in relation either to their colleagues (such as managers) or to groups in Level 1'. These needs are often for training or 'may be conducted to meet the information needs of an emerging field of technology'.

At Level 3 the focus of INA is the needs of the organization in relation to the resources or solutions it provides. However, Level 3 needs may be confused with Level 1 needs (Witkin and Altschuld, 1995, 12). For example, library managers might assert that their library needs more public access computers, but this would be a solution to a Level 1 need; and, while there may well be reasons for conducting INAs at Level 3, we agree with Witkin and Altschuld (1995, 13), who contend that Level 1 needs must be understood prior to investigating needs at Level 2 or 3.

Reasons for conducting an information needs analysis

Again we look at the general literature on needs analysis (and needs assessment) to inform our discussion of the reasons for conducting an INA. Here we use the second term ('needs assessment') only because the cited authors employ this term, and we admit that this can cause some confusion. Nevertheless, the reader should keep in mind that we are consistently discussing needs analysis according to the definition provided earlier.

According to Soriano (1995, xv), needs assessments are conducted for a variety of reasons: some are due to requirements imposed externally on an organization, such as by a funding agency, while others are related to internal reasons. Among the most common, as identified by Soriano, are:

◆ justification for funding
◆ regulations or laws that mandate needs assessments
◆ resource allocation and decision making – determining the best use of limited resources
◆ assessing the needs of specific, under-served sub-populations as part of programme evaluations.

Reviere et al. (1996, 2) point out that 'needs assessments are tools used by a variety of organizations, agencies and social scientists with differing needs for information'. As examples, they state that needs assessments are sometimes mandated by governments to document needs in relation to specific programmes to maintain or allocate funding or are used to determine community sentiments with respect to certain issues. Social scientists use needs assessments 'to track population status, analyze statistics, and answer basic questions'. Service-providing agencies use needs assessments to gauge the use of their service, to identify gaps in service to plan for the future; and advocacy groups conduct assessments to justify their services.

Rossi and Freeman (1985, 107) suggest that needs assessments are sometimes required to determine the magnitude of a problem or to verify that a problem actually exists, 'because those who are concerned about the issues involved often tend to exaggerate the extent of a problem'. In the same vein Witkin and Altschuld (1995, 4–5) point out that needs assessments are sometimes conducted because populations that seem demographically similar believe that their needs are unique, and an assessment can clarify whether the claim is true. These same authors also mention that needs assessments are sometimes used 'as a guide to policy making and program decisions that will benefit specific groups of people'.

Another of their key points states that needs assessments 'are shaped by and take their characteristics from their specific contexts'.

As mentioned earlier, these authors discuss three levels of needs and in doing so point out that needs assessments are conducted to determine the needs of service receivers, service providers and policymakers, and the needs of organizations in terms of the resources and solutions used to address the needs of the service receivers. When information needs are viewed in the context of Witkin and Altschuld's three levels of needs, it is easy to see that the reasons for conducting INAs are similar to the reasons for conducting needs assessments – but they will be shaped by, and take their characteristics from, their specific information-related contexts. When we examine the reasons given by various authors for information needs assessment, we can observe that this logic holds true.

Biblarz, Bosch and Sugnet (2001, 7), for example, identify the reasons for needs assessments for integrated information resource management and collection development:

◆ maximizing the potential of programmes, collections and services to support user needs
◆ providing data that assist in the allocation of resources
◆ providing data that support programme planning
◆ providing verifiable justification for requesting new resources
◆ supporting the development of verifiable performance and quality measures
◆ ensuring that resources are serving the clientele's/users' objectives
◆ supporting strategies that combine access and ownership to provide the best service
◆ providing justification for reducing collective activities in subject areas where materials are not heavily used.

Similarly, the broad-ranging reasons provided by Nicholas (2000, 37) for conducting an INA for the purpose of designing, evaluating and managing information systems also make sense in this light:

◆ to benchmark the needs of a [sic] chosen information communities and make comparison between them
◆ to monitor and evaluate the effectiveness and appropriateness of existing information systems from a user perspective…

◆ to detect gaps in information service provision and to remain vigilant to changes in need
◆ in the designing of on-going information support system for the individual (personalized information services)…
◆ in the assessment of the never-ending tide of new information products
◆ to ensure that the reference interview, an essential part of the delegation process, is conducted on firm footing and in a systematic and comprehensive manner
◆ to bring the user and the information professional closer together….

And finally, Westbrook (2001) provides the following reasons for conducting community information needs assessments:

◆ to provide insight on non-users
◆ to support general budget planning at both the immediate and mid-range levels
◆ to set priorities among collection elements, services and missions
◆ to position the library among its competitors
◆ to determine the optimum allocation of scarce resources
◆ to plan for inevitable changes
◆ to help staff develop a new vision of the library
◆ to support long-term growth and development
◆ to market the library.

We can see from these lists that an INA is a critical tool for many information-related contexts, including planning new services, evaluating existing services, setting priorities and allocating resources for services and establishing policies. These lists not only demonstrate the variety of reasons for conducting different types of INAs, but they also demonstrate the possible diversity of scope, size and complexity of these analyses and draw attention to the range of potential stakeholders to be involved in such exercises. At the end of the day it all comes back to one basic truth: 'the key to it all is the ongoing exploration and analysis of people's needs, which, alone, can ensure that they connect effectively to information' (Herman and Nicholas, 2010, 251). In information management contexts 'people' can be clients or staff or stakeholders, and also organizations.

Review of Chapter 1

This is admittedly a highly conceptual introduction to INA, and more practice-based readers may well be frustrated by it. Nevertheless, we stand by our view that without grasping the key concepts and theoretical underpinnings those who conduct INAs are both failing in their responsibility as professionals and probably missing many nuances of an investigation. Therefore, it is essential to understand the content of this chapter before proceeding into the field.

In Chapter 1 we have explained why 'information needs analysis' is preferred over 'information needs assessment' in our context, arguing that the former is more specific and focused and therefore more suited to the kinds of investigations that need to be conducted in libraries and other information organizations. We have also sought to distinguish among several commonly confused terms: 'need', 'want' and 'demand'. 'Need', we have suggested, is the most objective choice, because it incorporates the idea of value judgements being made by external observers. A clear understanding of need is essential if one is to make sense of the following chapters, and it must never be confused with either want or demand.

We have also defined 'information needs analysis' and have provided some discussion of types of information needs through summaries of ideas from Maslow, Nicholas, Bradshaw and Witkin and Altschuld. In particular the three-level model of Witkin and Altschuld (primary, secondary, tertiary) is singled out as perhaps the most user-friendly way to understand information needs in our context.

Why should we conduct an INA? This most basic question was addressed in the final section of Chapter 1. From the discussion it should be clear to any reader that the answer may be at the macro level, or down to the finest micro level – from gaining a 'big picture' of the overall information needs in an organization, ranging from resources to services to technology to personnel, down to analysing the needs related to a specific activity, such as the length of time taken to acquire and process information resources. In the end why we conduct an INA comes down to the specific context in which the need exists, and the issue of context is the focus of Chapter 2.

Further reading

On the theoretical side one could of course turn to Maslow and read his entire work, *Motivation and Personality* (1954), as this seems to underpin much thinking since the 1950s on needs. But if one prefers to put this in an information context, then two books cited in this chapter are more useful: the first chapter of Witkin and Altschuld's *Planning and Conducting Needs Assessments* (1995), especially pages 10–14; and Nicholas' *Assessing Information Needs* (2000), primarily Chapters 2 and 3. Both works help fill in some of the summary discussion in this chapter about the nature of needs and why one should conduct needs analyses.

If still more practically stated background is desired, one way to approach this is to look at a specific part of an information service. In *The Basics of Library-Based User Services* Whittaker (1993) deftly overviews the types of needs that might exist in a user-centred service, from current awareness to personal problem solving. His Chapter 5 may provide a usefully practice-based background in which to situate an INA. While Whittaker brings the discussion down to a manageable level, an alternative view is presented by Troll Covey (2002). In 'Academic Library Assessment' she describes the significant difficulties faced by libraries when assessing (or analysing) components of their work and also shows what a steep learning curve is involved when a library takes on the task of needs analysis or assessment – sobering but worthwhile reading.

While Troll Covey offers a good example of how information needs infiltrate many aspects of an information organization, this is stated more formally and fully by Choo (2001) in Chapter 2 of *Information Management for the Intelligent Organization*, which presents a process model of information management that starts with information needs and ends with information ecology and culture. This chapter is worth reading by anyone who is trying to place information needs in a more structured setting.

References

Adams, D. (1984) *The Hitchhiker's Guide to the Galaxy*, Pan Books, London.

Biblarz, D., Bosch, S. and Sugnet, C. (eds) (2001) *Guide to Library User Needs Assessment for Integrated Information Resource Management and Collection Development*, Scarecrow Press, Lanham, MD.

Bishop, K. (2007) *The Collection Program in Schools: concepts, practices and information sources*, 4th edn, Library and Information Science Text Series, Libraries Unlimited, Westport, CT.

Bradshaw, J. (1972) The Concept of Social Need, *New Society*, 30 March, 640–3.

Broadus, R. N. (1981) *Selecting Materials for Libraries*, 2nd edn, H. W. Wilson, New York.

Charles, S. and Webb, A. (1986) *The Economic Approach to Social Policy*, Wheatsheaf Books, Brighton.

Choo, C. W. (2001) *Information Management for the Intelligent Organization: the art of scanning the environment*, 3rd edn, ASIST Monograph Series, Medford, NJ, Information Today.

Gupta, K., Sleezer, C. M. and Russ-Eft, D. F. (2007) *A Practical Guide to Needs Assessment,* 2nd edn, John Wiley and Sons/Pfeiffer, San Francisco, CA.

Herman, E. and Nicholas, D. (2010) The Information Enfranchisement of the Digital Consumer, *Aslib Proceedings: new information perspectives,* **62** (3), 245–60.

Huitt, W. (2007) Maslow's hierarchy of needs, *Educational Psychology Interactive,* Valdosta State University, Valdosta, GA, www.edpsycinteractive.org/topics/regsys/maslow.html. [Accessed 5 November 2014.]

Maslow, A. (1954) *Motivation and Personality,* Harper & Row, New York, NY.

McKillip, J. A. (1987) *Need Analysis: tools for the human services and education,* Applied Social Research Methods, 10, SAGE Publications, Newbury Park, CA.

Nicholas, D. (2000) *Assessing Information Needs: tools, techniques and concepts for the internet age,* 2nd edn, The Association for Information Management and Information Management International, London.

Nicholas, D. and Herman, E. (2009) *Assessing Information Needs in the Age of the Digital Consumer,* 3rd edn, Routledge, London.

Norwood, G. (1999, rev 2014) Maslow's hierarchy of needs, *Deepermind,* www.deepermind.com/20maslow.htm. [Accessed 5 November 2014.]

Oxford English Dictionary 3rd edn Online (2010) Oxford University Press, Oxford. [Accessed 5 November 2014 through Victoria University of Wellington Library.]

Percy-Smith, J. (1996) Introduction: assessing needs – theory and practice, in Percy-Smith, J. (ed.), *Needs Assessment in Public Policy,* Open University Press, Milton Keynes, 3–10.

Reviere, R., Carter, C. C., Berkowitz, S., and Ferguson, C. G. (1996) Preface, in Reviere, R. et al. (eds), *Needs Assessment: a creative and practical guide for social scientists,* Taylor & Francis, Basingstoke, xi–xiii.

Rossi, P. H. and Freeman, H. E. (1985) *Evaluation: a systematic approach,* SAGE Publications, Beverley Hills, CA.

Soriano, F. I. (1995) *Conducting Needs Assessments: a multidisciplinary approach,* SAGE Publications, Thousand Oaks, CA.

Stufflebeam, D. L., McCormick, C. H., Brinkerhoff, R. O. and Nelson, C. O. (1985) *Conducting Educational Needs Assessments,* Evaluation in Education and Human Services [series], Kluwer-Nijhoff Publishing, Boston, MA.

Troll Covey, D. (2002) Academic Library Assessment: new duties and dilemmas, *New Library World,* **103** (1175/1176), 156–64.

Westbrook, L. (2001) *Identifying and Analyzing User Needs: a complete handbook and ready-to-use assessment workbook with disk,* Neal-Schuman Publishers, New York, NY.

Whittaker, K. (1993) *The Basics of Library-Based User Services,* Library Association Publishing, London.

Witkin, B. R. and Altschuld, J. W. (1995) *Planning and Conducting Needs Assessments: a practical guide*, SAGE Publications, Thousand Oaks, CA.

The importance of context in information needs analysis

Introduction

In Chapter 1 we discussed the meaning of 'need' as distinct from 'want' and 'demand' and used this discussion as a platform for defining INA. However, we did not discuss the essentially contextual nature of those situations in which information needs arise, and therefore the contextual nature of all INAs. This is the purpose of Chapter 2: to place INA in a contextual framework, whether this is a more general cultural context or specific to a particular level (users, providers, resources). The variety of contexts is the overriding theme of this chapter. The second theme is that data do not exist in a vacuum, and on their own they have no intrinsic value – that is, the data of INA are also context-specific.

> What does not seem to have been publicly acknowledged is that sometimes the needs and interests of different groups are mutually exclusive. Until we accept this, information managers will struggle to meet these conflicting demands. What is needed is a more realistic vision which provides different things to different people at different times, and perhaps in different venues . . ..
>
> Roddy, 2005, 41

This statement reminds us that different groups have different needs, and these needs are serviced in a variety of ways in varying contexts according to specific local requirements.

For example, there are x entries beginning with the letter 'J' in the Manchester telephone directory (available at www.whitepages.co.uk/england/white-pages-manchester.html); that number is a datum, but without any intrinsic value. If, however, we were seeking a list of names and addresses of medical practitioners in Manchester, this would be a different matter. As this book is being written nowhere near Manchester, such data have no value to us; but should we be in

Manchester in the near future, then it could well become information that accords with a need at that time, thus becoming of value. The worth, or value, of information and information services depends on context.

No individual or group has an information need *per se* (Nicholas and Herman, 2009). That is, any community, group or individual has an information need for a specific purpose and within a particular context. Information needs are most likely to be associated with contexts such as the demands of employment, formal or informal study, the need for more efficient operations within an organization, or some social or cultural activity. It may appear that the need for information is of a lower order than the need to earn a living or to find a place in society, but the one may depend on the other, and often these needs cannot be satisfied without access to relevant information.

Helping people, organizations and communities meet their information needs depends on understanding the reason for which they seek information. For example, if the origins of a request for information lie in the requirement for members of the Royal Institute of British Architects (RIBA) to understand local building regulations, then it will only be through knowing the origins of the information request that the information manager can begin to understand the information need of the RIBA members. If the information need is more personal, such as a health issue, then there is more to meeting the need than simply answering questions about an illness; someone with an illness may also need information about mobility, employment opportunities, networking and so on. In other words the person with an illness has a context, too.

Obviously communities and organizations can be deemed to have information needs, though in practice it is individuals within the community or organization that need and use the information in relation to specific contexts. If, however, the organization is treated as an entity with information needs, which it is in practical terms, then context also applies to the organization.

Usually an organization faces external and internal pressures of various kinds, and these are bound to be significant in developing, planning and operating services. The size of the problem may increase with the size of the organization:

> The greater the number of people to be served, the more complex the
> organisation, and the more critical the needs and issues appear to be, the more
> likely that political factors will play a part. That is, decision makers may take certain
> positions for reasons of ideology, protection of 'turf', or commitment to certain
> courses of action, or to be an advocate for a particular cause.
>
> Witkin and Altschuld, 1995, 35

These constraints can influence the scope of problems that are investigated, and it is entirely possible that an organization will make a decision either to analyse or *not* to analyse its own information needs as a result of various pressures exerted on it (Reviere et al., 1996, 6). Thus the environment of the organization or the individual is part of the context that must be investigated and understood.

To summarize this introduction to Chapter 2, what we seek to do is extend the discussion of INA into the real-world context of culture, society and other key variables by addressing these questions:

◆ What is the role of contexts, and especially cultural contexts, in information needs analysis?
◆ Do people always recognize an information need when they have one?
◆ How can individuals be grouped into communities with information needs?

The cultural context

Perhaps the most powerful and overarching context is that of culture – the culture in which individuals, organizations and communities have information needs. It is our contention that culture colours not only the information needs but also how those needs are expressed and how they are satisfied. For each of us cultural factors determine how we think, how we conceptualize problems and information needs and how we seek to satisfy those information needs.

The cultural 'onion'

Cutler (2005) maintains that culture is much like an onion, multi-layered and increasingly intense as each layer is peeled away (see Figure 2.1). The outer layer consists of subjective elements such as visible behaviour, relationship styles, thinking and learning styles, organization and work styles, communication styles, as well as objective culture in the form of artefacts, buildings, etc. Beneath this surface layer are value systems and norms, shared values and accepted standards of

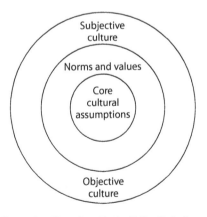

Figure 2.1 The cultural 'onion' [after Cutler]

behaviour; and at the deepest level are core cultural assumptions, which Cutler (2005, vol. 1, 76) calls "basic truths" about human identity and purpose, space, time, social organization, ways of thinking and communicating that, for the most part, groups and their members are wholly unaware of'.

The onion image of culture can be applied at many levels – individuals, groups, organizations, institutions, regions, nations – in some sense reflecting the various levels (primary, secondary, tertiary) discussed later in Chapter 3. Note that each level tends to anchor its sense of culture in a different layer. For example, a teaching team culture (or indeed any 'team' of individuals) exists primarily at the level of behaviour (the outer layer of subjective culture) and much less at the level of core cultural assumptions, whereas 'national culture often resides less in practices and more in taken-for-granted values and assumptions' – that is, the inner layer of core cultural assumptions (Cutler, 2005, vol. 1, 77).

The culture onion's relevance to INAs

Why is this relevant in terms of INA? When we seek to analyse information needs, it is necessary to understand the personal, organizational or community 'cultural onion' in which these needs exist. Not to do so is to lift the information needs, and therefore their analysis, out of context and detach them from real life. When this happens, any attempt at analysis is unlikely to address the genuine information needs of a group or organization that can actually be met by an information manager or library. That is, we are operating in another world: our world, which may be significantly different from their world, where the actual information needs reside.

Taking information literacy in a developing country as an example of an information need, these two different sets of cultural assumptions ('their world', 'our world') may well be setting up any INA, and subsequent training based on this analysis, for failure. A Western-influenced information literacy programme, based on Western norms and taught according to Western pedagogical practices, may not succeed in a developing society when the programme focuses on behavioural changes (as indeed it must, according to how we currently assess educational results in terms of outcomes). This potential for failure is because, beneath the outer layer of visible behavioural styles and learning and thinking styles, the core cultural assumptions, which may well run counter to the surface changes, remain untouched. And it is these core values that ultimately determine the long-term success of any information literacy programme.

Another example of contextually unaware INA lies in science education; in fact this area has received considerable attention over the years, with a common recognition of the disparity between science and daily cultures. This was put most succinctly by Aikenhead and Jegede (1999, 269):

> One major influence on science education identified by students in developing countries is their feeling that school science is like a foreign culture to them (Maddock, 1981). Their feeling stems from fundamental differences between the culture of Western science and their indigenous cultures.
>
> (Aikenhead, 1997; Jegede, 1995)

The results of such an approach are entirely predictable. When educational programmes are imported without change, without due consideration for local culture and without any attempt at context-based INA, two worldviews develop. There is a 'school view' of the world, or at least the world of a specific discipline or learning style, that is essentially foreign; students 'put on' this view when they are in school and engaged in what passes for learning, and it has little to do with their culturally based worldview and therefore has little meaning (Waldrip and Taylor, 1999). In effect students are saying '*this* is what I am taught in school, yet out here *this* is the way life really is'. In terms of information needs analysis, the person could well be saying, '*this* is what I am told my information need is, yet in reality I know that in my world my *actual* information need is quite different'. This kind of clash occurs when we are insensitive to the cultural context in which the information needs exist and are expressed.

In common with many others, among them Aikenhead and Jegede (1999) and Waldrip and Taylor (1999), we believe that what occurs in this situation is a downward spiral to failure, or rather the failure of classroom learning to become embedded in the learner's way of life. At the outset, a disparity develops between the learners' worldviews and their school views; this gives rise to conflicting sets of values, one from within the culture, one imposed from without. To cope with this the learners compartmentalize their values, as suggested above, with one set for the classroom, and another, real, set for the world. Thus real-life learning fails, and whether we are discussing science education or the identification and servicing of information needs, above all else we want our programmes to be embedded in real life so that understanding becomes part of a lifelong learning process. Scenario 2.1 gives an example of learning failure.

Scenario 2.1 HIV/AIDS information needs

A team of professionals is engaged by an international health agency to provide HIV/AIDS education for teenagers in a Southeast Asian country at the invitation of the agency's regional office for SE Asia. The team consists of a medical doctor, a nurse-educator and a teacher-librarian. The programme is carefully prepared at the agency's European headquarters by the team and fully vetted by staff in the regional office. The content is medically sound, pedagogical methods are pitched at the right level, and all necessary information sources are provided (in English and French, the two Western languages spoken by people in the host country). The team arrives in the host country and sets itself up in the library of a government school in a country town. After-school classes are organized and advertised by word of mouth, and the sessions are hugely over-subscribed. Included as part of the classes are a free medical examination, a light meal and prizes for attendance at each session – in a country where medical care is minimal and many people cannot afford proper meals.

The team is naturally delighted with the turnout and the regular attendance of the same young people at class after class. After the three-week sessions have been run twice, the team begins an ex post (i.e. retrospective) evaluation of the programme. The findings astonish them:

1   The young people who engage in (necessarily clandestine) sexual activity use no protection, even though condoms, etc. are provided to the participants.
2   They have not studied or even read the carefully prepared information packs, nor do they access resources they have been told about.
3   Actual behaviour has not changed, learning has not occurred, and information needs have not been met.

A group of the more open-minded teenagers is asked what has happened. The answers are simple:

1   We do not have a problem with HIV/AIDS in our country, because the government and our families have told us so.
2   We do not engage in sexual activities outside marriage, because this is illegal.
3   We do not keep the condoms because we would be punished if they were found, and we do not read the information packs because we do not really understand English or French well enough.
4   But we like to come to the classes because we have a good medical exam and medicine if we are ill, and we have something to eat, which saves our families money.

In retrospect we can see that the information needs were analysed both out of their cultural context and in a most insensitive manner, with the result that the entire approach to meeting these needs was inappropriate. The local cultural values were such that HIV/AIDS could not be admitted as a problem, and the cultural norms formally forbade premarital sex. The health education team, however, assumed that HIV/AIDS was a known problem, and they 'knew' that young people are pretty much the same worldwide. But the team failed to take account of the power of the local cultural context. This scenario is based on an actual case.

As Scenario 2.1 emphasizes, the need for information is socially constructed and culturally determined, and local communities have the capacity to understand information needs on their own terms and in ways that do not counter the local political economy of knowledge ownership and control. Therefore, as INA specialists, it is critical that we behave in a culturally sensitive manner – whether we are functioning in an organizational or a societal culture – and that we analyse information needs within the confines of that specific cultural context. Not to do so brings results that, in another context, Luke and Kapitzke (1999, 483–4) term 'at best anachronistic and dysfunctional, at worst counter-productive'.

Information needs awareness in context

From the preceding discussion it should be obvious that the information needs awareness of an individual or an organization depends on context. However, awareness itself is often a problem; individuals and organizations do not always recognize their information needs or do not necessarily know they face an information gap. Herman and Nicholas use the term 'information malnutrition' to describe the condition felt by individuals in the digital age who lack the information they need for competent decision making. These authors point out that one of the main reasons for information malnutrition is because 'people are frequently altogether unaware of having a need for some information, especially nowadays, when the information professional is increasingly absent from the picture' (Herman and Nicholas, 2010, 248).

A need that is not identified is sometimes referred to as a *dormant* need, and there are many contexts in which such a need might arise. For example, an individual might require information to overcome a financial problem but does not know that the local public library offers both relevant information and educational and information services to help resolve this need. It is worthy of note that 'Smart investing@your library' is an educational and information service offered by some public libraries and community colleges in the USA. It is a grant-funded programme administered jointly by the FINRA Investor Education Foundation and the American Library Association (see http://smartinvesting.ala.org). Monsour (2012) provides profiles of some of the approaches to financial education provided by several public libraries participating in the programme.

One might think this situation is more likely to occur in lower level socio-economic communities, but it can occur anywhere. In the corporate sector ineffective processes are often slow to change because of a lack of adequate information, though information management and knowledge management professionals assist in overcoming information gaps in many private sector and government organizations.

Known or predicted needs

The problem with most systems intended to satisfy information needs is that they are designed to meet known or predicted information needs that can be specifically articulated within a known and understood cultural context. When the end-users are familiar with concepts assumed by the system designers, then this can work well enough, as school librarians watching children use library catalogues to make successful searches for authors can testify. But one only has to watch a typical undergraduate student trying to coax a recognizable response from a library's databases to appreciate that finding a useful answer in an information system is not that easy unless the enquirer knows exactly how to pose the question. Or consider the behaviour of a newly formed group of some sort, such as environmentalists or hot-air balloon enthusiasts: the members will have quite specific concerns but will not know the nature of the information needs within those concerns. Being able to ask the question presupposes that the environmentalists or hot-air balloon enthusiasts know precisely the nature of the information need and that the context is such that they are able to address the specific need.

Unexpressed needs

Another sort of information need is the *unexpressed* need. People may feel that they lack knowledge or awareness of matters that concern them, but because there is some obstacle or constraint (which may be as simple as lethargy or inertia), they make no attempt to satisfy that information need. Many students fall into this trap, so they tend to 'satisfice' their information gathering in order to just pass a course rather than achieve excellence. Their need may remain unexpressed because it is hard to convert into terms that others will recognize. Similarly, residents of retirement homes often feel that they do not understand many aspects of modern life and that they do not understand because they do not possess the requisite information. Yet their attempts to gain this information are often limited to what they see on television or hear during afternoon tea in the common room. The late Elfreda Chatman's *The Information World of Retired Women* (1992) is superbly insightful in this regard.

Recognizing true needs

A further kind of information need will occur when an organization or individual is *unaware* of the true need. This state of affairs will be familiar to many information professionals. The user may express a need to read all of Shakespeare's plays to find a suitable quotation for a forthcoming speech, whereas the librarian might recognize that the real need was for the quotation, not for Shakespeare's plays, and the need would be better be met by a dictionary of quotations. Such situations may occur in any environment; a corporate example might be a manager annoyed that staff spend time looking for forms to request annual leave, to book meeting rooms and to ask for taxi chits. The manager does not recognize that the information problem does not lie with the staff, but in the absence of a service such as an intranet that allows the easy discovery and downloading of forms for all internal purposes.

Purpose and perceived importance

All communities, organizations and individuals have information needs. Information needs, information-seeking behaviour and information use have been the subject of scholarly attention in many environments, and a wide variety of groups with different motives has been placed under the microscope. It is clear that for some situations information and information services are more vital than in others, and higher stakes (as judged by the individual or society) are more likely to create situations that attract research. As a result, the literature contains much more about, for example, the information needs of health professionals, lawyers and academics than about the information needs of the unemployed, unskilled workers or people suffering from illnesses or mental disorders. One of the rare exceptions to this was the work of Chatman, noted above, who conducted research into the information needs and behaviour of various marginalized groups, including cleaners, the elderly in care and the poor (Chatman, 1990; Chatman, 1992; Chatman and Pendleton, 1995). Society may place a greater value on information provision for lawyers and doctors than it does on anything similar provided for cleaners or the elderly, but to the individuals concerned their information needs are very important, so the INA investigator must treat them with the same respect given to professional groups.

The spectrum of information needs

It is possible to construct a simple spectrum of information needs, ranging from the relatively simple to the far more complex. At the simple end would be the needs of one individual requiring information for simple actions or decisions. When is the next train going into the city? Which is the best tablet computer for less than £300 that suits my lifestyle? Though to society these may be insignificant needs, to the individual they may represent something truly important. Neither of these information needs is likely to be the subject of academic research, but they could be important to organizations such as (a) a transport company trying to increase the use of train services, (b) hand-held device manufacturers and retailers needing to know more about consumer preferences and how they make purchasing decisions and (c) publicly funded information services such as public libraries that ought to be aware of information needs, no matter how small or trivial they may seem, among the population they are expected to serve.

Moving from the individual to a wider context, consider a national referendum on a subject such as taxation or changing the manner in which elections are conducted. The end result will affect every citizen of the country. Presumably they will require, at the very least, *some* information for and against the propositions that will help people decide how to vote. An information needs investigator might be asked to consider the means by which the population finds out about its government and the extent to which e-government information services can help inform the public. The first question, then, might investigate how significant this is as an information need. Some might say it is extremely important, whereas others, perhaps more cynically, believe that voters make decisions without close attention to information for and against the propositions. And the second question might address how well e-government services penetrate various sectors of the voting public. In both questions the importance of context is obvious.

Seeking common ground

These examples also allow for context to be described in other ways – that is, the cultural contexts of various professions. Often information needs are examined by studying groups of people who have something in common, particularly an occupation or profession. Research scientists working in the field of nanotechnology would be an extreme example of such a grouping; more typical, though, would be medical practitioners (Davies, 2009; Younger, 2010), architects (Makri and Warwick, 2010) or design engineers (Allard, Levine and Tenopir, 2009) – the list goes on. The assumption is that individuals belonging to a profession or occupation will have information needs in common with other members of the same profession, and studies of group information needs tend to bear this out. People who share interests, e.g. backpackers, may also share information needs (Chang, 2009). Groups can also be segmented by ethnicity and their common information need; there have been numerous studies of the information needs of several ethnic groups – two classic examples being Metoyer-Duran's analysis of Native Americans and other communities (Metoyer-Duran, 1993) and MacDonald's study of New Zealand Maori (MacDonald, 1993).

Determining the communities

By this point we will understand that in most cases it is inefficient to attempt an INA of every individual within an organization or a profession, so an INA typically focuses on a specific group or community. The group may be apparent from the task set or the consultancy brief, an example being 'analyse the information needs of the paediatric nurses working the night shift at the local hospital'. On the other hand a general brief to 'discover the unmet information needs of staff within this company' leaves much still undefined. Do they *all* share the same needs? If not, which individuals share the same need and hence can be analysed as a group? As a starting point, the functional divisions of the organization may help, but we must remember that a company department or division will include senior staff whose information needs may be mainly of a professional nature, such as new accounting methods, and other staff with more task-based needs, such as how to use a particular piece of software. This makes the analysis more difficult, but still feasible.

Community segmentation

The general way of determining the sections of the community or groups to analyse lies in segmentation, which is something we have learned from marketing experts; a market segment consists of a group of individuals whose requirements for the product or service (in this case, information) are broadly similar. Identifying common characteristics helps sort out initial groups, with the warning that one of the traps is to go overboard with detail too early in the process (Coote and Batchelor, 1997, 8), for if the result is too many segments, it becomes impossible to do much with the results. Marketing theory suggests using four types of data to create segments:

- Needs and desired end benefits,
- Purchase behaviour,
- Value/lifestyle measures,
- Classifying characteristics.

Guiltinan, Paul and Madden, 1997, 77

A needs approach to segmentation starts with the identification of the needs that clients attempt to satisfy when using information services or resources. Within the general population this will be a huge range, but for an INA it might be possible to reduce the range, because at least *something* must be known about the target population in advance. This could start with a review of the likely situations in which people will need information (Rowley, 2006). Among occupational groups, such as police officers or opticians for example, some common reasons for using information can be assumed. In each case it should be possible to identify a benefit for the whole segment to be gained by using information.

'Customers do not purchase products and services for the features of the products, rather customers purchase the benefits the product provides' (Lehmann and Winer, 2002, 114). In information use the same applies: information seekers want the benefits the information will bring, rather than the product or service that provides it (such as an e-book, a database or a government advisory service). Does a team of accountants in a company seek information on current Inland Revenue tax-reporting requirements so they can complete a specific task at work? Is an individual looking for a job? Neither the team of accountants nor the individuals who are looking for information are much bothered about the 'bells and whistles' of the information source; rather they simply want valid content that meets their information needs.

Behavioural segmentation

Is this client a regular user of the organization's services, and, if so, is he or she a heavy, moderate or light user? Is that client informed or unaware of the range of services available? These are different kinds of behaviours, and in INA it helps to have some information about the clients' use of services. Behavioural measures ask people or groups to indicate which services they have used over a certain time period, say the last month or six months. From this information the investigator can deduce segments based on actual behaviour rather than supposition. Repeat use can help to categorize clients (Clark, 1983), thereby enriching our understanding of the context for a needs analysis. Typical categories might be social use, such as borrowing recreational fiction from a public library; business use, such as referring to Bloomberg for stock quotes; professional use, such as engineers accessing building standards; or even other categories such as cultural (perhaps using indigenous language materials) or recreational (travel and accommodation). One of the problems faced by the reflective information professional is that use of services tends to closely match provision of services simply because clients cannot use what is not provided, so the information service focuses on satisfying known demand at the expense of potential demand. They are not, in other words, capitalizing on the full context in which they exist through conducting an INA.

Values/lifestyle segmentation

For values/lifestyles measures one should look for activities, opinions and interests. Some individuals, organizations and communities might characterize themselves (or be characterized by others) as conservative (residents of Tunbridge Wells, members of l'Académie française, a Tory MP), rebellious (rock stars of a certain vintage, up-and-coming futures traders), fashionable (those who frequent Rodeo Drive in Hollywood), etc. People use services that they see as characteristic of themselves in their social self-image, and these services give shape to their lives. Such attitudes are shaped by experience and interaction with others in the community. In other words cultural contexts play a large part in some choices; hence groups of people tend to share the same values. Some will share information via Facebook, while others will feel that LinkedIn is a better match with their professional profile (and indeed many people use both according to the kind of information they wish to share). Typically, some older, middle-income people will regard the public library as something that matches their self-image, whereas other social classes and social groups, maybe younger and upwardly mobile professionals, or perhaps recent immigrants, will not identify closely with it. The INA investigator might see that such groups could satisfy their information needs if they would use the public library, but equally there is a problem if these groups will *not* use the public library even if told that is where their needs could be satisfied.

An INA might look at this from two perspectives: either from the public library perspective in which the library wants to promote services to non-users, in which case it might provide more electronic services sent to the mobile devices no doubt already in the bags and pockets of the upwardly mobile professionals; or from the perspective of identifying whether the public library can or cannot meet the specific information needs of these groups, in which case some alternative information service might need to be developed distinct from the public library. There are tests to establish where individuals will fit into a categorization of values and lifestyles, such as SRI's VALS program (www.strategicbusinessinsights.com/vals), that can be used if the INA investigator wishes to go in this direction.

Making use of existing data

When setting out to conduct an INA, it is often possible to make use of already existing data, particularly geographic and demographic information about individuals; such data also can be adjusted to apply to groups and organizations. Demographic data can range over age, gender, income, education, ethnicity, religion, family status and so on. In employing such data to determine the context of an INA it is important to recognize that training has a role to play, especially at the secondary level of service providers and policymakers (Witkin and Altschuld, 1995, 10). In the context of needs analysis among low socio-economic groups in less developed countries, for example, it is hardly useful to recommend the provision of computer-based information resources unless there is a matching recommendation for the provision of computer literacy (or better yet, multiple literacies) training. Competency in multiple literacies is a challenge in most societies: multiple literacies encompasses 'both the new forms of literacy associated with ICT (e.g., media literacy, print literacy, computer literacy, multimedia literacy) and the culturally-specific form of education such as cultural literacy, social literacy, and ecoliteracy' (UNESCO, 2005, cited in Li and Rao, 2009, 270). As one might imagine, such a broad range of literacies requires learning environments that are resource-rich, and teachers with high levels of ICT skills, which is often not the case in many countries, developed or otherwise.

Producing initial contextualized segments

Because existing demographic data are fairly easily obtained and easily aggregated (often from a national census or from a professional association census), it is common to use these as a means to produce initial contextualized segments. The first pass using demographic characteristics can be combined, for example, with data on needs and values or data about desired benefits. Thus combining demographic data with desired benefits data might produce groups such as school children doing homework, members of a professional association interested in continuing professional education, support groups of the Association of Breastfeeding Mothers seeking new information on breastfeeding.

Coming to an understanding of the context

Once these segments have been formed they are profiled by the behavioural information. It would be useful to know what services and resources are already in common use in each segment and the pattern of that use. How often do the school children use books from their school library for homework, how often do they go to the public library, and how often do they use the internet at home (though these are not mutually exclusive categories)? It would also be instructive to compare the data with information about values and lifestyle. In some urban areas, for instance, it might be rare for school children to use a public library for whatever reason – peer pressure, lack of awareness, distance to the library, disenchantment with school and so on. Along with these possible explanations some of these school children might not use the public library because they simply ignore their homework, despite this being a 'need' that will be expressed by teachers, parents and others.

The example of the previous paragraph clearly illustrates that the INA investigator must understand the environment, that is, the context in which numerous social, economic and political issues are operating (Coote and Batchelor, 1997, 10). Not only are human limits, such as computer skills, present, but there are also issues related to legislation, market forces and other factors to be considered. The investigator can employ a common method such as PEST (for Political, Economic, Social, and Technological changes) as an aid to the understanding of such issues (see De Saez, 2002, 29–38).

The impact of context on decision making

Preliminary identification of the demographic data for a community to be examined can affect decisions made on several aspects of the study. As an example, a study of citizenship information needs in the UK found that 'the doorstep interview method has reached greater proportions of those groups deemed to be in danger of social exclusion, providing results that are particularly revealing' (Marcella and Baxter, 2000). In other words the nature of the demographics suggested to these INA investigators that the best method of reaching the intended population was by doorstep interviewing, rather than some other method such as a postal questionnaire.

How an understanding of the various contexts and ways of using existing data might come together is illustrated in Scenario 2.2.

Scenario 2.2 Advice to the Service for Students with Disabilities

---

In this situation you are advising the Service for Students with Disabilities (SSD) of a typical publicly funded university. The staff have told you that they want a better understanding of the information needs of students with impairments.

The university provides much of the specific environment for these students. Can you provide more detail on where you would look for the specific environment, such as the relationship between the SSD and the university library? What is the general environment – for example, social acceptance of students with impairments in the general university community, or advances in adaptive technology that might make students less dependent on direct assistance?

Although about 300 students are enrolled with the SSD, staff know that there are still some students with impairments who have chosen not to register with the service. How will you gather data on students who have not registered with the SSD?

SSD staff believe that many hearing-impaired students have not registered with the SSD. These hearing-impaired students have found that the university campus has no hidden access problems for them, they can use all the print materials in the library, and they communicate with quite a few others by using sign language. To them, their impairment does not seem to be a major disability. Do they come into the target population for your INA? It could be that more information resources will use audio as the technology develops, or that recorded lectures are being signed to enable the hearing-impaired students to benefit from them.

Some students with impairments will have clearly expressed information needs, but others may have dormant or unexpressed needs. Although it is too early to make an accurate assessment of these different needs, it should be possible to make preliminary assumptions as to what some of the expressed, dormant and unexpressed needs might be.

Some needs might change with time. It could quickly become apparent that a key time for the students is orientation, during which they will form clear ideas about what information is available and what, they think, is not. It could well be that the information they think is not available actually is available, there for them to use if they were willing to find it. This point suggests that time is a factor in the information needs of these students. Do you think there would be other changes in their information needs over time?

Review of Chapter 2

This chapter has shown that context, including the cultural context, is an all-important consideration when dealing with INA, for needs do not exist in a vacuum. There are specific contexts that influence needs, such as organizations where people work or communities in which they live. Within these contexts we have seen that individuals or organizations are often unaware that they have information needs, and part of the function of an INA is to tease out these unrecognized needs.

It is important to be aware of the wide spectrum of needs for information and information services; from the perspective of such awareness one is better prepared to seek and recognize common ground among specific communities (groups in society, employees within organizations, etc.). Community segmentation is the result: this is useful in classifying information needs of identifiable groups. Equally important are behavioural measures of these segments, as these greatly determine the quality and depth of services that community segments might be thought to require.

Of course, one should never ignore the value of more traditional categories, such as demographic and geographic data; these, too, are contextual in the sense that age, gender, level of education and so on exist in a specific space and time. The space and time dimension greatly determines the information services that segments of the population are likely to demand.

All of this is by way of saying that INA is never context-free and that it always exists in a specific sector of the time-space continuum. The better the INA investigator recognizes this feature, the more reliable data he or she will collect about the environment, and the more adequate will be the resulting analysis of information needs of specific groups within that environment. One principal result of a clearer understanding of the context of INA is that we are in a better position to develop our own, contextually relevant, types of INA. These are discussed in the following chapter.

Further reading

On the issue of cultural context, perhaps the most fascinating work is that by Geert Hofstede, who addresses both national and organizational cultures and has developed five independent dimensions of national culture differences. The robustness of his findings has been tested in many contexts and warrants close study; the most up-to-date resource is by Hofstede and Hofstede, *Cultures and Organizations* (3rd edn, 2010).

More specific to INA, the book by Nicholas and Herman, *Assessing Information Needs in the Age of the Digital Consumer* (2009), is a good starting point, for it provides some simple definitions that have utility for most INA contexts. But it is also important to be aware of relevant marketing literature, for much of this informs the content of Chapter 2. For our specific context we recommend two standard marketing titles for information organizations: De Saez's *Marketing Concepts for Libraries and Information Services* (2002), though now rather dated, still conveys marketing basics clearly and succinctly; Rowley's *Information Marketing* (2nd edn, 2006) is a newer work on the topic and also provides useful background on marketing from an information perspective. If one is seeking a more current work on information marketing, then Smallwood, Gubnitskaia and Harrod's *Marketing Your Library* (2012) is a sound alternative that offers practical advice on marketing methods. More focused on marketing plans is *Marketing Your Library's Electronic Resources* by Kennedy and LaGuardia (2013).

But for the most up-to-date discussion of social media and marketing, at the time of writing the most broadly descriptive and thorough work is Thomsett-Scott's *Marketing with Social Media* (2014), which covers the full range of available tools, from Facebook and wikis to OR codes and Twitter, and describes their use and functions in some detail.

Segmenting the market so that a more specific analysis can be attempted is dealt with more adequately in many recent titles. One of these worth looking at is Potter's 2012 work, *The Library Marketing Toolkit*. Its main strength lies in the author's practical application of marketing theory, with three chapters devoted to online marketing, social media and new technologies, and 27 case studies interwoven into the text. Another worthwhile work is Nancy Rossiter's intriguingly titled *Marketing the Best Deal in Town: your library: where is your purple owl?* (2008). A particular strength of this book for the INA investigator is the way in which Rossiter combines theory and practice. Finally, another valuable publication that warrants study is *Bite-sized Marketing: realistic solutions for the overworked librarian* by Dowd, Evangeliste and Silberman (2010). Of value to the INA investigator are chapters dealing Word of Mouth Marketing (WOMM) and also such recent marketing tools as blogs, wikis, Twitter, mobile marketing and podcasts.

References

Aikenhead, G. S. (1997) Toward a First Nations Cross-cultural Science and Technology Curriculum, *Science Education,* **81**, 217–38.

Aikenhead, G. S. and Jegede, O. J. (1999) Cross-cultural Science Education: a cognitive explanation of a cultural phenomenon. *Journal of Research in Science Teaching*, **36**, 269–87.

Allard, S., Levine, K. J. and Tenopir, C. (2009) Design Engineers and Technical Professionals at Work: observing information usage in the workplace, *Journal of the American Society for Information Science and Technology*, **60** (3), 443–54.

Chang, S-J. L. (2009) Information Research in Leisure: implications from an empirical study of backpackers, *Library Trends*, **57** (4), 711–68.

Chatman, E. A. (1990) Alienation Theory: application of a conceptual framework to a study of information among janitors, *RQ,* **29** (3), 355–68.

Chatman, E. A. (1992) *The Information World of Retired Women*, Greenwood Press, Westport, CT.

Chatman, E. A. and Pendleton, V. E. M. (1995) Knowledge Gap, Information-Seeking and the Poor, *Reference Librarian*, **49–50**, 135–45.

Clark, P. M. (1983) *New Approaches to the Measurement of Public Library Use by Individual Patrons*, University of Illinois, Graduate School of Library and Information Science, Urbana, IL.

Coote, H. and Batchelor, B. (1997) *How to Market Your Library Service Effectively*, 2nd edn, Aslib, London.

Cutler, J. (2005) *The Cross-cultural Communication Trainer's Manual*, 2 vols, Gower Publishing, Aldershot.

Davies, K. (2009) Quantifying the Information Needs of Doctors in the U.K. Using Clinical Librarians, *Health Information and Libraries Journal*, **26** (4), 289–97.

De Saez, E. E. (2002) *Marketing Concepts for Libraries and Information Services*, Facet Publishing, London.

Dowd, N., Evangeliste, M. and Silberman, J. (2010) *Bite-sized Marketing: realistic solutions for the overworked librarian*, American Library Association, Chicago, IL.

Guiltinan J. P., Paul, G. W. and Madden, T. J. (1997) *Marketing Management: strategies and programs*, 6th edn, McGraw-Hill, Boston, MA.

Herman, E. and Nicholas, D. (2010) The Information Enfranchisement of the Digital Consumer, *Aslib Proceedings: new information perspectives*, **62** (3), 245–60.

Hofstede, G. and Hofstede, G. J. (2010) *Cultures and Organizations: software of the mind. Intercultural cooperation and its importance for survival*, 3rd edn, McGraw-Hill, New York, NY.

Jegede, O. (1995) Collateral Learning and the Eco-cultural Paradigm in Science and Mathematics Education in Africa, *Studies in Science Education*, **25**, 97–137.

Kennedy, M. R. and LaGuardia, C. (2013) *Marketing Your Library's Electronic Resources: a how-to-do-it manual*, Facet Publishing, London.

Lehmann, D. R. and Winer, R. S. (2002) *Analysis for Marketing Planning*, 5th edn, McGraw-Hill/Irwin, Boston, MA.

Li, H. and Rao, N. (2009) Multiple Literacies: beliefs and related practices among Chinese kindergarten teachers, *Knowledge Management & E-Learning: An International Journal*, **1** (4), 269–84, www.kmel-journal.org/ojs/index.php/online-publication/article/viewFile/40/31. [Accessed 31 October 2014.]

Luke, A. and Kapitzke, C. (1999) Literacies and Libraries: archives and cybraries, *Curriculum Studies* **7** (3), 467–91.

MacDonald, T. (1993) *Te Ara Tika: Maori and libraries: a research report*, New Zealand Library and Information Association, Wellington.

Maddock, M. N. (1981) Science Education: an anthropological viewpoint, *Studies in Science Education,* **8**, 1–26.

Makri, S. and Warwick, C. (2010) Information for Inspiration: understanding architects' information seeking and use behaviors to inform design, *Journal of the American Society for Information Science and Technology* **61** (9), 1745–70.

Marcella, R. and Baxter, G. (2000) Citizenship Information Needs in the UK: results of a national survey of the general public by personal doorstep interview, *Aslib Proceedings*, **52** (3), 115–23.

Metoyer-Duran, C. (1993) *Gatekeepers in Ethnolinguistic Communities*, Ablex Publishing, Norwood, NJ.

Monsour, M. (2012) Libraries Innovate with New Financial Education Programs, *Public Libraries* **51** (2), 36–43.

Nicholas, D. and Herman, E. (2009) *Assessing Information Needs in the Age of the Digital Consumer*, Routledge, London.

Potter, N. (2012) *The Library Marketing Toolkit*, Facet Publishing, London.

Reviere, R., Carter, C. C., Berkowitz, S. and Ferguson, C. G. (eds) (1996) *Needs Assessment: a creative and practical guide for social scientists*, Taylor & Francis, Basingstoke.

Roddy, K. (2005) Community Profiling, *Library + Information Update*, **4** (5), 40–1.

Rossiter, N. (2008) *Marketing the Best Deal in Town: your library. Where is your purple owl?* Chandos Information Professional Series, Chandos Publishing, Witney.

Rowley, J. (2006) *Information Marketing*, 2nd edn, Ashgate Publishing, Aldershot.

Smallwood, C., Gubnitskaia, V. and Harrod, K. (2012) *Marketing Your Library: tips and tools that work*, McFarland and Company, Jefferson, NC.

SRI Consulting (2005) *VALS Psychology of Markets*. Available at www.sric-bi.com/VAL. [Accessed 31 October 2014.]

Thomsett-Scott, B. C. (ed.) (2013) *Marketing with Social Media: a LITA guide*, Facet Publishing, London.

UNESCO (2005) *EFA Global Monitoring Report 2006: education for all, literacy for life*, Paris, UNESCO, www.unesco.org/new/en/education/themes/leading-the-international-agenda/efareport/reports/2006-literacy. [Accessed 31 October 2014.]

Waldrip, B. G., and Taylor, P. C. (1999) Permeability of Students' World Views to Their School Views in a Non-Western Developing Country, *Journal of Research in Science Teaching*, **36** (3), 289–303.

Witkin, B. R. and Altschuld, J. W. (1995) *Planning and Conducting Needs Assessments: a practical guide*, SAGE Publications, Thousand Oaks, CA.

Younger, P. (2010) Internet-based Information-seeking Behaviour amongst Doctors and Nurses: a short review of the literature, *Health Information and Libraries*, **27** (1), 2–10.

CHAPTER 3

Models and types of information needs analysis

Introduction

In this chapter we identify different levels, models and types of needs analysis generally (as distinct from INA specifically) that are discussed in the literature across a variety of disciplines. The purpose of this is to distinguish key features and themes related to needs analysis models. We also examine the application of some of these models to information management (IM) contexts, and ultimately we draw upon the key elements of these models to develop our own models of INA.

When reading this chapter it is important to note the following points. Because we are often referring to the literature, we use the term 'needs assessment' when it has been used by the authors we are referencing, and we use the term 'needs analysis' when providing our own points of view and when developing our own models. And, when discussing IM contexts, we are generally talking about situations in which information services, programmes or products are being considered, planned, implemented or evaluated. However, rather than continually repeating the terms 'services, programmes or products' we simply use the term 'services' as shorthand for all three.

The purpose of this chapter, in brief, is to address three questions:

1 What are the levels of INA?
2 How do we identify different models and types of INA?
3 What contextual factors must be considered when undertaking INAs?

We begin our search for answers to these questions with a brief analysis of relevant literature.

The literature

When scanning the literature on needs analyses and assessment, we soon recognize that there are many perspectives used to group needs analyses into different categories or types. Some writers categorize needs analyses into levels based on the scope or coverage with respect to the target groups, whereas other writers identify models based on the breadth of outcomes expected or the extent or types of changes that are possible with respect to the specific contexts giving rise to and INA.

We now examine specific examples from the broader literature that illustrate various ways in which models of needs analysis have been categorized. Primary focus is on literature from international development and management, human resources development and especially education, with particular attention to the work of Kaufman and English (1979) and Witkin and Altschuld (1995).

In the management literature Watkins et al. (1998, 41) argue that 'needs assessments offer performance initiatives as unique opportunities to approach performance improvement'. Similarly, in their book on needs assessment for international development agencies, Watkins, West Meier and Visser (2012, 22) explain that they use 'the phrase *improving performance* to represent the results that are the focus of a needs assessment'. Both sets of authors identify three levels of performance relevant in needs assessment: (1) individual or team, (2) organizational and (3) societal. Watkins et al. (1998) point out, however, that usually only two levels of organizational planning and decision making are defined by conventional 'business wisdom': the organizational (or macro level) and the individual (or micro level). They also contend that most models of needs assessment related to performance initiatives do not address the societal or even the organizational level. Hence organizations fail to take into consideration the broader context of the potential societal outcomes of needs assessments and they miss out on '"a societal bottom line" as well as a societal (or mega) level of planning and decision-making' (Watkins et al., 1998, 41).

Using this manner of framing needs analysis levels, we can argue that a city library seeking to improve its services to a particular group, such as an indigenous community or a minority ethnic group, must conduct an INA at the societal level, with the entire community as the target, rather than simply evaluating existing services. The INA in this instance could be used as a starting point in a strategic planning exercise that would extend management thinking outside the limiting confines of the existing services.

In the human resources development literature Leigh et al. identify criteria for determining a variety of training needs assessment models. Each of the models 'serves a particular purpose, is intended for a specific audience, and employs differing definitions of need and needs assessment that, although not always made explicit, drive the form and function of each model' (Leigh et al., 2000, 88–9). These authors identify models at the mega (society), macro (organization) and micro (individual/small group) levels, as well as models based on processes (efforts and activities) and resources (inputs). The first three categories focus on results, ends and consequences, whereas the final two categories focus on the methods and means.

In the education literature Burton and Merrill (1977, 28) argue that needs assessments can cover the full spectrum of educational need from 'a global level down to the level of a module within a course'. Kaufman and English (1979) focus on needs assessment for educational programme planning and identify types that range from the highly open to the very specific and simple. These authors link needs assessment to a *system approach* to general problem solving and planning, which they adapt to assessing needs in educational settings.

The system approach

The system approach emphasizes the importance of identifying the ends before determining the means. The six types of needs assessment defined by Kaufman and English (1979) are similar to some of the levels discussed earlier, but their levels also reflect different stages in the system approach to planning as well as the amount and type of possible change relative to the specific context.

1. The *Alpha type* is at the highest level, one with the potential for any amount of reasonable change because there are 'relatively few "givens" and no "sacred cows" in terms of organizations, personnel, history – or even existing laws' (p. 56). It requires the most risk taking, since it is 'the most direct route to the identification and achievement of "deep" change' (p. 57).
2. The *Beta type* is a more restrictive level in which boundaries to the amount of possible change are set by the goals, objectives and policies of the system of the agency that is the focus of the analysis (p. 344).
3. The *Gamma type* is at the level of prioritizing existing goals and objectives with a view to emphasizing alternative programmes or materials (p. 58).
4. The *Delta type* is used to manage the outcome process. The amount of change involved at this level is within the context of implementing previously determined alternatives (p. 58).
5. The *Epsilon type* is aligned closely with summative evaluations in that this level is used 'to determine the extent to which required results have been

accomplished' (p. 58).

6. The *Zeta type* can be associated with formative evaluations, since it is used to make decisions to modify or continue all or part of a programme or service (p. 58).

Table 3.1 summarizes the levels and relates them to the system approach of educational planning espoused by Kaufman and English (1979).

It is useful here to consider more closely the scope of each of Kaufman and English's six types of needs assessment. The Alpha type is both the broadest in terms of the extent of possible change and also the only level where the context's scope extends beyond the boundaries of the individual organization or entity. Thus the focus of Alpha needs assessments is external (that is, on the broader community or society), whereas the other five levels focus internally, on an organization's programmes or services or one of their components.

Kaufman and English note that the six types of needs assessment can be used in non-educational settings; we can easily relate these types and corresponding levels to IM contexts. It is essential for an INA to focus on the level that is appropriate for the task at hand. At the Alpha level we can conduct an INA to identify and examine the broadly based information needs of a particular community, such as the immigrant population of a city, for the purpose of strategic planning within a public library system. At this point in the planning process there is a clean slate in terms of what may or may not be entertained in terms of possible inputs and outputs. Consultations would occur with members of the immigrant community, library managers and staff, the policy staff within the local authority and so forth. In this level of INA any existing policies, programmes and related matters can be questioned and changed.

Scenario 3.1 provides an example of the application in a university library setting of five of the levels of needs analysis in Table 3.1.

Scenario 3.1 A systems approach INA project at the King's Lynn University Library

The School of Earth Sciences (SES) at King's Lynn University received approval to commence a new degree programme for a research-based master's degree in Environmental Science (MES). The University Library, working with the SES, undertook an INA project to determine the needs for library resources and services for the new programme. The investigator (and project team) used a systems approach to the INA and divided it into five stages.

The aim of the initial stage was to identify any gaps between the information resources and services that the University Library already provided and those that would be required to support the new programme. A Beta level analysis was required for Stage 1 because the University Library system already had established goals, objectives and policies that set boundaries for the level of possible changes. The analysis from Stage 1 supplied the project team with the programme requirements and the range of alternative solutions to the problem.

For Stage 2 the project team conducted a Gamma level analysis to select the most efficient and effective solutions from among the alternatives. A database providing access to raw scientific data was deemed to be the highest priority as the most effective and efficient means for meeting a significant need of the target group (i.e. the Environmental Science masters' students and the academic staff teaching and researching in that area).

Based on the decision to provide access to the database, the project team then undertook a Delta level analysis as Stage 3 of the INA. During this stage the team identified some gaps in hardware and software (i.e. specialized equipment and programmes required for viewing and manipulating the large datasets retrieved from the database) and in-library staff knowledge, which resulted in additional training for the librarians supporting the new MES programme.

During the implementation of the new resources and services the investigator and project team undertook Stage 4 of the INA project – a Zeta level formative analysis to determine the extent to which the processes involved in providing online access to the large statistical datasets were achieving the required outputs. As a result of the Zeta level analysis, the project team identified several additional shortcomings with respect to library staff competencies, and additional training was undertaken. The project team also developed a plan to carry out a similar level of data gathering and analysis on an ongoing basis to ensure the resources and services supporting the MES continued to achieve the desired outputs.

At the end of the first year of the MES and the commencement of the new services the project team undertook Stage 5 of the INA project by conducting an Epsilon level analysis. This concluding stage provided the library management as well as the SES with a summative evaluation of the efficiency and effectiveness of the new services and resources. The outcomes of the Epsilon evaluation confirmed that the new services had achieved the desired results but also identified some minor discrepancies which were quickly rectified, and allowed for the successes of the project to be documented for future reference.

Table 3.1 Levels of needs analysis [based on Kaufman and English (1979)]

Level	Corresponding function in system approach	Purpose	Referents	Parameters and extent of possible changes
Alpha	Identify problem based on need	To identify a 'need' as the starting point for organizational efforts in policy development, programme planning, etc.	External: societal focus looks outside the organization at the gap between what is and what should be; it is partnership based and requires input from all stakeholder groups	There are few or no givens relating to conditions and ground rules for operation or problem resolution; deep change is possible, including to policies, organizations, legislation, etc.
Beta	Determine solution requirements and identify solution alternatives	To analyse output gaps when there is certainty with respect to the system's goals, objectives and policies	Internal: focus is on the output gaps of current programmes, services or products and is partnership based	Planned change is set in the context of present goals, objectives and policies and is based on gaps between current and required outputs
Gamma	Select solution strategies from among alternatives	To prioritize existing goals and objectives with a view to emphasizing alternative programmes or materials	Internal: focus is on determining discrepancies concerning methods and means for problem resolution and is partnership based	Change is within the context of the present system but is aimed at determining the most efficient and effective solution for achieving ranked objectives
Delta	Implement	To administer jobs to be done and manage the overall organizational mission	Internal: focus is on identifying gaps relative to implementation of selected methods and means	This is used when what has to be done and how to do it are known; change is within the context of task management and accomplishment
Epsilon	Determine performance effectiveness	To evaluate the effectiveness of a programme, service or product	Internal: focus is on determining discrepancies between results and objectives	This is used when a project has been completed; the context is to examine gaps in results derived from the internal planning
Zeta	Revise as required	To evaluate processes and progress towards desired outcomes and implement corrective actions if needed	Internal: focus is on determining discrepancies between goals and objectives while en route	This is conducted during a project or when a segment is completed; gap identification may result in changes to inputs or outputs in a programme, service or product

The target group approach

Unlike Kaufman and English (1979), who differentiate the scope of needs assessments based on when and where the assessment occurs in the planning process and the type and amount of change possible as a result of the assessment, Witkin and Altschuld (1995, 10) focus 'on the people in the system' when determining the scope of needs analyses. As discussed in Chapter 1, these authors consider the system to include people who are inside (service users, providers and policymakers) as well as outside (non-users); and they differentiate three levels of information need, each related directly to a different target group:

◆ Level 1 (primary) – service receivers
◆ Level 2 (secondary) – service providers and policymakers
◆ Level 3 (tertiary) – resources or solutions.

By differentiating the level of need based on the target group Witkin and Altschuld are able to establish whether the analysis involves gathering data from and/or about people who are inside or outside the system.

At Level 1 the target group (service receivers) can be either inside or outside. For example, a public library that wishes to assess the needs of the city's ethnic minority groups will need to focus on members of the target groups who are users of the library system (internal to the system), as well as those who are not users (external to the system).

In all cases Level 2 and Level 3 needs relate to groups who are inside the system. Witkin and Altschuld define a *system* as 'a regularly interacting or interdependent group of people forming a unified whole and organized for a common purpose . . . [that is] the organization or group involved with the NA [needs assessment]' Witkin and Altschuld (1995, 13). In each needs assessment the boundaries and scope of the system will be defined by the specific context.

The contexts of needs assessments

Another key aspect of Witkin and Altschuld's approach is their identification of different contexts in which needs assessments are conducted. This aspect of their approach is in a sense similar to the way in which Kaufman and English (1979) identify the different types and corresponding levels of needs assessments.

One of the most common contexts, according to Witkin and Altschuld, occurs in an iterative planning cycle, which the authors describe as follows:

NA [needs assessment] precedes program-planning and is followed by implementation of the new program. Concurrently, the program is monitored and formative evaluation takes place. If necessary and feasible, revisions are made, the revised program is monitored, and, toward the end of the cycle, there is a summative evaluation. In turn, the data from the evaluation give information for a new stage of NA [needs assessment], which may lead to various outcomes: continuation of the program, continuation with radical modifications, termination, or branching programs.

Witkin and Altschuld, 1995, 61

They identify three separate contexts within an iterative planning cycle: the planning context, the evaluation context and the cyclical needs assessment context. They say that in planning, needs assessment 'is the first essential step in documenting needs and developing programs or other strategies to meet them' (Witkin and Altschuld, 1995, 61). The needs information provides the basis on which to decide priorities and to develop plans for resolving those needs.

Needs assessments in the context of evaluations serve a variety of potential roles. Witkin and Altschuld (1995, 61) point out that in summative evaluations needs assessments can be used to determine whether a programme has achieved its goals, whereas in formative evaluations they can be used 'to identify goals, problems or conditions that should be addressed in future program planning'. They also contend (p. 66) that in both planning and evaluation contexts decisions to determine priorities for allocating resources follow the needs assessment. In an iterative programme planning process needs assessment performs a specific role, as shown in Figure 3.1, which is based on an idea in Witkin and Altschuld (1995, 62). The needs assessment begins in Cycle 1 with Step 1 (Action plan) and concludes with Step 5 (Summative evaluation). This is then followed by Cycle 2, beginning with Step 6 (Update needs assessment) and concluding with Step 10 (Programme revisions). Cycle 2 could be followed by further recursive cycles as required.

The third context within the iterative planning process is cyclical needs assessment. Witkin and Altschuld (1995, 66) state that this context occurs when organizations, typically larger ones, conduct needs assessments regularly, such as annually or biannually. A cyclical needs assessment might be part of ongoing strategic planning or part of regular evaluations of parts of an organization.

Two other contexts identified by Witkin and Altschuld are ongoing needs assessments tied to management information systems (1995, 68–9) and collaborative (i.e. interagency) needs assessments (69–73). The former context takes advantage of the capabilities provided by management information systems, which gather data continuously and allow managers to manipulate these

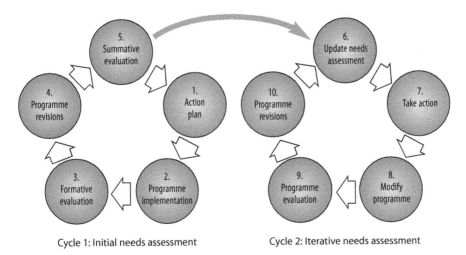

Cycle 1: Initial needs assessment   Cycle 2: Iterative needs assessment

Figure 3.1 The role of needs assessment in iterative programme planning evaluation

data for different purposes. A collaborative needs assessment involves collaboration between two or more agencies or organizations – for example, when a city's social services agency and public library system work together on a needs analysis to address issues of common concern with respect to a target population served by both organizations.

Comparing the perspectives

At this point we might usefully examine key similarities and differences between the perspectives of Kaufman and English (1979) and Witkin and Altschuld (1995). Both sets of authors argue there is a critical starting point for ensuring the success of needs assessment processes. For Kaufman and English the Alpha-type needs assessment forms the basis for all other types of needs assessments and has few or no set criteria with respect to conditions or ground rules – thus 'deep change' is possible. The Alpha-type needs assessment requires an organization to look at the outputs of the current system ('what is') and compare them to the target group requirements with respect to the outside world ('what should be'). Witkin and Altschuld take a somewhat different approach, stating that needs assessments for strategic planning processes differ from those for other planning processes. These authors contend that strategic planning processes require an organization to determine needs based on an examination of both internal and external environments. Thus, while the approaches of the two sets of authors are somewhat different, their underlying principles are essentially the same.

Witkin and Altschuld nonetheless differ from Kaufman and English in one key element of needs assessments. Using the system approach, Kaufman and English include the Gamma-type of needs assessment for selecting solution strategies and the Delta-type for implementing them. Witkin and Altschuld, on the other hand, consider the solution selection and implementation phases of the process to be in the post-assessment phase. We wish to emphasize the point made in Chapter 1: INA includes the identification of information needs, the analysis of the needs so that they are understood and the assessment of the needs with respect to impending decisions. We believe that, in IM contexts, INAs are critical to the initial parts of selection and implementation processes and that decisions based on those needs are made in ex post intervention stages.

We now describe a variety of types of INA for use in different types of processes.

Information needs analyses in information management contexts

From our examination of needs assessment models we can see that different models of INA are required for different purposes and in different IM contexts. These purposes and contexts are shaped by factors related to the three levels of needs identified by Witkin and Altschuld (1995). Here we discuss INAs in relation to the following six processes used in IM contexts:

1   Open planning processes
2   Closed planning processes
3   Solution selection processes
4   Implementation processes
5   Formative evaluation processes
6   Summative evaluation processes.

INAs conducted in relation to the six processes discussed here are similar to the six types of needs assessment defined by Kaufman and English (1979) in the system approach for education programme planning.

Needs analysis related to these six processes are not unique to IM contexts and are discussed in the literature of other disciplines and professions. For example, McKenzie, Neiger and Thackeray (2012) devote a chapter to needs assessment in their book, *Planning, Implementing, and Evaluating Health Promotion*

Programs: a primer (6th edn), and Posavac (2013) identifies the use of a variety of different types of needs assessments related to service receivers as well as service providers.

Our purpose here is to provide an understanding of the factors that set the contextual parameters of INAs. As Witkin (1984, 31) points out, 'the choice of models, procedures and instruments should be guided by the purposes and context of the assessment and the decisions to be made on the basis of the findings'. In the following discussion we group related processes: the two planning processes together, the solution selection and implementation processes together, and the two evaluation processes together. At the end of our discussion we provide a comparative table summarizing the contextual elements that establish the parameters of INAs conducted in the contexts of the six processes:

◆ the constraints of the analysis
◆ the scope of the analysis
◆ the intended output
◆ the target group for the analysis
◆ who should be consulted.

We conclude our discussion of these processes with six scenarios, one to illustrate each of the six types of contexts in which INAs can occur.

INAs in planning processes

In IM contexts there are two main types of planning processes, both of which aim to obtain a clear understanding of Level 1 (service receiver) needs: open planning processes (OPP) and closed planning processes (CPP).

Open planning processes are suited to contexts involving broadly based exercises, for example during strategic planning, or when developing policy, or when planning a completely new service. In an open planning situation the INA is an essential first step to ensure that the problem to be resolved is identified prior to determining the solution. Because the investigator's thinking must not be constrained by the parameters of the current system, these are the most complex of all INAs. The investigator must drill deeply into the situation and ask what the members of the target group actually need in order to be able to function in, and contribute to, their community (Scenario 3.2).

Scenario 3.2 An open planning process INA in the Simon, Peters & Kravitz
Information Centre

The Information Centre (IC) in Simon, Peters & Kravitz, a mid-sized law firm, is
undertaking a strategic planning exercise to shape its future direction. Because this is a
strategic planning exercise, all of the Centre's existing services, as well as its goals,
objectives and policies, are open to change. In this scenario an OPP is occurring, and
the target group of the INA is within the system, that is, the barristers, solicitors and
legal assistants in the firm who receive the services provided by the IC. The results of
the OPP INA will be a clear understanding of the target group's current information
needs; this understanding will then become the basis for ex post intervention actions,
which will not be restricted by any preconceived notions and therefore can be a set of
recommendations for radical changes to the IC's operations – or even a
recommendation to close it. The parties to be consulted include the firm's partners, the
other lawyers and legal staff in each of the firm's legal divisions, its administrators,
members of the IT group and the IC manager and reference person.

In closed planning processes INAs perform the same function as in open
planning processes, but the goals and objectives of the current system set the
basic parameters for any decisions. For example, when planning one or more
subsystems or service areas in an existing system, an INA must be undertaken
to understand the target group's needs, but the investigator must work within
the parameters that have already been established by the current system.

In some instances an INA in a closed planning process could be a logical
second step following an initial INA in an open planning process. This situation
would occur, for example, when the investigator during an open planning exercise
has identified a problem related to the target group, and the planners have then
decided that a new service would be the best way to resolve the problem. The
planners then set the parameters of the new service. When the planners have
received approval to move forward with the new service, they then conduct a
closed process, and the investigator conducts a second INA using the established
parameters of the new service to identify the specific needs of the target group
(Scenario 3.3).

Scenario 3.3 A closed planning process INA in the Yeltsin Library at the
University of Zhivago

The Yeltsin Library at the University of Zhivago is considering a new information
literacy (IL) programme specifically targeted at undergraduate business students. The

University already offers a range of pamphlets, web guides and orientation sessions, as well as a number of short workshops aimed at helping first- and second-year students learn how to find and evaluate information for their assignments. However, a recent survey of employers revealed a relatively high level of dissatisfaction with the abilities of recent business graduates to find and use appropriately sourced information in their work projects. The directors of both the undergraduate and postgraduate business programmes have discussed the situation with the University Librarian, who has recommended a new IL programme specifically for first- and second-year students. This would begin with a trial programme embedding IL into the business curriculum, but to do so would require a clear understanding of the information needs of academic staff as well as those of the students.

A CPP INA is very well suited to the process of planning a new IL programme that will operate within the parameters of the Yeltsin Library's existing policies and resources. The target group in this scenario is the full complement of first- and second-year students in the Faculty of Business, as well as the academic staff teaching these students. The academic staff are included in the target group because they also have information needs related to the courses they are teaching, and they create the information needs of the students in relation to the course-related assignments. The output from this CPP INA will be an understanding of the needs of both students and academic staff that subsequently will be used in the ex post intervention activities to determine the requirements of, and the range of possible solutions for, an IL programme. This CPP INA will require consultation with the complete range of stakeholders, including the students, the academic staff, the reference librarians and business liaison librarian, and the employers of graduates.

INAs in solution selection and implementation processes

Information needs analyses in solution selection processes are used predominantly for analysing Level 3 needs, and those in implementation processes are highly suited to analysing Level 2 needs. Nonetheless, the ultimate aim in all INAs contexts is to meet Level 1 information needs, that is, the needs of the particular target group for which the information service has been established.

In a solution selection process an INA investigator must focus on the needs of the organization in order to select the most efficient and effective of several possible solutions for meeting the needs of the target group, i.e. the service receivers. Here an INA is usually undertaken as a second step in planning for a new information service or to prioritize the objectives and outcomes of an existing service when the organization is confronted with new financial circumstances (Scenario 3.4).

Scenario 3.4 A solution selection INA for Malvernshire County Council

The results of an INA project conducted earlier in the year showed that a significant portion of the unemployed population of Malvernshire lacked the resources and skills needed to access the increasingly digital information about the range of services available to help them find work and/or obtain government support. The County Council therefore has decided to undertake an INA to determine the most efficient and effective solution to provide unemployed people with access to the required information through current service providers, including the Malvernshire Library Service and a number of government agencies, such as the Department for Work and Pensions and the Community Development Foundation.

The INA in this example is the second step in meeting the needs of Malvernshire's unemployed population for access to work- and benefits-related information. The County Council has already announced its desire to improve access for unemployed people to this information; therefore the focus here is on understanding the resource implications for the potential service providers with a view to determining which provider or providers will offer the most effective and efficient option.

The target group in this example is the County Council, since the analysis focuses on understanding its needs with respect to the resource implications (Level 3 needs) related to meeting the needs of the unemployed population for improved access to information. The INA process will involve consulting and gathering data from the Malvernshire Library Service, the Department for Work and Pensions, the Community Development Foundation and all other relevant stakeholders in both local and national government.

An INA in an implementation process is conducted when an organization is implementing a selected solution for resolving the service receivers' information needs. In this context the INA is internally focused because the aim of the investigators is to determine the needs of the service providers and/or the providing organization (Scenario 3.5).

Scenario 3.5 An implementation process INA for schools in South Wales

TeachConnect is an online service for teachers in South Wales. It provides a central database of full-text and online resources to support the curriculum across different levels and subject areas, and it makes available several social networking tools for teachers to share their professional expertise and discuss curriculum issues and ideas. The service has been in operation for five years, but responsibility for providing support is being decentralized to the school libraries in South Wales. The libraries are staffed by a mixture of qualified librarians, teachers with library responsibility and parent volunteers.

An implementation INA is required in this context to determine the needs of the service providers. The constraints are clear: the goals and objectives of TeachConnect have been established, and key decisions have already been made. The scope of this project includes the needs of the library staff (Level 2 needs) for skills to meet their new responsibilities and the needs of the school libraries for ICT resources (Level 3 needs) for use by staff and teachers. The output will be used in the ex post intervention stages to decide on solutions to meet the service providers' needs. Consultation will be required with all library staff and other stakeholders, including the school administrators, principals and teachers and the TeachConnect staff.

INAs in evaluation processes

Evaluation is a necessary course of action when determining whether new or existing services are achieving their goals and whether further actions are needed. INAs undertaken as part of evaluations are therefore primarily aimed at analysing Level 1 needs because they focus on how well the target group's needs are being met by a new or existing service.

A formative evaluation process (FEP) is usually undertaken during or soon after the implementation of a new service, or when an existing service is in operation, to identify where improvements can be made. In an INA undertaken as part of a formative evaluation, the investigators seek to understand the needs of the information service's target group (Level 1 needs) and the actual outputs of the service with a view to improving its performance (Scenario 3.6).

Scenario 3.6 A formative evaluation process INA in Washbourne County Library
Service

The Washbourne County Library Service is implementing Free Spirit, an open-source 'next generation' OPAC to provide its users with a single point of access for searching its online information resources. These resources include the Library Service's current OPAC, a range of full-text databases provided by commercial aggregators, some full-text resources created internally such as the digitized collection of local newspapers and pamphlets, plus the digitized content of the oral history collection. The Library Service's online systems currently have a wide range of users, with the main groups being genealogical researchers, secondary school and university students and academic staff from the University of Washbourne's Departments of History, Literature and Gender Studies.

A formative evaluation INA is being undertaken by the system implementers to ensure that the 'Free Spirit' software achieves its maximum potential for meeting the users' needs. The existing constraints for this INA are the established objectives for this new interface to the library's resources along with parameters such as the timeline for its implementation. The intended outputs of this INA are understandings of: (1) the main user groups' needs in relation to searching across the County Library's online information resources, and (2) how these needs relate to each of the functional options available in the Free Spirit software. These understandings will be used to make decisions in the ex post intervention stages about the search interface's appearance, preferences for displaying retrieved information, de-duplication processes, etc. The consultation process for the FEP analysis will include representatives from each of the main groups of users and from other existing and potential user groups, the reference staff who are providing the support for the users, and the systems support staff who are responsible for maintaining the service.

A summative evaluation process, on the other hand, is conducted to evaluate an existing service or programme and may be part of a regular review or an ad hoc review. There are many reasons for undertaking a summative evaluation: for example, to determine whether an existing information service should continue or be terminated, or at the conclusion of an information services training programme to understand which parts worked well and which did not, with a view to using the findings in future decision making. In both examples the INA investigator's aim is to gather data to compare the target group's information needs (Level 1 needs) with the actual outputs of the service or programmes.

The data from a summative evaluation INA are used to identify any gaps between the target groups' information needs and what the service or programme has actually provided in order to evaluate it and/or its parts. In some instances the understanding gained through the analysis will be used in an ex post intervention stage to make decisions about a service's future, whereas in other instances it will be used in the future as input to decisions about related services (Scenario 3.7).

Scenario 3.7 A summative evaluation process INA for MacRitchie City Library

---

Two years ago the staff of MacRitchie City Library (MCL) recognized that the growing number of immigrant families from Eastern Europe was changing the demographics of the Library's client base; as a consequence, MCL hired an INA investigator to identify and analyse the library needs of these clients. Last year, after assessing the needs, MCL obtained a grant from The Angus Foundation for a three-year project to build a print and e-book collection of Eastern European language resources for these immigrant families and their bilingual children, and also to establish an outreach programme to attract members of these communities to the MCL. The funding body has asked MCL to provide feedback at the end of each year during the project.

In this scenario a summative evaluation process INA at the end of each one of the two years is suited to the funding body's requirements and to MCL's own needs for managing the project. The objectives of the funded programme will set the constraints for each of the first two annual analyses, but there should be no constraints related to the third and final summative evaluation process INA. The outputs of the annual INAs will be reported back to The Angus Foundation in terms of how well the target group's needs have been met by the programme during the year. The output from the analyses after Years 1 and 2 will also be used in ex post intervention stages to make decisions about any required modifications, while the output for the Year 3 analysis will be used by the organization in ex post intervention stages to determine whether to continue the programme. If a decision to continue the programme is made, the information from the summative evaluation process INA will be used to determine any modifications required and to provide information for when future funding is sought.

Establishing the contextual parameters for INAs

Table 3.2 provides information about six processes that establish the contextual parameters for INAs.

Review of Chapter 3

The literature from a range of disciplines provides a variety of models and types of needs assessment. Based on an analysis of this literature, Chapter 3 has identified six different processes in which information needs analyses are essential – two processes used for planning information services and programmes (the open planning process and the closed planning process), two processes used in selection and implementation (the solution selection process and the implementation process) and two processes for evaluating information services and

Table 3.2 Processes that establish the contextual parameters for information needs analyses

Type of processes	Constraints	Scope	Intended output	Target group	Who should be consulted
Open planning	None – all options for changes or developments are open for consideration	The whole community, because the aim is to identify the needs of all possible members of the target group	A clear understanding of the information needs of the target group for different possible uses	All current and potential service receivers	All stakeholders, including those inside and those outside the current service
Closed planning	The policies, goals and objectives of the current service	People within the organization, because the aim is to identify the target group's information needs in relation to the organization's current goals and objectives	A clear understanding of the target group's needs (the actual set of requirements and the range of solutions to resolve the needs are determined in the ex post intervention stages)	The current service receivers	All stakeholders, including those who are inside and those who are outside the current service
Solution selection	(1) The goals and objectives of the new service or (2) the changed financial circumstances of an existing service	The organization providing (1) the planned service or (2) the affected service	A clear understanding of the organization's needs for choosing a solution to meet the target group's identified needs	The organization providing the service	All stakeholders inside the organization
Implementation	The existing goals and objectives for the selected solution	The service providers and/or the organization providing the planned or affected service	A clear understanding of the needs of service providers	The service providers and/or staff responsible for decisions about new services	All stakeholders inside the organization
Formative evaluation	Existing goals and objectives for the service	The organization, because the INA aims to determine whether the target group's information needs are being met by existing processes in relation to desired outcomes	A clear understanding of how well the service receivers' needs are being met by each part of the service to determine requirements for improving its performance	The service receivers	The service receivers and providers and stakeholders with perspectives on the effectiveness of the service
Summative evaluation	(1) None when deciding whether an existing service should be continued or discontinued; (2) existing policies, goals and objectives when the aim is to improve an existing service	The organization, because the INA aims to identify the information needs of the service receivers	A clear understanding of how well the service receivers' needs have been met, either (1) to decide whether to continue or discontinue the service, or (2) to determine the requirements for improving it	The current and potential service receivers	The target group of the service, the providers of the service and other relevant stakeholders

programmes (the formative evaluation process and the summative evaluation process). It is important to bear in mind that there is no single method of INA that suits all contexts. As Witkin points out with respect to needs assessment, the designs of different assessments are based on the following premise:

> that there is no single one right way to conduct a needs assessment that is applicable to all cases; that the data should be related to the purposes of the assessment, the organization's present knowledge, and the decisions that will be made; that needs assessment is not an isolated activity but part of a broad planning or development effort; and that after answering key questions, the needs assessor will be in a better position to make an informed judgment regarding the choice of data-collection approaches and instruments.
>
> Witkin, 1984, 32

This discussion has set the stage for Chapter 4, which examines the different stages involved in conducting an INA. Included in the stages to be discussed is, as one might expect, the requirement to select which of the six processes discussed in Chapter 3 might be applicable to the particular analysis to be conducted following the stages in Chapter 4.

Further reading

As the foregoing discussion indicates, the matter of models and types of INA is somewhat complex, and it arises primarily from the rather extensive literature on needs assessment. Unfortunately, we know of no simple guide to models for INA, so for further reading one must rely on materials looking more generally at needs assessment. Several of these have been used in this chapter.

Probably the best starting point is the literature review by Watkins et al. in *Performance Improvement* (1998); although now more than 16 years old, this paper still offers a sound overview of the key ideas related to needs assessment. This might usefully be followed by Sue Henczel's (2005) short piece in *Information Outlook*, which looks briefly at client needs identification in a simple and straightforward manner.

It is then necessary to move on to the heavier end of the spectrum, and here the paper by Leigh et al. (2000) on alternative models is probably the most accessible of the readings. Because this paper looks at alternatives, it is important not to stop here but to go on to the two comprehensive guides used in this chapter, Kaufman and English (1979) and Witkin (1984). The former is useful for its focus on the application of needs assessments, whereas Witkin is more comprehensive, covering both theory and practice.

The chapter on lifestyles in Grover, Greer and Agada (2010) provides useful details about the range of information and information sources relevant to understanding the culture of a community and the implications of a community's culture on its information needs. The various characteristics of a community (its history, values, customs, traditions, topography, climate, leisure activities, communication patterns, economic situation and social issues) are all discussed. The chapter is a useful resource for anyone undertaking an INA in an open planning process, especially in a public library setting.

For a more focused discussion of information needs and needs analysis in the context of information users and user studies, we recommend Gobinda and Sudatta Chowdhury's *Information Users and Usability in the Digital Age* (2011). Finally, we suggest that you conclude your further reading with a 'real-life' needs assessment in a library setting: the excellent study by Marchionini, Plaisant and Komlodi (1996) for the Library of Congress. This document shows how comprehensive and detailed a high-level information needs assessment can be and offers a model for needs analysis discussed in subsequent chapters of this book.

References

Burton, J. K. and Merrill, P. F. (1977) Needs Assessment: goals, needs, and priorities. In Briggs, L. J. (ed.), *Instructional Design*, Educational Technology Publications, Englewood Cliffs, NJ.

Chowdhury, G. G. and Chowdhury S. (2011) *Information Users and Usability in the Digital Age*, Facet Publishing, London.

Grover, R. J., Greer, R. C. and Agada, J. (2010) *Assessing Information Needs: managing transformative library services*, ABC-CLIO/Libraries Unlimited, Santa Barbara, CA.

Henczel, S. (2005) To Be Truly Accountable to Your Clients, Identify Their Needs, *Information Outlook*, **9** (2), 32–3.

Kaufman, R. and English, F. W. (1979) *Needs Assessment: concept and application*, Educational Technology Publications, Englewood Cliffs, NJ.

Leigh, D., Watkins, R., Platt, W. A. and Kaufman, R. (2000) Alternate Models of Needs Assessment: selecting the right one for your organization, *Human Resource Development Quarterly*, **11** (1), 87–94.

Marchionini, G., Plaisant, C. and Komlodi, A. (1996) *Users' Needs Assessment for the Library of Congress' National Digital Library*, Computer Science Technical Report Series, University of Maryland, Human-Computer Interaction Laboratory, Center for Automation Research, College Park, MD.

McKenzie, J. F., Neiger, B. L. and Thackeray, R. (2012) *Planning, Implementing and Evaluating Health Promotion Programs: a primer*, 6th edn, Pearson/Benjamin Cummings, San Francisco, CA.

Posavac, E. J. (2013) *Program Evaluation. Pearson New International Edition: methods and case studies*, 8th edn, Pearson, San Francisco, CA.

Watkins, R., West Meiers, M. and Visser, Y. L. (2012) *A Guide to Assessing Needs: essential tools for collecting information, making decisions and achieving development results*, The World Bank, Washington, DC, DOI: 10.1596/978-0-8213-8868-6.

Watkins, R., Leigh, D., Platt, W. and Kaufman, R. (1998) Needs Assessment – a digest, review, and comparison of needs assessment literature, *Performance Improvement*, **37** (7), 40–53.

Witkin, B. R. (1984) *Assessing Needs in Educational and Social Programs: using information to make decisions, set priorities and allocate resources*, Jossey-Bass, San Francisco, CA.

Witkin, B. R. and Altschuld, J. W. (1995) *Planning and Conducting Needs Assessments: a practical guide*, SAGE Publications, Thousand Oaks, CA.

CHAPTER 4

The stages of information needs analysis

Introduction

Following the definition of needs analysis in Chapter 1 –

> information needs analysis is the process of making value judgements regarding
> solutions to an information-related problem faced by a client group, service provider
> or facility in order to facilitate fulfilment of a necessary, useful and defensible purpose

– we now turn to the practical elements of this definition. Specifically, needs analysis in information settings is a process that involves delineating, obtaining and applying information to determine what is needed to serve a specified (defensible) purpose. These three key words – delineating, obtaining, applying – are at the core of all needs analyses and should be evident throughout any INA activity or project.

In an information setting the needs analysis process should be seen as contributing to two essential activities in the proactive management of services, facilities and staff. First, the process should help determine what needs exist and how they might best be met. Second, the process should provide benchmark criteria for evaluating the merits of whatever is being investigated (systems, buildings, staff, services, collections) to determine the extent to which the specified needs are being met.

It is against the background of these activities that we set out to address three main questions in this chapter:

1 What are the principal stages of INA?
2 What are the main activities in each of these stages?
3 How are these activities interrelated?

Four stages of needs analysis

To meet the needs of either type of activity just noted the needs analysis process typically embodies a four-stage set of activities, with an additional pair of post-intervention activities that are not properly part of the analysis process; this process is visualized in Figure 4.1. An INA *per se* ceases when the data about the needs have been gathered and analysed, and a range of possible context-specific solutions suggested. Putting these solutions into operation and then evaluating the results belong properly to ex post analysis.

The recursive nature of INA research

Each of these four principal stages is now outlined in turn. However, the investigator must remember that this is not a strictly linear process and that in fact a number of activities may occur simultaneously because of the complexity of the target group, community or organization. Further, as with all research, there is always a recursive element involved as the investigator finds that one stage leads back as well as forward. Suppose, for example, that during the analysis of information gathered about needs related to levels of information and communication technology (ICT) available to staff in a regional tourism authority the investigator finds that some of the stakeholders (for example, staff dealing with online enquiries) were overlooked during the preparation stage. At this point it would be essential to go back to those stakeholders and make sure that data are gathered from them in order to ensure the fullest possible dataset for analysis.

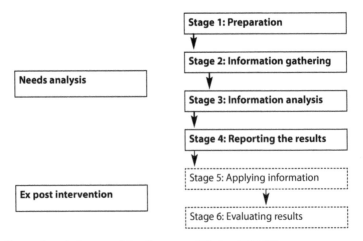

Figure 4.1 The needs analysis process [after Gorman and Clayton, 2005, 35]

Thus the stages of preparation and information gathering have a recursive relationship, as do the stages of information gathering and information analysis. Once the analysis is completed, however, it is unusual to find a recursive relationship between the initial three stages and the reporting of results. But at the ex post intervention stage of applying information (based on the findings of Stages 1–4) one may find that more information analysis is required, or perhaps even more information gathering, which means that there may well be movement between the stages. This reality should not be overlooked, nor should it be regarded as a sign of ineffective needs analysis. It is simply part of the reality that scenarios change rapidly and that an analysis of a month ago may need to be revised to take account of such changes. For example, suppose an unexpected budget cut in capital expenditure is announced by the university finance directorate shortly after a needs analysis for a new student learning commons has been completed. When this type of event occurs, it is pointless to continue with the application stage under the old scenario. Rather, the investigator must return to the information-gathering stage to consider how the changed circumstances will affect the information required for decision making.

Stage 1: Preparation

In this schema of needs analysis Stage 1 is equivalent to the 'delineating' aspect of our explanation of the INA process. This equivalence is because Stage 1 includes all preparatory steps undertaken to ensure the success of the overall process. These steps involve asking and answering six interrelated questions:

1 For what purpose are we doing this?
2 What questions do we need to ask, and of whom?
3 Who will ask them?
4 What methods will we use?
5 What resources are available to us?
6 What is a realistic schedule?

The purpose

The first question is of primary importance, for unlike needs analysis in education, for example, which tends to confine itself to programme evaluation, it is possible to investigate a wide range of activities and levels in information organizations – of services, collections, staff, physical plant, systems, ICTs, etc.

These activities are relevant to the three levels (service receivers, service providers, resources) in our model. While it is possible to undertake an INA across all three levels (what one might term a macro-analysis), it is more usual in the information sector for a micro-analysis to be undertaken, where the investigator focuses primarily on issues in one of the levels. At the same time, however, we should recognize that such an analysis within one level will have implications for other levels. For example, analysing the information needs of potential clients of a business information service (Level 1) will very likely lead to an impact for the information providers (Level 2) and to an alteration in resource provision (Level 3).

Therefore, unless one is undertaking a macro-analysis it is essential to have a clear focus on the specific context and situation requiring needs analysis; and for this there must be a purpose – a problem to be solved, a shortcoming to be improved, a new protocol to be implemented, etc.

The questions

Having identified the purpose and the type of INA to be conducted, we are then in a position to move on to the second of the six questions: 'What questions do we need to ask, and of whom?' (already partially addressed in the first step).

As in any research activity, accurately answering this two-pronged preparatory question is the key to success. First, to establish the more detailed questions we must determine which individuals, groups or organizations should be approached. Who are the key stakeholders in this particular needs analysis exercise? When an exhaustive list has been compiled, the investigators then need to establish good working relationships with all of those who will participate in the needs analysis or (and note this well) who may be affected by the analysis process and outcomes. If, for instance, an investigator is conducting an INA in preparation for upgrading the bibliographic and retrieval software that underpin the functionality of the library's search services (Level 3), whom would we include in our analysis process? The obvious answer is the key managers responsible for the system within the organization as well as senior management, who will make the final decision, and perhaps also the wider institution's finance team – also Level 3. These, however, are just the tip of the iceberg; what of the vendors, the operational staff who select and who catalogue the print and online resources that are accessed through the search services (Level 2) and even the users (Level 1), for whom, ultimately, the system exists? All of these are stakeholders to be consulted, and none should be ignored.

Having determined the purpose of the analysis and whom we must consult, we can then identify the principal research questions that will drive the process forward (as distinct from the specific questions asked during data gathering) and the ways of stating the principal research questions that best reflect the purpose of the analysis in light of the intention of the institution and stakeholders. In other words the principal research questions in an INA should reflect not only the purpose of the analysis but also the mission and objectives of the institution within which the analysis is being conducted. Scenario 4.1 (based on Westbrook, 2001, 52) expands on this idea.

Scenario 4.1 Mission of the Creswick Joint Public-School Library

The context of this scenario is an INA to determine the community's needs within the Creswick Joint Public-School Library. The issue is that the school library, after many years of neglect, had been more-or-less 'tacked on' to the well established and heavily used public library. Now, however, new members of the school community feel that their voice should be heard. The investigator for the project might begin the process by looking at Creswick Library's mission statement. This approach would help determine the main research questions to be addressed in the investigation. Questions regarding the mission include:

◆ What is the role of Creswick Library within the community?
◆ Is it possible for the INA investigator to refine that role based on community needs?
◆ Would the library management and staff be open to such refinement?

In this instance, because two communities are involved, it would be essential to determine whether both would support a revision of Creswick Library's mission: (1) the school principal and teachers, as well as parents of children, on one hand; and (2) the local authority, library board and members of the public on the other. If both communities are agreeable to such revision, then the investigator could proceed and frame the principal research questions accordingly. If, however, either community responded negatively, then another approach not relying on the mission statement as a starting point, or even abandonment of the project, would be necessary. Here it pays to remember that, in the words of Westbrook (2001, 51), 'research questions are *not* the actual questions posed to subjects in the study; instead they function like goals in that they are the large questions that the study must answer'.

Once the purpose, the stakeholders and the principal research questions have been determined, in Stage 2 the investigator can consider the reality that different stakeholders will be asked different questions and in different ways. This is the point at which all possible questions are determined, matched to likely respondents and organized in the approximate manner they are to be asked – all part of the Stage 2 process.

Choosing the person to gather the data

Equally important is the issue of who will do the asking. Here a word of advice is in order: select someone who can make respondents feel at ease and free to talk. This is a particular stumbling block in many INAs conducted within or on behalf of information organizations. Put another way, one might say 'never send a passive, withdrawn person to do the work of an extrovert'. In short, the person sent to gather the data should be someone who can elicit the fullest responses from those being surveyed.

The resources and time needed

The last two questions in Stage 1 deal with basic practicalities: resources and time. What resources are available for the investigation in terms of personnel, funds, equipment and time? Every INA works within these constraints, and the pattern used must fit the cloth that is available. This may mean that some staff require training in data collection or analysis, for example, or that special funds must be accessed, particular data analysis software purchased or outsourcing of the analysis considered.

Finally, time constraints should be embodied in a clear, accurate schedule that everyone agrees on from the beginning. For this a Gantt chart is especially useful. Margaret Rouse (2014) clearly defines a Gantt chart as 'a horizontal bar chart developed as a production control tool. . . . Frequently used in project management, a Gantt chart provides a graphical illustration of a schedule that helps to plan, co-ordinate, and track specific tasks in a project.'

Several websites provide useful tools to help investigators understand and create Gantt charts; here we mention only two examples that we have found useful in INA projects. The Gantt pages at What Is Gantt? in SmartDraw.com (2014) offer several types of charts that investigators might find helpful in INA project planning; and Project Management with an Interactive Online Gantt Chart (2014) at Smartsheet.com allows the investigator to create a fully workable

Gantt chart which can be used as a practice run for an INA project. The simplest form is generally the most useful, as it is readily understood by anyone engaged in the INA. The Appendix to this chapter provides further discussion of this and a sample Gantt chart.

Stage 2: Information gathering

During this stage the investigator develops his or her plan of how, precisely, the information is to be gathered. The investigator also determines the exact procedures by which and sources from which the information will be collected, the actual collection and storage of data. Westbrook (2001, 51) refers to this planning as essentially a 'two-step process, framing the research questions for the study and choosing the data-gathering techniques'. The 'research questions' here are more specific than those principal research questions determined in Stage 1, which were aimed at reflecting the purpose of the analysis in a manner that supports the mission and objectives of the institution. Rather, at this point the investigator is concerned with determining the specific research questions and then choosing the data-gathering techniques best suited to the conditions (i.e., the questions and the environment).

Formulating the research questions

Specific research questions in an INA arise from several sources: the principal research questions or focus of the investigation; the characteristics of the activity, process or entity being studied; the characteristics of the stakeholder groups, including the population involved. Putting these variables together, the investigator should be able to develop a set of questions that will:

◆ address the principal research questions
◆ determine the needs related to the activity, etc., being analysed
◆ suit the characteristics of the population.

Formulating the right questions in the right way is at once complex and essential. In *Social Research Methodology* Gomm (2008, 208) reminds us that 'the data collected are shaped by the way the questions are posed and the manner and context in which they were asked'. In other words the process of questioning and answering affects the data, and this in turn affects validity and reliability. Validity (or construct validity) refers to the level of accuracy between the received responses and the actual reality those responses were intended to capture (Gomm, 2008, 33), and obviously the investigator will want to ask questions in such a way that the received responses and actual reality fit as closely as possible. Additionally, reliability must be retained, and this is done by asking questions of participants in the same way and under the same conditions every time. Gomm's Chapter 10, entitled 'Questions and Answers', provides considerable detail on issues related to question formulation (Gomm, 2008, 208–38).

Choosing the data-gathering technique(s)

When the questions have been appropriately and clearly formed and tested, the investigator is then in a position to determine which data-gathering technique or techniques might be most appropriate. Here it is often useful to create a simple matrix, as in Table 4.1.

Table 4.1 Matrix of data gathering and data analysis

The question	Asked of whom?	By what means?	How is it analysed?
What is your experience of using the online databases in this library?	Undergraduates and postgraduates (Alreck and Settle, 2004)	Focus groups for each type of student (Gorman and Clayton, 2005)	Open coding of dialogue in transcripts (Gibbs, 2002)

Note in the top row of this matrix the questions that are being asked – these embody the key issues in needs analysis: the participants, how data are gathered and how the data are analysed. If there is more than one INA investigator on a particular project, it is essential that all understand and agree with each of these critical components, for then the process ought to proceed smoothly. The matrix is simply one means of keeping everyone on track and, along with the Gantt chart, is an especially useful device for all but the simplest INA projects.

Many would say that the most difficult of these questions to answer is 'By what means?' That is, exactly what method should be used and why? Some years ago McKillip (1987, 99–100) addressed this question by means of a 'need identification method matrix'. Table 4.2 is derived from McKillip. Note in particular the two types of attributes to be considered when selecting a method: resource implications and analytical focus. Ideally one would like the resource implications to be minimal, in other words low cost, short time and no special skills required. These criteria are clearly relevant across the INA spectrum and should be considered for any data-gathering method. The analytical characteristics are applicable in most INA investigations, although there are some criteria that do not apply in every method.

Table 4.2 Abbreviated needs identification methods matrix [after McKillip, 1987]

Attributes for choosing between methods														
Needs identification methods	Resources			Analysis							Audiences		Compatibility	
	Low cost	Short time	Skill need	Flexible	Problem oriented	Solution oriented	Relevant	Credibility	Detail	Ideas	Stakeholders	Interested parties	Prerequisites	Overlap
Observation	—	—	+	++	+	+	+	+	+	+	-	-	-	+
Focus group	+		-	++	+	+	+		++	++	-	-	-	+
Social indicator analysis	+	+	-	+	+		-	++	-	-	-	-	—	+
Client survey	-	-	-	++	+	-	+	+	+	+	++	+	-	+

Key
++ = very characteristic criterion of the method
+ = somewhat characteristic criterion
— = very uncharacteristic criterion of the method
- = somewhat uncharacteristic criterion

It should be noted at this point that the matrix in Table 4.2 may be somewhat misleading, for it suggests that observation, focus group, social indicator analysis and client survey are the only means of gathering needs information. Indeed, McKillip lists an impressive 22 methods of needs identification, but this is in relation to the analysis of 'human services needs' rather than 'information needs' *per se*. Also, some of his methods are subdivided – surveys, for example, are listed as training, key informant, client and citizen surveys. For the purpose of INA the number of methods is rather traditional, and these methods are discussed in Chapter 5.

While the criteria in the analytical focus may seem excessive to some, the important point to be gleaned from this is that some sort of matrix is an ideal way to help determine the most appropriate method(s) to employ – specific sets of criteria may be devised for INA projects. However accomplished, a key to success is how well the preparation addresses the strengths and weaknesses of respective data-gathering techniques in a specific INA context.

At this point it is worth asking, and here the matrix concept may be helpful as well, whether the mixed methods approach might be appropriate. Most likely the response would be 'yes' (but being sure to take account of financial and personnel constraints), because complementary methods of gathering and analysing needs analysis data can add much to the value and understanding of the data. Every method has strengths and weaknesses, and every method allows the introduction of certain types of bias into an investigation. By combining compatible methods with different strengths and weaknesses, it is possible to build a more accurate picture of the needs being analysed. It is for this reason that McKillip (1987) includes 'compatibility' among his criteria for assessing data-gathering methods; the investigator, in determining which methods to employ, wants to ensure their compatibility as well as their complementary nature.

Stage 3: Information analysis

We now come to the core of any INA undertaking: analysis of the information gathered in order to make a judgement about whether an actual need is evident. Depending on the data-gathering method selected, the analysis will involve sorting or counting (the basic approaches of qualitative and quantitative investigations) and then describing the results through narrative and/or statistical calculations. As this is not a book on research methods, it is inappropriate to enter into lengthy technical discussions of different types of data analysis. Rather, anyone unfamiliar with this should consult standard research texts, some of which are noted in the final section of this chapter, as well as in Chapters 6–9 of this book.

If the research world is divided into qualitative and quantitative halves (mixed methods simply adopts both) – and this is about as accurate as saying that Europe is divided into Northern beer-drinking and Southern wine-drinking populations – then we can say that data analysis is divided into essentially two types. This is a simplistic but nevertheless productive way of deciding how collected data might be analysed. For those interested, a balanced discussion of divisions in the research world is provided by Bryman (2008) in 'The End of the Paradigm Wars?'

Qualitative and quantitative frameworks for data analysis

In the qualitative framework data analysis involves the classification and coding of information (words) from participants. This means 'working with data, organizing it, breaking it into manageable units, synthesizing it, searching for patterns. Discovering what is important and what is to be learned, and deciding what you will tell others' (Bogdan and Biklen, 2003, 147). In this paradigm interpretation is integral to the analysis, and the two occur contiguously. In the quantitative framework analysis and interpretation are usually seen as discrete actions, or at least this is the ideal. Quantitative analysis is essentially statistical, and statistical analysis is a means by which we apply techniques for organizing and analysing data, nothing more (Connaway and Powell, 2010). The important point is that statistics *per se* do not equal interpretation; the results of statistical analysis must still be interpreted, but this interpretation is not part of the analytical (or 'number-crunching') process – rather, it occurs subsequently, whereas in the qualitative framework the two are more integrated.

The principal issue to note here is that information analysis goes well beyond tabulations and calculations; these result in descriptions, whereas we are seeking *analysis*. It is the meaning we attach to the results, and our judgements, that determine whether the results can be said to constitute a need for a defensible purpose. And effective judgement generally means that we have to consider a range of factors within the specific context of our investigation in order to make a justifiable judgement about the supposed need. In the words of Stufflebeam et al. (1985, 17), 'a statistical finding, regardless of its objectivity and empirical basis, does not equal a need. A need is a resulting decision coming out of a process that should include the compilation and review of several bits of information that culminates in a judgment of what constitutes need'.

Scenario 4.2 provides one situation in which other 'bits of information' usefully supplement the raw percentages derived from a needs survey.

Scenario 4.2 Information literacy needs analysis in Rutland University

---

In Rutland University one library staff member has been charged with conducting an INA pertaining to information literacy competencies among students (Level 1). Rutland University Library has already adopted the information literacy standards formulated by the US-based Association of College and Research Libraries (ACRL), and these standards are being used to guide the data gathering and analysis process. The ACRL standards are publicly available as *Information Literacy Competency Standards for Higher Education* (Association of College and Research Libraries, 2000). This document includes not only the standards but also performance indicators and outcomes for each standard.

Take Standard One as an example: 'The information literate student determines the nature and extent of the information needed' (Association of College and Research Libraries, 2000, 8). For this standard there are four performance indicators, the first of which states: 'The information literate student defines and articulates the need for information.' There are six outcomes identified for this indicator, including 'Identifies key concepts and terms that describe the information need'. Given this level of specificity, it has been relatively simple for the investigator to construct and conduct a survey seeking data on the information literacy outcomes achieved by students at various levels.

One finding has been that 41% of undergraduates have achieved fewer than half of the outcomes associated with any performance indicator. One might be tempted to see this as revealing a critical information need, but this would be leaping to conclusions. The investigator would want to look first at a range of other factors. For example, what has been the level of information literacy achievement in past years? What is the general educational level of the students accepted into first year, and has it perhaps changed? What percentage of the student population is international or speaks English as a second language? What sort of information literacy instruction has been provided, at what levels, and has it been voluntary or compulsory?

Such additional information would allow for a broader view of information literacy performance and might lead to a more informed judgement about the extent of the need indicated by the figure of 41%, as well as to a more general approach to solving the need. In any context one must consider what additional information should be sought and how to incorporate it into a plan to solve the identified need.

Stage 4: Reporting the results

Once the gathered data have been analysed and interpreted, it is time to report the findings. One may think that such reporting should be done after Stage 5 (application of the information), but in fact the needs *analysis* is actually completed with Stage 3, and it is this analysis that is reported in Stage 4. Applying the results of the analysis to solve an information need occurs subsequently to the analysis and forms a different set of activities.

It is at the stage of reporting that the investigator reviews the results of the findings and seeks to determine a range of likely cause-and-effect relationships. Looking again at Scenario 4.2, for example, the investigator (accepting that 41% is a significant finding) might determine that inadequate information literacy instruction is an important cause of the poor information literacy rate among undergraduates. One possible suggestion arising from this might be that, based on data from the analysis, more and better information literacy instruction is required. To accomplish this outcome a range of interventions might be suggested: intensive library-based information literacy instruction as a required first-year course, information literacy instruction tied to specific disciplines in second year, co-operative teaching of information literacy by librarians and academics in each undergraduate year and so on.

The identification of a set of strategies is articulated in the report. The selection and implementation of specific strategies occurs later through the design of a programme to solve problems identified in the INA, and this should be followed by an evaluation of the implementation. Both implementation and evaluation may be the subjects of a further report, but this again is outside the scope of an INA and reporting on such analysis.

Thus the INA report covers what has occurred to date: how the preparation was conducted; what methodology was selected, and why; how the actual needs analysis occurred (including background information collected, people interviewed, analytical techniques); and most importantly the probable cause-and-effect relationships that emerge from the analysis, and a set of proposals by which these relationships might be addressed and solutions reached.

In short the intention of an INA report is to describe, for all concerned audiences, the needs analysis process and findings in a timely, understandable and accurate manner. To do this well the reporter(s) must take into account the specific audience for the report, or the several audiences as is often the case, and the purpose to be served by the report. It is the audience and purpose that determine the presentation of the report's content, including amount of detail, level of language, format, etc. All of this is considered in some detail in Chapter 10.

The stages of ex post intervention

As we have suggested above, what happens after the INA has been conducted is outside the scope of the process. To highlight this point we return to the definition of information needs analysis:

> Information needs analysis is the process of making value judgements regarding solutions to an information-related problem faced by a client group, service provider or facility in order to facilitate fulfilment of a necessary, useful and defensible purpose.

That is, once the process of making value judgements about an information-related problem is finished, the investigator's task has been completed; this process will *facilitate*, not actually *undertake*, the fulfilment of a specific purpose. Nevertheless, it would be foolish to assume that there is no relationship between the four stages of INA and the two stages of ex post implementation of solutions to the identified information needs. Of course there is, as what is planned in these last two stages is wholly determined by the results of the preceding analysis, which suggests a range of possible solutions. But because the implementation and evaluation of any problem-solving solution are uniquely contextualized, we cannot offer specific guidelines about how to solve specific information needs-related problems.

An excellent example of this separation of ex post intervention stages from the needs analysis stages is provided in a paper by Ryan and Valverde (2005), 'Waiting for Service on the Internet: defining the phenomenon and identifying the situations'. Note the subtitle – the investigation, a kind of casual needs analysis, ceases with identification of situations that contribute to waiting for service on the internet. Initially it was believed by most investigators that the basic source of frustration to e-commerce users of the internet was 'download delay'. Ryan and Valverde's investigation identified an additional 13 factors that contribute to waiting on the internet. 'Service providers and other online entities are now much better equipped to identify the specific causes of waiting and to tackle the associated problems that have been hindering the commercial development of the internet and of their own particular businesses' (Ryan and Valverde, 2005, 237). While a genuine INA might have suggested possible solutions to the 14 causes of delay, it would be up to an individual enterprise to apply solutions and evaluate the results.

Basically, how INA information is used will of necessity vary with each information context and according to the purposes that the solutions proposed by the analysis seek to address.

Review of Chapter 4

This chapter has sought to provide a blueprint, or perhaps more of a vaguely outlined mind-map, of how the INA process actually occurs. As such, it is intended to help guide readers through subsequent chapters, which look in more detail at methodologies, as well as at different scenarios and how they are handled.

We have made the point that an INA *per se* consists of four stages (preparation, information gathering, information analysis, reporting results) and that the subsequent ex post intervention (applying information, evaluating results) occurs after the needs analysis, but with some possible linkages through the recursive nature of these activities.

Each of the four INA stages has been shown to be relatively complex, but still achievable if the key deliverables are kept in mind. Thus in Stage 1 (preparation) the investigator must carefully consider all aspects to be planned in the analysis and prepare accordingly. Whatever is overlooked in this stage will affect how well the process succeeds, or at least how smoothly it occurs. Likewise, with information gathering there is a suite of significant issues to be addressed: what questions should be asked, and of whom? How are data to be collected – and here there is a daunting range of possibilities – and subsequently analysed? We have emphasized that collection and analysis of data must be considered as part of a single activity, much like breathing in and breathing out, in order to derive results that are valid, reliable and accurate. And thus data analysis must be considered with special care, using means appropriate to the information gathered and able to inform the ultimate judgements that form the actual analysis of the need(s) being investigated. The results of all this work are then reported appropriately for the intended outcomes, the presumed audience and desired exposure.

Further reading

Most aspects of this chapter are discussed or exemplified in the chapters that follow, so there is much more to be learned about every stage of the INA process within the covers of this book. Still, it can be productive to draw on other sources of expertise to help embellish the bare bones of INA presented to this point.

Essentially we are outlining a specific focus for research, so it will not be surprising that much of the further reading comes from research texts. For anyone interested in some of the research techniques touched on in this chapter, excellent guidance is provided by Bryman in *Social Research Methods* (4th edn, 2012), which is a heavy-duty and thorough treatment of research techniques. Bryman is not for the faint-hearted, and a perhaps gentler but nevertheless valuable treatment of research is Chambliss and Schutt's *Making Sense of the Social World* (2013).

For some INA investigators these general research texts, which provide excellent and varied examples to illustrate the discussion of research methods and techniques, may require supplementation by works with a specific focus on information environments. This focus is provided by Connaway and Powell (2010) in *Basic Research Methods for Librarians*. Especially valuable for the present context are Chapters 3–5 and 7, which address a variety of data collection and analysis techniques. Equally useful is Pickard's *Research Methods in Information* (2nd edn, 2013), which devotes Part 3 to data collection and some of Part 4 to data analysis. If neither of these works is available, then Beck and Manuel's (2008) *Practical Research Methods for Librarians and Information Professionals* is worthy of consultation.

Chapter 2 (Instruments and Instrument Design) and Chapter 10 (Questions and Answers) of Roger Gomm's 2008 text, *Social Research Methodology*, provide a very thorough guide to the ins and outs of setting questions to ensure validity and reliability, and also reflect on how the context affects the answers. Finally, McKillip's 1987 work on needs analysis includes a brief Chapter 10 titled 'Communication of Results' that might usefully supplement the discussion of Stage 4 in this chapter.

Barbara Wildemuth's *Applications of Social Research Methods to Questions in Information and Library Science* (2009) provides breadth rather than depth of coverage about research design, data gathering and analysis methods. The book, which has 38 chapters (many of which Wildemuth has co-written with colleagues), is divided into six parts. The most relevant and largest parts are Part 3: Research Designs and Sampling (nine chapters); Part 4: Methods for Data Collection (13 chapters); and Part 5: Methods for Data Analysis (nine chapters). The range of research designs and data collection methods is extensive, though some are inappropriate for INAs. However, some chapters, such as Chapter 15: 'Studying Special Populations' by Perryman and Wildemuth (2009), can provide very useful insights that are applicable to INA research.

Finally, to have a flavour of the kinds of data structures and analysis that follow the data collection procedure, this is an appropriate moment to scan a clear and straightforward discussion of qualitative data analysis. To this end, look at Bazeley and Jackson's *Qualitative Data Analysis with NVivo* (2013).

There are many works such as those cited that add to the information presented in Chapter 4, but most of them are general research texts or guides to other types of needs analysis rather than specifically to INAs. What we lack is a collection of solid INA case studies that readers could refer to as a means of making concrete the abstractions presented in this chapter.

References

Alreck, P. L. and Settle, R. B. (2004) *The Survey Research Handbook*, 3rd edn, McGraw-Hill/Irwin Series in Marketing, McGraw-Hill/Irwin, Boston, MA.

Association of College and Research Libraries (2000) *Information Literacy Competency Standards for Higher Education*, American Library Association, Chicago, www.ala.org/ala/mgrps/divs/acrl/standards/standards.pdf. [Accessed 5 November 2014.]

Bazeley, P. and Jackson, K. (2013) *Qualitative Data Analysis with NVivo*, 2nd edn, SAGE Publications, London.

Beck, S. E. and Manuel, K. (2008) *Practical Research Methods for Librarians and Information*

Professionals, Neal-Schuman Publishers, New York.

Bogdan, R. and Biklen, S. K. (2003) *Qualitative Research for Education: an introduction to theory and methods*, 4th edn, Allyn & Bacon, Boston, MA.

Bryman, A. (2008) The End of the Paradigm Wars? In Alasuutari, P., Bickman, L. and Brannan, J. (eds), *The SAGE Handbook of Social Research Methods*, SAGE Publications, London, 13–25.

Bryman, A. (2012) *Social Research Methods*, 4th edn, Oxford University Press, Oxford. Companion website http://global.oup.com/uk/orc/sociology/brymansrm4e. [Accessed 8 November 2014.]

Chambliss, D. F. and Schutt, R. K. (2013) *Making Sense of the Social World: methods of investigation*, 4th edn, SAGE Publications, Thousand Oaks, CA.

Connaway, L. S. and Powell, R. R. (2010) *Basic Research Methods for Librarians*, 5th edn, Library and Information Science Text Series, ABC-CLIO/Libraries Unlimited, Santa Barbara, CA.

Gibbs, G. R. (2002) *Qualitative Data Analysis: explorations with NVivo*, Open University Press, Milton Keynes.

Gomm, R. (2008) *Social Research Methodology: a critical introduction*, 2nd edn, Palgrave Macmillan, Basingstoke.

Gorman, G. E. and Clayton, P. R. (2005) *Qualitative Research for the Information Professional: a practical handbook*, 2nd edn, Facet Publishing, London.

McKillip, J. A. (1987) *Need Analysis: tools for the human services and education*, Applied Social Research Methods, 10, SAGE Publications, Newbury Park, CA.

Perryman, C. L. and Wildemuth, B. M. (2009) Studying Special Populations. In Wildemuth, B. M., *Applications of Social Research Methods to Questions in Information and Library Science*, Libraries Unlimited, Westport, CT, 138–44.

Pickard, A. J. (2013) *Research Methods in Information*, 2nd edn, Facet Publishing, London.

Project Management with an Interactive Online Gantt Chart (2014) Smartsheet.com, www.smartsheet.com/online-gantt-chart. [Accessed 5 November 2014.]

Rouse, M. (2014) *Gantt Chart*, SearchSoftwareQuality.com, http://searchsoftwarequality. techtarget.com/definition/Gantt-chart. [Accessed 5 November 2014.]

Ryan, G. and Valverde, M. (2005) Waiting for Service on the Internet: defining the phenomenon and identifying the situations, *Internet Research*, **15** (2), 220–40.

SmartDraw.com (2014) What Is Gantt? www.smartdraw.com/articles/gantt-chart/what-is-gantt-chart.htm, [Accessed 21 October 2014.]

Stufflebeam, D. L., McCormick, C. H., Brinkerhoff, R. O. and Nelson, C. O. (1985) *Conducting Educational Needs Assessments*, Evaluation in Education and Human Services [Series], Kluwer-Nijhoff Publishing, Boston, MA.

Westbrook, L. (2001) *Identifying and Analyzing User Needs: a complete handbook and ready-to-use assessment workbook with disk*, Neal-Schuman Publishers, New York.

Wildemuth, B. M. (2009) *Applications of Social Research Methods to Questions in Information and Library Science*, Libraries Unlimited, Westport, CT.

Appendix 4.1: Gantt chart

The following description is based on Margaret Rouse (2014). A Gantt chart is constructed with a horizontal axis for the project timeline, divided into appropriate increments (days, weeks, months) and a vertical axis for the specific activities that constitute the project from outset to completion (an example is offered in Figure 4.2 below). Horizontal bars of varying lengths represent the sequences, timing and time span for each activity. Each specific activity is then listed sequentially on the vertical axis, beginning at the top and finishing at the bottom; a bar is shown on the graph to represent the amount of time the investigator expects to spend on each activity. Overlapping bars are quite common, as one activity may begin before the preceding activity has been completed. Gantt charts are not inviolate once constructed, and indeed there will normally be adjustments along the way as slippage occurs because of unforeseen circumstances.

Start date: 1 July 2014	Project: Sample INA Gantt Chart														
Current Week															
Weeks / Tasks	01/07 to 08/07	08/07 to 15/07	15/07 to 22/07	22/07 to 29/07	29/07 to 05/08	05/08 to 12/08	12/08 to 19/08	19/08 to 26/08	26/08 to 02/09	02/09 to 09/09	09/09 to 16/09	16/09 to 23/09	23/09 to 30/09	30/09 to 07/10	07/10 to 14/10
Consult with stakeholders commissioning the INA	▓														
Observe the context/situation to be analysed		▓													
Prepare draft of analysis procedures			▓												
Submit draft and receive feedback from stakeholders				▓											
Begin data collection – observation					▓	▓									
Continue data collection – interviews							▓	▓							
Collate data from observations and interviews									▓						
Analyse data										▓	▓				
Draft recommendations											▓				
Prepare draft report												▓			
Submit report to stakeholders for approval													▓		
Revise report if required														▓	
Submit final report to stakeholders															▓
Weeks / Tasks	01/07 to 08/07	08/07 to 15/07	15/07 to 22/07	22/07 to 29/07	29/07 to 05/08	05/08 to 12/08	12/08 to 19/08	19/08 to 26/08	26/08 to 02/09	02/09 to 09/09	09/09 to 16/09	16/09 to 23/09	23/09 to 30/09	30/09 to 07/10	07/10 to 14/10
Current Week															

Figure 4.2 Sample Gantt chart [generated from http://associate.com/gantt (2014)]

CHAPTER 5

Gathering data for information needs analyses

Introduction

The data-gathering stage is central to any INA project. As noted in Chapter 4, information gathering is the second of four stages in the INA process, and it has a recursive relationship with the delineation or planning stage – that is, decisions about the means by which the data will be gathered must be based on careful planning. The centrality of the data-gathering stage is further evident by its recursive relationship with the subsequent data analysis stage.

This chapter provides an overview of the main methods for gathering the data necessary to identify and understand information needs in different information management contexts. As is the case in any research project, the method(s) selected in an INA project will depend on a wide range of contextual variables. Accordingly, in this chapter we seek answers to a number of data-gathering questions, specifically:

- ◆ How is the choice of data collection method related to the purpose of the INA?
- ◆ What factors should be considered when choosing a data-gathering method?
- ◆ How will existing data be used?
- ◆ What are the advantages and disadvantages of surveys in needs analysis?
- ◆ What are the advantages and disadvantages of interviews in needs analysis?
- ◆ What are the advantages and disadvantages of focus groups in needs analysis?
- ◆ What other methods can be used?

How we have reached this juncture

In Chapter 1 we identified three general levels of needs from Witkin and Altschuld (1995):

◆ Level 1 (primary) – the needs of the service receivers
◆ Level 2 (secondary) – the needs of the service providers and policymakers
◆ Level 3 (tertiary) – the needs related to the resources or solutions.

In Chapter 2 we discussed the importance of context in INA. We stated that an INA is never context-free and that the better the investigator recognizes this feature, the more reliable data he or she will collect about the environment, and the more adequate will be the resulting analysis of information needs of specific groups within that environment.

In Chapter 3 we noted that the three general levels of needs provide a framework for contextualizing information needs. These levels allow us to establish whether the analysis involves gathering data from and/or about people who are inside (service users, providers and policymakers) or outside the system (non-users). We then described six different types of processes in which INAs are essential: two processes for planning information services and programmes, two for selecting and implementing them and two for evaluating them. Although some methods for gathering data are used more frequently than others to determine the information needs relevant to each type of process, we cannot predetermine which method should be used until we understand the full context. Five key factors that must be understood early in any needs analysis project are:

◆ constraints of the analysis
◆ scope of the analysis
◆ intended output
◆ target group for the analysis
◆ who should be consulted.

In Chapter 4 we stated that specific sets of criteria may be devised to determine the most appropriate method(s) for gathering data for an INA suited to a particular context. We provided an example of a simple matrix in Table 4.1 (based on McKillip, 1987, 99–100) with criteria for establishing the key issues in an INA:

◆ the question(s) to be answered

◆ the participants who are to answer the question(s)
◆ the means by which the data are to be gathered
◆ the method to analyse the gathered data.

These issues must always be considered in relation to the purpose for undertaking the analysis. Resolving these issues is done in the Preparation Stage of an INA. The other stages are Information Gathering, Information Analysis and Reporting Results. Following the INA are two ex post intervention stages: Applying Information and Evaluating Results.

The primary research question

As discussed in Chapter 4, in the Preparation Stage of a project, once the investigator has clarified the purpose of the INA, it is necessary (1) to articulate the principal research question(s), (2) determine who is to be consulted, and also (3) gain agreement from team members (if there are any). (For the sake of simplicity we will use the singular 'principal research question' henceforth. However, while many projects will have one principal research question, some projects might have more than one, depending on purpose and scope.) This step is the most critical one, because it articulates the core of the problem to be investigated, and it establishes the basis upon which the specific contextual issues identified in Table 4.1 will be resolved. In essence the principal research question encompasses the purpose of the INA and therefore sets parameters for the range of possible outcomes.

The research population

Having specified the principal research question, the investigator then identifies the research population and the method for gathering data. The research population consists of the individuals or groups who can provide the information required to answer the research question. Choosing the population may seem a simple task, but the investigator must consider carefully who will have the required knowledge and/or experience, and who is actually in a position to participate given practicalities, such as their availability, the costs involved in the required interactions and so on.

The data-gathering method

The interactions mentioned above form the basis of the method(s) that will be used to gather data from the research population. The ease, cost and speed of collection (discussed later in this chapter) are among the practical issues that must also be considered when determining the data-gathering method to be used in an INA. This point is clearly evident in the two examples at the end of this chapter. Factors such as the staff skill levels, the available budget, etc., all come to bear upon the decision making for determining the data-gathering method. Because details about these factors were not evident in the information available in Scenarios 3.2 to 3.7, the column for data-gathering methods in Table 5.1 has been left blank.

Table 5.1 Principal research questions and populations in Scenarios 3.2 to 3.7

Scenario	Type of Process and Context	Level of Need	Principal Research Question	Research Population	Data-gathering Method(s)
3.2	Open planning process: Strategic planning exercise in a law firm's information centre	1	What are the information needs of the law firm's staff?	Law firm staff	?
3.3	Closed planning process: Information literacy initiative after employers were dissatisfied with skills of new graduates	1	What are the information literacy needs of students and academic staff?	1st and 2nd year students and academic staff	?
3.4	Solution selection process: Determining which provider or providers will offer the most effective and efficient option for assisting the unemployed in accessing work and benefits-related information	3	What are the resource requirements to meet the needs of the unemployed population for work and benefits-related information?	Staff in Library, Department of Work and Pensions, Community Development Foundation and other stakeholders	?
3.5	Implementation process: Responsibility for providing support for a service that is being decentralized and transferred to new providers	2	What are the needs of new service providers for skills and resources to meet their responsibilities?	School library staff, school administrators, principals, teachers and TeachConnect staff	?
3.6	Formative evaluation process: Assessing whether a newly implemented OPAC is achieving its maximum potential in meeting user needs	3	What are the target group's needs and how do they relate to the functional options available in the software?	Genealogical researchers, high school and university students, faculty from the University of Washbourne	?
3.7	Summative evaluation process: Annual evaluations for a funding body of the language resources and outreach programme established for an immigrant community	1 and 3	How well have the target group's needs been met by the programme during the year?	Members of immigrant families including children, relevant library staff, funding body staff	?

Data analysis

When deciding on the data-gathering method(s), the investigator must also consider the most appropriate method or methods for data analysis. In many INAs this can be relatively straightforward, but data analysis also can be highly complex, depending on the amount and type of data gathered and the research question to be answered. We cover the analysis and integration of INA data in Chapter 9.

These four components – (1) principal research question, (2) research population, (3) data-gathering method(s) and (4) data analysis method(s) – are highly interdependent. However, decisions related to these components are not the end of the matter, for the investigator must also be thinking about how to report the results of the study while data are being analysed, because the nature of the report has implications for the level and forms of analysis undertaken.

Validity and reliability

Consideration must also be given to validity and reliability. Validity refers to the production of results that are accurate and that actually measure what is supposed to be measured. Care must always be taken to choose a research question for an INA project that actually will both allow and facilitate gathering of the required data. Reliability refers to the production of results that would be replicated if the study were to be repeated, even by other researchers. In other words the investigator must be objective and logical when designing the project. The investigator must ask precise questions that address the principal research question and record the results accurately. The concepts of validity and reliability are closely tied to the quality of data gathered and the accuracy of the results in INAs.

Ethical considerations

Ethics also must be considered in all INA projects. The underlying principle here is the obligation to conduct an INA responsibly, and in most instances this aspect involves review by an authority of some sort: a research ethics committee in a research institution, or management oversight in a service organization. In many situations these administrative structures make it difficult for INA investigators to maintain enthusiasm in the face of criticism of sampling, data-gathering and analysis protocols and so on. In reality there are four rather straightforward areas of ethical concern for INA investigators to consider: 'conflicts of interest, informed consent, cultural equivalence and the use of monetary incentives' (Fisher and Anushka, 2008, 97). It is worthwhile to address each of these very briefly, with the recommendation that for greater detail readers should consult:

◆ *The Research Ethics Guidebook: a resource for social scientists* (www.ethicsguidebook.ac.uk), made available by the Economic and Social Research Council, the Researcher Development Initiative, and the Institute of Education at the University of London; or,
◆ chapters in research methods texts such as 'Research Ethics in Social Science' by Fisher and Anushka in *The SAGE Handbook of Social Research Methods* (2008) or 'Ethics in Research' in Pickard's *Research Methods in Information* (2nd edn, 2013).

In INAs conflicts of interest are not as pervasive as they can be in scientific and social science research, when corporate sponsorship might lead to expectations that findings will support a particular bias or product. In an INA, for example, a conflict of interest might arise when an employer hopes that a commissioned INA will reveal the value of a particular programme or service. Fisher and Anushka (2008, 99) suggest that investigators 'anticipate and educate the [organization] to the conflict of interest issues that may emerge and establish agreements about data collection, interpretation and dissemination that permit the investigator to act ethically'. This point is particularly important to ensure that all involved parties share a common understanding of what will happen should conflict of interest issues arise.

In informed consent procedures the INA investigator seeks to maintain 'the autonomy and privacy rights of those recruited for research participation' (Fisher and Anushka, 2008, 99). To do this it is essential to obtain consent from participants that is 'informed, rational and voluntary' (Fisher and Anushka), which means the investigator must provide potential participants with all the information about the investigation that might influence their willingness to participate:

◆ objectives of the INA
◆ data-gathering method to be used
◆ amount of time it will take
◆ whether the data will be gathered anonymously and, if not, whether confidentiality is ensured
◆ what precautions will be taken to ensure that access to the raw data is restricted to the investigator.

All of this means in effect that participants must be fully informed about what their involvement in the project entails and the consequences of this involvement. Participation must be on a voluntary basis, and confidentiality must be maintained when promised.

Finally, offering rewards is ethically acceptable, provided they are small and unlikely to affect the validity of the data collection. A very small token of appreciation to everyone participating is one way of encouraging responses. Another is to offer a prize, such as a voucher, to be won by one person completing the survey or interview. This is common in market research, and it is increasingly used in academic research as well. Provided the personal information needed for this sort of prize draw can be collected without it being associated with the data collected, then there should be no ethical issues with this form of incentive. For more on incentives, we recommend that you read the section 'Compensation, rewards or incentives?' in the ESRC's *Research Ethics Guidebook: a resource for social scientists*.

Practical issues to consider when choosing a method

The decisions about which data to collect and which method to use require the investigator to consider a range of factors. Practical issues also come into play, and here we address the three most important ones:

1 ease of collection
2 cost of collection
3 speed of collection.

Ease of collection

Some data are easy to collect and gather. Computer systems generate data, often more than we might wish to use, but the data are there all the same. Automated 'housekeeping' systems in libraries and information services contain large amounts of data that are easily available. In many instances staff might be unaware that end-user data have been collected by their automated system, but with a bit of effort the data can be accessed. Websites generate log data that tell much about the use of electronic sources of information. With the agreement of end-users log data about their usage can be kept for a selected period of time, for example, three months, then analysed to see how often the selected clients used information sources such as Google, the library catalogue, and perhaps a corporate intranet. There is no need to ignore such information simply because it is easy to gather, but equally the investigator should not become overly reliant on it. What such information can do, and do very well, is provide a relatively straightforward start to an INA. The use of existing data is dealt with more fully in Chapter 6.

If the INA is being conducted within an organization, especially one that wishes to co-operate with the analysis, then staff should be available to assist. Staff will be familiar with existing service provision (that is, what services the organization provides); indeed, they will be the very best source of this information. Many staff will work very closely with clients on a daily basis, and such frontline staff will be far more knowledgeable about the clients than the managers (Cullen and Calvert, 2004). Again, it will be in-house staff who can provide data about service usage and will most likely have opinions about which data contain flaws and the reasons why the data may show bias or errors.

In-house staff can also be asked to explain irregular data, such as why a particular service was very popular in one month but not in any other. Managers remote from a library might not understand why, for example, circulation data peaked in May then dropped rapidly in June, but frontline staff will usually know the reason: there was a reading competition on at that time, and children who never normally borrowed books came to the library in May trying to win the prize. Unless the investigator understands the full set of circumstances the data can be misleading. In the example just given the context also starts to explain the motivation behind some current information use which the bare statistics do not tell.

Cost of collection

Collecting data involves time, and time costs money. It takes time to identify, read and then synthesize community or social indicator data. When it comes to surveys, interviews and other data collection methods, the significance of cost will be considered sooner or later, and many information managers will be antipathetic lest it cut into the materials budget, which is so often considered untouchable. This might be exacerbated when information professionals assume that they are already fully acquainted with what their users want and need, and that the service they provide is already meeting those needs as far as the budget will allow. But if they are wrong, then money is being poured into providing a service that does not meet client needs. Systems are bought that end-users do not want. It is hard to prove the negative, but 'the correct and only view must surely be that it is too costly *not* to collect needs data' (Nicholas and Herman, 2009, 11). The time and effort it takes to conduct an information needs survey might appear to be considerable, but if the results help with the identification and analysis of needs, then the manager can redirect resources into meeting those needs, and the investment will pay off.

Using in-house staff to assist can lower the costs of an INA considerably, though the reasons for this need to be understood. The savings do not come from using staff already on the payroll, for if they are being paid then they are already a cost. The cost savings come from the organizational memory and the skills and knowledge that the staff already have, as was described earlier in the example of fluctuating circulation data. Rather than operating alone, the investigator must do what the manager ought to do, that is, maintain a dialogue with frontline staff and use the knowledge they have gained from experience.

Staff can also help explain data that the investigator might never otherwise understand. Simple data might say that a data archive has been used 10 times in the past week, but only a staff member with knowledge of this usage could say precisely who used the archive and for what purpose. Cost savings turn to losses if staff are expected to carry out tasks that are beyond their skills, as might be the case if a willing staff member tried to analyse data with a software package such as SPSS when it was not really within his or her skill sets.

Speed of collection

An INA takes time, and this is a serious consideration in data collection. Scanning for data cannot be allowed to continue ad infinitum, and it must not become an end in its own right, although this is tempting for large projects. An investigator must remember that data collection is only part of the INA process. There must be time for data analysis and incorporation of the results into the INA report. If the results are inadequate, then more data collection can be done during a new iteration of the whole process. It is also a trap to spend too long on data collection and then discover that there is too much to sift through and comprehend. This situation is quite likely to happen in a large-scale community INA, where there is potentially a huge amount of relevant data.

To make some sense of what ought to be done, serious thought must be given to the purpose of collecting the data. Although this is, to an extent, an art rather than a science, the investigator must focus on identifying which data are going to be the most useful and reluctantly leave the rest. Many investigators have completed data collection and then realized just how much data have been collected – decisions on how much data are enough should have been taken earlier.

The main data-gathering methods

There are many data-gathering methods that can be used in INA projects. These methods can be grouped in different ways, depending on the reasons for classifying them. For example Westbrook (2001) divides the methods for gathering data in community INAs into person-to-person techniques (e.g. focus groups, in-depth interviews and unobtrusive observation), and person-to-document techniques (e.g. questionnaires, a Delphi study, diaries, journals and logs). She also discusses the use of in-house data in an INA.

In *Planning for Integrated Systems and Technologies* Cohn, Kelsey and Fiels (2002) state that a needs assessment (not analysis) specifically in system selection and implementation usually involves one or more of the following:

- Analysing information on existing use
- Distributing written user surveys
- Holding focus groups, interviews or informal discussions with users
- Analysing services provided by comparable or competitor libraries.

Cohn, Kelsey and Fiels, 2002, 17

In a similar vein Witkin and Altschuld (1995) suggest five main data-gathering methods:

1 Using existing records, social indicators and other databases
2 Surveys, interviews and the critical incident technique
3 Basic group processes (for example, community fora and focus groups)
4 Specialized surveys and group techniques (for example, a posted Delphi survey, electronic discussion groups and concept mapping)
5 Future-oriented procedures (such as strategic planning, scenarios and trend analysis).

Among these methods are some very specialized techniques for which the necessity would arise only very occasionally with respect to INA contexts.

In the next three chapters of this book we examine the main data-gathering methods in INAs and refer the reader to other sources for details about the very occasionally used specialized methods. The methods discussed in this book are:

1   Gathering data from existing sources (sometimes referred to as 'classifying data')
2   Gathering data through surveys
3   Gathering data through interviews.

Other methods, such as observation, are touched upon only briefly, given that they are used primarily to gather information informally about the target population.

We now briefly introduce the three main data-gathering methods and provide some examples of when they are used. In Chapters 6–8 we provide detailed information about these methods.

Gathering data from existing sources

Often there are contexts in which the analysis of some existing data either leads to insights that spawn new INA projects or informs the early planning decisions in a project under development. Data generated for other purposes, such as community or social indicators (for example, changes in population, employment, crime rates or education outcomes), may be of value in identifying information needs in the early stages of planning processes for new services. Data available in published reports of relevant research, library usage statistics generated by automated library systems or websites and information gathered by information centres and libraries for their annual reports may be highly relevant for identifying information needs for more detailed planning of new information services or for evaluating existing ones.

Information managers are often able to find existing information relevant to all three levels of information needs, that is, the needs of service receivers (Level 1), the needs of service providers and policymakers (Level 2) and the needs associated with resources or solutions (Level 3). As noted by Witkin and Altschuld,

> Many kinds of records provide information on the current status of target groups – characteristics of people in Levels 1 and 2, and information on resources at Level 3, as well as what services are being provided, to whom, in what quantities. Social indicators are variables that describe conditions or states of a population. They are helpful in assessing needs, and they can be accessed through or derived from records.
>
> Witkin and Altschuld, 1995, 103

Social indicators are found in census data, educational assessment programmes, employment statistics and so on and can be examined for variables to determine 'trends over time, that is, persistence of needs' (Witkin and Altschuld, 1995, 104). The three types of social indicator information can be easily extrapolated to INA contexts. The first provides evidence of 'the current status (the "what is" condition) of a group or the delivery of services to the group'. For example a public library's membership data can be compared with census data to determine what percentage of the various ethnic groups in the community are library members.

The second type can be identified in actual or implied standards or norms to determine 'discrepancies between current and desired statuses', that is, to determine how well a target population performs compared with the average of the population as a whole. An INA example here would be the lower scores of international students compared with the average score in a test of first-year university students' information literacy competencies. The lower performance of the international students would be an indicator of a training need.

The third type is found in data from which future needs can be predicted. For example, when an engineering firm is planning to increase the number of mechanical engineers on staff, the statistics measuring the current use of the relevant databases (the 'what is') along with the number of current and future mechanical engineering staff can be used to predict the future use (the 'what will be') by the expanded team.

Making use of existing data as early as possible helps to eliminate duplication of effort and to reduce costs. Existing data, however, have drawbacks, because they usually have not been gathered for the purpose of an INA. Fisher and Anushka (2008, 100) state that 'the purpose of archived data is to provide a rich set of data that can be used by future investigators to examine empirical questions about populations that may not be anticipated when information is first collected'. It is this 'that may not be anticipated' aspect that requires careful consideration, as Witkin and Altschuld infer:

> The use of existing records is generally cheaper and requires less time than creating new datasets. On the other hand, such records are rarely designed expressly for the purpose of needs assessment; consequently, needs must be inferred from them, with inferences subject to value judgments and questions of interpretation and validity.
>
> Witkin and Altschuld, 1995, 103

Nonetheless, in all INA contexts some investigation of existing data must be undertaken as a key part of the preparation stage – even if simply to confirm that there are no existing data. When relevant information about the target population can be found in existing records, it can save valuable time and effort if used with care.

Gathering data through surveys

As might be expected, surveys are a frequently employed data-gathering method in INAs. Surveys allow the investigator to gather responses to open or closed questions from people who have direct knowledge of the information need under investigation, whether they are members of the target population itself or individuals who work with or are otherwise knowledgeable about the target population.

Though survey questions can be asked face to face or distributed on paper, today they are most often sent to participants in e-mail attachments or made available as web-based surveys. Web-based surveys are now relatively easy to administer with the use of online survey software such as SurveyMonkey®, which offers a basic package free of charge along with enhanced paid products and services (see www.surveymonkey.com).

As noted above, in the preparation stage of all INAs it is necessary to clarify the issues in Table 4.1 (p. 74): the principal question to be answered, the participants who are to answer the question, the means by which the data are to be gathered and the method(s) for analysing the gathered data. The INA investigator examines the preliminary evidence to determine whether a survey is the best method. If it is, the investigator must then determine whether the individuals who can answer the survey questions are available to do so, and can do so using the chosen method of survey distribution. The investigator must also be certain that the data analysis methods will produce results that are valid. (These steps will involve some knowledge of statistical methods.) Other factors, including the cost, the skills needed and time constraints, must also be considered when choosing to conduct a survey in an INA project.

Surveys are frequently referred to as a quantitative data-gathering method because they are designed to generate numeric data, for example, about a target group's perceptions of a particular issue. Based on these numbers, inferences can be made about the population as a whole. Thus, in a survey conducted in an INA the number of responses from a representative sample of the target group can provide the basis from which conclusions may be drawn about the information needs of the whole target group.

The investigator, prior to selecting the survey method, must examine existing data to determine what kind of new data are required. In some situations the investigator will identify an issue or problem for which there are no existing data and a survey would be the most appropriate method to gather the required data.

Any or all of the three levels of information needs can be the subject of surveys. Witkin and Altschuld (1995, 130) state that surveys 'furnish data for system-specific, time-based decisions about priorities for planning, resource allocation, or program evaluation'. These authors also point out that for needs analysis 'the most effective type of survey . . . asks respondents for informed opinions based on personal experience, background, expertise, or knowledge, or for facts about themselves and others about which they have direct knowledge' (130–1).

Surveys have both strengths and weaknesses. Among the strengths identified by Burns (1997, 482) are the fact that surveys are relatively inexpensive, are easy to administer, and can be distributed to small or large groups locally or at a distance. Chowdhury and Chowdhury (2011, 41) note that, as a method for gathering data for determining information needs, surveys are impersonal and unobtrusive, thus allowing participants to respond anonymously and the researcher to remain uninfluenced by the respondents' personal appearances, accents and so forth. These authors also comment that surveys can pose questions to all respondents in exactly the same way and can be completed by the participants at their own pace and convenience.

Among the disadvantages of surveys Burns (1997, 483) states that the researcher has little control over the rate of response and from whom the responses are received. Thus it might be impossible to generalize with a high degree of confidence from the sample population to the larger population. Burns points out that complex, ambiguous or vague questions can lead to poor responses, and when questions are misinterpreted, the responses can be misleading. Burns further observes that surveys using closed questions are inflexible and do not allow free expression of thoughts and opinions by respondents, whereas surveys using open questions may produce results that are extremely varied and difficult to merge for systematic analysis.

Chowdhury and Chowdhury (2011, 41) identify three additional problems with closed questions in INA questionnaires:

1 They might require participants to choose more than one option to provide the correct response.
2 The respondents might not be able to identify an appropriate option among those provided.

3 Respondents might feel uncomfortable being subjective in their response to certain questions.

However, it is important to bear in mind that these problems usually can be overcome with careful planning.

Nonetheless it is important not to underestimate the complexity of surveys. Witkin and Altschuld (1995, 129) note that many of the steps involved in designing surveys require specialized knowledge and skills that might not be available in smaller organizations. They mention that in needs assessments surveys are often used inappropriately – for example 'to determine people's wish lists, rather than as a means of determining needs'.

There are also some contexts in INA projects when surveys are not well suited to data gathering. For example in the early stages of an open planning process (OPP) situation the investigator usually focuses on understanding the broader issues relevant to a target group's information needs; therefore, direct observation of current practices or consultation with key stakeholders would be more appropriate methods than a survey.

Gathering data through interviews

The third main method for gathering data in INA projects is the interview. Often the simplest and most direct method of gathering end-users' views of needs, services and resources is simply to ask them. This makes interviews the 'bread and butter' of INA data collection (Nicholas and Herman, 2009, 139).

The interview method relies on asking people about their first-hand experiences of the information needs of the group of individuals who are the focus of the INA. The interviewees either are themselves members of the group or are people who interact closely with the group. Interviews are usually conducted in face-to-face situations, though they may also be conducted over the telephone, through e-mail conversations or online chats, or via video calls using a web-based tool such as Skype. Web-based tools are convenient and generally easy to use, making it possible to interview individuals at no or low cost, even when they are located across long distances. It is also relatively easy to record the interviews (both sound and video) for later transcription and analysis.

Interviews can be conducted with individuals or with groups of people. For example in focus group interviews the investigator poses questions in a group setting where the interviewees or participants can discuss ideas and generate new understandings from each other's observations. Blogs and wikis, and tools such as Skype which allows conference calls, make it possible for participants to meet virtually to respond to research questions and to discuss issues and ideas, offering the potential to augment and possibly replace face-to-face focus group sessions. However, the context and complexity of the specific situation will again be the deciding factors in how a focus group session should be conducted.

Especially when done in the early stages of a project, an interview need not be tightly structured, and an experienced investigator will allow respondents to go off on tangents provided the discussion might arrive at some useful information relevant to the INA's objectives. Totally unexpected data will appear this way, particularly if the interviewee has been associated with the service or organization for some time and is recalling ideas, conversations, plans, proposals or events from the past that might not have not been recorded in any formal way.

More structured interviews are also often used in later stages of INAs for probing deeper into findings discovered in earlier data-gathering stages. An investigation into citizenship information needs in the United Kingdom opened with a large-scale questionnaire survey designed to elicit preliminary data on the needs for and methods used to find citizenship information (Marcella and Baxter, 1999). In a second stage people around the country were interviewed in order to gather more qualitative, in-depth and individual responses with a view to improving citizenship information dissemination by public libraries (Marcella and Baxter, 2000). The two-stage approach employed by Marcella and Baxter is widely used in INAs and involves asking clear-cut questions in a survey as the initial stage, followed by semi-structured interviews to tease out the reasons behind, or the potential effects related to, the key results in the initial stage.

There are other information-gathering methods discussed in the following chapters, such as the use of diaries and direct observation. These are employed infrequently in INAs, but in some IM contexts one of the lesser-used methods might well be better suited to gathering information to answer the research question than would a survey or interviews.

Examples of data-gathering methods selected in INAs

In Chapter 3 we discussed six different information management processes in which INAs are used. In this section we look at two INA projects, one in an open planning process (OPP) and one in a solution selection process (SSP), that provide examples of the contexts which give rise to the selection of various data-gathering methods. It is essential to bear in mind here that the specific methods chosen for an INA will depend on a range of factors, some of which become known only as the project unfolds. Therefore, the methods selected in the examples below might not be appropriate for other similar contexts due to the specific issues and the evolving nature of each INA.

An INA in an open planning process

As explained in Chapter 3, 'open planning processes are suited to contexts involving broadly based exercises, for example during strategic planning, or when developing policy, or when planning a completely new service'.

In 2005 an INA was conducted as one of several processes in an OPP exercise at the Malibu Community Library to revise its service goals. This example is described in Scenario 5. 1.

Scenario 5.1 Malibu Community Library community needs analysis

---

The Malibu Community Library (MCL) is within the County of Los Angeles Public Library (CoLAPL), one of the largest library systems in the USA (Malibu Community Library, 2005, 1). Malibu's existing public library was characterized by high staff turnover, a facility in great need of renovation and an aged collection that had deteriorated under severe California state budget cuts. In May 2004 the CoLAPL notified the City of Malibu that it had a continuing surplus of funds for the provision of library services that were being generated from property taxes.

Given this anomaly, the County Librarian recommended that the CoLAPL and the City of Malibu conduct a community library needs assessment 'to determine the library service goals and enable CoLAPL to provide service more closely tailored to the community's needs' (Malibu Community Library, 2005, 1). In other words the INA would be extensive, that is, at the community level, to determine the needs of the citizens of Malibu for library services specific to their community.

An advisory committee was appointed, and a consultant was hired to work with the committee on the project, beginning in February 2005 (Malibu Community Library, 2005, 2).

The goals were to identify community characteristics and assess community strengths, weaknesses and needs as well as library strengths, weaknesses and needs. The study would identify community-specific service goals for the Malibu Library, including how these goals related to the physical plant of the Malibu Community

Library and the overall service objectives. Service goals become the basis for resource allocation – staff, the facility, acquisition budgets and technology.

The INA process was designed to secure broad community involvement and 'included regular meetings of the Advisory Committee, a community survey, town hall meetings, stakeholder interviews, focus groups, site visits, facility and services analyses, and a comparative analysis of library service to similar jurisdictions' (Malibu Community Library, 2005, 2). Stakeholders represented a broad cross-section of residents, including city employees and elected officials, library staff, school personnel, parents, business people and supporters of the library.

Data for the facility and service analyses were augmented by a survey that was 'distributed at focus group meetings, library programs and events, citywide events, via the City of Malibu website and the City of Malibu Parks and Recreation quarterly newsletter' and was also made available at the library itself and other public locations, including schools, churches and service organizations (Malibu Community Library, 2005, 34). Library non-users had some representation through the survey, although with only 350 valid responses non-user input appeared to be rather limited.

The results of the Malibu INA were then used by the advisory committee in the ex post intervention stage to refine MCL's service goals and develop an implementation strategy for improving library services (Malibu Community Library, 2005, 3). This latter process required the advisory committee to establish priorities and to establish a schedule for service improvement.

Because of its broad scope, the wide range of stakeholders consulted and the need for developing an understanding in a step-by-step process, the MCL case is a good example of the broad array of data-gathering methods used in some OPP INAs. However, not all OPPs will be as extensive as the one in Malibu. Scenario 3.2 (p. 56) provides an example of a relatively small OPP INA – a strategic planning exercise in a law firm's information centre. In that scenario it is likely that a much simpler approach would be required.

An INA in a solution selection process

As noted in Chapter 3, INAs in solution selection processes (SSPs) 'are used predominantly for analysing Level 3 needs', that is, the needs of the organization for resources or solutions to meet the information needs of the target group. Scenario 5.2 describes how this occurred in an actual INA project. This example is for an INA undertaken as part of the Digital Electronic Library Integration within Virtual EnviRonments (DELIVER) Project. The aim of the DELIVER

Project was 'to integrate digital libraries and virtual learning environments (VLE)' (Secker, 2005, 39). It was funded by the Joint Information Systems Committee (JISC) and undertaken co-operatively by the London School of Economics (LSE) and De Montfort University (DMU), with additional support from two integrated library management system software companies – Sirsi and Talis.

Scenario 5.2 The DELIVER Project INA

The DELIVER Project was carried out between October 2002 and July 2003, which meant the INA 'needed to be planned and carried out within a short timescale' (Harris, 2003, 2). The project team selected a staff member from each of the partnering organizations 'with extensive consultation experience within their home institutions' to provide advice on the best methods 'to obtain relevant and useful results'. Because of the unique circumstances of each institution, two different data-gathering methods were used.

To identify user needs the DMU team conducted two focus groups with staff, one at each of its two campuses (Harris, 2003, 5). The sessions 'began with an open and lively, directed discussion, to record issues that users had with any current system of producing reading and learning materials lists'. In the second part of the meeting participants were asked to rank the issues as Very Important, Important or Useful. 'The purpose of the rating activity was to focus the functionality of the DELIVER system on resolving those issues that were Very Important and Important to the end users'. The project team sent e-mails to the people who had recorded an interest but were unable to attend the focus group sessions and asked them to rank the issues. In total the views of 24 staff were taken into account.

The DMU team started the project using the Delphi technique; this is best described as 'a method for structuring a group communication process so that the process is effective in allowing a group of individuals, as a whole, to deal with a complex problem' (Linstone and Turoff, 1975, 3). However, the DMU team had to change its plan after the first stage due to the tight time frame and 'the associated problems with getting academic involvement during teaching semester time' (Harris, 2003, 5). Instead of using the complex and time-consuming Delphi technique, the project team decided to discuss in turn each of the issues identified in the focus groups and e-mail responses 'to determine if it was a requirement or a more general comment. These were then converted into recommendations.' The recommendations were subsequently used as statements that could be converted into functions to be supported by the DELIVER system.

The LSE project team took a different approach. It originally considered using mixed focus groups to bring the various stakeholders together but decided this plan would be impractical due to the time constraints and commitments of both students and staff (Harris, 2003, 4). The team also felt that 'certain stakeholders may feel intimidated or restricted within a large, mixed group and that these users may respond to questions more freely within small peer groups'. As a result, the team employed a variety of techniques. It used semi-structured interviews with academic staff and course designers, either individually or in pairs. It conducted two focus groups with library staff, one for Taught Course Support staff and one for Information Services staff. A focus group was also used with students, whereas project team members consulted informally with staff from the Centre for Learning Technology. The LSE project team chose data-gathering methods that were best suited to the characteristics of each of the stakeholder groups and to the types of questions each had to answer to provide the information required to achieve the aims of the INA project.

The DELIVER INA project team then summarized and undertook a detailed analysis of the scripts received from the two partner institutions, translating the comments and ideas from the various sessions into 78 recommendations. 'These recommendations were further classified into institutional recommendations (to be passed across to the partner institutions for information and progression) and system recommendations that were passed to the technical development team' (Harris, 2003, 6).

The DELIVER Project is an interesting example on three fronts. First, it illustrates the types of issues to be considered when choosing the most appropriate method or methods for determining the requirements for selecting or developing a system to meet the information needs of a target group (a Level 3 need). Second, the project demonstrates that different methods might be necessary when different partners or groups are involved in a project because of their unique contexts. And third, in Scenario 5.2 the decision made by the DMU team to change its plan illustrates that, even though the choice of data-gathering method may seem the best choice during the preparation stage, the investigator must be amenable to change when it becomes apparent that something is not right. This is particularly important when the chosen method is proving to be impractical, and continuing with it will lead to delays or even to project failure.

Review of Chapter 5

In this chapter we have introduced the main data-gathering methods employed to identify and understand information needs in INA projects. We emphasized the importance of the articulation of a very clear principal research question as a necessary precursor to the selection of any data-gathering method(s). We then discussed the interdependent nature of the decisions in INAs related to:

1 The principal research question
2 The research population
3 The data-gathering method(s)
4 The data analysis method(s).

We then examined the issues of validity and reliability and looked closely at the ethical issues that investigators in INA projects must resolve, including how to deal with conflicts of interest, how to obtain informed consent and what is involved in offering incentives to participants.

We subsequently moved on to three practical issues that must be considered when choosing a data-gathering method: the ease, cost and speed of data collection. The organization paying for the INA will want to get the best return on its investment, and ensuring that these issues are taken into consideration will certainly help on that front.

In the major part of the chapter we introduced the main data-gathering methods used in INAs:

1 Gathering data from existing sources
2 Gathering data through surveys
3 Gathering data through interviews.

We then concluded the chapter with two examples of INAs, one in an open planning process, and the other in a solution selection process. These examples demonstrated the range of methods used, the circumstances that led to the choices and the need to be open to the possibility that, if something goes amiss, it might be necessary to change tack and employ a different method.

Further reading

There are, of course, many works that provide full details of how to gather and analyse data, and these more appropriately appear in further reading sections in Chapters 6–8, and to some extent in Chapter 9. At the same time, however, books that provide brief overviews are less common, and among those that do exist there are precious few that offer quality summaries appropriate for readers of this book.

One of the better works aimed at a student readership is Chambliss and Schutt's (2013) *Making Sense of the Social World: methods of investigation*. In the context of this chapter Chambliss and Schutt offer four very useful chapters: Ethics in Research, Sampling, Survey Research and Qualitative Methods: observing, participating, listening. Each chapter draws on examples from various fields and includes online and video support to augment the text discussion. Another, more detailed discussion of research ethics is offered in a 44-page chapter of *Research Methods, Design and Analysis* (11th edn, 2011) by Christensen, Johnson and Turner; this is notable for its extension of ethics to writing the research report, and for realistically showing when informed consent is not necessary, when it can be passive consent and so on – sticklers for bureaucratic procedures may not like this, but the authors do offer a much needed real-world reality check.

A higher-level discussion of research ethics, with particular focus on the online environment, is Natasha Whiteman's *Undoing Ethics: rethinking practice in online research* (2013). Not for the faint-hearted, this book does give pause for thought and encourages one to reconsider the whole ethical aspect of research. A final recommendation for understanding the importance of ethics in INA is Fisher and Anushka's 'Research Ethics in Social Science' (2008), which is especially good on conflicts of interest and how these should be handled.

Other reasonable summaries of data-gathering and analysis methods may be found in a number of general research texts. For example a discussion of surveys may be found in Chapter 8, 'Ethics in Research' of Pickard (2013, 87–96); observation is clearly addressed in Chapter 10 of Gomm's *Social Research Methodology: a critical introduction* (2nd edn, 2008); and a strength of Neuman's *Social Research Methods: qualitative and quantitative approaches* (7th edn, 2011) is his Chapter 13 on interviewing and focus groups. None of these references has a focus on INA research, but then that is the purpose of the book you are now reading.

There is also a range of valuable online resources available that should assist investigators in becoming more competent in their data gathering. Here we recommend just a few.

◆ *Strengthening Nonprofits: a capacity builder's resource library* (2014). Conducting a Community Assessment, http://strengtheningnonprofits.org. [Accessed 6 November 2104.]

Although the focus is on non-profit organizations, there is much here that is valuable training for those new to INA. Individual sections relevant to our purpose cover how to conduct a community assessment and how to create and implement a data collection plan. The training videos are simple and straightforward, and they offer very useful advice for the newcomer to needs analysis. This resource also offers some ancillary guidebooks pitched at the beginner.

◆ United States. Department of Justice. Office for Victims of Crime (2010). *Guide to Conducting a Needs Assessment,* www.ovcttac.gov/taResources/OVCTAGuides/ConductingNeedsAssessment/ step4.html.

Although it is not immediately obvious why the Office for Victims of Crime (US Department of Justice) created this series of four training programmes, the site does say that these are 'tools for victim service providers and allied professionals, like you, who want or need to conduct program evaluations or needs assessments'. One part of the series is the Guide to Conducting a Needs Assessment, which is not specifically on INA, but it contains useful ideas that an investigator could use. Step 2 tells the reader how 'to review existing resources', and Step 3 is on collecting new data (specifically interviews, focus groups and surveys). Step 4 covers (in simple terms) the analysis of qualitative and quantitative data. The final sections describe how to use the findings.

◆ University of Kansas. Work Group for Community Health and Development (2014). Community Tool Box, http://ctb.dept.ku.edu/en. The website for the Community Tool Box (CTB) states that it is 'a free, online resource for those working to build healthier communities and bring about social change. Our mission is to promote community health and development by connecting people, ideas, and resources'. Within this broad brief the CTB covers community assessment and planning, intervention and evaluation and other aspects of community practice. In these areas the CTB offers more than 300 educational modules to assist users in developing skills needed in community development. For example there are modules on ethical issues in community interventions, conducting interviews and surveys, qualitative assessment methods, using public records and archival data and so on. This is an excellent resource relevant to many aspects of INA and should be consulted for Chapters 6–9 as well as this chapter.

References

Burns, R. B. (1997) *Introduction to Research Methods,* 3rd edn, Addison Wesley Longman Australia, South Melbourne.

Chambliss, D. F. and Schutt, R. K. (2013) *Making Sense of the Social World: methods of investigation*, 4th edn, SAGE Publications, Thousand Oaks, CA.

Chowdhury, G. G. and Chowdhury, S. (2011) *Information Users and Usability in the Digital Age*, Facet Publishing, London.

Christensen, L. B., Johnson, R. B. and Turner, L. A. (2011) *Research Methods, Design and Analysis*, 11th edn, Allyn & Bacon, Boston, MA.

Cohn, J. M., Kelsey, A. L. and Fiels, K. M. (2002) *Planning for Integrated Systems and Technologies: a how-to-do-it manual for librarians*, 2nd rev. edn, Facet Publishing, London.

Cullen, R. and Calvert, P. J. (2004) Organisational Factors Affecting the Delivery of Service Quality in Academic Libraries. In Parker, S. (ed.), *Library Measures to Fill the Void: assessing the outcomes*, Emerald, Bradford, 166–72.

Economic and Social Research Council, the Researcher Development Initiative, and the Institute of Education at the University of London (n.d.). *The Research Ethics Guidebook: a resource for social scientists*, ESRC, London. www.ethicsguidebook.ac.uk. [Accessed 5 November 2014.]

Fisher, C. B. and Anushka, A. E. (2008) Research Ethics in Social Science. In Alasuutari, P., Bickman, L. and Brannen, J. (eds), *The SAGE Handbook of Social Research Methods*, SAGE Publications, London, 95–109.

Gomm, R. (2008) *Social Research Methodology: a critical introduction*, 2nd edn, Palgrave Macmillan, Basingstoke.

Harris, N. (2003) *DELIVER: user needs analysis report*, www.jisc.ac.uk/whatwedo/programmes/divle/finalreports.aspx. [Accessed 5 November 2014.]

Linstone, H. A. and Turoff, M. (1975) *The Delphi Method: techniques and applications*, Addison-Wesley, Reading, MA.

Malibu Community Library (2005) *Community Library Needs Assessment*, County of Los Angeles Public Library, Los Angeles, CA. www.malibucity.org/AgendaCenter/ViewFile/Agenda/10302013-324. [Accessed 5 November 2014.]

Marcella, R. and Baxter, G. (1999) A National Survey of the Citizenship Information Needs of the General Public, *Aslib Proceedings,* **51** (4), 115–21.

Marcella, R. and Baxter G. (2000) Citizenship Information Needs in the UK: results of a national survey of the general public by personal doorstep interview, *Aslib Proceedings,* **52** (3), 115–23.

McKillip, J. A. (1987) *Need Analysis: tools for the human services and education*, Applied Social Research Methods, 10, SAGE Publications, Newbury Park, CA.

Neuman, W. L. (2011) *Social Research Methods: qualitative and quantitative approaches*, 7th edn, Allyn & Bacon, Boston, MA.

Nicholas, D. and Herman, E. (2009) *Assessing Information Needs in the Age of the Digital Consumer,* 3rd edn, Routledge, London.

Pickard, A. J. (2013) *Research Methods in Information*, 2nd edn, Facet Publishing, London.

Secker, J. (2005) DELIVERing Library Resources to the Virtual Learning
    Environment, *Program: electronic library and information systems,* **39** (1), 39–49.

Westbrook, L. (2001) *Identifying and Analyzing User Needs: a complete handbook and
    ready-to-use assessment workbook with disk,* Neal-Schuman Publishers, New York.

Whiteman, N. (2013) *Undoing Ethics: rethinking practice in online research,* Springer,
    Heidelberg.

Witkin, B. R. and Altschuld, J. W. (1995) *Planning and Conducting Needs Assessments: a
    practical guide,* SAGE Publications, Thousand Oaks, CA.

CHAPTER 6

Gathering data from existing sources

Introduction

This chapter provides guidance on using existing data in INAs. Existing data can be obtained from a wide variety of sources and can take many different forms. In some INAs the gathering of new information might not be required because enough data already exist. In many INAs the investigators will use existing information to establish the background and context as the first step in their planning. And, bearing in mind the complexities as well as the staffing and other costs involved in employing the quantitative and qualitative methods described in Chapters 7 and 8, using existing data can be an effective and efficient approach for conducting all or part of an INA.

Useful INA data can be found in such existing resources as published statistics documents from government agencies and professional associations, from local sources such as chambers of commerce and in internal administrative forms and records, including those generated by computer systems. The wide variety of existing data is reflected in the many uses to which they are applied in INAs. In some instances the data can be very recent, whereas in others data can go back over a lengthy period of time. As a result, existing data can be what is sometimes referred to as historical data, and an investigator might be required to undertake some historical research for all or part of an INA. For example in the chapter 'Historical Investigation' in Gorman and Clayton's *Qualitative Research for the Information Professional*, Shep points out that 'historical data on an information service's evolving client service priorities may be essential as a basis for decisions concerning services to, say, particular ethnic groups in a multicultural social context' (Shep, 2005, 161).

The benefit of using existing data in a needs analysis requires little explanation. Data created within an organization (or community) can tell us much about the nature of the organization itself, for example: the way the organization sees itself through its mission, objectives, products and services; its clients; the way communication takes place within the organization; and what it values. An analysis of what data are created, who sees it, how they use it and transform it, and to whom it goes next ought to indicate how information flows reflect information needs, although this is something that an analysis will sometimes reveal is flawed, i.e. the information people most need is not reaching them in a timely manner. Finding the weaknesses in the current situation is significant to an INA.

The discussion in Chapter 6 addresses three key questions:

1   What are the most common types of existing data used in INAs?
2   What is the best practice for identifying sources of existing data for collection?
3   What different methods can be used for analysing existing data?

With regard to the final question, it is Chapter 9 that provides a more detailed account of the analysis and integration of data in INAs.

The data

This section illustrates that existing data uncovered for a needs analysis can have different facets. It is not simply a matter of deciding to 'find all the existing data', because it might reside in many different locations within the organization or community, and it might take different forms of electronic, print and even tacit knowledge. It is important for the investigator to appreciate the variety of existing data sources, because the solution to some problems may be much easier to determine if the most appropriate data are identified in time. This chapter cannot be comprehensive, but an attempt is made to illustrate the wide variety of data that can be utilized in an INA, no matter what kind of organization or community is under the microscope.

External data
Social indicators

Information managers should be familiar with the plethora of data available about the country and community being analysed. All governments collect data about their citizens, partly for the all-important reason that they want to collect taxes from them but also for planning purposes, and in some countries so that democratic elections can be held. For the most part such data help with Level 1 and Level 2 analyses. A Level 3 analysis might require data on resources, and that information can often be found in existing sources.

Government agencies keep numerous records that are the result of various data collection activities. Perhaps the starting point should be census data, data collected regularly and systematically from and about a population, not only because it contains great detail but also (a) because it is usually reliable, and (b) there is an historical record against which it can be compared. Census and other demographic data reveal much potentially useful information about people (ages, ethnicity, gender, income, educational attainment) that provides an excellent starting point for a community INA. In some countries the national statistical service provides tools that help collect and arrange data in a form useful for analysis; the Australian Bureau of Statistics (2014), for example, provides a tool called TableBuilder online with a basic version available at no cost and an advanced version available as a charged product. TableBuilder allows users to construct tables of varying complexity with data drawn from the Australian census.

At this point it is appropriate to give an example of how demographic data can be used. Suppose a Level 3 INA is being undertaken to investigate the availability of public access computers in a public library, and a question has been asked about who is using them. If data could be collected on who is using the computers, these data could be compared with demographic data to show which groups used them more and which less than the proportions in the general population. A very large-scale study in the USA did just this by first collecting data on public access computer use across the country by a combination of telephone surveys and point-of-service web surveys (Manjarrez and Shoembs, 2011). The data on usage were then compared with census data first by age, then by educational attainment. The findings revealed more use of public access computers by 14–19 year-olds than the proportion of people of that age range in the population (16.4% use compared with 8.8% in the population), though perhaps this might be expected if members of this age group do not own a computer and need to access information resources for homework. Perhaps surprisingly, the 25–34 year-olds used it less (11.7% use but with 16.5% in the population). Another comparison showed that educational attainment is correlated with use of public access computers: people with some tertiary education use them more, while those with only some secondary school education use them less.

Unobtrusive measures

Other centrally collected data can include the use of transport, health care, social services and much more. Not all of this information is relevant to every INA; the key point is that it might be in some cases, and the investigator needs to be aware it is available, and where. Most of these data are quantitative, though some exist as evaluations and reports. Here a possibly obvious point should be highlighted: that there is seldom a direct relationship between social indicators and an information need, simply because in any social environment there will be numerous factors at play. Suppose the investigator is examining information needs connected with deaths by drowning, e.g. what do people need to know about water safety, and why can't more people swim? National data will give the bald figures for how many people have died by drowning over a period of years. This information can be matched with what Witkin and Altschuld (1995) call 'unobtrusive measures', which could in this case be the number of enquiries received by swimming clubs for beginner classes. This example is offered because even a casual reading will suggest the tenuous link between drownings and beginner swimming classes; but there *could* be an information need in there somewhere, and if something must be done, then promoting swimming classes with better publicity and awareness campaigns could be one recommendation.

Scenario 6.1 shows how existing data from government departments, community organizations and libraries might assist in part of an INA.

Scenario 6.1 Local youth library needs in Chaplin

The City of Willingdon recently conducted a Level 1 INA to investigate the needs of local youth (teenagers and young adults) in Chaplin, a suburban area of the city which did not have a branch library. Mary Senior, Chief Librarian of the Willingdon Public Library Service, met with the Youth Services staff after the local newspaper reported that Chaplin's two secondary schools had the highest dropout rates in Willingdon, and its unemployment and crime rates exceeded all other suburbs. John Junior, Head of Youth Services, reported that very few local youth used the library services. Mary and John decided to contract an investigator to conduct an INA of the needs of Chaplin youth for library services.

As a first step, the investigator visited a range of organizations to obtain data relevant to the target group. The visits began with the Department of Statistics for data from the national census: the numbers of people in the target age range, their ethnicity, their level of education, their household incomes, languages spoken, their access to ICTs (particularly the internet) and so on. The investigator then obtained data from the Ministry for Social Development that provided a demographic breakdown of individuals receiving different types of government benefits. Further, the Ministry of Justice provided crime statistics for the area, and the Ministry of Education provided data that showed how many young people were in schools in the area. In addition the same Ministry offered data on the 'decile rating' for each local school (the lower the decile, the higher proportion of students from low socio-economic communities).

The investigator then contacted the local Chamber of Commerce for data related to small businesses: how many young people they employed and whether there were skills shortages in selected parts of the workforce. The investigator also drew on the Willingdon Public Library's own statistics to verify the number of Chaplin youth who were actually members of the branch libraries in their area and their borrowing statistics.

From the census and other government data the investigator found the following:

◆ A high proportion of the residents were from two immigrant communities.
◆ Many spoke languages other than English as their first language.
◆ Occupational achievement was low compared with nearby communities.
◆ Local high schools were Decile 1.
◆ The number of local youth convicted of petty crimes far exceeded the national average.
◆ Far fewer households than the national average had access to the internet.

Local business data pointed to the need for higher levels of literacy so that young people could look beyond only the most menial forms of employment. And the library's own statistics showed that only 25% of Chaplin's residents were registered public library users; among Chaplin's youth aged 12–20 only 15% were library members, and few of them were regular users.

The investigator knew that under existing policies a new branch library could not be built in Chaplin, because an existing branch was situated less than 5 kilometres from the suburb's centre. While Chaplin did not meet the criteria for a new branch library, the existing data showed the Chaplin's youth needs were so different from youth needs elsewhere in the city that an exception to the rules had to be considered. By using a variety of existing data to demonstrate the potential need for a new youth library in Chaplin, the INA investigation then moved to the next step: undertaking an Alpha-type Level 3 INA (see Chapter 3) as the basis for developing an evidence-based policy for high-need branch libraries – and gaining approval to build the Chaplin Youth Library.

Internally created data
Existing input data

Input measures are those that count the resources put into the organization ('how much' and 'how many') and are commonly used in assessing the current state of an information service. Many different aspects of library/information management operations can be counted as inputs; unfortunately, there is no agreed classification, but Matthews (2004) lists five types of operations for input measures:

◆ income and expenditures
◆ staff
◆ collection
◆ library information system
◆ space.

For most libraries and other information providers the simplest and most important input measure is the amount of money granted by the primary funding agency (for example, the local government authority, the university, company or government department). An indicator of this might be 'budget expenditure per capita'. Other common input measures are staff numbers, collection size, physical facilities (building space) and the number of workstations provided for public use, which Matthews (2004) included in the category 'library information system'. In practice the major use of input measures is to report back to the funding agency on how the budget has been spent, so the data often appear in annual reports. Though not *immediately* relevant to an INA, the organization will always expect to see such data about its information service in a report.

A Level 3 analysis might be conducted by an organization to see how the services it provides compare with those offered by other organizations. This example is a type of performance benchmarking, which in the context of a library involves comparing inputs and outputs initially against a standard and thereafter against selected peer libraries (Powell, 2006, 109). The *Standards for College Libraries* (American Library Association, 2000) suggest that a library could compare itself with 'aspiration peers', that is, libraries currently ahead in terms of input measures.

Existing usage data

Outputs are the end-result of a service; they are the uses to which the information service is put by its clients, such as finding the answers to questions arising in an organization's daily business activities or discovering the arrival information of family members from the inward passenger manifests for ships when conducting genealogical research. Again, the view is an internal one despite the actual consumption of a service by an end-user. While the following quote is about libraries, it could just as easily be stated in the context of any type of information service: 'Output measures reflect an inward orientation in that they measure how much the library is used. However, there is no clear innate or implied value in activity *per se* without context' (Matthews, 2004, 86). Output measures can reveal useful information about efficiency, that is, the organization's capacity to use its human and material resources efficiently.

Output measures, in contrast to input measures, are sometimes regarded as direct indicators of performance (Powell, 2006, 106), and the same would apply to any part of the organization or community that ingests resources and turns them into something considered useful (making this type of data very suited to a Level 1 analysis). Circulation counts seem to have a great attraction for library managers, having been used as output measures since lending libraries were first opened; for example, circulation counts are factored into the Hennen American Public Library Rating system (HAPLR) at least six times (i.e. cost per circulation, collection turnover, circulation per FTE hour, circulation per capita, circulation per hour, circulation per visit) (Hennen, 2002). This use of circulation data seems somewhat ironic given that user studies suggest that the socio-economic level of the local community affects library use to a greater degree than does the library's own activity (Ballard, 1989). For an INA the connection between organizational objectives and organizational outputs can be significant. Even circulation data, often considered mundane stuff, can be enlightening if employed to assess how much the target group is using existing resources.

When compared with input measures, output measures have the advantage that they can be applied to a wide variety of information services. Matthews (2002, 56–7) identifies five categories of output measures:

◆ services
◆ quality
◆ collection use
◆ online catalogue/portal use
◆ building activity.

To allow for inter-organizational comparisons, service output measures are often calculated on a per capita basis. There must be a service element in the activity; as examples, this might cover the number of hits on a website or the number of questions answered in response to client requests for assistance in finding information. Client use of an archive's online finding aids indicates how much its collection descriptions are being used, though it does not tell us how easy the descriptions are to use or how much they assist clients in finding the information sought. The number of people entering a library or working at desks, and even the number stopping to view a display, are all indicators of types of activity and may be useful in an INA.

Number of documents retrieved

Public and academic library managers have always favoured simple output measures as a gauge of the organization's 'performance'; hence such libraries will always count and publish circulation data, though this is less relevant in information services for companies or for professions, where enquiries answered or documents delivered might be considered more relevant. Some other data on retrieval might not reflect well on the service. If a document is requested from the stacks or offsite records store, should it ever have been relegated there, and why the delay in meeting the needs of the staff member or client? When an inter-library loan request is received, it can only be because the library does not have that item. No one expects a library, even the very largest, to be able to meet all document requests, but data of such service 'failures' (if they can be recognized as such) help in an INA.

The use of online full-text databases has made the collection of data on document provision much more difficult and in the process has made it harder for information managers to watch for information needs. The problem is that the information service becomes only a third-party provider of many such databases, with the key interaction now between the database host and the end-user. The information service only acts as an intermediary to the extent that it pays the subscription and will then provide access to the database through its website or a mobile app, and once the customer accesses the database the service provider loses almost any control over the interaction. Not only is the provider then dependent on the database host for service, but it is also totally reliant on the host for usage data. It is helpful if vendors agree to supply data in agreed formats, such as COUNTER (Counting Online Usage of NeTworked Electronic Resources)(2014). Typical measures will be the total number of searches in a set period of time, the number of times one article has been downloaded and the useful measure of 'turnaways' (i.e. the number of people not being allowed to access the online resource) that might point to the organization needing to make a change to its licence to permit more synchronous users.

Transaction logs record information about searches undertaken on electronic resources. These data, however, are not always as precise as may be thought, because searches can be interrupted and then resumed, or simply abandoned before anything is retrieved; but the numbers do have some value as measures of transactions. It may be possible to measure the amount of time spent on each search, although skilled searchers can be expected to search faster than unskilled searchers. Another category of searchers, however, searches rapidly, including those who are so unskilled that they will take whatever they find with their first attempts, or those who feel they are so busy that they cannot spare time for searching. Nicholas (1997, 124) places journalists in this latter category.

Care must be taken when analysing transaction logs. For example, the number of *records* retrieved by the system's users might be interpreted as the number of *documents* retrieved by them. This can be a useful measure, but only if the searcher actually wants several records. It is likely that a scholar will want numerous documents, but in many other areas of life the opposite is true. The busy marketing executive wants only a few documents, but they must contain just the 'right' information. No CEO will thank the organization's information manager for delivering 200 records of potentially relevant information sources when only one or two documents are wanted. So how many would be a good match for information needs? In academia it often can be assumed that the more the better, provided the academic has the ability to determine which ones are the most useful. However, by observing end-users directly, even those who said they wanted a 'comprehensive' search, Nicholas (1997, 127) found that one-third of them were looking for only 1–10 records. This finding demonstrates that comprehensiveness is only a relative term, and any attempt to assess it by measuring the number of searches, records retrieved and documents retrieved can result in some dubious assertions. One suggestion is to divide the number of records retrieved by connect time to give a rough measure of productivity.

Number of users

The number of registered users tells us something of the overall use of the information service, and longitudinal data can show trends in usage, but little more than that. If, while collecting these data, the affiliation of the end-user were added, we might then begin to understand much more about the existing service.

Take a software company as an example. The data might show that software engineers have been active users of the information service, but sales and marketing staff have not. There may be many more software engineers than sales and marketing staff, so if the ratio is taken into account and this still shows less use by the sales people, does it tell a more useful story?

The investigator must then consider the available resources. Are the resources heavily geared to the software engineers? A collection based on usage data reinforces usage by those already using the service at the expense of those not currently using it, so the profile of the service needs consideration. Low use by one group of potential users might raise the question of whether they have an alternative source of information that they find easy to access and relevant to their needs. Commonly, there will be those happy in the belief that everything they could need to know can be found somewhere on the web. There will be others who use in-house knowledge communicated only by word of mouth. Yet others may have found some other formal information service that seems to suit them better than the organization's internal information service for reasons of subject information available, better personal service or convenience of opening hours and location. An instinctive reaction is to compete for the custom of those users and try to prise them away from other information providers, but an INA investigator will do well to enquire just why end-users have chosen to use an alternative to the 'preferred' resources, and then perhaps to imitate some of the better features of those services.

Enquiries

A simple figure for the number of enquiries made by clients of an information service tells about volume but little else. An obvious question to ask is, how many of the enquiries receive an accurate answer, or an answer that satisfies the enquirer (the two are not always the same)? An information need is not resolved simply by asking the question; it must receive an answer that supplies the information that makes a real difference to the enquirer. It is also worth examining the nature of the enquiries, for this aspect can say much about the information needs and the information system's ability to meet those needs. For example, are clients asking questions that are relevant to the organization's purpose, or are they expecting the information service to meet other, less defined information needs? An example might be a schoolteacher embarking on a higher degree going to the school library in the expectation that it can provide her or him with study materials at a much higher level than the school library would normally stock.

Most information services count the number of enquiries they receive as a measure of user information needs, and the rationale for this measure hardly needs further explanation. Why would people ask a question unless they felt they needed to know the answer, and why would they ask the question if the service made the answer so simple that there was no need to ask the question? Information services such as libraries usually encourage questions by providing an information desk or something similar. Whole departments in some university libraries are devoted to the reference function, and such reference services are now commonly available by e-mail or text messaging. Simple numerical data can be collected even at a busy desk by using a 'clicker' each time staff deal with an enquiry, but obviously this number says nothing of the nature of the enquiries. The next level up is to check off each enquiry into pre-set boxes for the type of enquiry. Some are simply directional, whereas others might be about membership and rules of use, and at the higher level of usage they will be bibliographic, document retrieval, and informational. It is the last category that needs deeper analysis, so during an INA staff might be required to record each enquiry in full so that its content can be analysed later in conjunction with the full set of enquiries for, say, one month, and also put in conjunction with other data gathered during the INA.

Automatically created web data

As a sweeping statement, it can be said that all computer systems create usage data. The computers that manage circulation in a library, for example, will generate plentiful data about client behaviour. Online reference questions can be stored for later analysis. Yet another kind of data, that collected by our use of interactive digital channels, is often undervalued. The Digital Analytics Association (2014) defines digital analytics as 'the science of analysis using data to understand historical patterns with an eye to improving performance and predicting the future. The analysis of *digital* data refers to information collected in interactive channels (online, mobile, social, etc.).'

A basic premise of digital analytics is that this end-user generated data can provide some insight into how people, for example, use websites or apps to seek information or to communicate. This sort of data deals with the 'what' of usage; that is, it is behavioural and tells us what end-users are doing when they visit a site or use an app. It does nothing to explain the 'why' of the activity, which means other methods, such as interviews, must be used to gather a fuller picture of website or app use.

A common type of digital analysis starts by using the logs that all websites create automatically. The most common form is transaction log analysis, and another is search analysis. There are other methods, such as using cookies and what is called 'packet sniffing', but this section concentrates on log analysis because of its popularity in data gathering. Every web server keeps a log of page requests that can include (but is not limited to) visitor IP address, date and time of the request, request page, referrer and information on the visitor's browser and operating system. The actual data collected depend on the type of log being used, e.g. NCSA or W3C. When conducting a web log analysis, it is important to know the specifics of the logs being used.

Although this all sounds very precise, in practice log data are far from it. The common web count of hits is far too simplistic, because it does not distinguish between first-time visitors and repeat visitors; eliminating that error and counting only the number of separate individuals who visit the site is much more desirable. This can be done by counting the number of different IP addresses – but then, does this number include IP addresses for shared computers with many users? What of visits by search engine bots (which can account for a large number of visits)? These factors make precise counts impossible. The data are nevertheless useful, provided they are employed with some understanding of their potential vagaries; Scenario 6.2 offers an example of how log data might contribute to an INA. For those who wish to use log analysis and who need more detail than is provided here, useful guidance can be found in *Understanding User–web Interactions via Web Analytics*, edited by Jansen (2009).

Scenario 6.2 Abel Tasman University resources on Thailand

Abel Tasman University (ATU) in New Zealand created a digital library of resources on the Isan region of Thailand. Its main purpose was to support postgraduate research in Isan cultures, a subject area that was very popular at ATU, but the creators also hoped the digital library would be used by researchers elsewhere, including Thailand. Using digital analytics, the ATU Library staff were able to see how many unique users were accessing the site over a set period. The data showed only the country in the IP address of the end-user, but this was sufficient to show that the majority of hits came from New Zealand, as might be expected, for the resource was primarily designed for ATU's research students. It was also possible, however, to see a significant number of end-users living in Thailand, many more than from nearby Malaysia or Vietnam. After some tests for statistical significance the ATU Library staff were satisfied that information needs of researchers in Thailand in particular were also being met by the digital library. To find out more about the end-users the staff of the digital library plan to put a survey on its website to gather more precise data about who is using the digital library, and why.

An emerging form of analysing information needs by using web-based data examines the use of social networking tools. In an exploratory study of BibSonomy, a social bookmarking tool, the data were analysed to assess the use of information by academic researchers (Borrego and Fry, 2012). If this method is sufficiently accurate, then it can supplement data collected in interviews and surveys. The results show that academic journal titles are the most frequently bookmarked type of resource, which matches what we would intuitively expect, and also are similar to results in more conventional studies. Because most social networking tools are free to access, this type of analysis is becoming more widespread and may well be a significant part of INA data gathering in the near future. It has a wider reach than citation analysis, because it collects data from readers as well as authors; and this gives a clearer picture of the information actually being used by the target community. It is an unobtrusive data collection method, and because of this it should not suffer from low response rates. There are weaknesses, mostly in the metadata in the bookmarks – insufficient and even incorrect bibliographic data reduce the value of the collected data.

At the time of writing this method of gathering information goes far beyond bookmarking and bibliographic data, extending to information use, information exchange and data sharing among groups. Although understanding this in terms of the potential in an INA context is in its infancy, as the techniques are refined data from social networking tools can be analysed and utilized more accurately. When we say 'as the techniques are refined', we are not referring to a leisurely, well paced development, but rather to something that is happening quite rapidly even as we write.

Part of this development with particular potential in our context is social media analytics, which is

concerned with developing and evaluating informatics tools and frameworks to collect, monitor, analyze, summarize and visualize social media data to facilitate conversations and interactions to extract useful patterns and intelligence.

Zeng et al., 2010, 14

The potential for social media analytics as a means of analysing social networking and social media data relevant to information organizations and other contexts should not be underestimated – the ubiquity of smartphones and other devices in information services is testimony to the potential here. As the number of users on social media sites grows so does the opportunity for us to utilize these in INA data gathering. Clearly this growth must affect how we perceive not only information services but also the study of these services. Accordingly, followers of INA are well advised to keep a watching brief on how social media analytics develops, and its potential as a data-gathering tool in INAs.

Documents and similar resources

In almost any organization there are documents that are relevant to an INA, and quite often these are easy to access. If the needs of staff within a company are being investigated, there will be documents that describe the production, marketing and managerial processes that can be read to increase understanding. Inevitably some managers will be coy about showing some documents to an outsider – and perhaps even more reluctant to let insiders see them – but the investigator needs to press for access. Typical documentation in an organization or formalized community (a club or church) that the INA investigator may want to read includes annual reports, policies, reports from any previous investigations, organization charts, forms (for entering data, making requisitions, etc.) and so on.

Documents can reveal much about what data are collected and stored and also can tell the investigator something about information flows. For example, if a form is completed, to whom must it be sent? Do the acquisitions librarians see the inter-library loan requests? When an architect makes a change to a drawing, how is it documented and who then knows what changes were made, who made them and when? In a case known to one of the authors, when architects in one company started to use new technology, changes to drawings were made directly onto the drawings, yet no record was being kept of who did what and when. Architects said this was a loss of information that they needed, but the system was failing them. In this case an investigator might recommend that the security in the system be upgraded to ensure version control – that is, that the original drawings are stored separately from the versions with changes and that appropriate authority levels are established to control access to the drawing files.

Recognizing that existing quantitative data alone might be insufficient, we suggest that there are many cases where it makes sense to use a two-stage data collection and analysis. The first level is for 'relatively gross, quantitative measures, suitable only for macro-evaluation' (Baker and Lancaster, 1991, 19). This level might include use, time and costs but will not necessarily include data about quality. The gathered data may not offer any explanation of why the numbers are what they are, what failures there might have been or whether clients find the service satisfactory. To take the analysis to the second level (the micro-evaluation stage) requires more diagnosis of the simple data. The example in Scenario 6.3 gives some ideas about how raw data can be analysed at a micro-evaluation level by adding more data (or additional relevant factors) to the mix.

Scenario 6.3 Rockfall Public Library database tutorials

The interrelated nature of most services provided by a library is illustrated in the following scenario. The reference staff in Rockfall Public Library (RPL) have been offering tutorials for clients interested in using some of the online databases that the library regularly adds to its services. The existing data showed that the uptake of the tutorials is low, only five per month, suggesting to management that clients do not need, and therefore are not interested in, the tutorials and that they should be abandoned as a waste of staff time.

However, this is not the whole picture, which a fuller INA might reveal, and unless managers are ready to look at the bigger picture then mistakes are easily made. In this case a factor might be the quality and relevance of the online databases being offered to the public, which could be discovered by asking for an external expert opinion or by questioning different groups of clients who both use and do not use the databases. It might be that the selection of databases is the problem rather than the teaching provided by the reference staff. Taking an even broader view, the public library might be located close to a university at which a large number of databases can be accessed, thus reducing the demand for all but the most general of resources for the non-student part of the population. Two more potential problems could be the quality of the equipment that clients use to access the databases and the amount of bandwidth available and the consequent speed of access.

By using only existing data as the basis for an INA decision leading to the discontinuation of the tutorials on online database searching, RPL staff would be making a major error of judgement, which ultimately would be a disservice to its clients.

One young staff member, Maryam Nazari, was rather alarmed that the clients themselves were not consulted and raised this point with her manager. The manager then addressed Maryam's concern by appointing her to lead an INA to investigate the training needs of RPL's online service users. After determining the purpose of the INA and assessing the existing data, Maryam decided that interviews with a cross-section of the community would help to obtain a clearer picture of the training needs of RPL clients.

The methods

Existing data can be used in an INA in several different ways, and two will be mentioned here.

First, they simply provide the investigator with basic data upon which to base the next steps in the evaluation. If the data say that this is a younger-than-average population, then this could be a suitable case for using new technologies (e.g. location-based social networking) that younger people take to with ease. It is also useful to check assumptions made by the investigator and the people who provide information. For instance, one of us was told by a library manager that the community served by his public library was primarily an elderly population, a statement he used to justify a considerable proportion of the library's resources being used to provide services for seniors. A quick check of national census data showed that this assumption was false. Was the manager genuinely mistaken? In the end the motivation may not really matter, but the investigator used the census data in his final report to show services to be skewed towards a segment of the population already well served, with the consequence that resources were denied to some sectors (the young, ethnic minorities) needing more than was being offered.

The second way that existing data can be employed is as a source of information for statistical analyses such as in the example given earlier. In that example statistically significant differences were found when census data were compared with data gathered in a survey on library computer use. An analysis of the data showed that the proportion of users of public access computers who were between 14 and 19 years old was significantly higher than the proportion of people in that age category in the general population and that it was significantly lower for those in the 25–34 year-old category (Manjarrez and Shoembs, 2011, 2). The analysis also found a positive correlation between educational attainment and the use of public access computers. These types of analyses are often of great value to the people who are making resource allocation decisions related to information needs.

Desk research

The secondary literature (that is, published material) is a rich source of information relevant to an INA. Those working in the academic world will be immediately familiar with the concept of a literature review (see, for example, Oliver, 2012) conducted prior to a research project, no matter how great or small, though it is worth adding that the secondary literature is also commonly used in the corporate world for diverse purposes, including competitive intelligence and environmental scanning. Some INAs can be conducted entirely by desk research in the existing literature. While desk research is not precisely the same as a literature review, anyone skilled in searching the literature will adapt to desk research quickly.

Typically desk research starts with a specific question. In an INA it might be something such as 'What is the educational level of the population being analysed?' This is typical of some general data that might be very relevant to the INA. Demographic data, for example, can be essential for an evaluation of information provision to a community: gender, age, income and so on, although increasingly marketing agencies want to know about 'psychographic' variables, that is, any attributes relating to personality, values, attitudes, interests or lifestyles. An example of this might be 'What proportion of the target population is interested in "green politics"?' Another simple but relevant dataset might be the number of people within the target population who access information via tablets and smartphones on a regular basis. Such data might already be available, so the investigator need not try to find it by experimental methods, although the data collection method will depend on the nature of the population. This raises a point worth noting: sometimes the information needed to answer an investigator's question might *not* exist at present, so it has to be discovered some other way, such as by a survey.

The basic technique is to find documents and sources pointing towards the information being sought, and the approach most likely to succeed is one that initially identifies several documents. This is where experience can help the investigator make intuitive judgements about where to start, and when 'enough' documents have been discovered. The first document consulted might not contain what is wanted, but it could point to a much more relevant source.

A great deal of useful data is available on the web, often at no charge, so being able to use search engines (Google, Bing, etc.) and directories (Yahoo, and specialist subject guides such as those maintained by Library and Archives Canada at www.bac-lac.gc.ca/eng/Pages/home.aspx) is a necessary skill. Experience also teaches us that some apparently simple information can take a long while to find on websites, yet it can be retrieved very quickly with a simple telephone call or e-mail. The postal address of an organization, for example, may not appear on its website, but the phone number or an e-mail address usually does.

Libraries are the traditional base for desk research, and there is still much that can be found in libraries and not elsewhere, or at least not so easily. Although many Western countries have moved national data sources to electronic formats on the web, many local sources are still only accessible in print, so the local library or local government offices are the most likely sources. Another benefit of a local library is that most services are provided at no charge, although some libraries do charge a fee for their business information service. There are, of course, other sources of business data, such as the local Chamber of Commerce or its equivalent, trade associations and retail associations.

Analysing service usage

It has already been stated that an information need may exist without necessarily being clearly articulated. Sometimes those needs are converted into an enquiry posed to a library system or database as expressions of demand, and because they have been posed formally, they can be captured and analysed.

Demand is based to some extent on expectation. Library clients have quite strongly formed impressions of what libraries can and cannot do for them. They will expect a public library to have a copy of the latest John Grisham novel, so they will demand it. They will expect a university library to hold key texts for the curriculum, so they will demand them. Staff of an engineering company will expect the corporate information service to hold relevant technical standards, and they will ask for them. What clients cannot do, however, is expect the unexpected. They will not necessarily anticipate a public library having an extensive collection of digital audiobooks, even though some do. Will they expect a university library to provide them with a mobile app so they can access the catalogue and databases on their smart phones? Maybe they would like it to be available because they have heard that some libraries provide a mobile app, but would they *expect* it? Well, they will – if not today, then tomorrow! Similarly, the engineering company's staff would not anticipate a news service such as the BBC being available, but it happens in some special libraries (and public libraries, for that matter).

The point about the unexpected is that such services may be used to a limited extent by the clients who have learned about them by diligence or accident, but they are not likely to be demanded much by the majority of potential clients. And this is a pity, because, to take the first example, it may be that there are some people who do not use the public library while they think it only contains John Grisham novels and the like. If they knew they could find audiobooks there, it just might induce them to 'visit' the library (even in a virtual sense) for the first time in many years.

There is a further flaw within use analysis. Generally speaking, information use is in response to a need that has been translated into a question asked of an information service. The snag is that not all information use has been anticipated in advance. Information is discovered accidentally while browsing, so here the counter-argument has to be put. Some people browse because they have no other option. They cannot articulate their information need to the degree that it can be put to the system as an enquiry, so they scan the web or browse through books and journals more in hope than expectation of locating information that will meet their needs.

Another weakness of analysing usage is that use can only follow provision. If a specific resource is not available or cannot be accessed, it cannot be used. Some will recall the case of an information services department in a national police force that did not expect the ordinary constable on the street to want access to an online database of legislation, so they did nothing about providing one. However, when a commercial supplier produced just such a database, police across the country spent time and effort trying to access it. Eventually the information services staff agreed to host it on an internal server. An INA should have discovered this unmet expectation of the police rather than them having to wait until the organization responded to their circumvention of internal resources.

In another example a public library manager devised a collection management policy driven solely by circulation data. If many books on gardening were borrowed, then more gardening books were bought. Because poetry books were not borrowed, no more poetry books were purchased. The method has some validity because it is based on empirical data, and it is also transparent for all to see and understand. That said, this method would also become self-fulfilling. For example, as the gardening section increases in size and quality, naturally more clients who enjoy gardening will hear the good news about the library's collection and borrow the newly purchased titles. At the same time, if the poetry collection shrinks, then obviously no one will expect to find a title they want in the collection and so use will fall even further. Another problem with this method is that 'use' is interpreted as *borrowing*, but any library user knows that use can be much more than borrowing. Poems are sometimes short enough to be read in the library without any need to borrow the book, or alternatively selected poems might be photocopied. This in-house use needs to be counted and considered alongside other use data, and there is guidance on this in ISO 11620 (International Standards Organization, 2008).

Conclusion

Some of the difficulties in analysing usage data are easy to describe but rather harder to avoid. There is a natural tendency to collect data that are cheap and easy to collect rather than data that are relevant to the discovery of information needs, met and unmet. Library systems, for example, generate enormous amounts of data at the push of a button, and websites generate no less than four logs of activity (although just because it is there is not a reason for the information manager to draw on it). Assuming that the investigator has asked for usage data pertinent to the INA, how can the analysis be conducted?

Some authors recommend the use of a simple two-dimensional matrix to analyse usage data. Matrix analysis is a useful tool, because within it a complex problem area can be broken down into its various components. The starting point is a thorough breakdown of user groups served by the library or information service. This is none too difficult in the corporate sector, where the groups might well be finance, sales and marketing, engineers, etc. The second matrix is a list of resources. It is unlikely that the groups or the list of resources will be correct initially, but iteration will make both lists more appropriate to the INA.

Usage data will be employed to plot the matches between user groups and resources. Overlaps between groups will be seen and groups merged or even split. Some 'typing' of resources may need to be refined. The key is that ultimately the groups should reflect common information needs rather than simply being taken straight from an organizational chart. As an example, marketing staff may have very similar information needs to product development staff despite working for a different manager. Another use of the matrix approach will plot subject topics on one arm and user groups on the other. The data in the cells will be the means of delivery.

The investigator could then use the simple five-step process for mapping information flows suggested by Hibberd and Evatt (2004). The first stage is an organization chart that shows current users of information and those groups who apparently do not use information provided for them. The second stage delves into non-use, perhaps by interviews, to identify the organizational goals of the target group and thus what sorts of information could be useful to the group. After a mapping of potential clients for the information service, the fourth stage ranks priorities, and the final stage converts the findings into an 'information map' that shows each department and the suggestions for their information needs.

Review of Chapter 6

There are two main benefits of using existing data in an INA. First, in many situations there is no need to collect new data using surveys, interviews or other methods described later in this book. Second, existing data reveal a great deal about the organization or community being analysed. There are numerous types of existing data; while this chapter could not be comprehensive, it has pointed to social indicators, such as census data, that can be used as a starting point for an analysis or for providing variables that can be used with data gathered by other means. Data found within the organization can be the result of transactions, such as library circulation numbers, or from the use of websites. Finally, we looked briefly at finding data in social bookmarking sites, which could open up a huge area for uncovering information needs data.

Further reading

As we have seen in this chapter, the use of existing data in an INA is complex and wide ranging, from historical records to social media. Thus further reading in this field can be equally broad and complex, but in this brief note we can but point to a handful of resources – please bear this in mind when seeking further information on the topic.

There is no obvious place to start reading about existing data for an INA. Prior to the publication of this book, probably the best starting point was Chapter 5 ('Records and Social Indicators') in Witkin and Altschuld's *Planning and Conducting Needs Assessments* (1995). This remains a useful initial reading, although now rather dated.

Shep's chapter (2005) on historical investigation in *Qualitative Research for the Information Professional: a practical handbook* treats existing data within the context of historical research, obviously the parent discipline of studies involving extant data. Shep's chapter is valuable in that it is written by a historian from an information management perspective and therefore resonates with using existing data in an INA context. There is a similar chapter ('Historical Research') in Pickard's *Research Methods in Information* (2nd edn, 2013), as well as a chapter titled 'Analysis of Existing, Externally Created Material' by Andrew Shenton (note, however, that this deals with analysing rather than collecting existing data). A more standard historical approach is available in Williams' *The Historian's Toolbox* (2003), but it is perhaps more useful for students than practitioners.

On the matter of locating and using demographic data there is no standard text on this related to INAs, so we turn to web resources. In most developed countries the relevant government statistical authority provides considerable online information. Taking Statistics New Zealand (2014) as an example, on their website at www.stats.govt.nz one can find not only census data but also research papers and documents related to survey design and data collection, data analysis and so on. In less centralized countries there will also be provincial, state and local authority demographic and census data available on the web.

Outside the government sector, many universities and training institutes offer freely available online resources. Especially helpful here are those produced by Cornell University's Community and Rural Development Institute (2014). Although exclusively US-focused, some of these resources provide a good starting point on finding, understanding and using census data. They also run an interesting series of workshops and webinars, some of which are uploaded onto the CaRDI website (see, for example, Blakely, 2009).

For a discussion of web tracking, and particularly the software aspects and criteria for selecting appropriate software, readers might want to look at Fourie and Bothma (2007). While some of the software will be superseded, their discussion of the literature and both strengths and weaknesses of web tracking remains valuable.

When we come to the newer area of social networking, social network analysis and social media analytics, we are well served in Scott's *Social Network Analysis* (2013), now in a third edition. The real advantage of Scott is that it discusses the key techniques thoroughly and in this regard is a key resource. For social media analytics we do not yet have a single text for reference; rather, there are several articles on which to draw, even though none of them is specific to the information world. Worth consulting here is Fan and Gordon (2014); although written from a business perspective, the authors 'explore how the explosion in social media necessitates the use of social media analytics, . . . explain the underlying stages of the social media analytics process, . . . describe the most common social media analytic techniques in use . . ..' (Fan and Gordon 2014, 2). With this as a starting point, one should have a basic grounding in social media analytics and begin to understand the value in INAs.

To conclude our further reading recommendations for this chapter, we offer these websites for consideration:

◆ Statistics New Zealand (2014), www.stats.govt.nz.
   United Kingdom National Statistics (2014). Publication Hub, www.statistics.gov.uk. Government statistical data are usually available from the government agency responsible for collecting them, such as Statistics New Zealand and the United Kingdom's National Statistics.
◆ Harvard University. Kennedy School. Library and Information Services (2014). *U.S. Government Information Sources*, http://guides.library.harvard.edu/hks/us_government_information. Many universities provide guides to government statistical sources. For the USA the premier resource is Harvard University's guide. This guide is detailed, comprehensive and thorough. However, the reader may not be able to connect to all the sources through this site.
◆ Search Engine Watch (2014), http://searchenginewatch.com.
   Because so much information seeking is done using search engines, some familiarity with how these applications work and what sorts of results can be expected from different search engines is invaluable. The INA investigator might log in regularly to Search Engine Watch, possibly the oldest and usually considered the most trustworthy site on the subject. This site has changed somewhat since it was first launched in 1997, yet even now it continues to provide tips about searching the web and offers a thorough analysis of the search engine industry.
◆ How Stuff Works (2014). *How Microsoft Bing Works*, http://computer.howstuffworks.com/internet/basics/microsoft-bing2.htm. The ever-reliable How Stuff Works has a section on Bing vs Google that might help the analyst choose which search engine is more likely to produce the desired results.

References

American Library Association (2000) *Standards for College Libraries*, American Library Association, Chicago, IL.

Australian Bureau of Statistics (2014) *TableBuilder*, www.abs.gov.au/websitedbs/

censushome.nsf/home/tablebuilder. [Accessed 5 November 2014.]

Baker, S. L. and Lancaster, F. W. (1991) *The Measurement and Evaluation of Library Services*, 2nd edn, Information Resources Press, Arlington, VA.

Ballard, T. H. (1989) Planning and Output Measures, *Public Libraries*, **28**, 292–4.

Blakely, R. (2009) *Understanding and Using Demographic Data*, Cornell University, Community and Rural Development Institute. PowerPoint presentation, http://cardi.cornell.edu/cals/devsoc/outreach/cardi/training/loader.cfm?csModule=security/getfile&PageID=552346. [Accessed 5 November 2014.]

Borrego, A. and Fry, J. (2012) Measuring Researchers' Use of Scholarly Information through Social Bookmarking Data: a case study of BibSonomy, *Journal of Information Science*, **38** (3), 297–308.

Cornell University. Community and Regional Development Institute (CaRDI) (2014), http://cardi.cornell.edu/. [Accessed 5 November 2014.]

COUNTER (2014) www.projectcounter.org. [Accessed 5 November 2014.]

Digital Analytics Association (2014) *The Official DAA Definition of Web Analytics*, www.digitalanalyticsassociation.org/. [Accessed 5 November 2014.]

Fan, W. and Gordon, M. (2014) Unveiling the Power of Social Media Analytics, *Communications of the ACM*, **57** (6), 74–81, http://cacm.acm.org/magazines/2014/6/175163-the-power-of-social-media-analytics/abstract. [Accessed 5 November 2014.]

Fourie, I. and Bothma, T. (2007) Information Seeking: an overview of web tracking and the criteria for tracking software, *Aslib Proceedings*, **59** (3), 264–84, http://137.215.9.22/bitstream/handle/2263/5834/Fourie_Information(2007).pdf?sequence=1. [Accessed 5 November 2014.]

Harvard University, Kennedy School, Library and Information Services (2014) *U.S. Government Information Sources*, http://guides.library.harvard.edu/hks/us_government_information. [Accessed 5 November 2014.]

Hennen, T. (2002) Great American Public Libraries: the 2002 HAPLR rankings: the eagerly awaited – if overdue – measure of the nation's public libraries, *American Libraries*, **33** (9), 64–8.

Hibberd, B. J. and Evatt, A. (2004) Mapping Information Flows: a practical guide, *Information Management Journal*, **38** (1), 58–64.

How Stuff Works (2014) *How Microsoft Bing Works*, http://computer.howstuffworks.com/internet/basics/microsoft-bing2.htm. [Accessed 5 November 2014.]

International Standards Organization (2008) ISO 11620: *Information and Documentation – Library Performance Indicators*, Geneva.

Jansen, B. J. (2009) *Understanding User-Web Interactions via Web Analytics*, Morgan & Claypool, San Rafael, CA.

Manjarrez, C. and Shoembs, K. (2011) *Who's in the Queue? A demographic analysis of public access computer users and uses in U.S. public libraries*, Institute of Museum and Library Services, Washington, DC.

Matthews, J. R. (2002) *The Bottom Line: determining and communicating the value of the special library*, Libraries Unlimited, Westport, CT.

Matthews, J. R. (2004) *Measuring for Results: the dimensions of public library effectiveness*, Libraries Unlimited, Westport, CT.

Nicholas, D. (1997) Understanding End-users. In Scammell, A. (ed.) *Handbook of Special Librarianship and Information Work*, 7th edn, Aslib, London, 113–44.

Oliver, P. (2012) *Succeeding with Your Literature Review: a handbook for students*, Open University Press, Maidenhead.

Pickard, A. J. (2013) *Research Methods in Information*, 2nd edn, Facet Publishing, London, chapter on Historical Research, 167 –77.

Powell, R. (2006) Evaluation Research: an overview, *Library Trends*, **55** (1), 102–20.

Scott, J. (2013) *Social Network Analysis*, 3rd edn, SAGE Publications, London.

Search Engine Watch (2014) http://searchenginewatch.com. [Accessed 5 November 2014.]

Shenton, A. K. (2013) Analysis of Existing, Externally Created Material. In Pickard, A. J., *Research Methods in Information*, 2nd edn, Facet Publishing, London, 251–61.

Shep, S. (2005) Historical Investigation. In Gorman, G. E. and Clayton, P. R., *Qualitative Research for the Information Professional: a practical handbook*, 2nd edn, Facet Publishing, London, 160–81.

Statistics New Zealand (2014) www.stats.govt.nz. [Accessed 5 November 2014.]

United Kingdom National Statistics (2014) Publication Hub, www.statistics.gov.uk. [Accessed 5 November 2014.]

Williams, R. C. (2003) *The Historian's Toolbox: a student's guide to the theory and craft of history*, M. E. Sharpe, Armonk, NY.

Witkin, B. R. and Altschuld, J. W. (1995) *Planning and Conducting Needs Assessments: a practical guide*, , SAGE Publications, Thousand Oaks, CA, Chapter 5, 103–27.

Zeng, D., Chen, H., Lusch, R. and Li, S.-H. (2010) Social Media Analytics and Intelligence, *IEEE Intelligent Systems*, **25** (6), 13–16, http://ieeexplore.ieee.org/stamp/stamp.jsp?tp=&arnumber=5678581. [Accessed 5 November 2014.]

Gathering data through surveys

Introduction

Chapter 5 introduced several methods for gathering data for INAs. Following that introductory chapter, Chapter 6 then began the in-depth discussion of methods by addressing the use of existing, or historical, data. Chapter 7 now continues the in-depth discussion by focusing on the survey, a quantitative data-gathering tool frequently used in INAs. Before continuing it is necessary to say that surveys are not the only source of quantitative data; numerical data can be collected from a variety of sources ranging from interviews and observations to web server log files. The survey, though, is by far the most common method for collecting quantitative data for INA.

A well designed quantitative study can produce reliable, robust, generalizable results. Chapter 5 noted that surveys can produce data for an INA to show, for example, that end-users favour one kind of information resource over another, or that clients are dissatisfied with a specific element of the information service. Another common method of collecting data for an INA, the use of structured groups, is discussed in Chapter 8; and the analysis and integration of data are covered in Chapter 9.

In this chapter the focus on surveys as a data-gathering method addresses three principal questions:

1 Most basically, what is a survey, and how do surveys fit into INA?
2 What are the planning procedures for conducting a survey?
3 How do we conduct a survey?

What is a survey?
Surveys as part of an INA project

The methods used to collect data within an INA may be simple or multi-faceted. Sometimes in an INA a survey is the only method of data gathering employed, but often a survey is used in conjunction with other research methods in a mixed methods process (introduced in Chapter 5). Thus a survey of a particular client group may be used as part of a concurrent or sequential series of data-gathering exercises that might include examining existing data (see Chapter 6) and gathering qualitative information through interviews, focus groups and other methods (see Chapter 8).

Survey results can suggest patterns in actions and behaviour (telling us what is happening), while the qualitative methods of data gathering are more appropriate for exploring why something is occurring based on the opinions and attitudes of the people involved. An investigator might conduct a survey of a representative sample of the population (defined in the section headed 'Populations and sampling'), identify patterns in the resulting data and then use qualitative data gathering with a smaller group to explore in depth why these patterns are occurring. An example of a situation in which results of a survey led to the use of a qualitative data gathering technique for further exploration is provided in Scenario 7.1.

Scenario 7.1 Researcher perceptions of the Institute for Yeti Research library facilities

---

Paul Foot, Director of the Institute for Yeti Research (IYR), wanted to know his researchers' perceptions about the quality of the library facilities as part of a budgeting exercise, so he asked the library staff to conduct a survey on the matter. One question in the survey was about noise in the building, and after the data were collected and put through a simple statistical analysis the mean showed that most researchers had no concerns about noise. However, the standard deviation was high, giving an inkling that something else was to be found in the data. On looking at the data in detail it became apparent that the majority of respondents found little problem with noise, but a small number believed it to be a major problem and made that clear with their responses (technically this is called 'bimodality'). There would be different methods open to the library for exploring this issue: one might be to hold focus groups to assess the impact of the noise problem, another would be to ask engineers to undertake acoustical tests in different parts of the library. If focus groups were held to investigate this issue further, they would have a 'closed' structure (see Chapter 8), and all the questions would concentrate on the noise issue identified in the survey.

Alternatively, a qualitative process such as focus groups may identify trends and patterns which the investigator chooses to test on a larger sample, so the results from the qualitative data are used to guide the design of a quantitative survey. A third approach is to incorporate some element of descriptive data collection into a chiefly quantitative survey by including some open questions. This approach can provide some useful additional information but generally falls short of the in-depth understanding possible in an interview or focus group. Whichever approach is used, an investigator must remain open to the possibility that additional exploration may be required once insights are gained through the different types of data gathering. However, for now the focus is on surveys.

The advantages of surveys

In an INA survey a data-collection instrument, generally (though not exclusively) a questionnaire, is designed to gather data to help the investigator understand the information needs of a particular population. The chief attraction of surveys is that they allow data to be gathered relatively efficiently from many separate, even geographically disparate, participants. Also, and unlike qualitative methods, the results of a well designed survey can be generalized beyond the participants to the wider population, which makes the survey a very useful tool for some INA projects (Witkin and Altschuld, 1995, 130).

Gorman and Clayton define quantitative research as a search for patterns and causal relationships:

> The quantitative researcher is looking for patterns in events, for normative behaviour . . . . and for causal relationships among variables. For such purposes numerical and statistical approaches tend to be the most useful.
>
> Gorman and Clayton, 2005, 10

In an INA survey the purpose of the investigation is to discover the patterns of current behaviour or preferences of a specific client group or population in relation to their information needs – or, as Creswell (2014, 157) puts it, 'to generalize from a sample to a population so that inferences can be made about some characteristic, attitude or behaviour of this population'. This focus allows for the exploration of changing priorities and practices in information use and can indicate gaps in service provision. Through collecting and analysing data from a representative sample of the population understandings emerge that could not be identified in other ways. An example of this is a study that explored the level of use of print and e-books at University College London. When all responses were analysed, a preference for electronic sources emerged, but when the data were explored in relation to various demographic factors, it became clear that there were distinct trends by age, gender and academic discipline. While the overall descriptive analysis had considerable value, the more detailed analysis of the patterns in the data allowed the library to identify where further investigation or actions were needed (Lewis, 2008).

Planning for a survey

To reiterate a point made in Chapters 4 and 5, a survey, as with any part of the INA process, begins with thorough planning, and the time required for preliminary preparation should not be underestimated. As well as planning for the survey, the investigator is likely to be working within a wider INA project framework and therefore needs to ensure that a survey fits within the timeframe allowed for the project. Chapter 4 discusses the use of a Gantt chart to plan the whole INA project, and this tool is very useful for planning and monitoring the survey in fine detail.

Unlike qualitative data gathering, during which the investigator can modify and develop the research design as the project unfolds (see Chapter 8 in the section 'Thoughts on managing qualitative data collection'), the survey designer must be very clear about what is being investigated (and what is *not* being investigated), anticipate possible behaviours and attitudes, and construct a carefully written survey instrument that will generate usable data for statistical analysis in the way that best suits the project's objectives. 'The survey design makes critical demands on the researcher that, if not carefully respected, can place the entire research effort in jeopardy' (Leedy and Ormrod, 2013, 189–90). This rigidity may sound daunting to novices, but with experience and reflection the logic and rationale behind this systematic process become evident.

The specific context of the INA will guide decision making at every stage of designing the survey. Is it a one-off survey, or is it part of a wider INA process employing a range of data-gathering techniques? Will the investigation explore just one aspect of the information needs of a particular group, or will it take a broader approach? Is this a part of a longitudinal study requiring that the same data are collected over time to enable direct comparisons and explore changes in behaviour or perceptions? The annual satisfaction survey conducted by many libraries is a good example of this last approach (University of the South Pacific, 2013); if the wording of questions changes over time, results may become difficult to compare across years. A conscious decision may be made to leave out and/or add sections to a consistent core, as is done in national population censuses (Jackson, 2011, provides a detailed analysis of this issue).

No INA exists in a vacuum. The investigator needs to be aware of what is already known about the information needs of the target population, and this will require background investigation of data sources from industry and/or media reports. A preliminary analysis of existing data can be very useful here (see Chapter 6). Looking at the target population in its wider context can provide insights: What is the nature of the community or society? How is it changing? How is information currently being delivered, communicated and used? Not all of this will be known, but some will be, and this can provide valuable jumping-off points for subsequent investigations. In addition an investigator should scan relevant published and unpublished literature from prior INA studies about the group under investigation or similar groups. These can provide insights into patterns of behaviour in the target population(s) and it is also possible to pick up ideas for questions for the survey or identify gaps that justify further exploration (Pickard, 2013, 26). Knowing what has been done in the past increases awareness of problems that were encountered in earlier studies or helps avoid the collection of the same information again. One of the authors began an INA of school librarians and discovered that a significant report had been written about four years previously that had been largely forgotten by the funding agency, but fortunately not by the school librarians. This meant that some of the data collection planned for in the original research design was no longer needed, for the data already existed.

Because surveys require a systematic, logical process, investigators will find it valuable to seek guidance and feedback from someone with experience in conducting surveys. People have more exposure to surveys now than they did in the past, and so may offer more informed criticism. Kopycinski and Sandro (2007, 16) found in 2006 that 81% of librarians who were developing surveys in academic libraries 'sought out expertise on campus for assistance with formulating and implementing the surveys' compared with only 16% in an earlier version of the survey conducted in 1995.

Populations and sampling

A key part of the planning phase is determining exactly from whom data will be collected. For example a satisfaction survey will explore the extent to which a service satisfies the expectations of its current users; a non-user survey may explore why people do not use an information service and what might entice them to use it. But who exactly are these people? The key concepts here are the population (the client group) and the sample. The population is the whole body of potential participants, and being clear about the nature and boundaries of this population makes it easier to devise an appropriate data collection method. Being a little more precise, a population is an entire group of persons, things or events having at least one trait in common: 'a population is the universe of analysis, such as individuals, social groups, organizations, or social artifacts about which a researcher makes conclusions' (Pavlichev, 2004, 834). A population could, therefore, be a collection of documents (as social artefacts) that share some characteristics and about which we wish to collect and analyse survey data. Much more typically, though, the populations investigated in an INA are identifiable groups of people, such as all first-year undergraduates in a university, or all staff of a specified organization working 10 hours a week or more. Such attributes are frequently necessary in order to stipulate who is 'in' and who is 'out'. A population can, though, be easy to conceptualize hypothetically but be much harder to reach in practice, such as all the people in one country suffering from Ebola or all divorced males between the ages of 30 and 50 with children at school, yet such populations could very well be the subjects of an INA. Even something apparently straightforward, such as identifying an ethnic target population in a city, can be problematic, as Scenario 7.2 shows.

It may be possible to invite all members of the population to participate in the survey, which is then called a census. In the case of a professional body it might be possible to persuade the secretary to send a message to the association's e-mail list inviting all members to participate, or it may even be possible to access a membership list directly and invite members to respond to the survey, though there are privacy issues with this approach. While directly targeting individuals may seem to guarantee a high response, it is important to recognize that it is almost unheard of to get a 100% response.

Scenario 7.2 Bingham City Council and the local Polish community

Caroline Patel of the Bingham City Council is investigating the local Polish community, and in particular she wants to design new outreach programmes to meet the information needs of recent Polish immigrants. The initial problem is defining who belongs to (and therefore who does not belong to) the Polish community. The term 'Polish' refers to both citizens of Poland and those who claim to have Polish ethnicity. For some other communities the defining characteristic could be language or religion.

There will be Poles who have for several generations lived in Bingham and so will define themselves as part of the Polish community, and indeed some of these people will be very prominent members of it and are not to be ignored. Of the more recent arrivals Caroline will need to understand that some immigrants who have come from parts of the world such as Germany, Lithuania and Belarus may identify themselves as ethnic Poles. This makes it very difficult to define membership of the Polish community, but for the purpose of a survey it is very important to make a decision and have a clear definition of the target population. It aids practicality because the definition makes it easier to distribute the survey, and for reasons of data analysis knowing the size of the target population is necessary for calculating the response rate. If the reader needs a precise definition of who is a member of an ethnic group, the document from the United Kingdom's Economic and Social Data Service called simply *Ethnicity: introductory user guide* (Afkhami, 2012) is a good place to start.

Realistically, in most populations it is impossible to collect data from all members, and it is usually unnecessary. Instead it is convenient to use sampling to identify the number of responses necessary for a statistically representative understanding of the whole population: 'The purpose of sampling is convenience. It has no other purpose whatsoever' (Wallace and Van Fleet, 2012, 147). There are sample size calculators available (such as the one provided by the Australian National Statistical Service, 2012) to help determine an appropriate number for a sample: in small populations the aim is to gather data from as many people as possible, whereas in very large populations a sample of several hundred may be sufficient (Bryman and Bell, 2011, 187). There are different types of sampling, too, and the choice made will be dictated by the purpose of the survey and the nature of the population. Some of the most frequently used sampling types include random sampling, in which every member of the population has an equal chance of being selected; a stratified random sample that sets target numbers for different sectors of the population; and a purposive sample, in which individuals with particular characteristics are invited to participate – but there are many more approaches available (Pickard, 2013, 61–6). This reminds us that trying to achieve a large sample size is not always the best approach, for there are times when increasing the size of the sample can reduce its representativeness (Gerring, 2012, 89). Accordingly, one might prefer a small sample of in-case observations to give stronger grounds for causal inference.

In most surveys respondents are to some extent self-selecting, because people choose whether to participate; and the investigator must attempt to minimize the resulting biases in the data. Ensuring that the sample size is large enough is a key element in this. However, this is not always possible, and the investigator may need to acknowledge the bias. Penner (2009) illustrates this clearly by describing a survey of the information needs of students in the International Baptist Theological Seminary in Prague, Czech Republic. Here the population was small, so all 63 students were sent the survey as an e-mail attachment, and 48 (76.2%) completed surveys were returned. Although this is a high response rate, Pinner acknowledged the inherent bias in the results: 'those actively involved with the library, who were interested in and appreciative of its resources, were the first to respond and so added a bias toward a more positive evaluation' (Penner, 2009, 53).

Data collection

Once the population and sampling frame are defined it becomes easier to decide how best to gather data from the sample. Often in INA research the aim is to explore the needs of a specific group of people, so the investigator must choose the most appropriate survey format for that group. Factors influencing the decision about format include the amount of time available to conduct a survey, to what extent the answers require the participants to take their time and consider alternatives carefully, the level of trust between the information service provider and the participants, the need for anonymity or confidentiality in answers, and the general characteristics of the population. For example a verbal survey may be most appropriate to collect 'satisfaction' data from people who are using an information service on a particular day. A printed survey dropped into letterboxes throughout a neighbourhood may be the best way to collect data from both users and non-users of a community service. However, an online survey (or e-survey) may be more convenient to distribute if the aim is to explore the needs of people who use online communication routinely. A 2006 survey of 133 academic and research libraries in the USA found that only 31% used paper surveys to collect data, while 48% relied on computer-based surveys of some sort (Kopycinski and Sando, 2007, 14, 28) – one can safely assume that the proportion of e-surveys has risen since then.

It is advisable to expect a low response rate to a survey regardless of what method is used for distribution. Mangione (1995, 60–1) suggests that a response rate of 85% or more to postal surveys is excellent, while below 50% is not acceptable, but Wallace and Van Fleet (2012, 187) say that a response rate over 30% of a large sample can be considered 'impressive'. Bryman (2012) reminds us that responses to online surveys are typically very low, and it is good if 50%

or more of a target group responds. Our experience confirms that response rates to surveys in the region of 30–50% are quite respectable. To offset the lower response rate the survey should be distributed to many more people than are required for a statistically significant sample. This may mean printing 500 survey forms for a public library satisfaction survey in order to obtain 200 usable responses, or sending an e-mail invitation to participate in an online survey to an e-mail list with 3000 subscribers in order to receive something less than a thousand responses. Increasing the response rate can be done by offering inducements; in their 2006 survey of US academic and research libraries Kopycinski and Sandro (2007, 14) found that 54% had offered inducements to participate in user surveys. Even the time of day or week the survey is distributed may influence the response rate. For example an online survey invitation e-mailed throughout an organization at 0930 on the Tuesday after a bank holiday weekend is likely to achieve a higher response rate than one sent mid-afternoon on a Friday.

Sometimes investigators deliberately remove themselves from data collection, while at other times there is simply a pragmatic need to be involved to get the job done. As an example, problems may be caused by breakdowns in communication between the investigator and people collecting the data through telephone or face-to-face surveys. An example of this occurred in a client satisfaction survey conducted by a large public library system, for which data collection was delegated to the staff of each branch library with the instruction, 'invite a representative sample of your users to complete the survey. Aim to gather data from people of a range of ages, ethnicities, genders, etc.' Staff of one branch approached what they considered to be a representative sample of people entering the building but were highly selective and collected only 30 responses over a week, whereas the other branches each gathered 400 or more. Thirty was too few for the investigator to undertake statistical analysis with any confidence, and so it was not possible to compare trends among all the branch libraries. This could have been avoided by using a robust sampling framework, adequately training the staff who were undertaking the data collection and monitoring progress.

Chapter 5 introduced the ethical principles to follow in an INA. A key element in the ethics of data collection is the matter of identifiability of participants. Survey responses may be anonymous (the identity of individual respondents is never known to the investigator) or confidential (only the investigator knows who participated), or may lack these safeguards. If the respondents' identities are known to the investigator, this may inhibit potential participants from providing full or honest answers to some questions, particularly if the investigator works in the organization conducting the survey. There are several ways to avoid such problems, although not all will be possible or necessary. Examples include setting up the data collection methods to ensure anonymity of responses, for example having respondents place paper surveys in a sealed box. Online survey tools commonly allow for responses to be collected without the respondents' identities being visible, thus providing them with anonymity. As noted above, an external person may be hired to conduct verbal surveys or to enter data into a spreadsheet from written forms, with part of the job being to remove identifiable information such as contact details from the responses.

In some cases, of course, collecting contact details of participants is a key element of the study, but in other situations it is neither necessary nor desirable. Knowing who has and has not completed the survey allows for targeted follow-ups which are likely to increase the response rate, though this is rarely going to add more than 10% to the original number of responses.

Designing a survey questionnaire

Unlike qualitative research (discussed in Chapter 8), in which open questions form the starting point for a conversation designed to elicit rich, in-depth understanding, survey questions need to be very precise and unambiguous. Except when the survey is conducted verbally, there is no opportunity for the participant to seek clarification of a question's meaning or the differences between options provided for the answer. Consequently, careful design and testing of the questions is important before distributing the actual survey. This process tests whether the questions are unambiguous and will elicit the expected responses; it also explores whether the wording of individual questions allows for the most useful statistical analysis of the data and is an opportunity to check that the survey meets the needs of the overall INA process. It can take several drafts before the survey instrument reaches an acceptable format.

Question design is a very precise process. Typically most or all questions in a survey are phrased in a manner that allows for a choice of responses to be made from a pre-arranged list of possibilities. Question types vary: they can include yes/no statements, choice of options, ranking or weighting options, and questions that ask for a response on a predetermined scale. In addition many surveys include open-ended questions to which participants can provide free-text answers. The inclusion of these open-ended questions can result in useful insights, although not everyone provides unambiguous, full or carefully considered answers, and the survey should not be turned into a written interview. The information sought may be better explored using a different, qualitative data collection approach (Pickard, 2013, 219). However, if the investigator is conducting the survey face to face or via the telephone, it is possible to build a significant open-ended element into the survey design and engage the respondent in discussion to gain a more in-depth understanding of the answer.

It will help understand the situation being investigated if the data are analysed to see whether patterns emerge when the answers to two or more questions are combined or compared. The survey designer or investigator must therefore be clear what he or she intends to do with the data prior to the survey instrument being written and tested. The underlying purpose of the analysis should help determine what attributes (sometimes called variables) on which to collect data. It might be important to test for a variation in responses to specific questions by demographic factors (gender, age, qualification level, etc.). Is it useful to know whether people who rated one service highly also felt the same about another service? This is the starting point for deciding what to ask and how to phrase the questions. It can be tempting to ask a wide range of questions, but longer surveys may result in a lower response rate, so the process of choosing what to include is critical.

It is easy to assume that writing the questions for a survey is simple, yet harsh experience teaches us that it is not. It often takes many drafts to get even the instructions clear and unambiguous, and the questions may take even longer. Always keep it in mind that in many an INA this is the one chance for collecting data, and if the wording in the survey is not quite right, it will not collect the data needed to identify information needs.

Common mistakes in the wording of survey questions include:

◆ using jargon: 'How often do you use the OPAC?' (what's that?)
◆ using ambiguous time periods: 'Are you a regular user of the legal information service?' (what does 'regular' actually mean?)
◆ asking two questions at once: 'Were the information literacy classes enjoyable and useful? (well, they might have been enjoyable but not useful!)
◆ asking loaded questions, common enough when the question writer feels strongly about an issue: 'Do you think it fair that you should pay to borrow books when you are already paying for the library through your taxes?' (of course it isn't fair!)

It is usually possible to identify poorly worded questions, but a failing much harder to detect is simply not asking the *right* questions that collect the sort of data needed to satisfy the objectives of the INA. If, for example, the survey questions focus only on the actual use of information resources (behavioural data), it could be realized too late that not enough data were gathered on other important issues, such as the ease of access to the resources.

We strongly recommend – if not insist on – a pilot process to test the survey instrument. This is not very time-consuming, and it can result in a huge return on investment. Simply ask a few volunteers (even two may suffice) to complete the survey just as a participant would. The volunteers are given all the documentation and asked to proceed. In our experience such pilots are best done with the investigator present to discuss issues with the volunteers. They may point out that a word is a little ambiguous, or that the instructions for completing a question are unclear. Don't argue, just listen, and then rewrite the survey instrument to make it clear and unambiguous. As an extra incentive, conducting a pilot is one way of increasing the validity of the survey instrument (Leedy and Ormrod, 2013, 199).

The variety of data types

Not all data are created equal. There are different types of data, and the extent of the statistical analysis that can be done on each type of data varies. There are guides available to help clarify what types of statistical tests can be used on different types of data; for example, Vaughan (2001, 158) identifies how to go about exploring association or difference between variables of different types. An understanding of the different types of data (nominal, ordinal, interval and ratio) that specific questions will generate, and what statistical tests can and cannot be done with each, can make data analysis much more successful. A brief overview is given here, but it is important to consult quantitative research texts for greater detail on analysing the different types of data (see the 'Further reading' section at the end of this chapter).

Nominal data (data divided into categories) are the simplest type. Common examples are gender, neighbourhood, education level and so on. One can count how many people are in each group, calculate percentages and look at whether there is any statistical difference between how members of each of these categories answer other questions by using a test like Chi-square (Vaughan, 2001, 75–91). A library collects nominal data when bibliographic records are analysed to see how many books and DVDs are in the entire collection, and the same data can be used when circulation records (also nominal data) are examined to see how many items are borrowed each week. The number of books being borrowed as a percentage of the total collection of books is one example of how two sets of data can be used to calculate more data of potential use in a needs analysis. There are standards and guidelines for libraries that suggest collecting just this sort of data: for example, the Association of College & Research Libraries (2011) suggests a range of benchmarking templates that focus on expenditures, such as 'total library resources expenditures per faculty', and on reference activities such as the 'ratio of reference transaction to student enrollment (full- and/or part-time)'. As a word of caution, Brooks-Kieffer (2010, 7) says that these sorts of data will 'offer libraries little in the way of actionable information'. This suggests that the investigator must have a clear understanding of how to use these types of data if they are to be worth collecting.

Ordinal data ask participants to place items in order, for example, what service they use most or least, or how they feel about an item on a scale of, say, 1–5 (a Likert-type scale). These data have an order, but there is no way of measuring whether the distances between the points on the scale are the same. For example, if some respondents claim that they read mostly historical fiction, some romantic fiction and a little bit of science fiction, this gives a ranking of 1,2,3; but it does not provide any way of knowing that, in the last year, they read 20 historical fiction books, five romantic fiction and two science fiction (that would be ratio data, described below). There is an ongoing debate about whether scales should have a mid-point: an even number of choices does not have a mid-point, and the respondent is forced to come down on one side of the fence – there is more on this in Leedy and Ormrod (2013, 193).

Interval data are very similar to ordinal data: there is still a distinct order, but we know that the intervals between the different categories are the same. There is no absolute zero, however; the most common examples are time and temperature. More robust statistical calculations can be performed on this type of data because the difference between the categories is certain. Many researchers in the social sciences argue that Likert-type scales can be analysed as interval rather than ordinal data. It can be very convenient to be able to calculate the mean (average) of a Likert-type scale and report that to give a sense of the shape of the data, and it is often used this way in market research, although the most commonly held belief is that this approach is inappropriate (Gob, McCollin and Ramalhoto, 2007).

The fourth type of data is ratio data, which has an absolute zero and evenly spaced elements. Ratio data can be used to collect and represent data on ages, income, frequency of activities (e.g. how many times per week does the respondent use a smartphone to access an information service), and also additional data that can be used in an INA. The investigator can calculate the mean (average) and run a wide range of statistical tests on the gathered data (Vaughan, 2001, 4).

Scenario 7.3 provides an example of when the design of a survey question will result in a data type that is not suited to the desired statistical calculation. However, the scenario also shows that the resulting data might still be of value.

Scenario 7.3 Information use in Stubbs, Short & Broad

A consultant-investigator is reviewing staff information use in Stubbs, Short & Broad, a medium-sized architectural firm. Using a survey, the investigator collects data on how frequently staff use Google Search to find what they think they need. A question in the survey instrument requires a response on a scale of 'Several times a day – Once a day – Several times a week – Once a week – Less than once a week'. The investigator decides to count the number of responses to each point on the scale, then to weight them so that 'several times a day' is multiplied by 5, 'daily' is multiplied by 4, and so on. This gives the investigator what he believes to be the average (or mean) frequency for Google use. By comparing the average response from staff in different parts of the company, such as marketing, HR and legal, the investigator hopes to develop a feel for differences in how often staff think they need instant search results.

Unfortunately, the data gathered by the scale described earlier are not suited to calculating an average. It is ordinal data in which the 'distance' between the points on the scale is not even. If the investigator had planned to use the data this way, it might have been better for him to design a scale using interval data in which each point on the scale is equal to the others, though even that would not be acceptable to some. The data gathered can still be used, however, for they can be used to make a useful pie chart for the final report. The investigator may even find some unusual results in the data that can be highlighted just as they are, with no need for further calculation. One possibility is that the data might be 'bimodal' – that is, there are two different peaks, for example, a high number of responses to 'several times a day', much lower numbers for 'daily' and 'several times a week', but then another peak for 'once a week'. A column chart would display these data very well.

Conducting a survey

Discussion of the planning process has defined the problem being investigated and identified the research population and sample. It has identified the most appropriate method of distributing the survey to gather the required data and has created a survey instrument (questionnaire) that asks unambiguous questions phrased in ways that gather the most useful data for the investigation. The investigator now needs to gain approval for the plan from whatever bodies are involved (the INA team, organizational ethics committees, etc.), and then the plan can be implemented.

A survey typically begins with a cover page of information, which explains the purpose of the investigation, identifies the ethical conditions and provides contact details for the investigator and possibly for the person who has authorized the project (Connaway and Powell, 2010). If the survey is not anonymous, there will be information explaining the participants' rights to withdraw from the process before a given date, and a second section in which the participant includes his or her signature to indicate that informed consent has been given.

The layout of the survey is important, regardless of the format used to distribute it. Plenty of white space, clear page layout and easy-to-follow instructions all make it easier for the participants. Spelling, grammar and punctuation must be perfect, and there should be no ambiguous or confusing jargon either in the instructions or in the questions. These aspects should all have been tested and refined during the pilot.

Online survey software has become the most popular way of distributing surveys in many contexts, but they are not suitable for all INA populations, and they generally result in a low response rate. To get around this many researchers will offer the survey in more than one format (often called a 'multimode' design) to cater for the different preferences of the target population. For example those exploring the information needs of a public library's clients will need to provide suitable formats for people of all ages and levels of computer literacy (Hayslett and Wildemuth, 2004, 74). Some will respond to an online survey, but if it is known who has not responded after a set period of time, they could be sent a questionnaire by post or be contacted by telephone. The removal of barriers to participation is important to help ensure that the response rate will be acceptable and that all target groups have been reached. And often it is quite simple to remove such a barrier; it is easier, for example, to click through from a link in an e-mail message than it is to type a URL from a printed source into a web browser (Millar and Dillman, 2011).

Inducements (a reward for participants, the opportunity to enter a prize draw and so on), are often used to increase participation rates (see also Chapter 5 on the ethical aspects of incentives). Of course, the effectiveness of this depends on the group being surveyed. Knepp, White and McCormack (2011, 20) describe how the announcement of a 'restricted number of prizes greatly increased the number of participants and created a sense of urgency among respondents' in a survey of information needs in the US Agency for International Development. Bear in mind, however, that ways must be found to avoid one person making multiple entries and that data gathered may include some misleading responses from respondents whose only motivation is to gain entry to the prize draw.

There are many different online survey software products available, such as SurveyMonkey (2014), available free for small surveys or at several subscription rates for more complex or ongoing surveys. Different levels of functionality and security are available, but they all perform fundamentally the same purpose. Online survey software collects answers to a full range of question types and typically divides the survey into different pages that give the respondent a sense of progression through the survey, as well as the ability to move back and forth in the questionnaire. Online surveys can include branching logic, in which subsequent questions are revealed or hidden depending on the answers given to key questions, though this function must be used with care because an error in planning may result in useful data not being collected. The main advantage of online surveys is that data are immediately and automatically entered into a spreadsheet. Many online survey packages support sophisticated analysis and graphing, or the raw data can be exported and manipulated in other software applications. Nonetheless, the raw data need to be carefully managed to ensure that they remain secure.

Printed surveys may be distributed in various ways. They can be sent by 'snail' mail, handed out to people in a particular location (such as the entrance to a museum), left on a convenient counter or posted online to be printed for completion and return by the respondent. Reply-paid envelopes should be attached to printed questionnaires, or a sealed box provided in which completed forms can be deposited. Typically there is a low response rate for printed surveys, and this compounds the high cost of running them, because a large number need to be printed and distributed to gain an acceptable response rate. When printed surveys are returned, the data they contain need to be entered carefully into a spreadsheet, which can be very labour-intensive.

Verbal surveys are typically conducted in two ways: by telephone or face to face. They take more investigator time than online or printed surveys but have a higher participation rate, because it is harder to say no to a person standing in front of you than it is to ignore a letter or e-mail. However, due to the high volume of requests many members of the public refuse to participate in telephone market research surveys. Face-to-face investigators have different challenges. The investigator must attract the attention of potential interviewees and persuade them to invest a few minutes of their time. Consequently, this approach may be more appropriate for shorter surveys. When undertaking verbal face-to-face surveys, some researchers enter responses onto paper forms, while others use hand-held devices such as tablets to capture the answers directly into an online system. Telephone surveyors typically enter responses directly online, and some computer-assisted telephone interviewing systems make this very easy to do (Calvert and Pope, 2005, 140), which is a significant advantage of this data collection method.

When there is neither time nor capability to conduct a survey, there is the alternative of contracting it out. Survey companies offer trained staff with knowledge of the complex problems that can arise in the conduct of surveys, and some of whom may be able to travel to remote locations. Also, they can bring objectivity and a fresh viewpoint. One of the major advantages of contracting out is simply that the job is (or should be) completed on time, while the investigator works on other matters. There is cost involved, of course, though perhaps a bigger challenge is writing clear objectives for the survey and ensuring the work is done to a required standard and on time. This topic is seldom addressed in the literature, and one of the few sources with thorough attention to contracting out a survey is *A Guide to Good Survey Design* (2nd edn) from the New Zealand Department of Statistics (1995). It deals with preparing survey specifications, what the tender should contain and evaluating tenders, but due to its age does not cover the contracting out of online surveys.

Preparing for data analysis

This chapter has described the process of quantitative data collection. The crucial stage of data analysis is described in Chapter 9, and a reader interested only in quantifiable data could go on to that chapter now. The stages of data collection and data analysis must be treated as intertwined. Data collection should not be started until the investigator has a very clear idea of what sorts of data are likely to be gathered and that they can be subjected to meaningful analysis. It helps to know in advance what sorts of data will be produced (nominal, ordinal, interval or ratio), because there are statistical tests for each kind of data (see, for example, Vaughan, 2001) which should be known before the data collection phase commences.

Preparation for the analysis can start well before the data are collected. Preparing and (possibly) cleaning the collected data will take some time, and there is always the need to record what is being done, both for reporting purposes and in case something unexpected arises. Think ahead about where and how the actual data will be stored: this has both privacy and security implications. Plan for how the data will be coded. Quantitative data collection and analysis has a feel of 'the domino effect' about it when all goes well. If the initial stages are thought out thoroughly, then all subsequent stages seem to fall into place just like one domino falling on the next in line.

Review of Chapter 7

This chapter explores the use of quantitative data collection and analysis methods appropriate to an INA, especially the most commonly used method of surveys. The key point made early in the chapter is that using surveys is a robust and commonly employed means of collecting large amounts of quantitative data relatively quickly and painlessly for use in an INA. The type of data collected by a survey is useful for an analysis needing behavioural data, but the data are not so useful for one that needs to interpret less quantifiable issues such emotional responses to situations. The point is made that surveys can be used in conjunction with other data collection methods, such as focus groups, before, concurrently with, or after the other methods. Key issues for survey management such as identifying the population, developing the survey instrument with clear and unambiguous questions, and then determining the best way to distribute the survey to its intended recipients are all dealt with. The reader is alerted to the need to prepare in advance for the data analysis phase by thinking ahead about the questions to ask and what types of data they will produce.

Further reading

Remember to look at 'Further reading' in Chapter 9 for additional materials relevant to surveys. Survey methodology is covered most thoroughly in almost any standard text on quantitative research methods. Probably the most thorough of these, and one that makes excellent use of online adjuncts to the text, is Alan Bryman's *Social Research Methods* (4th edn, 2012). Less daunting but still thorough resources include *Practical Research: planning and design* by Leedy and Ormrod (10th edn, 2013), *Research Design: qualitative, quantitative and mixed methods* by Creswell (4th edn, 2014), and especially Keith Punch's *Introduction to Social Research: quantitative & qualitative approaches* (3rd edn, 2014). We say 'especially' because those chapters devoted specifically to quantitative methods (4, 10–12) are models of clarity and lucidity, making this work accessible to virtually anyone involved in INA projects. Like Bryman, Punch has a companion website. A useful, up-to-date text specifically for researchers in information contexts is Pickard's *Research Methods in Information* (2nd edn, 2013), which is particularly accessible with regard to survey design. And of course the standard work for many years within the information professions has been Powell's (now Connaway and Powell, 5th edn, 2010) *Basic Research Methods for Librarians;* it is still worth consulting on matters related to survey-based data gathering.

Beyond the standard texts there are also several more focused works worth consulting in the context of INA surveys. Most crucial is the need to create the best possible survey for the particular investigation being undertaken, and here the most helpful guide is undoubtedly Alreck and Settle's *The Survey Research Handbook* (3rd edn, 2004), which contains everything one might need to know about designing and using surveys. Perhaps less thorough, but more than adequate and with the advantage of discussing such statistical packages as SPSS and ATLAS.ti, *Designing and Doing Survey Research* by Lesley Andres (2012) is commended for its clarity and directness.

Then, when it comes to using statistical techniques to analyse survey data in an information context, perhaps the most useful guide is *Statistical Methods for the Information Professional: a practical, painless approach to understanding, using and interpreting statistics* by Liwen Vaughan (2001), which provides clear examples and explanations to guide decision making in the design of survey questions and the subsequent analysis of data. Those who are new to survey research will find it useful to study several such texts. In addition, Jason Osborne's *Best Practices in Data Cleaning* (2013) tackles an issue that we have only mentioned – the need to examine and clean data to decrease the likelihood of error in data analysis. We recommend that this be consulted early in the survey development process to help counter the desire to jump from data collection directly to data analysis without pausing to clean the collected data.

Finally, we wish to point to five online resources of value for their information on topics covered in this chapter.

◆ Excel Easy (2014) *T-Test*, www.excel-easy.com/examples/t-test.html.
   The Microsoft Excel spreadsheet is used widely and, although not as powerful as dedicated statistical packages such as SPSS, is perfectly adequate for many basic statistical tests. There are several Excel tutorials online, but we believe this site is one of the better ones. Look at the simple guide to the *t*-test as an example.
◆ Leland, E. (2011) *A Few Good Online Survey Tools*,
   www.idealware.org/articles/fgt_online_surveys.php.

◆ Mora, M. (2013) *Three Popular Online Survey Tools – what they give for free*,
www.relevantinsights.com/free-online-survey-tools.
For investigators wishing to conduct an online needs analysis survey the choice
of which survey tool to use is critical. There are many guides to online survey
tools on the web. Leland's review (on the IdealWare site) is good but becoming
dated; Mora's piece is newer and focuses on three well-known free online
survey tools, including SurveyMonkey, which we recommend for a simple INA.

◆ Pew Research Center (2014). Questionnaire Design,
www.people-press.org/methodology/questionnaire-design.
Most readers will be familiar with Pew Research, the authors of many
influential reports on American society. We have highlighted the section on
questionnaire design because it is a crucial element in a quantitative needs
analysis, but we could have also pointed to the sections on sampling and the
different methods for collecting data. It is interesting to note that Pew
Research regards much of this as more a science than an art, and the results
of its own work are evidence that they get it right almost all the time.

◆ Stat Trek: Teach Yourself Statistics (2014), http://stattrek.com.
This is a very full site that can be used in conjunction with this chapter and
also Chapter 9. It is an excellent site for statistical tables needed, for
example, when checking to determine whether the results of statistics tests
are significant. For the present chapter the section on sampling is relevant.

References

Afkhami, R. (2012) *Ethnicity: introductory user guide*, Economic and Social Data Service,
London.

Alreck, P. L. and Settle, R. B. (2004) *The Survey Research Handbook*, 3rd edn, McGraw-
Hill/Irwin Series in Marketing, McGraw-Hill/Irwin, Boston, MA.

Andres, L. (2012) *Designing and Doing Survey Research*, SAGE Publications, Thousand
Oaks, CA.

Association of College and Research Libraries (2011) *Standards for Libraries in Higher
Education*,
www.ala.org/acrl/standards/standardslibraries. [Accessed 10 November 2014.]

Australian National Statistical Service (2012) *Sample Size Calculator*,
www.nss.gov.au/nss/home.nsf/NSS/0A4A642C712719DCCA2571AB00243DC6?
opendocument. [Accessed 10 November 2014.]

Brooks-Kieffer, J. (2010) Yielding to Persuasion: library data's hazardous surfaces. In
Orcutt, D. (ed.), *Library Data: empowering practice and persuasion*, ABC-CLIO/Libraries

Unlimited, Santa Barbara, CA.

Bryman, A. (2012) *Social Research Methods,* 4th edn, Oxford University Press, Oxford. Companion website http://global.oup.com/uk/orc/sociology/brymansrm4e. [Accessed 8 November 2014.]

Bryman, A. and Bell, E. (2011) *Business Research Methods,* 3rd edn, Oxford University Press, Oxford.

Calvert, P. and Pope, A. (2005) Telephone Survey Research for Library Managers. *Library Management,* **26** (3), 139–51.

Connaway, L. S. and Powell, R. R. (2010) *Basic Research Methods for Librarians,* 5th edn, ABC-CLIO/Libraries Unlimited, Santa Barbara, CA.

Creswell, J. W. (2014) *Research Design: qualitative, quantitative and mixed methods approaches,* 4th edn, SAGE Publications, Thousand Oaks, CA.

Excel Easy (2014) *T*-Test, www.excel-easy.com/examples/t-test.html. [Accessed 8 November 2014.]

Gerring, J. (2012) *Social Science Methodology: a united framework,* 2nd edn, Cambridge University Press, Cambridge.

Gob, R., McCollin, C. and Ramalhoto, M. F. (2007) Ordinal Methodology in the Analysis of Likert Scales, *Quality & Quantity,* **41** (5), 601–26.

Gorman, G. E. and Clayton, P. R. (2005) *Qualitative Research for the Information Professional: a practical handbook,* 2nd edn, Facet Publishing, London.

Hayslett, M. M. and Wildemuth, B. M. (2004) Pixels or Pencils? The Relative Effectiveness of Web-based versus Paper Surveys, *Library & Information Science Research,* **26** (1), 73–93.

Jackson, N. M. (2011) *Questionnaire Design Issues in Longitudinal and Repeated Cross-sectional Surveys,* Duke University, Durham, NC, dism.ssri.duke.edu/pdfs/ Full%20report%20final%203-7-12.pdf. [Accessed 10 November 2014.]

Knepp, A., White, K. and McCormack, F. (2011) Leveraging a Needs Assessment to Enhance Service, *Information Outlook,* **15** (7) 19–21, 36.

Kopycinski, D. and Sandro, K. (2007) *User Surveys in College Libraries,* Association of College and Research Libraries, Chicago, IL.

Leedy, P. D. and Ormrod, J. E. (2013) *Practical Research: planning and design,* 10th edn, Pearson, Boston, MA.

Leland, E. (2011) *A Few Good Online Survey Tools,* www.idealware.org/articles/ fgt_online_surveys.php. [Accessed 10 November 2014.]

Lewis, S. (2008) E-book Discovery and Use Behaviour Is Complex, *Evidence Based Library & Information Practice,* **3** (2), 38–41.

Mangione, T. W. (1995) *Mail Surveys: improving the quality,* SAGE Publications, Thousand Oaks, CA.

Millar, M. M. and Dillman, D. A. (2011) Improving Response to Web and Mixed-mode Surveys, *Public Opinion Quarterly*, **75** (2), 249–69.

Mora, M. (2013) *Three Popular Online Survey Tools – what they give for free*, www.relevantinsights.com/free-online-survey-tools. [Accessed 10 November 2014.]

New Zealand. Department of Statistics (1995) *A Guide to Good Survey Design*, 2nd edn, Wellington, www.stats.govt.nz/methods/survey-design-data-collection/guide-to-good-survey-design-2nd-edition.aspx.

Osborne, J. W. (2013) *Best Practices in Data Cleaning: a complete guide to everything you need to do before and after collecting your data*, SAGE Publications, Thousand Oaks, CA.

Pavlichev, A. (2004) Population. In Lewis-Beck, M. S., Bryman, A. and Liao, T. F. (eds), *The SAGE Encyclopedia of Social Science Research Methods. Volume 2*, SAGE Publications, Thousand Oaks, CA, 835–6.

Penner, K. (2009) Information Needs and Behaviours of Theology Students at the International Baptist Theological Seminary, *Theological Librarianship*, **2** (2), 51–80.

Pew Research Center (2014) *Questionnaire Design*, www.people-press.org/methodology/questionnaire-design. [Accessed 10 November 2014.]

Pickard, A. J. (2013) *Research Methods in Information*, 2nd edn, Facet Publishing, London.

Punch, K. F. (2014) *Introduction to Social Research: quantitative & qualitative approaches*, 3rd edn, SAGE Publications, London. Companion website www.uk.sagepub.com/punch3e/main.htm. [Accessed 10 November 2014.]

Stat Trek (2014) *Teach Yourself Statistics*, http://stattrek.com. [Accessed 10 November 2014.]

SurveyMonkey (2014) *Create Surveys, Get Answers*, www.surveymonkey.com. [Accessed 10 November 2014.]

University of the South Pacific. USP Library Survey Team (2013) *The University of the South Pacific Regional (Campus) Libraries User Satisfaction Survey Findings and Analysis*, University of the South Pacific Library, Suva.

Vaughan, L. (2001) *Statistical Methods for the Information Professional: a practical, painless approach to understanding, using and interpreting statistics*, ASIST Monograph Series, Information Today for the American Society for Information Science and Technology, Medford, NJ.

Wallace, D. P. and Van Fleet, C. (2012) *Knowledge into Action: research and evaluation in library and information science*, ABC-CLIO/Libraries Unlimited, Santa Barbara, CA.

Witkin, B. R. and Altschuld, J. W. (1995) *Planning and Conducting Needs Assessments: a practical guide*, SAGE Publications, Thousand Oaks, CA.

CHAPTER 8

Gathering data through interviews

Introduction

In Chapter 5 we provided an overview of the main methods for gathering the data required for an INA in different information management contexts. In this chapter we look specifically at the use of individuals and groups as a source of data in INAs.

The main questions driving this chapter are:

◆ What is the value of gathering data from individuals in an INA?
◆ What are the main methods of qualitative data collection?
◆ How do focus groups function?
◆ What are the uses of observation in data gathering?

We thus begin by explaining the value of using individuals and groups in INAs, and then we describe the main methods of qualitative data collection, especially the use of focus groups.

Those familiar with qualitative research will find that it is relatively easy to transfer qualitative methods they have used in research to an INA. Both are processes for enquiry that gather data from the perspectives of the subjects of the investigation (or from key individuals who interact closely with the subject group) in order to help the investigator form a better understanding of what is happening and recommend improvements to the current situation. Both assume that meaning can be found in the context of relevant events, actions and interactions, which in the academic world would place most qualitative research in the interpretive paradigm. Both assume that the best way to understand such events and actions is through close engagement with people most directly involved in those events and actions. Further, both approaches assume that we can gather rich data from those most closely involved by talking with them or actually watching them while they are involved in the events of relevance to the INA.

Some aspects of qualitative research are not present in INA: often the investigator is not looking for 'new knowledge' to present to the world, nor is there necessarily any theory building involved. Given these points, it is somewhat paradoxical that the best definition we can find for qualitative methods for INA happens to come from a research methods text (thankfully, in this definition there is no reference to theory or any of the other elements commonly associated with academic research):

> Qualitative research is a process of enquiry that draws data from the context in which events occur, in an attempt to describe these occurrences, as a means of determining the process in which events are embedded and the perspectives of those participating in the events, using induction to derive possible explanations based on observed phenomena.
>
> Gorman and Clayton, 2005, 3

Where you read 'research' simply insert 'needs analysis'. It is all in this definition: needs analysis is a process of enquiry, the process draws data from the actual context in which events occur, and the purpose is to be able to describe those events from the perspective of the subjects. Lastly, the ultimate purpose is to be able to explain those events.

This sort of investigation usually takes place *in situ*, that is, within the organization being investigated or among members (individuals or groups) of the community. There is value in this approach because the investigator draws close to the situation and so gains a better 'feel' for the context. There is often something about the physical environment, or the dynamic between people in the community, that helps us gain better understanding of what is really happening, for sometimes data collected from individuals and groups will correspond with something else we have witnessed during the investigation. Even the simplest example shows what we mean: a focus group held with scientists at a research institute produces some comments about how rarely they actually visit the library. If the focus group is conducted within the library, a glance around the physical environment might tell the investigator how dull and uninviting the place is, or how far away it is from the scientists' laboratories. Nothing else can substitute for that immediate experience.

In gathering data from individuals and groups it is the investigator who is the research agent, and it is the human subjects who provide the data. Humans, of course, are complex entities, and hence human society is almost beyond comprehension, yet in an INA the investigator must try to make sense of this complexity. In many contexts reliance on individuals or groups for gathering the necessary data, and the employment of interpretive methods to analyse the data, are necessary in order to gain the depth of understanding required to identify and understand the information needs of the target group(s). No claim can be made that the results from such data are statistically significant; value lies rather in the particular perspectives seen within the context of a specific situation, so 'particularity rather than generalizability is the hallmark of qualitative research' (Creswell, 2014, 204). Using qualitative methods to gain relevant insights improves the chances of successful outcomes when compared with the sometimes 'thin' analysis of uni-dimensional quantitative data.

Some readers will be familiar with the term 'participatory research', a method used quite widely in community health studies, and occasionally for identifying information needs (Penzhorn, 2002). In this approach the investigator works with the participants while making key decisions. Preliminary administrative arrangements are made about the where and when of meetings, but more importantly the methods of data collection will be discussed and agreed upon with those who will take part as 'subjects'. Furthermore, analysis of the data is done in conjunction with the participants, with, for example, categories for coding (see Chapter 9) developed jointly. Finally, and perhaps most crucially, explanations for the information needs that were identified in the course of the enquiry are debated and recommendations for further actions agreed upon together by investigator and participants. Penzhorn's project exploring the information needs of South African women (2002) was a Level 1 analysis, and perhaps not everyone is willing to try participatory research with people previously unknown to the investigator; but a Level 2 analysis with staff of an information service might be easier. While not advocating participatory research whole-heartedly, we believe readers should be aware of the potential of this extension of traditional qualitative methods.

Thoughts on managing qualitative data collection

In many INA projects time is a considerable constraint. An organization may only permit data collection within a fixed period, so careful planning is needed to ensure that time is spent in the most productive way. Setting times to meet senior members of the organization or community is an obvious step. Having a schedule for interviews, focus groups and observation is something most investigators will try to arrange, either by themselves or through intermediaries.

Yet experience teaches us not to become too tightly constrained by a schedule. We cannot know in advance what we do not know, so the discovery of something that could be very important to the investigation is enough reason to change the schedule. Data collection design, therefore, has to be 'emergent' (Pickard, 2013, 16) rather than very detailed. Each new stage of the investigation will possibly be redesigned afresh in response to data analysis just completed that leads to the identification of ideas and concepts that require further and deeper investigation. It is the 'further and deeper' part of that previous sentence that will resonate with all those who have done much qualitative data collection and analysis.

Creating a research protocol is also something that should be considered seriously when preparing to gather qualitative data. According to Yin (2011, 103), a research protocol consists of a stated set of topics 'that you need to cover as a line of enquiry'. The role of the protocol is not to predetermine specific questions to be asked, but rather it should 'connote a broad set of "behaviours" that should be undertaken'. Yin says that the protocol

> should contain sufficient questions, central to the topic being studied, that guide one or more lines of inquiry – for example, what evidence to seek and from what sources. The broad lines of inquiry work toward revealing the issues for the entire study. Note carefully that these questions are *yours* to answer, based on evidence (including interviews) you will gather.
>
> Yin, 2011, 103

Although Yin contends that the research protocol should be carried in the researcher's head and not on paper, it actually can be beneficial to print a research protocol for each interview. It is advisable to add to the protocol the contact details of the person to be interviewed, as well as the time and location of the meeting. The content of the protocol can then be used as a checklist during the interview to ensure the essential topic areas are covered, and the interviewee's contact details will be invaluable to an investigator who is running late or is unfamiliar with the meeting's geographic location. In some instances the research protocol should be adjusted between interviews based on the responses to questions in the previous interview. Further, the ideas embedded in the research protocol can be of use during the data analysis stage, an aspect of the protocol which is discussed in Chapter 9.

In most cases it will not be possible to talk to every person in an organization or community. It therefore becomes essential that time is used effectively by meeting with the people who will be most useful to the conduct of the INA;

these might be called the Key Informants (KIs), a term used by Witkin and Altschuld (1995, 147). KIs perform two roles. First, they know the local situation well and have the authority to share information; second, they will speak for the benefit of the people they represent (see, for example, Assessment Capacities Project, 2011). In an organization it will probably be the senior staff who are KIs; in a community it might be 'gatekeepers', such as local government officials or church leaders, who should be approached for information.

It can be worthwhile spending time within the organization simply to be visible and become a 'known presence'. This can pay dividends when individuals (not necessarily the obvious ones we think are the KIs) come forward and identify themselves as having information or opinions that they want the investigator to hear. As an example, one of the authors found, while conducting an INA in a research organization, that appearing every morning at teatime resulted in some people making themselves known to him, sometimes providing comments suggesting that what was said by senior managers was not what the rank and file thought was the case.

Interviews

The structure of an interview is most likely familiar to all readers. The nature of the interview might be very structured, with little deviation from predetermined questions, or it could flow more naturally by allowing the interviewee to go a little off-track, which the interviewer then follows with some extempore questions to elicit further thoughts on the topic. The latter is good for studying perceptions, attitudes and motivation; although Bryman and Bell (2011, 213) caution against varying the order, because it can have an impact on replies, we believe the investigator will be able to see the possibility of this occurring and take steps to avoid it.

The advantage of the interview over other forms of data collection in an INA is simply the large amount of data that can be collected in a short period of time. A completed survey questionnaire may appear to contain a large amount of data, but there may be little in the way of context or explanation in the responses. It is the rich content that is the greatest value of qualitative data collection. A focus group compared with an interview can seem efficient, for perhaps eight people are giving their opinions in the same time that one person could in an interview, but the time is being shared by all eight of them. In fact it is the interaction among participants that is a particular benefit of focus groups, something that does not occur in one-on-one interviews. Each method has its advantages, so the investigator must think carefully about which best suits the needs of the INA being conducted.

Structured interviews were used in an INA project to understand nurses' information needs (Randell et al., 2009). The resulting data were used to identify information sources used by nurses in consultations, their accounts of topics where they felt more information was needed and their accounts of their use of electronic information tools. In the interviews it was noticed that nurses sought information more for background knowledge, and because databases were designed with the expectation of searches for clinical information, the nurses were often frustrated when using them. The recommendations that followed this INA were to move from 'pull' technology, in which nurses had to make a choice to search a database, to 'push' technology, in which information was provided directly to the nurses – a good example of a Level 1 needs analysis.

Questions need not always be targeted directly at the topic, and sometimes it is more productive to encourage people to explain their thought processes. In one project on redesigning an intranet, the questions were constructed almost to *avoid* asking staff what they wanted from the intranet. In explaining how to obtain an in-depth understanding of the needs of staff and the organization for an intranet, Robertson offers this advice about interviews:

> The interviews should not focus on the intranet itself, and it's not necessary to
> cover the intranet at all during the interviews. Instead, the interviews should
> explore how staff work, what this involves day-to-day, the information they need,
> and where they currently get this from.
>
> Robertson, 2005

The explanation for this apparently contrarian interviewing is the assumption that the expectations of those being interviewed will be limited to what they have already experienced, yet an INA should go beyond the participants' limited experience; in this case the design of a new or revamped intranet will offer an innovative level of service based on actual needs. Asking questions about what information people need in order to do their jobs better will help the investigator create something new.

Preparing for an interview will be little different from designing a survey instrument. Care must be taken to ask questions that elicit useful responses. There is not always a second chance to ask questions missed or to try clarifying misunderstood questions. When time and circumstances allow, piloting interview questions on a willing guinea pig can be invaluable for improving the format of the questions. If several interviewers are involved, then time is required to train them. It is also useful to pre-code possible responses, if this is an inherent part of the data analysis. Scenario 8.1 offers an example of how interviewing might proceed in a small tertiary institution.

Scenario 8.1 Interviewing faculty at Seeds Agricultural College

Jelena Herzog was invited by the Principal of Seeds Agricultural College to evaluate the information needs of the faculty. Having assessed the situation, she decided to use interviews as her primary data collection method; it was very difficult to find enough staff on campus at any one time to organize even one focus group. She was fortunate that the communications manager was willing to arrange times for interviews and book a small meeting room for the three days Jelena would need.

Jelena sent a brief information sheet to the communications manager in advance, which helped with the recruitment process. She produced a consent form at each interview and asked the interviewee to sign it; this was especially necessary because she had decided to record the interviews in case her memory proved to be fallible. She prepared a list of questions in advance and decided to stick to it closely.

The basic information needs were already well understood, but it was the detail she needed, especially the relative importance of information needs that were somewhat unpredictable – careers advice, travel information and so on. By assessing the mood of the responses she could assess whether it was worth the college investing more funds in resources to meet these needs. She also wanted to know whether staff avoided some information sources for whatever reason, because she suspected that some staff were uncomfortable using certain search interfaces. The predictable nature of the questions made it easy to prepare codes in advance, and subsequently that helped with the initial data analysis. After three exhausting days Jelena felt the interviews had gone well, attributing this to (a) careful preparation, (b) sticking to the questions and generally avoiding distractions and (c) recording the interviews, which helped her recall a few comments she would otherwise have overlooked.

It is a matter of debate whether questions should be provided to the interviewees in advance. We tend to agree with Connaway and Powell (2010, 170) that 'this may be inadvisable . . . if the interviewer is particularly concerned about obtaining frank, spontaneous responses. Giving respondents a lot of time to consider answers is likely to reduce their candidness.' This perspective supports our opinion and experience that interviews without interviewee preparation are more likely to reveal honest responses about topics that are complex or emotionally charged. Nason (2007) expressed a different view in reporting on the information needs of farmers. She sent her interview questions in an e-mail message prior to meeting the farmers face to face so that they could prepare for her visit, and we concede that this approach may elicit better response rates from people who are very busy or feel that unprepared answers might reveal sensitive information. It has to be said, however, that these are more often than not self-important individuals who are unlikely to reveal state secrets or commercially sensitive information. A more likely situation in which questions might be provided in advance is for those uncomfortable with providing information to strangers, such as farmers.

Using an audio recorder is also contentious. There are obvious reasons to record an interview – keeping notes can be challenging while simultaneously asking the questions and listening carefully to the responses for something unexpected that might lead to fresher fields. Our human nature is such that we listen for what we expect to hear, not the reverse, so, if we are not careful, then the interviewee only confirms what we already believe. An audio recording, however, should not lie, and the investigator has the chance to hear everything that was said, including some comments that might have been overlooked during the interview itself, thus giving the chance to correct any original bias. On the other hand a recorder can be intimidating or intrusive and may distract the interviewee (even though he or she will have given permission for it to be used). You will know this is happening if the interviewee constantly looks at the recording device while talking (actually quite common in our experience), so if that is happening try to do without a recording and rely on your notes.

The assumption underlying much of the above is that an interview is conducted face to face, but there are alternatives. Telephone interviews are still commonly used in market research. Compared with a face-to-face interview, a telephone or Skype interview will require less time for both parties, is almost certainly going to be cheaper (Calvert and Pope, 2005) and can be conducted soon after an event has occurred, for example a natural disaster (Connaway and Powell, 2010, 177). Computer-mediated communication channels such as 'chat' can be used and naturally make possible interviews that would otherwise be impossible when time and distance pose insurmountable obstacles. An advantage of the 'internet interview' given by Connaway and Powell (2010, 172) is the avoidance of bias; we can communicate in this medium, but it is difficult to see the emotions of interviewees. However, this method of interviewing is only advisable when all parties feel comfortable with the medium.

Focus groups

For many decades market research companies have used focus groups as a key tool in understanding how customers think about products and services. Politicians, too, or at least their advisors, have adopted focus groups as a means of determining which way the wind is blowing, especially before an election. In addition the use of focus groups in academic research is now well established (see Gorman and Clayton, 2005). Since this method is so well established, it is worth looking at the pros and cons of focus groups for INA.

A focus group is essentially a group interview, but it does not necessarily follow a sequence of question-and-answer, as would an interview. The key element is interaction among the participants, and if the investigator takes no part in the discussion for some minutes, then the session is probably going well, not badly. Participant interaction is every bit as important as the contribution of each individual, which is why focus groups have been called 'collective conversations' (Kamberlis and Dimitriadis, 2008, 375), and it means that some attempt at capturing the nature of the interaction has to be made (Belzile and Oberg, 2012).

The success of the method lies in the fact that we are social animals. Generally if we put people around a table in a non-threatening atmosphere, within no time at all they will be talking with each other. They will say what they are thinking, but they also will listen to other participants, mull over what they are hearing and then respond. A focus group should be designed to stimulate a relaxed, free flow of associations and avoid people's innate censoring mechanisms. This design gives focus groups their strength: interaction will take participants beyond their own initial thoughts to formulate new ideas as a result of the stimulation caused by what the others present have said. Thoughts that might never have occurred to them during a one-on-one interview might come to the surface during a focus group. In this way the focus group will mimic the settings in which most people form their opinions and attitudes (Millward, 1995). The interaction and discussion can be very discursive, yet most investigators want *some* sort of specifically focused outcome to emerge, which is where the name of the method originates – a wide-ranging discussion narrows down to the focus of the investigation.

The focus group is not truly 'naturalistic' as social scientists would use the term. What we know from experience, however, is that it is not so unnatural that it deters most people from speaking openly. Interaction in a focus group is almost entirely vocal, so the data collected are verbal; although this may seem limiting, it is not really a weakness of the method. Spoken data are especially good for collecting attitudes and opinions. There is no expectation that the members of the focus group reach complete agreement. It is sufficient that we hear their opinions and that they have the opportunity to discuss them freely. Some members of the group might prefer to qualify the responses given by others or give contingent answers (Stewart, Shamdasani and Rook, 2007, 42), and this characteristic is a strength of the method. The point made earlier about the data being almost entirely verbal can be overcome if there is a video record of the session, which will make possible an analysis of body language and possibly the degree of emotional engagement when participants speak about a topic, although it should be added that video recording of focus groups is uncommon.

Focus groups might be the sole source of data, or they might be a supplementary source in a study that uses a different method (for example a survey) as its primary source. Irrespective of whether the focus group is the primary source or a secondary source of data, the practical steps taken in conducting focus groups are basically the same. Later in this chapter we will discuss the use of structured groups with other data collection methods.

Focus groups work well in most contexts. Within an organization they allow staff to discuss issues of common concern, which may seem like a repeat of 'water-cooler' or tearoom conversations, yet experience shows that in a focus group we often discover how little staff may have been able to (or felt willing to) interact before. We can witness demographic groups such as young people talking about how they look for information related to their lives. Another group, scholars, can talk (and *how* most of them can talk) about information seeking, enabling the investigator to look for patterns in the behaviours they describe. No topic is off-limits for a focus group, although people may well be reluctant to talk openly about topics most of us find inhibiting, including sexual and financial matters (not often topics of discussion in an INA). To encourage free and frank discussion and to eliminate the possible dangers that might result if a focus group member says something embarrassing about himself or others, consent forms (see Chapter 5) for focus groups usually add a condition that the conversation must not be repeated to others.

The potential for one particularly vocal person to dominate the focus group is often cited as a disadvantage of this method. One might imagine that in a focus group held within an organization the senior managers present would speak the most, and this does sometimes happen despite group members being encouraged to speak freely. In these situations other group members may feel intimidated or may moderate their input for fear of being outspoken. This is especially likely in some non-Western cultures, in populations in which minority cultures figure significantly and in organizations with a traditional pyramidal hierarchy.

If the investigator finds one person dominating the discussion, he or she then must curb that person's enthusiasm by fair means or foul – by persuasion, by imposing a rule on how long anyone can speak or by steering the discussion to topics that are of less interest to the problem person. Kahle (2007) offers some excellent ideas on how to remove dominating or disruptive people from the group. Enlisting the help of other people in the group will usually calm a situation that has the potential to become unmanageable. Along the same lines there might be a problem with timid people on one hand and 'blatherers' who talk much but actually say very little on the other. These types of situations might result in simple consensus chat filling up the allotted time, but there is no need to fear 'groupthink' emerging from a focus group. Indeed, that is almost what we *want* to hear, for 'it can be useful . . . to find out not only what a specific group thinks, but why the group thinks as it does' (Connaway and Powell, 2010, 176). This will occur if we allow general chatter and then closely observe the interactions taking place in the group.

The role of the moderator

Before the first focus group meets the investigator should be fully immersed in the project and aware of why the meeting is being held. This point is especially important if a moderator (a term used here synonymously with 'facilitator') has been engaged for the purpose. The pros and cons of using an outsider as moderator are as might be expected: it takes time for the moderator to get up to speed on the issues being investigated, and this person will most likely expect to be paid, yet such an individual can bring an unbiased perspective and some communication skills not otherwise available (Wildemuth and Jordan, 2009, 250). Brown University Library used an outsider in a project investigating customer service processes. The staff were happy with the outcome, saying that it justified the time and money that went into the project (Shoaf, 2003). This kind of result will only happen if the external moderator becomes totally familiar with the topic of the investigation both before and during the focus groups.

The session starts with a brief welcome, the provision of necessary information about break times and toilet locations, and crucially, an introduction to the subject and purpose of the meeting. Then the moderator launches the session with the first question. It is up to the moderator to know when key discussions are taking place and to recognize when something unexpected has been said that can lead the discussion into new and exciting territory – these are the moments to prize, so one really must be prepared with adequate background knowledge. The moderator can employ the standard techniques for keeping the discussion flowing: probing for more complete responses, encouraging all to participate, occasionally using the 'pregnant pause' and so on. Conversely, the moderator must not be hectoring and should avoid asking leading questions unless absolutely sure of the territory.

It is not uncommon to have two people conduct the focus group session. One takes the moderator role of moving the discussion along, while the other takes notes and acts as a general factotum. This technique is common practice among market research companies.

Types of focus group

There are clearly many purposes for focus groups, and there are different ways to conduct them, which here are put into two simple categories: the closed structure and the open structure. In the former the moderator has a set of prepared questions and will work through them, allowing for discussion but not much divergence from the central topic. In the open format the moderator allows discussion to flow freely but ensures that the discussion does not stray too far from the central topic (which is a matter for judgement). The closed format suits discussion of matters that are already fairly well understood; discussion will not change the big picture, and it is the detail we need to know. An example might be a focus group being used to help interpret some rather puzzling results found in a survey. The open format, in contrast, is for 'big sky' thinking, when the moderator allows participants to wander to some extent because it is not possible to know where things might go.

The number of groups

As mentioned earlier, one of the apparent advantages of focus groups is that they might be cheaper and quicker than organizing several individual interviews. If this is a consideration, then the investigator will wish to avoid organizing numerous focus group meetings. At the same time, however, it is desirable to hold more than one focus group lest the collected data be skewed by the dynamic within a particular set of personalities in a focus group. Sometimes just one additional group will suffice. If, however, it is necessary to split the participants by some characteristic, say gender, then the investigator is looking at two groups of men and two of women, and the economy of the method starts to decline. However, it is unusual for more than four groups to be required – the generally agreed test is that once you have heard it all before (or very nearly all), then you have held enough focus groups. This assessment sounds imprecise, but anyone who has run focus groups knows what this means in practice. One of us once made a commitment to running seven focus groups for a single project, but by the time of the fifth group there was nothing much new being added, and the last two added only a little to the investigation – although in fairness the participants were eager and played their part. In summary the investigator ought only to have as many focus group sessions as it takes to capture enough data for the needs analysis, and experience tells us that four should be enough.

Numbers in groups

The purpose of the INA can change the desirable sample of participants in the focus groups. As an example, while searching for a better way to organize information flows within an organization, the investigator might choose to ask only the 'information-rich' to a focus group, as advocated by Krueger and Casey (2015). Others will disagree and say that the selection of participants in focus groups should minimize sample bias, but this view does not strike us as sensible practice. Take the example of an investigation into the ways that architects look for information on sustainable building materials: the investigator certainly wants to include architects who have actively searched for this sort of information in the past, but will it be useful to balance this in the focus group with architects who have never looked for such information but might wish to do later? It is worth stating again that statistical significance is not an issue here.

Once the general nature of the groups is determined, typical practice is to invite 8–12 participants for broad topics, but fewer members in a group if participants will have plenty to contribute on a narrower topic (Wildemuth and Jordan, 2009, 246). It is common to over-recruit by up to 100% in some cases, although 25% is more typical (Millward, 1995). Be prepared to offer incentives – tea and coffee, of course, and chocolate biscuits, or even shopping vouchers. Market research companies often give cash as compensation for the time participants spend in focus groups. Not every project can afford this largesse, of course.

There are arguments in the literature about whether it is best to have homogeneity or heterogeneity. In INA this issue is rarely a matter that requires consideration, for nearly all situations will result in homogeneity by default. Where there might be an option, for example in an academic setting, Young (1993, 391) recommends homogenous groups, for faculty perceptions could be quite different from student views.

Location

The location of the focus group meeting sometimes chooses itself. Within an organization, for example, there may be only one or two suitable meeting rooms. When the focus group involves members of the wider community, the location must be convenient for them, with factors such as public transport and personal safety high on the list of criteria. For an INA done by or on behalf of a library the most suitable location for a focus group is within the library. Location might become an ethical issue – for example, an investigation into the information needs of people with HIV. If the call has gone out that 'we would like to talk to individuals who have HIV', then to maintain confidentiality the focus group should be held somewhere more discreet than the library.

Commonly the members of a focus group sit around a table. That is a familiar way in which we conduct normal meetings, so people feel most comfortable seated this way. Some recommend a circle of chairs (Liamputtong, 2011, 72) 'to facilitate interaction'; although the logic of this is clear, will everyone feel quite comfortable seated this way? The circle is also recommended by Hennink (2007, 162) to remove the feeling of 'dominance' created if one person sits at the head of a table, whereas in a circle everyone is equal. Scenario 8.2 offers an example of how a focus group might be conducted.

Scenario 8.2 A staff focus group in Bingham Public Library

Jelena Herzog did such a good job with the INA at Seeds Agricultural College that she was recommended to the nearby Bingham Public Library for another INA.

The needs analysis this time concerned the library's staff and the quality of their client services. Management wanted to know staff perceptions of what constituted good service before any attempt would be made to change behaviours. Jelena opted for focus groups because the 'grey' nature of the topic might best be understood if staff could interact and bounce around ideas on what each one considered good service and how they might put their ideas into practice.

Jelena organized three focus groups with six staff in each one. No managers were invited. All the meetings were held in the central library during working hours, with staff given time off to attend. Jelena had picked out some statements describing good customer service in the literature and circulated these to participants in advance of the meetings.

After the initial welcome she asked the group members what they thought about the first statement on the list, and after a slow start they began to comment. A few words to encourage more comments and simple questions for more clarification furthered the discussion. Jelena then asked for examples of when and how staff had provided this kind of service. It was here that she began to receive some very useful comments, because a few participants were prepared to say that they had not been given enough training to provide some types of service, or there was too little support from management.

When the discussion turned to supporting the library's Wi-Fi, several staff said they had received requests to help individuals choose the correct settings on their tablets when they could not connect to the internet, but these staff had no idea how to go about it. It was here Jelena started to see some results of the needs analysis. Staff clearly needed more information about mobile devices if the library wished to provide good customer service in support of its Wi-Fi and the 'bring your own device' policy it preferred.

To conclude this section we provide a brief description of the use of focus groups in an INA undertaken to evaluate the effectiveness of a health sciences library's liaison programme and to gain a better understanding of the information needs of faculty in order to design new and improved library services (a Level 1 needs analysis). The study was conducted in the College of Pharmacy at the University of Arizona in Tucson (Kramer et al., 2011). Because the liaison librarians wanted answers to a number of open-ended questions (for example, 'Are there things that frustrate you when you're searching for information?'), it was decided to use qualitative data gathering. In order to allow respondents to bounce ideas off each other, the focus group was the chosen method. Three focus groups were held in small conference rooms within the college with 6–8 participants in each 90-minute session. The discussions were recorded, and the librarians also made notes. In the focus group sessions the liaison librarians learned how faculty looked for and used information related to their work and study. Faculty told them which databases were popular and which were not, how much they relied on Google and Google Scholar, how the library's website was used (primarily to find electronic journals), how little they used the catalogue and much more. Faculty also talked about what they thought the students needed to know and how the liaison librarians were helping improve student searching skills. The INA achieved its objectives through the use of focus groups.

Observation

The most natural of all data collection methods is watching people as they go about their normal business. It is the only method that brings the investigator into direct contact with the phenomenon being studied. If done well, it has a high potential for reliability (Wallace and Van Fleet, 2012, 213). To use observation as a data collection method the investigator-as-observer takes the role of the outsider looking in, trying to eliminate bias; but this separation cannot become too distant, for the observer must be accepted by the people who are the subjects. Being liked is not necessary, but being tolerated is.

In general observation will not be approached completely cold. The observer should be familiar to some degree with what will be seen, but not so over-familiar that prejudices and assumptions are hard to overcome. The need for observers to have some prior knowledge of what they are to investigate has led one writer to use the term 'Subject Matter Experts' (McClelland, 1994, 4). As an example, the observer watches librarians at work on a typical day in a public library; this environment is familiar to the observer, who therefore recognizes routine activities and the general purpose of what is being done. What is witnessed, though, might not be all as expected, because some unusual organizational culture is influencing the behaviour of the library staff in unproductive ways, and these conventions and mores are what the investigator-as-observer will need to investigate further and in more detail (Gobo, 2008). Usually the only way to achieve this is to focus on the 'how' of a process rather than the 'why', because 'how' can be observed, but answering 'why' involves interpretation best left until more data are available for analysis (Tolich and Davidson, 1999, 128). Outsiders can see structures of a culture that are invisible to insiders, because the latter are so familiar with the structures that they have become invisible.

On the occasions that the investigator-observer is not an outsider and therefore cannot be a stranger to the setting being observed, the way to deal with the problem is to use 'estrangement techniques' to suspend familiarity with the environment and to force the investigator to see only 'sets of activities' in supposedly social facts (Gobo, 2008, 150). In this case the focus must be on task analysis while trying to put the context into the background.

Observation as a method in INA is almost always time consuming, and time is not a resource the investigator has in abundance. Observing can take days if done thoroughly; hence it is not commonly used entirely on its own. When factors restrict the use of observation in an INA, other methods should be employed instead. While trying to understand the information needs of physicians, Davies (2011, 252) found that 'time scales, financial pressures, and patient/physician confidentiality discouraged the physical observation of physicians, to determine their information needs', so online questionnaires were used instead.

The most common way to record what has been observed is simply to take notes or to keep a log. A recording device can be inhibiting to those being observed, and sometimes actually impractical or not permitted for reasons of personal privacy. Being watched can also be disconcerting, and it seems to double the discomfort if the observer takes extensive notes in the presence of the subject. While good notes are invaluable, experienced investigators learn to observe and remember, writing only brief aide memoire notes that will be expanded later as soon as time permits. Not many of us, though, will end up like Barbour (2008), writing her notes in the hospital toilet to avoid embarrassing her subjects in the ward.

The observer is looking for three different elements in the environment: social structures, talking and context. Leedy and Ormrod (2013, 184) suggest that observation should focus only on one aspect of behaviour, and behaviour is to be quantified. While this suits some academic research, it is inappropriate for all but rare INAs.

The concept of structure was referred to earlier: in an INA this will mean the underlying culture of the organization or community. Organizational cultures reveal themselves through events such as rituals (morning tea) and through common routines (weekly newsletters). These apparently mundane activities sustain the organizations and sometimes alter them. During an investigation by one of us it was discovered that most of the staff of a public library spent more time mending books than they did on the enquiry desk attending to client needs. It had become such a part of the culture for staff to sit in the workroom and mend books that they were convinced that this constituted excellent client service. Needless to say, the investigators had different opinions on this, and it became one of the most contentious points in the final report.

The reader might wonder how this sort of invisible structure can be identified, in response to which all we can say is that experienced observers know it when they see it, and a typical work culture can be understood within a couple of days. Observation of structures can be done in almost the opposite way, if necessary; that is, an individual or an 'object' within the target organization/community can be identified and then assessed by the investigator. An 'object' could be a new policy document that is observed as it follows its trajectory through the organization and its environment. 'As it passes from central government to the local authorities, from office to office, from interpretation to interpretation, from negotiation to negotiation, it undergoes numerous changes' (Gobo, 2008, 166). Keeping detailed notes during this sort of observation is obviously essential.

To observe the second element in the environment (talking) we must listen. As with other qualitative methods, listening to the words of those being observed is a potentially rich source of data. What makes observational methods rather different from interviews and focus groups is that the words are heard in context, and sometimes the association of words and actions reveals meaning in ways that would not otherwise be possible. If an analysis focuses on training needs, then 'behavioural reactions, exhibitions of frustration, congeniality between employees . . . should be documented' (McClelland, 1994, 6). Words and gestures can be very revealing; for example, during an investigation of records management practices the observer notices that, while talking with staff on the telephone, the records manager grimaces regularly and frequently mutters 'oh, not again'. The observer would see this negative behaviour and make notes about it and also about the need to investigate possible causes.

The third important element in observation is context. What the investigator might need to consider here includes the physical place and the resources within the environment in conjunction with what is said and done, for 'social practices are always situated practices, in that they take place in an organized situation comprising an array of both resources for action and constraints upon it' (Gobo, 2008, 173). It is important that the investigator understands these constraints, lest the language and actions in the observation are misinterpreted. The use of smartphones, for example, can change the ability of individuals to seek information, but depending on the setting under observation there may be more or less access to smartphones than we might assume, making it necessary to ascertain the degree of access and factor that into the analysis.

We would argue that observation of context is a very useful method for gathering data for a Level 3 INA related to the use of existing information resources within an organization. The investigator could observe the use of existing resources (in whatever format and by whatever means accessed) by staff in their specific contexts to understand their specific needs and determine whether the current resources meet their needs, and whether the resources could be used more effectively. As an example of a typical observation within an organization, one might look at Scenario 8.3.

Scenario 8.3 Observing staff productivity at Cheetham & Prosper

Her growing reputation in Bingham led to another INA contract for Jelena Herzog. This time Cheetham & Prosper, a successful law firm in the area, approached her to investigate staff productivity. The partners did not believe the staff to be lazy, but probably in need of some assistance to do their work more effectively.

Jelena noticed on her first visit that staff were in and out of the office a great deal. She was told that the company did a lot of work with rural clients, and staff visited them at their homes and places of business rather than asking them to come to the main office. The partners endorsed this because it set them apart from other law firms in the town.

Jelena talked to some of the staff about their rural work, and they agreed to allow her to accompany them on some of their visits. She noticed immediately that the staff, who seemed diligent while in the main office, became very relaxed as soon as they set off to see one of the rural clients. Words and actions told her that this was part of the culture; a trip to see a rural client was considered to be a 'cushy' afternoon out of the office. The law staff told her that they could not do much work until back in the office, because they could access neither the legal databases nor their own files. Jelena saw that this could be overcome by providing the staff with better resources. She suggested they all be given iPads, and that the firm improve the security on its networks so that databases could be safely accessed out of town. Overcoming the culture took much longer than the technology 'fix' would take, but eventually some staff could see that, by working more effectively while out of the office, they could cut the hours they spent in it, so behaviours gradually changed.

An INA observation can be a useful way of ensuring that the information service is doing what it claims (and believes) it is doing. Although observation data may initially appear to be suited to a Level 1 analysis, in fact such data are very likely to be more useful in a Level 2 analysis for the service providers who would otherwise remain ignorant of how well or badly the information service is actually being delivered.

Other qualitative methods
Diaries

INA investigators have often overlooked the use of participant diaries or journals as a possible source of qualitative data, yet diaries or journals can perform at least two tasks. They can either confirm what the investigator has already discovered or give some ideas about what has so far been missed. They have a value in that the participant can record in them events that took place while the investigator was not present. As an example, a subject records the occasions when he required information and how he searched for it. The diary will allow him to record the situation in which he realized information was needed and the steps taken to retrieve it, including both successes and failures. In a typical use of diaries for data collection the investigator could facilitate this process by preparing diaries with sections for date, location, resource used and its intended purpose. Pickard (2013, 236), however, found that some of her participants were unhappy with the formal diary structure she presented them, so after a focus group meeting held to clear the air some continued with the structured diaries, some used very informal journals and others preferred the very formal structure of a database to record their attempts at information seeking. This example is evidence of how our INA data collection processes should be open to redesign at all times.

Related to diary keeping is the relatively new concept of photovoice. Participants are encouraged to take photographs of people, places – really anything they see while thinking about their information needs. In a very simple case with which we have worked volunteers were asked to take a photograph of the 'place' where they looked for information, whether it was a library, town hall, DVD shop or any other place. They were given instructions on how to upload the resulting images to Flickr and then to invite the investigator (and only the investigator) to view the photos. Because the participants were in their teens, they found this a fun activity and not at all irksome. They used the photos as an aid when recalling the process they went through while conceptualizing what information they would need, where they would most likely find it and what to do once they started an actual search. Most found this easier than writing notes.

A rather similar needs assessment project in the USA (not specifically an INA) asked female Hispanic undergraduates to take photographs to portray major aspects of their lives and then help the researchers to understand them (Scacciaferro, Goode and Frausto, 2009). It is important to add here that the maintenance of privacy is essential both in maintaining the trust of participants and in ensuring ethical conduct during this sort of investigation.

Participants make a considerable time commitment when agreeing to keep a diary or photo stream, so if possible some sort of reward could be offered to all participants, or to a 'lucky winner' as an incentive.

Usability testing

This INA method is particularly useful in Level 3 INAs, such as those that focus on the evaluation and testing of information systems (regardless of whether they are manual or digital). It might be appropriate to test the level of comfort felt by a target population when using an existing system, or to test how well a beta version of a new system is meeting the needs of a target population. Participants can be volunteers testing a new system or current end-users evaluating an existing system. Users are asked to perform some common tasks while using the system and (generally) they 'talk' the investigator through their behaviour. They are asked to indicate when the system is working as they expect it to, as well as to indicate when they are confused, when the system has not behaved as they anticipated it would and so on. The investigator can be passive throughout the test or can engage in a dialogue with the tester; there are no obvious rules for which is better. This method is a very practical one: 'User testing is usually concerned with implementing actual change, either at the design stage or to assist in creating systems specifications for a new design: it is not usually concerned with theory development' (Pickard, 2013, 129), which makes it better suited to an INA than for research.

Review of Chapter 8

In this chapter we have examined the use of individual and group participants to gather data in INAs. Such participants (the individual subjects selected for interviews, or the groups of individuals selected for focus groups) are at the core of qualitative data-gathering methods. Qualitative methods are here set apart from quantitative methods as a process of enquiry that draws data from the context in which events occur. The INA investigator will use data collected directly from participants to help explain events from the perspective of those participating in the events. This chapter has described the use of interviews and focus groups in some detail, plus the use of observation more briefly. Each method suits different types of analysis, both in terms of the match of data collection with the context and the sorts of data collected. The importance of planning and preparation has been emphasized. We have included practical suggestions on how to conduct each type of data collection. Methods for analysing the data collected from structured groups are discussed in Chapter 9.

Further reading

In addition to comments here that are specific to Chapter 8 materials discussed at the end of Chapter 9 may also be of relevance. The analysis of qualitative data is a topic covered in most texts on research methods, so, provided the investigator can make the relatively simple conversion from generic research to INA, almost any such text will do. Among the works covering research methods of all types our preference is for Bryman, *Social Research Methods* (4th edn, 2012), because of its detail and also the online resource centre accompanying the text, as well as actual student comments on the various methods. With its focus on information managers, Pickard's *Research Methods in Information* (2nd edn, 2013) will appeal to some investigators, although it lacks the detail and user-friendliness of Bryman.

While Bryman and Pickard both cover the full range of research methods, many texts focus specifically on qualitative methods. Here a clear and well-tested leader is Corbin and Strauss' (2008) *Basics of Qualitative Research*, recommended because of its thorough treatment of data analysis, which fits very well with INA.

For interviews we have an embarrassment of riches, but perhaps the key resource here is Gubriam et al. (2012), *The SAGE Handbook of Interview Research* (2nd edn), because it 'emphasises the dynamic, interactional, and reflexive dimensions of the research interview' (Gubriam et al., 2012, ix). That is, this collection of discussions on all aspects of interviewing sees the procedures in their evolving, more flexible dimensions more than most other guides to interviews, which in our view reflects the reality of interviewing for INA projects. Coverage is comprehensive, with 38 chapters by recognized experts covering context, methods, logistics, the self in interviews, analysis and ethics. There is little need to go beyond this work when seeking guidance on interviewing.

One of our favourite books on focus groups is the very informative, stylish and highly accessible *Focus Groups* by Krueger and Casey, now in a fifth edition (2014). This work offers a great deal of practical advice on all aspects of focus groups from a team widely experienced in this method. There is much practical advice in Greenbaum's *Moderating Focus Groups* (2000) and in Liamputtong's thorough text, *Focus Group Methodology* (2011). For a book specific to information management, we suggest the older but still useful *Focus Groups for Libraries and Librarians* by Beryl Glitz (1998).

On the matter of observation we are fortunate to have Gobo's *Doing Ethnography* (2008), which contains excellent chapters on how and what to observe, along with a large number of individual case study chapters that bring the field alive; there is also a companion website for the book. A much earlier work that covers observation is Kellehear's *The Unobtrusive Researcher* (1993), recommended because of its interesting and often amusing take on the craft of observation.

Finally, we conclude with recommendations for seven websites of value for their content on interviewing, focus groups and coding.

◆ Online QDA (2012), http://onlineqda.hud.ac.uk/.
 This site was created by staff of Huddersfield University and is a well-developed (but not recently updated) resource for the beginner, yet it still contains enough of value for the relatively experienced investigator. There is a thorough treatment of the range of qualitative methodologies that can be used in an INA, including techniques not covered in this book (for example, ethnography and narrative analysis). There are links to many useful online materials.
◆ Community Tool Box (2014) *Conducting Focus Groups*, http://ctb.ku.edu/en/table-of-contents/assessment/assessing-community-needs-and-resources/conduct-focus-groups/main.
 From the University of Kansas, this site is designed to provide tools and resources to support local community groups in their efforts to 'make a difference'. The page on focus groups is written in simple language that almost anyone will understand, yet it still manages to answer the key questions, such as why focus groups are different from other groups, when to use a focus group and how to manage a focus group.
◆ Digital Methods Initiative (2013) *Qualitative Content Analysis*, www.digitalmethods.net/MoM/QualContentAnalysis.
 This resource stands out for its explanation of the use of coding textual data. The treatment may be denser than is required for a typical information needs analysis, but this will be very useful for academics wanting to write high quality papers.
◆ Glaser, J. and Laude, G. (2013) *Life with and without Coding*, www.qualitative-research.net/index.php/fqs/article/view/1886/3528.
 This is another good guide to coding qualitative data, which is compared with qualitative content analysis. The authors argue that both techniques have their merits, but irrespective of that the investigator will find the

explanation of the methods useful enough to make this a resource worth visiting.

◆ Stanford Institute for Higher Education Research. National Center for Postsecondary Improvement (2003) *Tools for Qualitative Researchers: interviews*, http://web.stanford.edu/group/ncpi/unspecified/student_assess_toolkit/ interviews.html.

This is an interesting checklist that will be useful for anyone new to using interviews in an INA project. There are four parts to it, all equally important: an interview checklist for researchers to use before they start, an interview protocol checklist, a sample faculty interview protocol and a set of (very practical) interviewing tips. It is a shame the site has not been updated for many years.

◆ Open University (2014) *Conducting an Interview*, www2.open.ac.uk/students/skillsforstudy/conducting-an-interview.php. This simple guide to interviewing is part of a wider resource aimed at undergraduate students, yet can be applied to an INA with little adaptation necessary. The section on types of questions will assist those who have not conducted interviews before and may be wondering how to proceed.

◆ B2B International (2014) *Using the Focus Group in Market Research*, www.b2binternational.com/publications/market-research-focus-group. Who really knows how to use focus groups better than market researchers? They have been using this methodology for decades, and, as they are still using this technique, there must be something in it for them. This is a simple yet effective guide for businesses that can easily be adapted to an INA.

References

Assessment Capacities Project (2011) *Direct Observation and Key Informant Interview Techniques for Primary Data Collection during Rapid Assessments,*: ACAPS, Geneva, www.acaps.org/img/disasters/direct-observation-and-key-informants-interview-techniques.pdf. [Accessed 10 November 2014.]

B2B International (2014) *Using the Focus Group in Market Research*, www.b2binternational.com/publications/market-research-focus-group. [Accessed 10 November 2014.]

Barbour, R. (2008) *Introducing Qualitative Research: a student guide to the craft of doing qualitative research*, SAGE Publications, Thousand Oaks, CA.

Belzile, J. A. and Oberg, G. (2012) Where to Begin? Grappling with how to use participant interaction in focus group design, *Qualitative Research*, **12**, (4), 459–72.

Bryman, A. (2012) *Social Research Methods*, 4th edn, Oxford University Press, Oxford. Companion website http://global.oup.com/uk/orc/sociology/brymansrm4e. [Accessed 8 November 2014.]

Bryman, A. and Bell, E. (2011) *Business Research Methods*, 3rd edn, Oxford University Press, Oxford.

Calvert, P. and Pope, A. (2005) Telephone Survey Research for Library Managers, *Library Management*, **26** (3), 139–51.

Community Tool Box (2014) *Conducting Focus Groups*, http://ctb.ku.edu/en/table-of-contents/assessment/assessing-community-needs-and-resources/conduct-focus-groups/main. [Accessed 10 November 2014.]

Connaway, L. S. and Powell, R. R. (2010) *Basic Research Methods for Librarians*, 5th edn, ABC-CLIO/Libraries Unlimited, Santa Barbara, CA.

Corbin, J. and Strauss, A. (2008) *Basics of Qualitative Research: techniques and procedures for developing grounded theory*, 3rd edn, SAGE Publications, Thousand Oaks, CA.

Creswell, J. W. (2014) *Research Design: qualitative, quantitative and mixed methods approaches*, 4th edn, SAGE Publications, Thousand Oaks, CA.

Davies, K. (2011) Information Needs and Barriers to Accessing Electronic Information: hospital-based physicians compared to primary care physicians, *Journal of Hospital Librarianship*, **11** (3), 249–60.

Digital Methods Initiative (2013) *Qualitative Content Analysis*, www.digitalmethods.net/MoM/QualContentAnalysis. [Accessed 10 November 2014.]

Glaser, J. and Laude, G. (2013) Life with and without Coding: two methods for early-stage data analysis in qualitative research aiming at causal explanations, *Forum Qualitative Sozialforschung/Forum: Qualitative Social Research*, **14** (2), Art. 5, www.qualitative-research.net/index.php/fqs/article/view/1886/3528. [Accessed 10 November 2014.]

Glitz, B. (1998) *Focus Groups for Libraries and Librarians*, Forbes Custom Publications, New York, NY.

Gobo, G. (2008) *Doing Ethnography*, SAGE Publications, London. Companion website www.sagepub.co.uk/gobo.

Gorman, G. E., and Clayton, P. R. (2005) *Qualitative Research for the Information Professional: a practical handbook*, 2nd edn, Facet Publishing, London.

Greenbaum, T. L. (2000) *Moderating Focus Groups: a practical guide for group facilitation*, SAGE Publications, Thousand Oaks, CA.

Gubriam, J. F., Holstein, J. A., Marvasti, A. B. and McKinney, K. D. (eds) (2012) *The SAGE Handbook of Interview Research: the complexity of the craft*, 2nd edn, SAGE Publications, Thousand Oaks, CA.

Hennink, M. M. (2007) *International Focus Group Research: a handbook for the health and social sciences*, Cambridge University Press, Cambridge.

Kahle, R. W. (2007) *Dominators, Cynics and Wallflowers: practical strategies for moderating meaningful focus groups*, Paramount Market Publishing, Ithaca, NY.

Kamberlis, G. and Dimitriadis, G. (2008) Focus Groups: strategic articulations of pedagogy, politics, and inquiry. In Dinzin, N. K. and Lincoln, Y. S. (eds), *Collecting and Interpreting Qualitative Materials*, 3rd edn, SAGE Publications, Thousand Oaks, CA.

Kellehear, A. (1993) *The Unobtrusive Researcher: a guide to methods*, Allen & Unwin, St Leonards, NSW.

Kramer, S. S., Martin, J. R., Schlimgen, J. B., Slack, M. K. and Martin, J. (2011) Effectiveness of a Liaison Program in Meeting Information Needs of College of Pharmacy Faculty, *Medical Reference Services Quarterly*, **30** (1), 31–41.

Krueger, R. A. and Casey, M. A. (2014) *Focus Groups: a practical guide to applied research*, 5th edn, SAGE Publications, Thousand Oaks, CA.

Leedy, P. D. and Ormrod, J. E. (2013) *Practical Research: planning and design*, 10th edn, Pearson, Boston, MA.

Liamputtong, P. (2011) *Focus Group Methodology: principles and practice*, SAGE Publications, Los Angeles, CA.

McClelland, S. (1994) Training Needs Assessment Data Gathering Methods: part 4, on-site observations, *Journal of European Industrial Training*, **18** (5), 4–7.

Millward, L. J. (1995) Focus Groups. In Breakwell, G. M., Hammond, S. and Fife-Shaw, C. (eds), *Research Methods in Psychology*, SAGE Publications, London.

Nason, L. (2007) The Farmer in the Library: information needs of farmers and how the rural public library can fulfill them, *Rural Libraries*, **27** (2), 19–45.

Online QDA (2012) http://onlineqda.hud.ac.uk/Intro_QDA/what_is_qda.php. [Accessed 10 November 2014.]

Open University (2014) *Conducting an Interview*, http://www2.open.ac.uk/students/skillsforstudy/conducting-an-interview.php. [Accessed 10 November 2014.]

Penzhorn, C. (2002) The Use of Participatory Research as an Alternative Approach for Information Needs Research, *Aslib Proceedings*, **54** (4), 240–50.

Pickard, A. J. (2013) *Research Methods in Information*, 2nd edn, Facet Publishing, London.

Randell, R., Mitchell, N., Thompson, C., McCaughan, D. and Dowding, D. (2009). From Pull to Push: understanding nurses' information needs, *Health Informatics Journal*, **15** (2), 75–85.

Robertson, J. (2005) *Conducting Intranet Needs Assessment*, www.steptwo.com.au/papers/kmc_needsanalysis/. [Accessed 11 November 2014.]

Scacciaferro, J., Goode, S. and Frausto, D. (2009) Using Photovoice as Participatory Needs Assessment with Youth at a Latino Youth Action Center, *Undergraduate Research Journal for the Human Sciences*, **8**, www.kon.org/urc/v8/scacciaferro.html. [Accessed 10 November 2014.]

Shoaf, E. C. (2003) Using a Professional Moderator in Library Focus Group Research, *College & Research Libraries*, **53** (2), 124–32.

Stanford Institute for Higher Education Research. National Center for Postsecondary Improvement (2003). *Tools for Qualitative Researchers: interviews*, http://web.stanford.edu/group/ncpi/unspecified/student_assess_toolkit/interviews.html. [Accessed 10 November 2014.]

Stewart, D. W., Shamdasani, P. N. and Rook, D. W. (2007) *Focus Groups: theory and practice*, 2nd edn, SAGE Publications, Thousand Oaks, CA.

Tolich, M. and Davidson, C. (1999) *Starting Fieldwork: an introduction to qualitative research in New Zealand*, Oxford University Press, Melbourne.

Wallace, D. P. and Van Fleet, C. (2012) *Knowledge into Action: research and evaluation in library and information science*, ABC-CLIO/Libraries Unlimited, Santa Barbara, CA.

Wildemuth, B. M. and Jordan M. W. (2009) Focus Groups. In Wildemuth, B. M. (ed.), *Applications of Social Science Research Methods to Questions in Information and Library Science*, Libraries Unlimited, Westport, CT.

Witkin, B. R. and Altschuld, J. W. (1995) *Planning and Conducting Needs Assessments: a practical guide*, SAGE Publications, Thousand Oaks, CA.

Yin, R. K. (2011) *Qualitative Research from Start to Finish*, Guilford Press, New York, NY.

Young, V. L. (1993) Focus on Focus Groups, *College & Research Libraries News*, **7**, July/Aug, 391–4.

CHAPTER 9

Analysing and integrating information needs analysis data

Introduction

In this chapter we focus on the analysis and integration of data that have been gathered to identify and make decisions about the information needs being investigated. In an INA project the analysis and integration of data occur not only towards the end of the project but also must be done to varying degrees throughout the project and for different purposes at different times.

In Chapter 4 we identified the four stages of INA projects: (1) preparation, (2) information (or data) gathering, (3) information (or data) analysis and (4) reporting the results. (Note that here we will refer to 'data gathering' rather than 'information gathering' and 'data analysis' rather than 'information analysis'.) As explained below, the INA process is not strictly a linear one. It is iterative, so the information analysis stage may occur several times during a larger INA project, requiring the investigator to integrate several types of data.

In this chapter we examine when and how to analyse the information collected to determine the needs of the target group, bearing in mind that the project might involve several iterations of the various stages. We look at both qualitative and quantitative types of data and the processes used to analyse them. The extent of an analysis will depend on why the information was gathered, with analyses conducted during Stage 2 usually requiring more detail than those conducted during Stage 1 of an INA. Regardless of the stage at which data analysis is being undertaken, any issues that might affect the validity and reliability of the results must be considered.

Worth remembering is that INAs are not conducted solely to provide diagnostic data about the information needs of individuals; rather, they are conducted for a range of specific purposes, such as to determine priorities for providing new resources, programmes or systems, or to make improvements to existing ones, for groups in specific information-related contexts. The purpose must be kept in mind when making decisions throughout the INA. Also worth remembering is that the data analysis is intertwined with the kind of reporting expected from the investigation. If the INA requires formal reporting, then it probably will be necessary to apply procedures for analysing data that are recommended in academic research texts, but there will be times when other, perhaps less complex, data analysis methods are more appropriate.

In most INA projects the investigator who gathers the data will also be responsible for the analysis; this is important because the investigator will be well acquainted with the project's background and know what kind of outcomes are required for reporting the INA outputs. There will be cases, however, in which other people are brought in for the analysis – for example, because of their strength in conducting statistical analyses of survey data. When outsiders are brought in, it is essential to inform them fully about the INA's purpose and the reporting requirements.

The preparation stage in the INA process

While the main focus in this chapter is the data analysis stage, because of the iterative nature of the INA process we start our discussion with a look at the analysis and integration of information which occurs most frequently in the preparation stage.

Many INAs begin with the investigator gathering preliminary information to build a level of understanding that allows him or her to undertake more detailed planning. This phase is part of the initial stage and often involves integrating and analysing existing data with information gathered in preliminary interviews or focus groups. The result will be the identification of the gap between what is already known and what must be known about the information needs under investigation.

Uncomplicated INAs can be relatively straightforward, with one stage leading directly to the next. In more complex INAs, however, there are often recursive relationships between the stages. For example during the preparation stage, as a prerequisite to understanding the context in which the target group's needs occur, the investigator gathers and examines some existing information, such as census data relating to the local community. This information is then used as the basis for planning and conducting interviews with three or four key stakeholders who are knowledgeable about the target group. The investigator then analyses this preliminary data to make informed decisions about what information is required and what method(s) should be used during the main data-gathering stage of the INA.

During the data analysis stage the INA investigator must ensure that any relevant information from preliminary planning is also taken into consideration. By integrating this information with the data acquired in the main data-gathering stage, the investigator is ensuring that all leads have been explored so that the target group's needs are understood and can be expressed clearly in the reporting stage.

In some INAs, such as when Levels 1, 2 and 3 needs are all under investigation, there could be three or four iterations involving the preparation, data-gathering and data analysis stages. At the end of each of the data analysis stages the investigator must record the results and document the decisions. The final iteration will lead to writing the formal report. Some INA projects, however, might require a single data-gathering stage that involves drawing together multiple data types, with each type requiring its own analysis; upon completion of these analyses a final combined data analysis must occur to integrate the results.

The information analysis stage in the INA process

We have organized the following discussion about analysing and integrating INA data into two main parts: the first focuses on qualitative data; the second, on quantitative data. In some INAs, however, it is necessary to gather and analyse both qualitative and quantitative data using a mixed methods approach to obtain an in-depth understanding through the exploration of the situation from a variety of angles – some examples of this are provided below.

Qualitative data

In Chapter 8 we discussed the two main qualitative data gathering methods: (1) individual interviews and (2) focus groups. Each of these methods generates data that require their own type of analysis, and the depth and form of analysis depends on the purpose for gathering the data in the first place and the uses to be made of it. As Gorman and Clayton (2005, 206) point out, the researcher's task is to make sense out of the large amount of gathered data. They describe this task as 'the process of bringing order, structure and meaning to the mass of collected data'. Regardless of the complexity, the investigator must use intuition as well as critical thinking and creative abilities to analyse the gathered data.

When interviews, focus groups or observation are used to gather data, it is important at the start of the data analysis stage for the investigator to organize any notes taken during or immediately after each of the sessions. The next step is to reduce the mass of collected data into manageable units by identifying broad categories into which the gathered data can be divided for in-depth examination. When this step has been taken, the process continues by dividing the data further into more specific categories. Then, through the use of inductive reasoning, the investigator should be able to determine relationships between and within categories. Based on these relationships, the investigator should be able to draw some conclusions – for example, the potential causes of weak information retrieval skills among members of the target group, or the resources needed to provide the level of services required to meet the target group's information needs. Gorman and Clayton (2005, 207) point out that 'in qualitative data analysis the primary tool is the investigator's innate human ability to confront enormous amounts of information and to make sense of it'.

In *Qualitative Research from Start to Finish*, Yin (2011, 177–9) describes the process of qualitative data analysis as a five-phase cycle. He says that 'although analyzing qualitative research does not follow any cookbook, neither is it totally undisciplined' (177). Phase 1 of the cycle is to compile and sort 'the field notes amassed during your fieldwork' into a database (178). Phase 2 is the process of 'breaking down the compiled data into smaller fragments or pieces' (178), while the third phase entails using themes, categories or codes 'to reorganize the disassembled fragments or pieces into different groupings that might have been in the original notes' (179). Phase 4 involves 'using the reassembled material to create a new narrative', with initial interpretations 'leading you to recompile the data in some fresh way, or to disassemble or reassemble the data differently' (179). The fifth and final phase is the point at which the investigator draws conclusions from the study, conclusions which 'should be related to the interpretation of the fourth phase and through it to all phases of the cycle' (179). Yin makes the very important point that the five phases do not occur in a linear sequence but in fact 'have *recursive* and *iterative* relationships' (179). These relationships occur not only in the data analysis stage of qualitative research but are also part and parcel of the nature of INA research as a whole.

When conducting qualitative data analyses, it is important to keep the validity and reliability of the research in mind. With regard to validity there is a range of approaches that can be taken, the choice of which depends on the nature of the data and the project. Here we present five of these approaches which we believe are the most useful ones for INAs involving qualitative data. *Triangulation* is the process of checking that the key findings or themes drawn from the data are based on multiple sources, such as from several interviewees within the same organization, or from interviewees as well as from documents or direct observation. *Member checking*, sometimes referred to as *respondent validation*, involves presenting the major findings to the participants to see whether they perceive them to be accurate. Obtaining *feedback* is extremely important, so having at least one or more persons, such as colleagues, review the research can be a useful step in identifying anything that is unclear or questionable in the findings. The use of *thick description*, by providing an in-depth depiction of the research setting, allows the report readers to understand the context and thus come to their own conclusions. As noted above, there are other strategies that can be employed if needed, and these are covered in most qualitative research methods texts.

To achieve a high level of reliability in qualitative INA research we recommend applying the advice of Gibbs (2007), whose strategies are well suited to INA research. *Transcription checking* involves the laborious process of reviewing transcripts so that there are no obvious errors. Guarding against *definitional drift in coding* is done by constantly comparing the coding and writing memos about the codes during the analysis to identify any inconsistencies. (The coding process is explained in more detail below.) When a team is used to code the data, it is essential to ensure that the work is well co-ordinated and that there is good communication. By getting two people to develop codes for the same set of data the process can unveil researcher bias, the inadvertent omission of key issues, as well as a lack of consistency. In addition *code cross-checking*, that is, having two people apply the same predefined codes to a dataset and then comparing their work, is an effective way to reduce researcher bias and achieve a high level of consistency in the coding. These strategies help ensure that the analysis is consistent and that the same or similar findings would be achieved by other researchers.

Interviews

As indicated in Chapter 8, individual interviews are perhaps the most common method used to gather qualitative data in INAs. Either during or immediately after each interview the investigator will write notes about the key points made by the interviewee that shed light on the problem being investigated, such as details related to the target group, their specific circumstances and their information needs. If, for example, the interviews were part of preliminary planning, the investigator would analyse the notes along with the interview transcripts to determine whether to undertake a survey next or to conduct interviews with a wide range of stakeholders.

In the data-gathering stage of most INAs the interviews are usually semi-structured. The INA investigator will have developed a set of questions to ask about the identified issues, but during each interview the investigator is able to probe and ask additional questions or change the questions depending on the responses of the participant. While conducting the interviews, the investigator should undertake continual analysis of the data; that is, he or she will use notes and listen to key parts of the individual interviews to ensure that the required data are being obtained, either by sharpening the questions or probing newly identified issues.

In the data-gathering stage, usually when the required number of interviews has been completed, the analytical process becomes more prescribed. At this point the interview recordings need to be transcribed. Some investigators prefer to do this task themselves, because it gives them the opportunity to listen to each word and to make decisions about segments of the interview that need not be transcribed (for example, the information may be extraneous to the project). The investigator might also note the place in the interview when key statements were made. The place can be recorded as the hour, minute and second of the interview, or whatever calibration makes sense given the type of recording device used. If the investigator does not have the time or desire to transcribe the interviews, then a skilled transcriptionist might be employed. This person must be informed of any ethical issues relating to confidentiality, and it is good practice to have him or her sign a confidentiality agreement.

When beginning the analysis process, it is necessary to do some planning. The initial step should be to identify who or what is to be analysed in the interview data. In research jargon this step is called determining the *unit of analysis*. In an INA investigating Level 1 needs the unit of analysis might be the individual members of the target group or a particular segment of the target group. In an INA investigating the information needs of families caring for elderly parents the unit of analysis could be the individual parents who require the care and/or the individuals or family units who provide the care. The choices depend primarily on the purpose of the interviews and the questions asked.

If re-analysing interviews for a new purpose, it is necessary to identify a new unit of analysis. Using the previous example, after determining the information needs of the families caring for their elderly parents the investigators might re-analyse the interviews to identify gaps in information resources provided by the support agencies. In this context the new unit of analysis would be the information resources available from the support agencies.

After determining the unit of analysis it is necessary to decide how to break down the data in each interview into manageable and meaningful segments. In research jargon the process of dissecting the textual data into categories for analysis is called *coding*. Coding occurs in an iterative fashion, starting with the investigator identifying codes for high-level concepts and then categorizing the data using those codes. The investigator then closely examines the data within each coded category and establishes finer codes for breaking down the data into meaningful units. From these meaningful units the investigator comes to understand the information need being investigated.

One method for identifying high-level codes is to create a list of the key themes or the question topic areas in the protocols (see Chapter 8) used as a tool to guide the interviews. Beside each item in the list the investigator provides a brief definition or clarification of its meaning in relation to the data to be analysed. The investigator then uses this list and the definitions when reading through each interview to categorize the data into manageable segments for further analysis.

A second method is to start the analysis by reading through each interview transcript and using what Gorman and Clayton (2005) refer to as 'a form of selective perception' (p. 206) to identify key events or comments within the data, as well as relevant terminology and notable themes. Those events or comments considered significant are then selected as the high-level codes for categorizing the data. In an INA focusing on a Level 1 need, for example, a high-level code could be established to bring together data about the situations or causes that trigger the target group's information needs, with another code for the factors that enable or impede the target group's access to that information. In a Level 2 INA a high-level code could be established to identify the types of services provided, with another code for denoting data about the characteristics of the service providers that contribute to the target group's information-related needs, etc. For a Level 3 INA a high-level code could be created for identifying inadequate system-level resources. The investigator employs the codes to group together related units of data from within and across interviews.

Regardless of which method is chosen for determining high-level codes, the investigator's task on initially reading the transcripts is to categorize the data into manageable units. If there is no appropriate code for a specific unit of data, one must be created. At the end of this first pass through the transcripts the investigator should review the content gathered under each code. When finding a code that has been called upon only once or twice, the investigator should consider whether the data categorized by that code might be merged with the data of another code. The investigator should also be open to adding new codes for relevant data that does not fit comfortably into any of the initial codes. Though some data might fit with two or more codes, if there is a large overlap between the categorized data for two codes, consideration should be given to merging them and their related data under a single code. Figure 9.1 provides an overview of the initial coding process.

1. Examine interview protocol	➔ create a list of key themes or question topics (with definitions) to be used as high-level codes
2. Read unit of data	➔ assign a high-level code
	➔ if no appropriate code is found, establish and assign new one
3. Repeat Step 2 until all data have been analysed	
4. Aggregate data by assigned codes	
5. Examine aggregated datasets	➔ identify unique datasets or overlapping datasets, then merge if appropriate

Figure 9.1 The coding process

The next step is to analyse the units of data aggregated under each of the high-level codes. At this point the investigator must sharpen his or her focus in order to identify smaller units of data of varying size (words, phrases, sentences, paragraphs) that can be brought back together to identify trends, patterns or repeating relationships related to the level of need that is the focus of the INA. To achieve this level of analysis it is necessary to establish a list of more specific codes, that is, codes for concepts that are subsets of the higher-level codes. Again, each code must be defined in a sentence or two to help ensure consistency in coding.

In most INAs the coding scheme can remain relatively simple. Only in large, complex INA projects should the scheme reach three or more levels. In an INA project of any size, however, the analysis process is frequently not as straightforward as we would like; therefore, when working through the transcripts, the investigator must check the coding scheme several times, merging codes, adding new ones and perhaps deleting those that appear superfluous. The aim is to categorize the data so that it becomes possible to start understanding the information needs being investigated.

In very small projects the formalities of identifying the units of analysis and determining the codes for the analysis need not be highly formal. The main point to remember is that the investigator must have a clear idea of what steps to take when analysing the interview data, as illustrated in Figure 9.2.

---

1. Transcribe each interview.
   ↓
2. Determine who or what to analyse in each transcript.
   ↓
3. Establish concepts as code names under which you will note relevant parts of each transcript.
   ↓
4. Read through all of the transcripts, assigning relevant parts to each code.
   ↓
5. Carefully analyse the content under each code and, if needed, determine sub-codes into which you further refine the categorized data.
   ↓
6. Repeat Step 5 for each sub-code if necessary.
   ↓
7. Prepare the data for report writing.

Figure 9.2 Steps in analysing interview data

A simple approach to conducting the analysis is to print the transcripts onto paper and then read through them and code the passages using highlighter pens of different colours to represent the broad themes or topic areas. During the second reading of each transcript the investigator should be making notes about the key pieces of information, organizing them into one or more tables under the themes or topics and including the line and page number where the information is found. It also is possible to cut and paste into the table any particularly striking comment made by a participant about a specific point in case it has future value. For example, key quotes can be used later to assist with the wording of questions in a subsequent survey or when writing the INA report to highlight an issue or to clarify the reason for interpreting an important point from the data.

Another approach is to conduct the complete analysis using a computer. There is a variety of software products for analysing qualitative data. Gorman and Clayton (2005, 219), however, warn about the risk of data overload, citing Wolcott (1990, 35), who explains that by using the computer's full capabilities you can accommodate mountains of data – but you 'have to be careful not to get buried in avalanches of your own making'. And Yin notes that, even though the functionality of software for analysing qualitative data has improved considerably over the years, researchers need to be aware of complexities and dangers in using software to analyse qualitative data. He comments that, while the software now

> mimics the most essential steps of doing analysis . . ., with each new function also comes more complicated computer-based procedures and navigation rules. Nevertheless, the main caution in using such software still remains: You have to do all the *analytical thinking*. To do this will require an added burden because you will have to use the software's language while also keeping track of your own (substantive) analytical path.
>
> (Yin, 2011, 180)

Nonetheless, it is possible to keep the analysis process simple. Commonly used features of word-processing software such as font colours or text highlighting colours can be employed to identify broad topics within the text, and comments can be inserted into the transcript margins as notes, which can be assembled with the related text when the report is being drafted. Spreadsheet software such as Microsoft Excel can be used to create a database for organizing the analysed data. The drawback here is being able to see just a single screen of information at a time, whereas with paper copies multiple pages can be placed side by side on a large work surface, enabling the investigator to see similarities or differences in the content more readily.

Gorman and Clayton make the following useful points (but the formal analysis to which they are referring occurs in academic research projects such as those conducted by postgraduate students for their dissertations and theses):

> Formal analysis requires that you review all of the data collected (field notes, transcripts and online transactions), and it is commonly accepted among qualitative investigators that this review be undertaken at least three times. Preferably the review readings are done over a long enough period to permit substantive gestation and reflection. With each reading new insights, patterns and connections will emerge . . .
>
> Gorman and Clayton, 2005, 209–10

Whether the three times rule is necessary in straightforward INAs is open to debate, but the point remains that time is required for the data to be understood fully, and that the investigator must be totally familiar with the collected data. It is also worth questioning whether software need be employed when analysing qualitative data. Tips on how to select and use software for the analysis of qualitative data are available on several websites; some of these are noted in the 'Further reading' section below.

Focus groups

As discussed in Chapter 8, focus groups can be used for a variety of purposes in INAs. Regardless of the purpose for conducting a focus group session, the key element is the interaction among participants that stimulates new ideas or highlights important points about which they agree or disagree. The interviewer will have prompted this interaction with prepared questions, and then by probing something that a participant has just said. The dynamic nature of the interaction means that several people can be speaking at one time, or that one person will be providing his or her perspective which then motivates several other participants to speak because of new ideas that have occurred to them.

The flow of conversations in focus groups makes transcription almost impossible unless the session has been videoed to allow the identification of individual speakers. If it is considered necessary to video a focus group session, permission must be obtained from the participants. Be aware that the intrusiveness of a video camera can introduce an 'unwelcome visitor' into a session that impedes the flow of conversation; think carefully about whether video recording is worth the risk.

As already noted in Chapter 8, it is not uncommon for two persons to conduct a focus group session, with the moderator asking questions and the second person taking notes about key points during the discussion. If a second person is not present, then the moderator has the difficult task of guiding participants' conversation and taking notes (although notes are often made just after a session rather than during it). When two people have been involved in listening and gathering data in a focus group session, they must then meet to discuss the session and key points that emerged, with some agreement being reached as to which points seem most significant. Notes from this debriefing play an important role in guiding the data analysis.

If the INA project is at the data-gathering stage, and existing data or data gathered from interviews or surveys have already been analysed, the investigator will then have used the initial findings as the basis for planning the focus group sessions. The investigator will be able to categorize the questions asked in the focus group sessions into thematic areas, as outlined in the earlier discussion about analysing interview data. The investigator will also have the notes made during and immediately after the focus group sessions. These notes must be referred to prior to listening to the focus group recording to provide initial insights about what to listen for.

When listening to the focus group recording, the investigator's task is to identify the key issues pertinent to the purpose of the data-gathering session. These issues often arise when discussion is the most animated and there is strong agreement or disagreement among the participants. When analysing the data, it is important to note the place in the audio recording (the minute and second) where a key point was made. If a specific comment captures the essence of a key point, it should be transcribed verbatim, especially when made by a stakeholder who is highly knowledgeable about the target group and has given permission to be quoted.

If the purpose of the focus group session is to plan the data-gathering stage of an INA, then the analysis will be aimed at identifying the key issues to be addressed, the potential sources of information about those issues and the best method or methods for gathering the information. In some INA projects the use of qualitative methods will end here, and outcomes of the focus group analysis will be used to develop the survey questions. In other projects the focus group analysis will be used to identify the themes and question areas for gathering more qualitative data through individual interviews or additional focus groups.

If the focus group session lies within the data-gathering stage, the findings from the analysis will either be used on their own for making key decisions or will be integrated with other gathered information for further analysis. Findings from the focus group analysis will contribute to any reports for the project. It is in the final report that quotes taken during focus groups or individual interviews can be of most value, because the words of key stakeholders can clarify specific aspects of major issues in ways that comments by outsiders cannot.

Observation

Observation as a data-gathering method in INAs is generally done in conjunction with other methods, but occasionally as the sole method. The focus of observation is usually on three different elements within the environment: social structure, talking and context. Notes or a log are the usual way information is recorded when observation is used to gather data. Occasionally video recordings or photographs are used for capturing observations, with the investigator writing about what is being observed in the images.

The focus of note taking and data analysis must be directly related to the reason for undertaking the observations. If, for example, the INA is about information needs of medical practitioners and is aimed at determining how to help them manage patient information more efficiently, the observational notes might cover:

◆ the kinds of information that doctors need
◆ the information that doctors add to their patients' histories
◆ the various contexts in which the doctors' information behaviour occurs.

The subsequent analysis would be undertaken to categorize the various tasks that the doctors performed, the types of information they used and gathered and any contextual factors that arose. The observations on their own, however, might be insufficient for decision-making purposes, so another data-gathering instrument, such as a survey, might be required to triangulate the results.

Scenario 9.1 Full-text database usage at Warlock Law

After examining the usage data for the firm's expensive full-text legal databases, Joseph del Campo, Information Services Manager at Warlock Law, decided to undertake an INA to learn why these databases were not being more heavily used. After reading this book on INA Joseph conducted a focus group session with the four lawyers on the firm's Information Services Advisory Committee. From his notes on the focus group discussion Joseph developed an interview protocol to ensure that he would cover all of the key issues when conducting interviews with a cross-section of the firm's lawyers. After the first interview Joseph adjusted the protocol to factor in several new topic areas and made minor adjustments several times during the interviewing stage. By the end of the twelfth interview Joseph was hearing primarily responses he had already heard, so he felt confident that no further interviews were necessary.

While transcribing the relevant parts of each transcript, Joseph noted interesting points which he used in conjunction with the protocol to identify broad categories of issues and establish the initial codes for them. This step allowed him to approach the data analysis with a clear idea of how to code the text within the transcripts as he came across the relevant issues. He decided that the unit of analysis should be the individual lawyer, and he chose to use Microsoft Excel to organize the analysis process, creating a spreadsheet with a column for the codes, one for the interviewees, one for the relevant text and one for notes. During the coding of the first four transcripts he revised the initial codes, merging some where there were significant overlaps, adding some for new issues that arose during the analysis and creating some sub-categories when it became evident that an issue had several aspects to it. When Joseph came across a quote that highlighted an issue particularly well, he recorded its details for possible use later in the written report. After coding all 12 transcripts he went back through the coded data, creating several more sub-categories under some of the codes and adjusting several other codes and their related data.

By the end of the process Joseph was confident that he had identified the reasons for the lack of database use. (1) There were several databases that provided content of little relevance to the firm's lawyers, (2) while there were also some key topic areas for which no databases were being provided. And, just as important, (3) some of the lawyers said that online searching took too much of their time because they had difficulty narrowing their searches to identify a manageable set of retrieved items.

Quantitative data

This is not a book on research methods, nor is it a book on the use of statistical methods; hence what can be said here about quantitative data analysis is essentially limited, but some key methods are introduced.

As discussed in earlier chapters, quantitative data are gathered in INAs for a wide variety of purposes. An investigator, for example, might integrate census data about population trends with information about a public library's membership to develop an initial understanding of the local context in the planning stage of an INA. Or an investigator might employ a mixed methods approach, conducting a survey to determine patterns of behaviour in a target population, then undertaking interviews with a smaller group to explore the underlying causes of those patterns. The analysis undertaken by the investigator must be directly tied to the type of data as well as to the purpose for which it was gathered.

Unlike the qualitative data analysis process, validity and reliability are less of an issue during the *analysis* of quantitative data but are highly important during the *planning and data gathering* stages. As stated in Chapter 5, validity refers to the production of results that are accurate and that actually measure what is supposed to be measured, whereas reliability refers to the production of results that would be replicated if the study were to be repeated, even by other researchers. In other words in the planning and information-gathering stages the investigator must ensure that the right questions are asked, the right variables are chosen to measure the relevant concepts and the right statistical tests applied to the data, so that if someone else chooses to ask the same questions they will derive the same or similar results.

Quantitative data analysis in INAs need not be highly complicated. As noted by Booth:

> Basic statistical methods of description and cross-tabulation are the foundation of the majority of library-based research, and neither calls for statistical expertise. Descriptives list the simple distribution of responses to an item (e.g., average number of Facebook applications used), while cross-tabulation segments these responses based on one or more demographic characteristics (e.g., number of Facebook applications used by age, gender, and academic major).
>
> Booth, 2009, 38

For larger, more complex INA projects, if the investigator is unfamiliar with statistical concepts and methods, we recommend that one begins by referring to relevant texts for more detail and/or by seeking advice from individuals trained in statistical analyses. A good starting point for understanding the processes for preparing quantitative data and the techniques for describing and analysing the data is Chapter 23 (Quantitative Analysis) in Pickard's *Research Methods in Information* (2nd edn, 2013).

The initial step in analysing quantitative data

As noted above, the choice of method for analysing quantitative data must be based on the purpose for which the data were gathered. In the following sections we explain the two main types of statistical data gathered in INAs and some of the main methods used to analyse them. Before beginning that discussion, we explain a basic initial step in all quantitative data analyses: data organization.

At the start of any quantitative analysis it is important to organize the data in ways that allow the numbers to be explored so that any patterns within them can be identified. This might seem a simple task, but it needs to be carefully planned with the final result in mind. Take, for example, a test of information literacy competencies of university students; by organizing the data first by the students' age, then by their gender, followed by their programme of study, the investigator might discover that students in social science programmes achieve much higher results than students in the arts and humanities and in the hard sciences on questions involving information sources from government agencies. Other findings might be that female students are much more knowledgeable about citation software such as EndNote and Zotero than their male counterparts, and that, when compared with older students, those aged under 25 perceive the information in Wikipedia to be trustworthy and indicate that they would use Wikipedia-sourced information for a course assignment. This example shows that looking at the numeric data from only one perspective might prevent the investigator from determining the full range of meanings within that data.

As long as appropriate questions have been asked, it will be relatively easy for the investigator to make these discoveries by using spreadsheets to organize the data in different ways for analysis. Indeed, organizing the data in multiple ways is relatively easy when using spreadsheets or specialist software.

A spreadsheet is basically a matrix of rows and columns. Each row is used for one of the units being analysed (called 'cases'), whereas each column is for data representing one of the characteristics (called 'variables') of interest and upon which the descriptions or comparisons will be based. Easily accessible spreadsheet software such as Microsoft Excel or Calc can be used for entering and analysing quantitative data gathered for most INA projects. Calc is a component of LibreOffice, an open-source suite of software, with details available at the Document Foundation (2013).

Spreadsheets can be used to arrange the data in different ways – for example to sort the variable of interest from the largest to the smallest number of occurrences in order to determine the amount of use by individual staff members of their organization's intranet. Or the usage data could be arranged by groups of staff based on the type of position they hold or by the department in which they work. Calculations might also be performed on the data using the spreadsheet's pre-programmed formulae for commonly used statistics; or, when a statistical function is not pre-programmed, the spreadsheet software usually allows the formula to be specified and the calculation to be performed.

There are also options in most spreadsheet software for producing graphs and charts from the data. The range of chart types available is usually quite large and will likely include bar and column charts, pie charts, area charts, scatter charts, line charts, bubble charts, donut charts and net charts (sometimes called spider, web or radar charts). These are relatively straightforward to create as long as the data are organized and sorted appropriately. Line graphs are also relatively easy to create with spreadsheet software – for example to plot the changes to a variable of interest over time. Graphs and charts generated from spreadsheets are also useful for presenting the data in any reports that are written for the INA. The use of graphs and charts in written INA reports is discussed briefly in Chapter 10.

In more complex INA projects quantitative analyses can be done using specialist software commonly used in academic contexts such as SPSS (IBM,

2014) or ADaMSoft (2014) – the former is available on many university websites, while the latter is a free open-source system in Java. These programs also give options to produce graphs and charts to help analyse the data and to report the results.

With regard to online survey products such as The Survey System (Creative Research Systems, 2014) and SurveyMonkey (2014), the good news is that they allow the gathered data to be exported directly into spreadsheets and/or statistical software packages. The Survey System includes a free, downloadable version called Evaluation Edition, which is suitable for all but the most complex INAs. There are many online tutorials available for SurveyMonkey, including one on its own website; these are useful for anyone unfamiliar with this tool.

Analysing quantitative data

Quantitative data analysis involves manipulating numbers, and the simplest way to do this is usually by means of a spreadsheet. When analysing data gathered in a survey, for example, each response (a case) is entered into a line on the spreadsheet, and the answer to each question (a variable) has its own column. When creating a spreadsheet from scratch, the axes need to be set up manually prior to the entry of data, but an online survey should allow the data to be automatically entered into the spreadsheet. The investigator should download a copy of the spreadsheet and save it. It is very easy to scramble data in a large spreadsheet, so it is highly advisable to work on a copy, never on the master spreadsheet, and to make frequent backups.

It is easy to assume that only one or two people will ever need to use a spreadsheet created for an INA, so little by way of labelling or other explanatory information needs to be added. This assumption could be false, however; for example, if one member of the team falls ill and has to be replaced at short notice, or if the spreadsheet might be reviewed at a later date to see whether more information can be extracted from the data. For these reasons the spreadsheet must be clearly labelled so that anyone familiar with the purpose of the project will be able to open it and understand what data have been entered, how they are being manipulated by the formula, and where the results of calculations can be found. Details of the coding must also be easily accessible. For example, rather than just entering a number for a question (e.g. Q13) it is better to enter the whole question into the spreadsheet. If a cell includes data used in a calculation (e.g. the currency exchange rate used to determine how much money is needed to purchase material from a particular country), then that cell must be clearly labelled so that someone arriving at it fresh will know where to edit that particular datum.

Once answers have been entered into the spreadsheet, the data need to be coded. In online survey software this may be done automatically, but an investigator needs to understand what is happening behind the scenes and be able to make manual adjustments as necessary. The answers to almost all questions in a survey are in words, but the coding process requires that these be translated into numbers to allow for statistical manipulation of the data. A simple example is gender: *Female* coded as 1, and *Male* coded as 2. In a question that asks respondents to choose one option from a list of five, the choices are coded as 1, 2, 3, 4 or 5. All such coding must be recorded and be accessible for subsequent use with the spreadsheet.

There are some tricky situations in coding, and you will need to do some reading to get advice on how to handle these. Questions that allow respondents to tick all answers that apply can be complex to analyse and require a systematic approach. If you are coding Likert-type attitude scales, then you must remember that negatively phrased statements need to have the coding reversed in order to convey the sentiment correctly. If there are 'other comments' or open-ended questions in the survey or other instrument, the answers must be coded as qualitative data, as described in the qualitative data section of this chapter.

There are different levels of analysis applied to quantitative data. The simplest approach is to describe the answers to single questions and to identify the basic patterns in the data through graphing and the use of percentages, means (averages) and other measures of central tendency. There is a brief description in Chapter 10 of graphing and how to use it to convey the analysis in the final report. More sophisticated statistical analysis can explore whether there is a statistically significant difference in the answers between groups of respondents (such as whether more men than women read historical fiction), or whether there is any relationship or association between answers to certain questions. This type of analysis cannot determine for certain that one event or factor has caused another to occur, but it can indicate that there is a pattern (that, for example, people who have higher levels of education tend to read more historical fiction than people with lower levels of education).

Of course, many online survey software packages will allow researchers to do quite sophisticated analysis that combines the answers to different questions. Specialist data analysis software such as SPSS and spreadsheet programs such as Excel provide a medium level of functionality which can be supplemented by add-ins. There is also a range of web-based statistical calculators; more than 100 of these are listed at DanielSoper.com (2014) – all 'free to be used by anyone in the research community at large'. When using these tools, the investigator must understand what calculation is being done and be able to interpret the results appropriately, picking up errors in logic that may occur.

Types of quantitative data and statistical tests in INAs

In Chapter 7 we briefly discussed the different types of quantitative data (nominal, ordinal, interval and ratio) and the statistical analyses, often called statistical tests, that can and cannot be done with each of them. Detailed explanations of the data types and statistical tests along with examples of their use can be found in most research textbooks; several of these are noted in the 'Further reading' section at the end of this chapter.

The type of statistical test selected for analysing quantitative data in an INA is of necessity directly related to the investigation's purpose and the nature of the data. In quantitative research there are two broad categories of statistics that perform different functions: descriptive and inferential. In many INA projects both types are employed.

Descriptive statistics

Descriptive statistics are used to provide numerical descriptions of the basic features or to summarize the key attributes of the gathered data. The most common descriptive statistics are the measures of central tendency: the mode (the most frequently occurring value); the median (the mid-point value); and, the mean (the average value). Each of these statistics provides a single value which is meant to represent the full dataset.

Another type of descriptive statistics is variability measures, which include the range and interquartile range, the variance and the standard deviation. The range is the spread from the bottom figure to the top figure among the recorded values, while the interquartile range covers the middle 50% of values within the full distribution. These two statistics are often used in INAs to describe datasets that do not follow a normal distribution due to outliers (values that lie outside the expected range). The variance and the standard deviation (SD) also provide insights into the level of variation within a dataset and are useful for understanding the degree to which individual scores vary from the mean. Variance measures the spread of the numbers in the data, while the SD measures the level of consistency, with a low SD showing high consistency and a high SD showing considerable variation. McNabb (2008, 350) points out that both 'are used in higher level statistical tests' and 'are two of the most important of all statistical measures'.

The two other types of descriptive statistics are 'measures of relative position in the set' and 'measures of correlation between two or more variables' (McNabb, 2008, 123). The former measures include percentiles and standard scores (of which the z score is the most common), while the latter includes various correlation tests (of which the Pearson product moment correlation, or simply Pearson, is the most common). Correlations tell us both the strength and the direction of the relationship between two or more variables (McNabb, 2008, 123). Correlation numbers range between -1 and +1, with those on the minus side being negative correlations and those on the plus side being positive ones. When the correlation is closer to either end of the range, the stronger it is: thus a correlation of -.89 is a strong negative correlation whereas +.78 is a strong positive correlation.

Given that the correlation indicates a relationship between two variables, it is important to realize that a positive correlation indicates that, as the value for one of the variables increases, so does the value of the other variable. Assume, for example, that a positive correlation exists between secondary school information literacy classes and students' independent learning; that is, students who have taken more information literacy classes receive higher grades for their independent research projects. A negative correlation indicates that, as the value of one variable increases, the value for the other decreases. Assume, for example, that when the staff in a consultancy organization take a longer time to complete a report for a client, the lower the organization's profit will be for the work undertaken.

Rather than going into detail about how to calculate these measures, it is sufficient here to say that they can be easily computed using the statistical tools available, such as Excel and SPSS. The formulae for calculating these are explained in statistics textbooks and on many websites (see 'Further reading' below). It also should be said that many investigators, without knowing the finer details of statistical analysis, are quite competent in utilizing spreadsheet software and statistical packages to make the necessary calculations. (The trick here is to know enough about statistics to avoid making egregious errors when using common statistical packages, and to avoid misinterpretation of statistical analyses.)

Scenario 9.2 provides an example of how data can be organized and analysed to use descriptive statistics in an INA.

Scenario 9.2 Statistics about rural veterinarians

The National Association of Veterinarians and Veterinary Surgeons (NAVVS) requested its information services manager, Natalie Pearson, to investigate the information needs of rural veterinarians when working in the field. Following some initial research in which Natalie used existing data to gain an understanding of the types of practices and the range of practitioners, she then undertook a Level 1 INA by conducting an online survey of a random sample of rural vets across the country from the NAVVS membership list. The survey contained some demographic questions, some questions about the type of practice in which the vets worked and the type of work they did, as well as questions related to their specific information needs. Natalie used an online survey tool that allowed her to enter the results directly into spreadsheets.

Natalie thought carefully before deciding which statistics she should use to start the analysis. From the responses to a multiple-choice question on practice type (there were four choices offered) she quickly determined that the mode was 'Small Practice', with 54% of respondents (198 of 365) making this choice. She sorted the data from the question that asked the respondents for their age into a sequence showing the number of respondents at each age, from youngest to eldest. From the data she could see that the ages of the rural vets ranged from 26 to 70 years old, and she calculated the mean to be 42.5 years old.

When Natalie plotted the data onto a graph using five-year age groups, she could easily see that there were more younger vets than older ones. She calculated the median age as 39.4 years old and decided that the median would probably be of greater utility than the mean, because the dataset had a disproportionally large group of practitioners between the ages of 26 and 45. From these basic descriptive statistics Natalie began to understand that the composition of the vets whose needs she was analysing was not standard; that is, the group was skewed to the younger end of the scale. These results are displayed in Figure 9.3.

In the survey Natalie included questions to identify the information needed by the vets, as well as how they accessed the information. One question asked whether they used smartphones or tablets to access information while in the field, and she found that 64.9% of the sample were using these devices. When she organized these data by age group (Figure 9.4), however, she found that nearly all of the vets under the age of 45 had adopted the technology and were using it in the field, but the majority of vets over the age of 45 were not.

After analysing the descriptive statistics, predominantly through the use of spreadsheets and graphs, Natalie realized that she should learn why the older practitioners were not using smartphones or tablets. Based on what she would glean from the interviews, Natalie would then be able to decide what the next step should

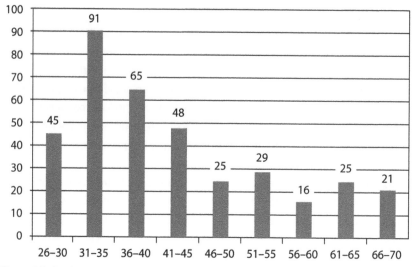

Figure 9.3 Rural veterinarians by age group

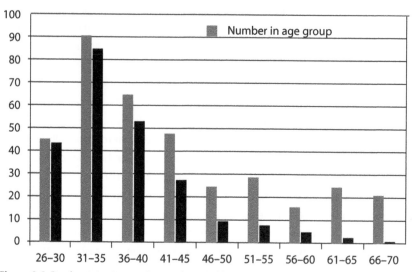

Figure 9.4 Rural veterinarians and smartphone/tablet users by age group

be: perhaps her attendance at NAVVS meetings in a range of locations around the country to explain how new ICTs and networked information services can be used to assist practitioners in the field. These sessions could then be followed by a series of workshops to train the practitioners in how to use these new ICTs.

Inferential statistics

Inferential statistics are used to draw inferences or make predictions about a population by analysing data gathered from a representative sample of that population. For example the likelihood of a new service's success can be inferred from the results of a survey of a representative sample of the population of potential users; or the level of e-reader usage among a university's undergraduate students can be estimated from data drawn from a representative sample of those students. Trochim provides this overview:

> Most of the major inferential statistics come from a general family of statistical models known as the General Linear Model. This includes the *t*-test, Analysis of Variance (ANOVA), Analysis of Covariance (ANCOVA), regression analysis, and many of the multivariate methods like factor analysis, multidimensional scaling, cluster analysis, discriminant function analysis, and so on. Given the importance of the General Linear Model, it's a good idea for any serious social researcher to become familiar with its workings.
>
> Trochim, 2006a

As can be deduced from this quote, when inferential statistics are involved in an INA project, several factors must be considered together to determine the statistical test best suited to resolving the problem or answering the research question. It is because of this complexity when using inferential statistics that an investigator must be well versed in statistical methods or must consult someone who is.

According to Creswell, in the planning stage of a research project whose aim is to test inferential questions or hypotheses a key step is to identify the statistics and the computer program to be used. He advises to

> base this choice on the nature of the research question (e.g., relating variables or comparing groups as the most popular), the number of independent and dependent variables, and the number of variables controlled . . .. Further, consider whether the variables will be measured on an instrument as a continuous score (e.g., age from 18 to 36) or as a categorical score (e.g., women = 1, men = 2). Finally, consider whether the scores from the sample might be normally distributed in a bell-shaped curve if plotted out on a graph or non-normally distributed.
>
> Creswell, 2014, 163

In INAs statistical tests will be used most often to 'prove' that sets of data are either alike or unalike. The key decision for the investigator is which test to use, and that, not surprisingly, comes back to the original purpose of the INA. What, when all is said and done, is this analysis trying to determine? Because it is more often useful to know that datasets are similar in some way, the tests used for the 'hypothesis of association' will be given rather more coverage here than the 'hypothesis of difference'.

A very common test involving inferential statistics in an INA is to see whether two variables can be said to be related. Suppose we want to determine whether more females than males use a university library's mobile app for the virtual reference service. A survey has already produced data that seem to show more females than males using the university library's virtual reference services, but how can we be sure? The best test for this is Chi-square, which is common in INAs because it tests for association and works with nominal or ordinal data. In this case there are two variables, gender and the use/non-use of the virtual reference services. The Chi-square test compares the data that would be expected if there were *no* relationship between the variables (that is, males and females would use the services in the same proportions) with the actual data in which there *is* a difference in use by gender. The actual process of calculating the association between the variables can be found in most books of statistical tests, but what matters here is the outcome. The Chi-square score shows the discrepancy between the expected data and the actual data. The larger the Chi-square score, the more likely it is that the two variables are related. One of the strengths of this test is that the investigator can use it to determine an association at a selected strength. Commonly scores are said to be significant if they exceed a known score at 0.05 probability.

If we wish to show association between datasets with interval or ratio data, the best test is correlation. To put it simply, correlation compares two sets of data and indicates how close the relationship is between them. In a survey of, say, 30 questions the mean response for each question can be put into a list. If there are lists for the responses of two different sectors of the population, say undergraduate students and postgraduate students, the two lists can be compared and the strength of the relationship shown with a correlation score. There are several correlation tests, but the most commonly used are Spearman's for skewed data and Pearson's for data that are not skewed. Joubert and Lee (2007) used the Pearson correlation coefficient to test whether library user satisfaction was related to the library's institutional reporting structure, and in this case the test showed a low relationship between the variables.

There are several tests for measuring difference, but these are less commonly used in an INA. The *t*-test (or Student *t*-test) for two datasets merits some description here. Any two sets of data can be compared with the *t*-test, although it is generally used on interval or ratio data. An INA of clinical specialists and biomedical researchers was conducted at the US National Institutes of Health (NIH). A sample of 500 NIH scientists was surveyed, and the results were analysed for statistical significance using the *t*-test and Chi-square. Then the findings were compared with published studies and an aggregated dataset of information users in business, government and health care. The study results highlighted similarities and differences with other studies and the industry standard, providing insights into user preferences (Grefsheim and Rankin, 2007). Scenario 9.3 offers an example of how Chi-square might be employed as part of a decision-making process; this scenario is based on the study by Wilmoth (2007) of the effect of the Axis Card on library use at Griffin Technical College.

Scenario 9.3 Smartcard use in the Updike University Library System

---

Helen Hague, Director of the Updike University Library System (UULS), recently read several reports that focused on the positive feedback from students when libraries had initiated smartcards. She wondered what effect the introduction of a smartcard would have in UULS, so she decided to conduct a quasi-experiment to find out. The purpose of the study was to determine whether the smartcard would affect use of the UULS technologies, resources and services, and whether the effect was significant and positive enough to support adoption of the smartcard across all libraries in the UULS.

For the study the students enrolled in SOC0100, an introductory sociology course, in the autumn semester were all issued with smartcards. The smartcard served as their official student identification and offered multiple functions, including storage of login information for multiple websites, bookmarks for frequently visited sites, personal information for automatically completing online forms, library-recommended URLs and multiple user profiles for use of online resources. At semester's end the students were surveyed to see how frequently they used 13 specific library resources recommended in SOC0100, and a satisfaction survey was also conducted to assess the cardholders' attitudes towards the smartcard and its usefulness.

In the winter semester a new group of students who enrolled in SOC0100 were not given access to smartcards. At the end of their semester they were given the same survey on the frequency of use of the 13 library resources. A Chi-square test was done on the frequency of use data from the two groups to see whether access to a smartcard was associated with library use. The results showed that there was a significant association for only two of the 13 library resources. While these results were disappointing for Helen, the satisfaction survey of the first group of students indicated a strong acceptance of the smartcard, with 77% indicating they would recommend it to others. For these students password storage was the most used storage service, followed by personal bookmarks. In addition these students indicated that they would use a wide range of other university services in conjunction with the smartcard if they were available.

Even though the survey did not show a significant association between possession of a smartcard and library use, Helen decided to implement the smartcard across the UULS and recommended that the university begin to allow payments for vending machines, photocopying and printing via the smartcard.

A decision about which method of data analysis to use, not surprisingly, comes back to the original purpose of the INA. What precisely is this analysis seeking to determine? If the investigator is attempting to use the gathered data to describe the sample population or to compare components within it, then the analysis will require descriptive statistics. If the investigator is trying to infer or predict something based on data from a representative sample of a population, then the analysis will require inferential statistics.

Review of Chapter 9

In this chapter we have examined when and how to analyse and integrate the information (or data) gathered in an INA project. Although such analysis is considered principally as the third stage in the INA process, we have also emphasized that such analysis during an INA project must not be confined to a single stage, but rather be understood as a recurring process throughout an INA. Therefore, an investigator might initially analyse data gathered for preliminary planning at the start of a project, as well as subsequently analysing data gathered later in the project to identify the information needs of the target group.

We have proffered advice on how to analyse both qualitative and quantitative data gathered in INA projects. For qualitative data we advised about the specific types of analyses for data gathered in interviews and focus groups and through observation. For quantitative data we provided a brief overview of both descriptive and inferential statistics and the types of tests that can be performed with them, and we advised on some simple methods for managing these types of analyses.

Further reading

Remember to look back at 'Further reading' in Chapters 5–8 for works also related to Chapter 9. As already noted, most research texts discuss data analysis. In the context of INA it might help if we recommend four titles that we find particularly useful: Creswell's *Research Design: qualitative, quantitative and mixed methods approaches* (4th edn, 2014); Leedy and Ormrod's (10th edn, 2013) *Practical Research: planning and design*; Chapters 14 and 15 in Christensen, Johnson and Turner's *Research Methods, Design and Analysis* (11th edn, 2011); and Chapters 8 and 10 in Chambliss and Schutt's *Making Sense of the Social World: methods of investigation* (4th edn, 2013). Trochim's *Research Methods Knowledge Base* (2006b) is recommended because it is a freely accessible, web-based social research methods textbook that covers data analysis as well. All of these recommended texts provide relatively easy-to-understand guidance on both qualitative and quantitative data analysis. Texts that focus on research in public administration (such as McNabb, 2008) also can help with understanding both types of data analysis, and many data analysis questions can be answered on a variety of high quality websites (see below).

Specifically for qualitative data analysis we recommend Yin's *Qualitative Research from Start to Finish* (2011), which includes two excellent chapters on data analysis. In addition Gorman and Clayton's *Qualitative Research for the Information Professional: a practical handbook* (2nd edn, 2005) is also worth consulting for its chapter on data analysis, which has the added benefit of setting the research process in the context of information management organizations.

For quantitative data analysis we suggest Vaughan's *Statistical Methods for the Information Professional* (2001), older but still useful for its approach from the perspective of information professionals. More current and also very accessible is Yang's *Making Sense of Statistical Methods in Social Research* (2010). Chapter 24 on quantitative analysis in Pickard's *Research Methods in Information* (2nd edn, 2013) is also worthwhile for its concise overview of this topic.

Among the software packages for data analysis the grandfather of them all is IBM's SPSS (IBM, 2014), recommended for more complex statistical tests. Much less known is the Italian ADaMSoft (2014), which has the advantage of being a free and open-source system (but in Java). Still, it is worth consulting various websites on how to select and use software to manage data analysis. Our recommendations for the most suitable websites for Chapter 9 are as follows:

◆ Content-analysis.de (2013) *Resources Related to Content Analysis and Text Analysis*, www.content-analysis.de.
  Created and managed by Matthias Romppel, this software directory covers

not only software but also research (institutions, topics, organizations) bibliographies and electronic texts. In the context of this work the most valuable section is that on software. Here are listed 21 software packages for qualitative data analysis at www.content-analysis.de/software/qualitative-analysis, and 27 for the quantitative data analysis at www.content-analysis.de/software/quantitative-analysis.

◆ The Listening Resource (2012), www.qualitative-researcher.com. This web presence is the creation of Susan Eliot, a 'certified listening professional'; it focuses on programme evaluation, professional development, needs assessment and case studies. Her blog (www.qualitative-researcher. com/blog) is the most valuable part of this project, as it covers, however briefly, 33 topics ranging from coding qualitative data and focus group guidelines to qualitative sampling and recording interviews. Taking the last of these as an example, Eliot offers us 540 words based on her own experience of recording and note taking, without providing much in the way of leads to other resources. There are also some excellent interviews, such as one with Richard Krueger on 'qualitative listening'. This site is a relatively painless and user-friendly introduction to many aspects of qualitative data gathering and analysis. One may also subscribe to the blogs.

◆ Web Center for Social Research Methods, www.socialresearchmethods.net. This is a valuable resource for quantitative data analysis in particular. It includes Trochim's *Research Methods Knowledge Base*, which is 'an online hypertext textbook on applied social research methods' dealing with all aspects of quantitative research and much less on qualitative research (www.socialresearchmethods.net/kb). In addition another of Trochim's creations, *Selecting Statistics*, is also available on this website (www.socialresearchmethods.net/selstat/ssstart.htm); this is an 'online statistics advisor' that takes the user through a set of questions and then suggests appropriate statistical tests for the data. In our experience this works very well. Trochim has been instrumental in founding Cornell University's Office for Research on Evaluation, and its web presence opens the way to a plethora of interesting resources on research (https://core.human.cornell.edu/about).

References

ADaMSoft (2014), http://adamsoft.sourceforge.net. [Accessed 10 November 2014.]

Booth, C. (2009) *Informing Innovation: tracking student interest in emerging library technologies at*

Ohio University, Association of College and Research Libraries, Chicago, IL, www.ala.org/acrl/sites/ala.org.acrl/files/content/publications/ booksanddigitalresources/digital/ii-booth.pdf. [Accessed 10 November 2014.]

Chambliss, D. F. and Schutt, R. K. (2013) *Making Sense of the Social World: methods of investigation,* 4th edn, SAGE Publications, Thousand Oaks, CA.

Christensen, L. B., Johnson, R. B. and Turner, L. A. (2011) *Research Methods, Design and Analysis*, 11th edn, Allyn & Bacon, Boston, MA.

Content-analysis.de (2013) *Resources Related to Content Analysis and Text Analysis*, www.content-analysis.de. [Accessed 10 November 2014.]

Cornell University. Cornell Office for Research on Evaluation (2014) https://core.human.cornell.edu/about. [Accessed 10 November 2014.]

Creative Research Systems (2014) *The Survey System,* www.surveysystem.com. [Accessed 10 November 2014.]

Creswell, J. W. (2014) *Research Design: qualitative, quantitative and mixed methods approaches,* 4th edn, SAGE Publications, Thousand Oaks, CA.

DanielSoper.com (2014) *Statistics Calculators Version 3.0,* www.danielsoper.com/statcalc3/default.aspx. [Accessed 10 November 2014.]

Document Foundation (2013) *LibreOffice 4.1. Calc Guide: working with spreadsheets,* https://wiki.documentfoundation.org/images/4/47/CG41-CalcGuideLO.pdf. [Accessed 10 November 2014.]

Gibbs, G. R. (2007) *Analyzing Qualitative Data,* SAGE Publications, London.

Gorman, G. E. and Clayton, P. R. (2005) *Qualitative Research for the Information Professional: a practical handbook,* 2nd edn, Facet Publishing, London.

Grefsheim, S. F. and Rankin, J.A. (2007) Information Needs and Information Seeking in a Biomedical Research Setting: a study of scientists and science administrators, *Journal of the Medical Library Association,* **95** (4), 426–34.

IBM (2014) SPSS software: predictive analytics software and solutions, www-01.ibm.com. [Accessed 10 November 2014.]

Joubert, D. J., and Lee, T. P. (2007) Empowering Your Institution Through Assessment, *Journal of the Medical Library Association,* **95** (1), 46–53.

Leedy, P. D., and Ormrod, J. E. (2013) *Practical Research: planning and design,* 10th edn, Pearson, Boston, MA.

The Listening Resource (2012) www.qualitative-researcher.com. [Accessed 10 November 2014.]

McNabb, D. L. (2008) *Research Methods in Public Administration and Nonprofit Management: quantitative and qualitative approaches,* 2nd edn, M. E. Sharpe, Armonk, NY.

Pickard, A. J. (2013) *Research Methods in Information,* 2nd edn, Facet Publishing, London, 283–310.

SurveyMonkey (2014) Create Surveys, Get Answers, www.surveymonkey.com. [Accessed 10 November 2014.]

Trochim, W. M. K. (2006a) Inferential Statistics. In *Research Methods Knowledge Base*, www.socialresearchmethods.net/kb/statinf.php. [Accessed 10 November 2014.]

Trochim, W. M. K. (2006b) *Research Methods Knowledge Base*, www.socialresearchmethods.net/kb. [Accessed 10 November 2014.]

Trochim, W. M. K. (2006c) Selecting Statistics. In *Research Methods Knowledge Base*, www.socialresearchmethods.net/selstat/ssstart.htm. [Accessed 10 November 2014.]

Vaughan, L. (2001) *Statistical Methods for the Information Professional: a practical, painless approach to understanding, using and interpreting statistics*, ASIST Monograph Series, Information Today for the American Society for Information Science and Technology, Medford, NJ.

Web Center for Social Research Methods, www.socialresearchmethods.net. [Accessed 10 November 2014.]

Wilmoth, W. S. (2007) The Effect of Smart Cards on Library Use: the Griffin Technical College case, *Georgia Library Quarterly*, **44** (2), Art. 5, 15–21.

Wolcott, H. F. (1990) *Writing up Qualitative Research*, Qualitative Research Methods [Series] 20, SAGE Publications, Newbury Park, CA.

Yang, K. (2010) *Making Sense of Statistical Methods in Social Research*, SAGE Publications, London.

Yin, R. K. (2011) *Qualitative Research from Start to Finish*, Guilford Press, New York, NY.

CHAPTER 10

Reporting on an information needs analysis

Introduction

We are now at the end of the process, both figuratively and literally. In this final chapter of the book we examine the last stage of an INA process – reporting the results. There is no single way to write such a report, so our comments here must be viewed as suggestions rather than specifications. Each INA will have a unique purpose and context, and there may well be organizational requirements for formatting or target audience expectations for terminology that prescribe aspects of the written project report. Therefore, it is best to clarify those prior to putting fingers to keyboard.

For some INA projects the requirements will be spelled out clearly, for example when the investigator has a contract containing specifications for the work. The contract might include instructions on the nature and extent of the final report and specify all the topics/problems that must be addressed and a maximum word length.

INAs can be presented in written format and/or verbally, so both are covered in this chapter, the majority of which concentrates on the formal report written at the end of the analysis. Other short sections discuss the use of draft reports, oral presentations and less conventional means of communicating findings to the stakeholders.

In Chapter 4 we stated that reporting the results is Stage 4, that is, the final stage, of the INA process, coming after preparation, data gathering and data analysis (see Figure 4.1, p. 68). At the reporting stage the investigator presents a review of the investigation's findings and seeks to determine a range of likely cause-and-effect relationships. On the basis of these relationships a range of possible interventions might be suggested to address the needs that the analysis has highlighted or exposed. That is, the recommendation of a set of possible context-specific solutions is articulated in the report. Thus one purpose of a report is to present the findings; another is to serve as a permanent record of the analysis.

Regardless of whether the INA has been requested internally or commissioned by an external body, it has been requested because someone believes that some sort of a problem exists. Therefore, the final document must, above all else, deal with the issues as perceived by the organization or community. The INA process may well uncover other matters that are considered important – indeed, our experience is that this very often happens; nevertheless, the key point is that the organization wants to have its questions answered.

Written documents, presentations and other forms of reporting all have the same basic function at heart: making results of the analysis respond directly and meaningfully to the information needs that were investigated (Alreck and Settle, 2004, 347). Regardless of whether the INA has investigated the information needs of a target population (a Level 1 need) or of the service providers (a Level 2 need) or of the organization with regard to its resource allocation (a Level 3 need), it will require a report of some sort.

As noted in Chapter 4, the primary intention of an INA report is to describe for all stakeholders the process and findings in a timely, understandable and accurate manner. To do this well, the investigator must take into account the report's specific audience(s) and its purpose. The audience and purpose determine the presentation of the report's content, including matters such as the amount of detail and level of language (all advice on report writing says this, but for an example see Forsyth, 2010). A secondary intention might be to present information to stakeholders that will generate feedback on selected issues.

To help focus our thinking on the somewhat complex and varied matter of reporting on an INA, this chapter addresses five questions:

1　For whom is the INA being reported? That is, what is the audience?
2　What is the process for writing an INA report?
3　How is a typical INA report structured?
4　How can graphics and other visuals be employed to good effect?
5　How else might INA results be presented?

The audience and its impact on the final report

As the final stage commences, it is necessary to keep in mind the audience and reason for preparing the report, whether written or verbal. Specifically, who forms the principal audience and what are their significant characteristics; what is this audience's level of domain knowledge and facility with specific terminology; what attitudes do its members bring to the INA, and what is the best way to 'reach' them in the style of the concluding report or presentation? It is never a matter of 'talking down' to the audience, but rather of speaking directly to the members in a way that is understandable and interesting. It is also never a matter of trying to show superior knowledge – key audiences are generally more aware than writers and presenters give them given credit for.

If presentation choices open to the investigator are determined by the nature of the audience, it is worth keeping an open mind regarding the media most appropriate for this audience: letters and memos, telephone calls, audio-conferences, e-mail messages, tweets and more. The medium employed need not necessarily be a formal written document or a formal presentation, though for the most part this chapter assumes that it is, and that it is prepared in electronic format. At the same time we recognize that there are benefits to be had from providing informal communication, especially if the intent is to generate feedback, so this can be considered as the project nears its conclusion.

Writing aimed at a specialized (expert) audience, perhaps if conducting an INA for a Level 1 need, should be characterized by clarity and attention to detail. In a typical report aimed at an expert audience we can expect to find a statement of the study's framework, a literature review, a discussion of methodological issues and the findings and recommendations. In short, when writing for expert readers, the investigator must be aware of formal expectations and specific institutional requirements. To go outside these is to court unwelcome criticism.

More flexibility is allowable with non-expert readers. Here we have in mind people who read reports in search of information and solutions to specific problems in the workplace or in their own communities. They are not experts who are immersed in the niceties of methodologies.

Validity and reliability

It is worth remembering that validity is concerned with the integrity of the conclusions generated from a piece of research (Creswell, 2014, 201) such as an INA. In our context external validity (whether the results can be generalized beyond the specific context) will rarely apply, since an INA is conducted in and for a specific purpose. But internal validity is important and asks whether a causal relationship established during the investigation actually holds true. If, for example, the analysis concludes that information needs in a community have a strong linguistic component, is it possible to show this clearly? Do the findings 'prove' that readers of Serbian have information needs that can be met only by providing material in Serbian? To give a different example, is it true that poor lighting in part of a building impedes access to information located in that section? These may be assumptions that many would believe, but the investigator needs to go beyond assumptions. The evidence (that is, the relevant data) must establish beyond reasonable doubt that there is cause and effect and that interpretation of the data is on sure enough ground to convince even the sceptic.

Reliability, on the other hand, is concerned with whether the results of a study are repeatable (Creswell, 2014, 201); in terms of INAs this means repeatable in the same context or one that mirrors it, for an INA is always linked to a specific context. Specifically, is the measure established by the analysis for gauging an information need at any of the three levels (service receivers, service providers, or resources) reliable and stable? If it is not, then the analysis is likely to be unreliable.

Qualitative data pose something of a problem, because by their very nature they cannot be replicated; yet this is not a barrier to the use of interviews and other techniques for data gathering, only a warning that there may be questions asked about the reliability of such data. If an investigator is questioned about the reliability of data from interviews or focus groups, it might be necessary to explain how respondents were chosen as a reflection of the population, how the data were collected, how transcripts were created and analysed – in short how the data are representative of what would have been gathered if different people had been used as respondents in different locations and at different times. One of us had his analysis questioned by a manager who did not like the direction the investigation was taking, and the target chosen for the criticism was the interviews. After hearing an explanation of how the interviews were conducted and how respondents were chosen, the critic was sufficiently mollified, if not exactly happy.

The writing process

When preparing to write the results of an INA, it pays to begin with a disciplined approach. When planning, enough time must be allocated not only for writing but also for such matters as receiving feedback, proofreading and printing. Once again we emphasize that there is no single way to write a report, so what follows are suggestions rather than specifications.

The final stage of the INA process is sufficiently important for it to be considered a sub-project within the project. Without communicating the results the value in what has been discovered would remain unrealized. If an organization has requested the INA, then the content of the report is all the staff really care about – to them the report *is* the analysis. As Sussams (1998, 109) has said, 'the presentation of information in the form of a report is actually the main objective'.

INA investigators should not overlook one obvious fact: the quality of the reporting is often interpreted as a surrogate for the quality of the work discussed in the report. Accordingly, it is crucial to allow enough time and energy for preparing the final presentation of the findings; even if the INA has gone extremely well it can still 'flop' if the final reporting is rushed. As a result, its intended audience might deem the whole project a failure.

Before beginning we recommend that the investigator develop a detailed schedule with firm deadlines. Gantt charts are addressed in Chapter 4; a Gantt chart prepared for an INA should include the time needed for writing the final report. It is important to work backwards from the completed report's due date and set realistic target dates for each preceding activity. If one is relying on participants for feedback, this needs to be included in the timing; experience shows it is often overlooked to the frustration of all concerned. As a rough guide, expect the focused data analysis and writing to take at least as long as the data collection phase. It can take considerable time to become fully immersed in the data and their full meaning as part of the overall writing exercise, and many reports have been less effective because the investigator did not leave enough time for this final step in the process. This does not mean that writing cannot start until all the data are in. Bryman and Bell (2011, 677) recommend starting earlier, because the writing process forces the researcher to think how best to present and justify the key points in the analysis.

When developing the schedule, the investigator must have a realistic understanding of his or her time management capabilities when under pressure, and be conscious of all other commitments that can and will distract from the writing. It is necessary to ask, given other commitments, how many days of the week will be productive. How many pages or words will be written at an average sitting? While some experienced INA investigators can produce about 1000 words of 'clean' text during a two-to-three hour sitting, the reality is that less experience usually means more time is required.

The investigator should keep the report outline close at hand (discussed below), and continually ask, 'What am I meant to be writing about at this point, and what am I trying to say?' These questions help to avoid the unfocused or tangential writing that often occurs. Above all else, the advice offered by Bartle

(2007) can focus the writing process: 'One over-riding principle that you should aim for in all report writing is to report on the results of your activities. This requires some analysis on your part that goes beyond a mere description of your activities'. In other words, the results should be supported with evidence derived from the data and commentary on the findings; this will be crucial for those who take the next step after the analysis.

At the draft stage the writer need not worry too much about grammar, syntax and spelling, although poor writing at any stage is inadvisable. Instead of looking for that piece of 'deathless prose' at this stage, it is more valuable to concentrate on expressing ideas simply and clearly and utilizing all the available data to do so. Experienced INA investigators find that writing flows more readily if they have in mind someone who may eventually read the report, especially if that person is known to be a sharp thinker who will criticize the report mercilessly if it is full of waffle. If the writer can think of someone from the commissioning agency who expressed considerable doubts about the value of the process, then writing to convince that person will require great attention to relevance and clarity. This technique gives a far greater reality to the report than writing for an audience that may be easily convinced by the writer's less-than-perfect arguments.

While advising novice writers not to worry unnecessarily about grammar and syntax at this stage, we also suggest having crisp prose as a goal. A writer should try to make the text vibrant and succinct by writing in the first person and using the active rather than the passive voice, avoiding abstract nouns, keeping sentences simple and limiting the length of paragraphs. However, it is necessary to bear in mind that the final choice of grammatical style must depend on why the report is being written, and especially for whom, as this can help determine the style most appropriate to the context. For the very best guidance on writing we cannot do better than refer the reader to the classics: Gowers' *Plain Words* (2014) and Fowler's *Modern English Usage* (Burchfield, 2004).

Here it seems appropriate to digress and discuss the purpose of a draft report. For the investigator-turned-writer the draft is a stage on the way to the final report in which to review the structure of the whole, to move some sections and strengthen or delete others; it is possible to add more data, to work on spelling and formatting and even to start creating the table of contents. Yet there can be a purpose for the draft beyond these considerations, and this is how the investigator of the draft report uses it in communicating with key stakeholders.

The investigator can submit a draft to the individual who has contracted the report (and it should go no further than that) as a means of 'flying a kite' or two.

The writer's question to this person is simple: 'Is this what you want?' Even if the response is not in the affirmative, it is valuable to know if the right focus has been achieved, and it helps to know this sooner rather than later. It can be humiliating (and time-consuming) to be told to change a final report because it has not met the expectations of the key stakeholders.

We have suggested that the most basic principle is for the investigator to begin writing with a carefully planned outline. However, it is equally important not to follow this outline slavishly when the data dictate differently – this is especially true of the results section (discussed below). Often, as familiarity with the data increases, it becomes possible to find previously hidden patterns and themes. When this happens, the data can be organized to give prominence to emerging patterns lately identified as important. How this approach might take place is suggested in Scenario 10.1.

Scenario 10.1 Information needs analysis in a government information service [based on an idea in Glesne (2011)]

In a major INA focusing on senior managers in a large government information service it becomes clear during the information-gathering stage that conflict resolution is an area of responsibility for which managers have a considerable information need. While analysing the data, under the heading 'conflict resolution information needs' the investigator, Cynthia Blackadder, has categorized information needs data by conflict resolution techniques, including 'holding section meetings', 'holding individual discussions', 'involving superiors', etc.

However, as Cynthia writes, it becomes apparent from the data that individual discussions are used in two ways. One way is confrontational, seeking to resolve the conflict by directing the relevant staff member to cease specific activities that create ill-will. The other approach is far more nondirective, in which the senior manager invites the staff member to discuss the problems, verbally reflecting on cause and effect, in the hope that this person will come to a personal understanding of an appropriate course of action. The 'holding individual discussions' data are subdivided accordingly, and she continues to write.

Then, as Cynthia writes about information needs regarding the nondirective approach, it emerges that male and female managers are treated differently in the nondirective scenario. With female staff the senior managers, usually male, take a passive, nondirective approach, whereas with male staff these same managers are much more directive, suggesting specific courses of action. Once again, then, Cynthia sorts the data into new sub-categories and continues to write, seeking to highlight this gender-based pattern in discussing the information needs of senior managers. Cynthia then reflects on what she read in Glesne (2011) while preparing for the report writing stage: 'through this . . . process, you increasingly impose order on your data. Yet, at the same time, the order is flexible; it continuously changes, shaped by the ideas that your writing generates'.

Because writing is an iterative process linked closely with data analysis, the writer may need to reconsider previously relegated data and incorporate some aspects as evidence. Retrieving data originally considered marginal but which on later reflection can be seen as relevant to issues that emerge during the analysis is a common occurrence during INA report writing. For this reason it is essential to keep all data well organized in files with logical names and to review data during the analysis. Nearly everyone who has conducted this kind of analysis will have gone back to previously discarded data and had a moment of discovery that casts new light on a theme within the project. No final report should be presented until all data have been reviewed one last time just in case a key point has been overlooked. This step takes time, and it is further reason for allowing plenty of leeway in the timeline for report writing. Conversely, other data that once seemed crucial might now be less relevant to newly discovered patterns and can be summarized instead of described in full.

The writer should focus on the information at hand and work through it so that the remaining data become progressively less. Non-existent data are not a concern at this stage; if there is a genuine gap in the data, it may be enough simply to admit it. On those rare occasions when such a gap cannot be ignored it will be necessary to attempt to collect the missing information.

The structure of an INA report

In reality Scenario 10.1 may be somewhat misleading with regard to flexibility. What we have tried to convey is that, when writing the report, it is necessary to be as true to the data as possible. Although the identification of different patterns in the data might require the report to be reorganized, the writer will very likely retain the standard structure of an INA report. First, there are basic conventions regarding content that should be followed in any good research report. Second, there are some useful organizational strategies that help guide the presentation of ideas in qualitative studies. We look first at the structure of a typical report, and then at some common organizing techniques.

Report organization

To the extent that we can speak of a typical INA report, the audience might expect to find four sections:

1 Executive summary
2 Scope and methods section
3 Findings section
4 Implications of findings.

From this list it is apparent that the outcome is a report, not a scholarly paper. For the academic who may serve as an INA investigator this is often difficult to comprehend. Therefore, our first word of advice is to avoid paying too much attention to guides on scholarly writing for advice on how to prepare an INA report, but instead to refer to the many good guides to report writing available on the web, as well as in libraries and bookshops. Completed INA reports available as public documents should also be consulted. Some are on the web, as are these examples:

◆ Colmar Brunton Research (2009) *Financial Investors' Information Needs*
◆ Harris, L. K. (2008) *Library User Needs Analysis Report*
◆ NHS Bolton Library (2012) *Public Health Information Needs Analysis*
◆ Verso Consulting (2007) *Information Needs Analysis*.

The four parts noted above are another way of saying that a report should begin with a summary and have a beginning, middle and end to provide (1) an overview, then to inform the target audience about (2) what the INA set out to achieve and how it was done, (3) what was found out and (4) why the results are relevant. Often different titles will be given to the various sections, but the content generally follows the same pattern.

Executive summary

The executive summary must perform the job that its name implies, to provide a summary of the whole report, including the major findings and recommendations. The aim is not only to provide a succinct overview, but also to capture the interest and attention of the audience, especially the principal stakeholders who are invariably busy and may forgo reading the rest of the report. Therefore, the executive summary should be brief and to the point –

usually no more than 10% of the whole report and certainly no more than 2000 words. In this limited space it is important to be engaging; this can be done by

◆ avoiding jargon and instead use direct, clear language
◆ expressing the findings simply and without embellishment, avoiding the natural tendency to qualify findings with 'ifs and buts'
◆ including expert opinion about the implications, employing qualitative assessment rather than quantification.

If this can be done succinctly and clearly, then the executive summary will have conveyed the essence of the INA for those who will read no further, and the hope is that it will have encouraged others to keep reading.

The executive summary is a common weakness in reports. Because it is usually the last part of the report to be written, it is often done quickly to meet a deadline or simply to get it out of the way. But the executive summary appears at the beginning of the report, so it is, quite naturally, read first. Judgements about the quality, merit and value of the report can be made very quickly, so a poorly written executive summary can have a damaging initial impact from which it may be difficult to recover. This only serves to emphasize that considerable effort and time should be devoted to its writing.

When writing the executive summary, the simplest way can be the best. We recommend that the writer list the main points in the same order as they appear in the report. A simple sentence should then be written about each of the main points and further sentences added to explain more if needed, always avoiding jargon. Then the summary should be read to ensure it makes sense to any reader unfamiliar with the subject. At this point the writer should ask a colleague who is unafraid to make critical comments to read the summary to ensure it is clear and to the point.

Other front material should be included in a report: a title page, acknowledgments (not necessary in a commercial report) and a contents page and a list of figures if relevant.

Scope and methods section

Typical readers of an INA do not want the detailed description of methodology and methods found in most academic research reports. The best advice here is to keep it simple and to provide just enough information so that the readers understand how data were collected and analysed. Even the most sceptical readers need to be reassured that the study is credible, and for this purpose it is important to provide the numbers of respondents in surveys, interviews and focus groups, but not the minutiae of their design.

The scope section can begin by stating the questions the analysis set out to address, and of course these will have been tailored to the particular audience being addressed. The questions should be stated clearly and in a manner that is conducive to being answered in the next part of the report. It is sometimes possible to write this section based on the questions set out in the contract or terms of reference for the INA. If necessary, the key terms should be defined and the limitations of the study noted.

The literature review, such as it is, usually comes next and sets the study in context. A brief overview should be provided of any documents that describe the relevant organizations, communities and individuals (see Chapter 6) so that the reader understands the background to the analysis. Discussing the literature early in the report allows the investigator to refer to relevant works in other parts of the report without disrupting the flow of description and analysis.

The description of the methods usually follows the literature review. Here the procedures selected for conducting the analysis should be described and explanations given for why they were chosen. The investigator should tell the readers about the participants and the setting and any other significant features of the INA's context, always bearing in mind the audience characteristics. The account of the data-gathering techniques can be kept short and to the point, because the technical issues that will preoccupy the investigator are much less likely to interest a typical reader. It is important, however, to report any issues arising from the use of a particular technique or method that may limit the validity or reliability of the findings. In other words the report should not pretend that everything went according to plan if this is not the case. Sometimes an appendix containing details of the methodology is provided in an INA report, but our advice is that it is usually unnecessary.

Findings section

This section is the core of an INA report, for here the investigator tells the target audience what has been found through the data analysis. When writing an INA report, the key is to keep in mind the message or content to be conveyed. How this content is presented might depend on the structure required by a contracting agency and on the style best suited to the information itself and the intended audience. Wolcott's short and readable volume, *Writing Up Qualitative Research*, is replete with handy ideas on how to juggle conflicting demands on the content (Wolcott, 2009). He provides a series of practical suggestions on starting the writing, keeping going and finishing – straightforward, entertaining and useful advice.

When reporting the findings, it is important to consider how to do this to best effect. The investigator might tell readers what he or she has read, seen and heard during the investigation. Pithy verbatim transcripts of participant dialogue could be included along with detailed descriptions of sites, activities and other relevant events (if these are essential to the analysis), computer-generated data and everything else that was collected. Field notes will provide concrete descriptive data that can be used to make the case for the recommendations. Often such data will not just help to make a case but will enhance it with colour. As an example, instead of simply describing an interview in which one participant said he did not like a specific activity, quoting his actual words, including the vernacular, might make his opinions very clear indeed! Put simply, evidence must be provided to support the points being made.

Throughout the findings information should be provided in a positive manner. This approach is especially true when reporting on the information needs of those with some form of disadvantage, such as people in a deprived socio-economic area or those with an illness. Those forced to live in such communities already know they have problems, and they do not need this to be reinforced. For example people with multiple sclerosis said that more of what they are told emphasizes the probable negative outcomes of the illness than what can be done about it, which is inevitably depressing for people who already have it tough enough (Hepworth, Harrison and James, 2003, 299). The communication of such an INA should therefore start with, and emphasize, all the positives that can be identified for the disadvantaged communities. This will also please funding agencies and parent bodies, who want to hear good news rather than bad. The tough messages can come later.

Findings are typically organized around the questions that the INA has set out to answer. With these questions serving effectively as subheadings, the data can then be organized in a number of ways, but again simplicity and clarity should be primary considerations. These characteristics are most often achieved when a report follows what might be termed a thematic approach; Glesne (2011) discusses this along with other approaches. An INA is much more than mere description, and reporting without interpretation, evaluation and projection is only reportage. An investigator has conducted an INA in order to increase understanding, and this is done first by interpretation of what was found, then by evaluation and finally by projection. Recommendations drawn from the analysis can appear within each themed section, although they should also be collated at either the beginning or the end of the report.

In the thematic approach, under each question there will be a set of themes that emerge from the collected data. The discussion of findings is organized under these themes. Details are not reported in slavish chronological fashion. As discussed in Chapter 9, observed relationships and events as well as content from interviews are drawn together to identify patterns in the data. If reporting the results of a survey, as an example, you need not report the results in the original order but can rearrange them so that what is considered the most important data can go first (Alreck and Settle, 2004, 347).

A point from May and May (2009) is that the investigator should aim to summarize a core idea in a single sentence (the topic sentence of a paragraph). All other sentences in the paragraph should be related to it. This approach is especially useful when seeking to draw conclusions that will inform concrete actions that may follow from the INA. However, an important point here is to avoid the dry presentation of each separate action that will be recommended. Referring back to Chapter 2, the writer needs to remember that it is not the information that the audience wants from an INA, it is the *benefits* of the information. Thus all results should emphasize the gains the audience will receive after the implementation of the recommendations.

As an example, we refer back to Scenario 10.1. In the scenario 'conflict resolution information needs' is a principal heading – perhaps derived from an initial question such as 'What are the information needs of senior managers with regard to conflict resolution?' Under this principal heading Cynthia, the investigator, subdivides data into the following themes: 'holding section meetings', 'holding individual discussions' and 'involving superiors'. But it also emerges that 'holding individual discussions' actually divides into two sub-themes, 'confrontational' and 'nondirective'. Whether these should be treated as specific sub-themes depends on the nature of the findings, but in terms of the INA the broader theme of 'holding individual discussions' may be adequate. At the same time, however, it also emerges that gender is an issue in conflict resolution, and it may be sensible for Cynthia to add 'gender issues' as a separate thematic category of the INA.

Whatever approach is taken, ease of use should drive the reporting of findings. The report should show that the writer has been thinking of the reader first and foremost rather than focusing on fine prose.

Implications of findings

In the final section of an INA report it is essential to focus above all on the value of the findings. The readers are looking for an answer or a solution, so we recommend starting the section by restating the question or problem that the INA has investigated.

In this section the writer presents the implications, conclusions and recommendations arising from the findings. When presenting the conclusions, it is essential to explain how they were derived from the analysis. Any implications arising from the findings should be raised, for example, addressing whether they suggest that some common assumptions about a target population need to be modified. At the practical level the implications need to be addressed in the form of recommendations which might well pertain to professional practice, organizational structures or policies and procedures. In other words at the conclusion of the report the investigator must present the readers with the meaning and value of what has been learned from the investigation.

Further, the investigator should keep in mind that the findings section must be succinctly written. Its purpose is not to review all of the evidence or to provide some simple suggestions for future steps; rather the function of the findings section is to address the key points from the investigation that can be used by readers and stakeholders to improve the present situation. Features such as bullet points can highlight key recommendations, and illustrations can demonstrate the relationships between the themes from the findings and the recommendations.

Just when you think you are finished

Reports generally have fewer references than academic publications. In the latter the authors must identify all sources that informed their thinking so that readers can trace the ideas back to the original items if they wish. This level of detail is unnecessary in the typical INA report, in which only the key documents referred to need be referenced.

It is important to remember that the final presentation of the report will influence how it is received. As already indicated, poor spelling, faulty punctuation and incorrect grammar have ruined many reports. Proofreading carefully, using skilled copy editors and relying on comments from colleagues, helps to make a report accurate and clear. Irving and Smith (1998, 80) offer these words of warning to anyone writing a report or dissertation: 'If you skimp at the end you will regret it when you see the errors in the final version'. Thus it is wise to leave enough time to do all the necessary checking before releasing the final report.

There is a range of elements that affect presentations. Page numbers are essential, and running headers and footers are useful in formal or long documents. Reports use numbering for each section, and for this a 'section' may be one, two or more paragraphs on a single topic. A common convention that works well is to use numbers starting with the chapter number, then a dot followed by a running number, so in the third chapter, sections will be numbered, e.g., 3.1, 3.2, 3.3, 3.3.1, 3.3.2, 3.4 and so on. The same numbers are used in the table of contents. Most reports are printed only on one side of the paper, and commonly 1.5 line spacing is used, though requirements may vary. Use margins of at least 2.5 cm on both sides, especially if the final document is to be bound – and allow more for the left hand margin if an especially thick binding will be necessary. On that matter, find out about requirements for binding well in advance and make suitable preparations. No one wants to discover that the binders cannot do the job in time to meet a deadline.

The use of graphics

Many INA reports and presentations stick to simple text, but this can be augmented and made more interesting by employing tables and graphs. A clear table or a simple graph can add visual impact to the text, provided the best form of graphical display is chosen.

While graphs and other visual aids add to the quality of data presentation, a graph is not a picture 'worth a thousand words'; rather, a graph does not speak for itself, and some of the content still has to be explained. But remember that it is the context that needs explaining, not the data; it is unnecessary to repeat data in the text that already appear clearly in a graph (for example there is no need to say 'only 20.5% said Yes' if that fact is already visible in the graph). It is much more important to attempt an explanation of why only 20.5% answered in the affirmative.

Bar charts, histograms and line charts lend themselves especially well to the sort of data comparison that is most useful in INAs. A bar chart is appropriate for displaying the frequency of categorical data. If the INA measured the use of a library by students, it would be possible to show the numbers of primary, secondary and tertiary student visitors in a bar chart (see Figure 10.1). This choice of graphic display (the bar chart) would also apply to, for example, data for the number of public, academic and special libraries in one county or state.

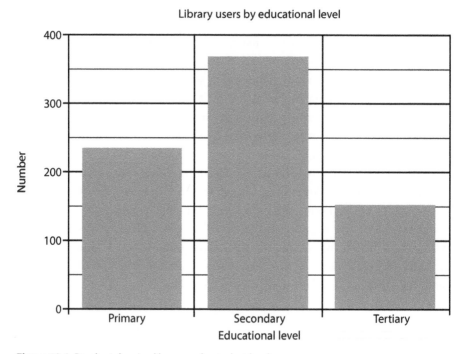

Figure 10.1 Bar chart showing library use by student level

As each category of data is not connected to the data in other categories, the columns should not touch, nor should the graph be 'enhanced' by the use of 3D columns (temptingly easy to generate in almost all spreadsheet software), for this would be representing data that simply are not there.

However, if the type of data to be displayed did not come from distinct categories but was instead continuous, then the columns should touch. If the data need to be reduced to groups for simplicity, then, for example, the cost of books in a collection might be best shown by putting all books that cost between £0.00 and £9.99 into one class, all those costing between £10.00 and £19.99 in a second class and so on. There are no gaps in these data, so the graph can display columns touching in a histogram.

Data collected over time are well suited to a time series plot, in which the horizontal axis shows time (years, days, seconds), and the variable data are shown in the vertical axis. As the data are connected, the points can be joined together to display a single line. If the purpose is to display the use of library books to show the recovery of lending activity after the borrowing fee was introduced, the time series plot could look like that in Figure 10.2.

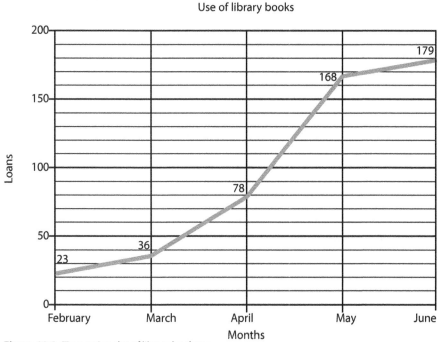

Figure 10.2 Time series plot of library book use

The final form of graph to suggest is employed when the data have two variables, and their relationship to each other is crucial. As an example, in a library weeding exercise the age of the book and its number of loans in the past year could be factors used in the deselection process. For this purpose a scatter plot can be used. The year of publication will be the horizontal axis, with the number of loans plotted in the vertical axis. Typically this will display a scatter of points travelling up from left to right, showing that the newer the book is, the more times it is borrowed. If sufficient data are used, then this graph can roughly predict how many times a book of a certain age will be borrowed.

The type of graph to choose depends on two factors: first, the type of data, with categorical data in a bar chart, numerical data in a histogram, time-based data in a line chart and pairs of numerical variables in a scatter plot; second, different types of graphs, as a particular type may assist in understanding the needs analysis better than another.

Creating graphs is no longer the chore that it once was, thanks largely to the availability of many software packages and websites to aid in the process of graphic representation of data. Microsoft Excel is one aid found on many desktop computers, and it is a passable means of creating very simple bar graphs. In addition there are literally hundreds of websites that facilitate graph creation.

All tables and figures should be numbered, and the numbers should be referred to in references in the text. One simple reason for this is that a figure can be moved just prior to printing so that it does not appear exactly with the relevant text. Note that readers will find it easier to follow the argument if a table or graph appears just after it has been referred to in the text.

The addition of images to a report can increase the reader's understanding of both the present situation and what might potentially be done in the future. Screenshots of web pages, for example, add to comprehension. Thus a study of mobile use among undergraduates, and how an academic library might improve the services it provides to mobile devices (a Level 3 case), can include images of present sites (such as in Seeholzer and Salem, 2011), although prototypes of new pages in the making are very useful, provided they can be released.

Other means of communicating the results
In person

Ultimately most organizations will want to see a formal written report emanating from the INA. Yet there will be reasons why managers will also ask for verbal reports. This situation is not necessarily a presentation, simply a talk among a few people. Typically this is where the most honest assessments are given, because the constraints of a semi-public written document can be forgotten. In face-to-face talks an investigator has the opportunity to be blunt about certain issues that could not be stated in writing. Suppose a manager is unwilling to allocate sufficient resources to an information service, and this is obstructing information flow; suppose a librarian is unable to handle the pressures of using a social networking tool; suppose an institutional partner is not performing to a required level – all of these might be cases in which the investigator must tell the clients exactly what has been found and what might be done about it. In cases such as these the investigator has to say something along the lines of:

> Look, the current manager is unable to provide the information service you desire because he won't shift resources away from service B to service A. He is too set in his ways, he doesn't have the technological knowledge needed, and the staff don't much like his style. If you really want to move the service ahead to provide your clients with what they need and deserve, you have to do something about the manager.

It is not necessarily the investigator's job as the writer to say exactly what might be done with the manager, but a client is quite likely to ask for suggestions, so it is wise to have some ready. And remember this is an information needs *analysis*, not an *assessment* – see the beginning of Chapter 1 if you have forgotten our distinction between the two.

Presentations

Many INAs will be adequately completed with a written report, but not all. There will be times when the investigator is called upon to give a verbal presentation, sometimes instead of a written report but often as a complement to one. The investigator might believe that some aspects of the findings need to be presented directly to the clients, perhaps for greater impact or because some members of the intended audience are likely to prefer a verbal report over a written one.

If the INA is seeking to alter core norms and values, then a verbal presentation that can contain almost theatrical elements might be more effective than the same content presented in written form. An INA of a disadvantaged group could be completed with a written report to stakeholders who need detailed findings to improve the information systems being analysed, but members of the group might want to hear (literally) about the outcomes of the INA. For people with an illness or mental condition, this itself could affect communication, and 'people with high fatigue and low concentration levels are going to require information in a succinct form with emphasis on a graphical rather than textual presentation of information' (Hepworth, Harrison and James, 2003, 301). This suggests the use of a presentation or perhaps electronic media such as a website or a podcast.

A presentation does some things better than a written report, but for others it is largely useless. A well written report might be densely packed with data and detail about each stage of the analysis. However, in a verbal presentation the investigator must be careful not to rely on excessive detail, especially if it focuses on shortcomings. Verbal presentations are usually better suited to upbeat reports in which the opportunities to bring benefits to the organization are emphasized (Orna, 2004, 79).

As with written reports, attention in a verbal presentation must focus on what the audience will want to glean from the presentation. It is important to remember that those in the audience are giving their time to be there and hope to learn something in return, so the focus must be on communicating the key message(s) clearly and directly. There is usually not much time available for this, so trying to do too much might end in failure. One tip is that presenters should keep reminding themselves why the *Readers' Digest* is so popular!

People have different learning styles, and some in the audience will favour text, while others will prefer, and learn better from, an auditory style. Hilyer (2008) is very good as a source for more about presentations and learning styles. In a presentation there is little chance for the listeners to check on definitions, so it is advisable to avoid technical terms and jargon unless they will be understood immediately. Graphics such as maps, drawings, photographs and diagrams can help the audience understand much better than words can, so if the topic lends itself to visual illustration, then it is worth the effort spent preparing good-quality images.

In writing the constant repetition of words and phrases can become tedious, but in a presentation it is acceptable to use the key nouns over and over rather than substituting a pronoun. Though the presenter will have been living with this INA for some time, it will be new to most of the audience, so when he or she says 'we measured it each month' or 'after a while they found it useful', what is 'it' and who are 'they'? By saying exactly what is meant, as in 'we measured the number of transactions every month' and 'after a while the nurses found it useful', the audience will comprehend the meaning more readily. When preparing the presentation, the investigator must ask the question: do the words make sense with no previous context? If they do not, the need for revision is clear.

Scenario 10.2 offers an example of a verbal presentation used as a lead-in to a training programme intended to resolve an information need discovered during an INA.

Scenario 10.2 Verbal presentation of an INA at Warlock Law

In Scenario 9.1 (p. 201), Joseph, the information services manager at Warlock Law, undertook an INA to find out why the full-text databases to which the firm subscribed were not being used to a greater extent and whether the firm's lawyers were being provided with the information they needed. After analysing the transcripts of the interviews with 12 of the firm's lawyers, he identified several databases that provided content of little relevance to the lawyers; he also identified some key topic areas unsupported by the databases that were being provided. He also concluded that many of the senior lawyers needed training to help them be more effective and efficient in their online searching.

As Joseph wrote the report, he decided to ask a trusted colleague from the Law Commission library to read the initial draft. He incorporated his colleague's advice about the findings and the recommendations into the next version, but as a final step before submitting the report and organizing a presentation to the firm's partners, he decided to make a verbal presentation to the head of HR. This proved to be a very wise move, because the HR head gave Joseph some critical advice on how to present the findings and the recommendations about training needs in a way that would not make the firm's partners feel that Joseph was saying their ability to retrieve information was inferior to every other member of staff.

After the presentation Joseph set up a one-on-one training programme with the firm's partners, from whom he received great praise. When the programme was completed, Joseph helped his colleague from the Law Commission to set up a large-scale INA to investigate the effectiveness and efficiency of senior lawyers in their region.

Electronic media

It is unusual for an INA to use *only* a website, or any other electronic media, as the primary medium for reporting the results. It is increasingly common, however, to find one or more types of electronic media used in conjunction with written reports and presentations. Immediacy is a major advantage of electronic media; cheapness is another, and ubiquity, thanks to the enormous popularity of mobile devices, is a third. A fourth reason for using electronic media is the capacity for immediate communication within a community, though this might not always be seen as an advantage.

Websites

A website as a source of information about an INA has some advantages over print media such as newsletters. It can be updated regularly to keep the information current, so end-users only need to know of the website rather than keeping a record of which newsletter contains the information that they most require.

Social media

Blogs are a better medium for announcing the results of an INA than their actual amount of use for this purpose would seem to suggest. Because a blog post can be published the same day it is written, it can have a currency difficult to match in hard copy. A blog allows for the insertion of a link to a copy of the full report and other relevant sites and has the potential for interactive communication with stakeholders – if this is seen as useful. A podcast is an interesting channel for publishing the results of an analysis. A purely factual report could be made in oral form, but devices such as interviews with key stakeholders make better use of the medium. Networking tools like Facebook can be used if there is a desire to maintain contact with a 'community', which might well be true of a Level 1 analysis.

Review of Chapter 10

The reader might now appreciate that various forms of reporting are appropriate in a single INA. As an example, when conducting an analysis in preparation for purchasing a new integrated library system, there are several different groups who will be interested in the results. Key managers (concerned about Level 3) will want to read a full and detailed written report. Library staff (potentially Level 2) may be interested enough, but not all will be sufficiently motivated or technically able to read a detailed report on system capabilities. What can be done for them? In this case a presentation might be the most appropriate means of communicating the central findings, but without all the detail. And what of the end-users? For them the most immediate and useful form of communication might be through Web 2.0 tools such as blogs, and perhaps even Facebook. Announcing the impending arrival of a new automated system will make for a popular blog post or podcast.

This chapter has suggested that a detailed schedule and clear deadlines for report writing should be established as part of the whole project timeline, even working backwards from the due date to calculate when writing must commence. Writing needs to be simple and clear, with the specific purpose of the study and its intended audience always the focus. Report writing starts with a carefully planned outline. An adaptation of the familiar 'tell them what you're going to tell them; tell them; and tell them what you've told them' approach can provide an overall structure, with the findings themselves probably presented using a thematic approach. This lends itself to the structure recommended in this chapter: Summary, Scope and methods, Findings, Implications.

Presentations are a lively means of communicating results and are well suited to some stakeholder audiences, particularly those who will not wish to read a final report; but presentations are not the best means to articulate complex ideas. Content should be to the point, using language that the audience can follow without difficulty.

Further reading

We begin this section by recommending Phil Bartle's *Community Empowerment Collective: report writing* (2007) because it is (1) an excellent, thorough guide to report writing and (2) readily accessible on the web. Bartle's guide is among the best for our purposes, partly because it has a community rather than a commercial focus, and partly because it is practical and filled with common-sense advice. It covers the following topics:

◆ report writing guidelines (why, how, for whom)
◆ report writing for co-ordinators
◆ why write reports?
◆ who should receive reports?
◆ how to write reports
◆ writing better reports
◆ 'the job is not finished, until . . .'
◆ a model for writing reports
◆ hand-outs and briefings
◆ monitoring and reporting illustrations.

There are many other web-based guides to report writing (some are listed below), and we suggest searching for one that is best suited to the task at hand. Again we would remind readers that there are only a few examples of completed INA reports that are publicly available, partly because of the internal and sometimes sensitive nature of such documentation. Of the four publicly available reports listed on page 227, one particularly worth consultation is from the NHS Bolton Library (2012), not because it is an example to be followed but rather because it shows how such a report can be tailored to the needs of a very specific clientele.

There are several books worth consulting on the topic of this chapter. McKillip (1987, 120–31) includes a chapter on communicating results that addresses most of the topics covered by Bartle. Also, the simple guide by Irving and Smith (1998) is very accessible and replete with sound advice. A more recent book on the subject is Forsyth's *How to Write Reports and Proposals* (2nd edn, 2010). Possibly the most comprehensive book on communication for librarians and information managers is by Ross and Nilsen (2013).

For guidance on written English, which seems to become more necessary with each new generation of graduates and professionals, two classic but modernized works stand out. The first is *Fowler's Modern English Usage*, revised and largely rewritten by Robert Burchfield (Burchfield, 2004); the second is Gowers' *Plain*

Words, released in a completely new edition by Rebecca Gowers (2014), great-granddaughter of Sir Ernest Gowers. With the new editions of both works we have up-to-date, no-nonsense guidance on the use of British English. For American English a similarly robust work is Jacques Barzun's *Simple and Direct* (2001), written in his engaging and stylish way and covering diction, linking, tone, meaning, composition and revision. More 21st-century in format is Rachael Cayley's *Explorations of Style* blog discussed below.

For a simple, readable and entertaining guide to making presentations, one can never overlook Antony Jay's *Effective Presentation* (1993). If this name is recognizable, it is because he was co-writer of the *Yes Minister* (1980–4) and *Yes, Prime Minister* (1986–8) BBC TV series, and this guide is presented in much the same tongue-in-cheek style. Also covering the basics, but adding some useful content about cognition and how to adapt presentations to suit different learning styles, is Hilyer's *Presentations for Librarians: a complete guide to creating effective learner-centred presentations* (2008). A more detailed guide is provided by Leech in *How to Prepare, Stage and Deliver Winning Presentations* (2004). By using several of these works in combination, all bases will be covered.

To conclude this chapter, and the book, we recommend four websites for their guidance on presentations and report writing.

- ◆ Cayley, R. (2014) *Explorations of Style: a blog about academic writing*, http://explorationsofstyle.com.
  Although aimed at an academic readership (Cayley is in the Office of English Language and Writing Support at the University of Toronto), this is a hugely helpful guide to style for both professional and academic writing, and very useful for INA reporting. Most notable is her Five Key Strategies, covering reverse outlines, paragraphs, transitions, verbs and subjects – all replete with practical and helpful advice. There are many other valuable resources and discussions in the blog; we recommend that serious writers and reporters subscribe.
- ◆ Haughey, M. (2013) *An Introvert's Guide to Better Presentations: improving your public speaking despite hating crowds*, https://medium.com/@mathowie/an-introverts-guide-to-better-presentations-be7e772b2cb5.
  Writing with a sense of fun, Haughey provides sensible guidance to making public presentations and does so in an entertaining way that will bring the introverts on board. Good on visuals, Haughey offers solid and simple advice on such matters as 'telling a story', timing (including giving breaks) and the use of slides. Although written for a general-purpose audience, this site is relevant

to those needing to present the results of a needs analysis at a formal meeting.
◆ University of Canberra (2014) *Report Writing*,
www.canberra.edu.au/studyskills/writing/reports.
Most universities offer online guides to writing, and most include advice on
the particular skills required by report writing. This one from the University
of Canberra is rather fuller than others we have seen, but investigators and
reporters should surf the web for other guides suited to their particular
contexts. The Canberra guide is quite detailed on the structure of a report,
including the importance of the executive summary, undoubtedly the most
visible part of a report, yet in our experience often the most overlooked.
The guide also offers good advice on the visual presentation of the final
report, which frequently comes as an afterthought in real-world reports.
◆ Verso Consulting (2007) *Information Needs Analysis: summation report*,
http://ilc.com.au/resources/2/0000/0008/verso_summation_report__f__
061007.pdf.
Readers might well decide that rather than finding a guide to writing a
report, they would rather see a good example of a needs analysis report and
use that as a template. This is a pragmatic approach, but the caveat is that,
while there are some good examples of INA reports on the web (such as
the one cited here), most are flawed and should not be relied on as a
template for uncritical replication. It is better to use an example of a report
in conjunction with one of the better guides to report writing.

References

Alreck, P. A. and Settle, R. B. (2004) *The Survey Research Handbook*, 3rd edn, McGraw-Hill/Irwin Series in Marketing, McGraw-Hill/Irwin, Boston, MA.

Bartle, P. (2007) *Community Empowerment Collective: report writing. Different kinds of reports for mobilizers: Part C, How to write reports*,
http://cec.vcn.bc.ca/cmp/modules/rep-how.htm. [Accessed 10 November 2014.]

Barzun, J. (2001) *Simple and Direct: a rhetoric for writers*, 4th edn, Quill, New York, NY.

Bryman, A. and Bell, E. (2011) *Business Research Methods*, 3rd edn, Oxford University Press, Oxford.

Burchfield, R. W. (2004) *Fowler's Modern English Usage*, rev. 3rd edn, Oxford University Press, Oxford.

Cayley, R. (2014) *Explorations of Style: a blog about academic writing*,
http://explorationsofstyle.com. [Accessed 10 November 2014.]

Colmar Brunton Research (2009) *Financial Investors' Information Needs: final*, Retirement

Commission, Wellington, NZ,
http://ndhadeliver.natlib.govt.nz/delivery/DeliveryManagerServlet?dps_pid=IE53
06574&dps_custom_att_1=ilsdb. [Accessed 10 November 2014.]

Creswell, J. W. (2014) *Research Design: qualitative, quantitative and mixed methods approaches*,
4th edn, SAGE Publications, Thousand Oaks, CA.

Forsyth, P. (2010) *How to Write Reports and Proposals*, rev. 2nd edn, Kogan Page, London.

Glesne, C. (2011) *Becoming Qualitative Researchers: an introduction*, 4th edn, Pearson,
Boston, MA.

Gowers, E. and Gowers, R. (2014) *Plain Words*, Penguin/Particular Books, London.

Harris, L. K. (2008) *Library User Needs Analysis Report*,
http://works.bepress.com/lindsay_harris/3. [Accessed 10 November 2014.]

Haughey, M. (2013) *An Introvert's Guide to Better Presentations: improving your public speaking
despite hating crowds*, https://medium.com/@mathowie/an-introverts-guide-to-
better-presentations-be7e772b2cb5. [Accessed 10 November 2014.]

Hepworth, M., Harrison, J. and James, N. (2003) Information Needs of People with
Multiple Sclerosis and the Implications for Information Provision Based on a
National UK Survey, *Aslib Proceedings*, **55** (5/6), 290–303.

Hilyer, L. A. (2008) *Presentations for Librarians: a complete guide to creating effective learner-
centred presentations*, Chandos Publishing, Oxford.

Irving, R. and Smith, C. (1998) *No Sweat! the indispensable guide to reports and dissertations*,
Institute of Management Foundation, London.

Jay, A. (1993) *Effective Presentation*, Pitman and the Institute of Management, London.

Leech, T. (2004) *How to Prepare, Stage, and Deliver Winning Presentations*, 3rd edn,
American Management Association, New York, NY.

May, C. B. and May, G. S. (2009) *Effective Writing: a handbook for accountants*, 8th edn,
Prentice Hall, Upper Saddle River, NJ.

McKillip, J. A. (1987) *Need Analysis: tools for the human services and education*, Applied
Social Research Methods, 10, SAGE Publications, Newbury Park, CA.

NHS Bolton Library (2012) *Public Health Information Needs Analysis 2012*, Bolton,
http://blogbhm.files.wordpress.com/2012/03/nhs-bolton-library-presents-public-
health-information-needs-analysis-2012.pdf. [Accessed 10 November 2014.]

Orna, E. (2004) *Information Strategy in Practice*, Gower, Aldershot.

Ross, C. S. and Nilsen, K. (2013) *Communicating Professionally: a how-to-do-it manual for
librarians*, 3rd edn, American Library Association/Neal-Schuman, Chicago, IL.

Seeholzer, J. and Salem, J. A. (2011) Library on the Go: a focus group study of the
mobile web and the academic library, *College & Research Libraries*, **71** (1), 9–20.

Sussams, J. E. (1998) *How to Write Effective Reports*, 3rd edn, Gower, Aldershot.

University of Canberra (2014) *Report Writing*,

www.canberra.edu.au/studyskills/writing/reports. [Accessed 10 November 2014.]

Verso Consulting (2007) *Information Needs Analysis: summation report: October, 2007*, Report to the Independent Living Centre of WA (Inc), Clifton Hill, Vic, http://ilc.com.au/wp-content/uploads/2013/08/verso_summation_report__f__061007.pdf. [Accessed 10 November 2014.]

Wolcott, H. F. (2009) *Writing Up Qualitative Research*, 3rd edn, SAGE Publications, Newbury Park, CA.

Bibliography

Adams, D. (1984) *The Hitchhiker's Guide to the Galaxy*, Pan Books, London.

ADaMSoft (2014) http://adamsoft.sourceforge.net.

Afkhami, R. (2012) *Ethnicity: introductory user guide*, Economic and Social Data Service, London.

Aikenhead, G. S. (1997) Toward a First Nations Cross-cultural Science and Technology Curriculum, *Science Education,* **81**, 217–38.

Aikenhead, G. S. and Jegede, O. J. (1999) Cross-cultural Science Education: a cognitive explanation of a cultural phenomenon. *Journal of Research in Science Teaching,* **36**, 269–87.

Allard, S., Levine, K. J. and Tenopir, C. (2009) Design Engineers and Technical Professionals at Work: observing information usage in the workplace, *Journal of the American Society for Information Science and Technology,* **60** (3), 443–54.

Alreck, P. L. and Settle, R. B. (2004) *The Survey Research Handbook*, 3rd edn, McGraw-Hill/Irwin Series in Marketing, McGraw-Hill/Irwin, Boston, MA.

American Library Association (2000) *Standards for College Libraries*, American Library Association, Chicago, IL.

Andres, L. (2012) *Designing and Doing Survey Research*, SAGE Publications, Thousand Oaks, CA.

Assessment Capacities Project (2011) *Direct Observation and Key Informant Interview Techniques for Primary Data Collection during Rapid Assessments*, ACAPS, Geneva, www.acaps.org/img/disasters/direct-observation-and-key-informants-interview-techniques.pdf.

Association of College and Research Libraries (2000) *Information Literacy Competency Standards for Higher Education*, American Library Association, Chicago, IL, www.ala.org/ala/mgrps/divs/acrl/standards/standards.pdf.

Association of College and Research Libraries (2011) *Standards for Libraries in Higher*

Education, www.ala.org/acrl/standards/standardslibraries.

Australian Bureau of Statistics (2014) *TableBuilder*,
www.abs.gov.au/websitedbs/censushome.nsf/home/tablebuilder.

Australian National Statistical Service (2012) *Sample Size Calculator*,
www.nss.gov.au/nss/home.nsf/NSS/0A4A642C712719DCCA2571AB00243DC6?
opendocument.

B2B International (2014) *Using the Focus Group in Market Research*,
www.b2binternational.com/publications/market-research-focus-group.

Baker, S. L. and Lancaster, F. W. (1991) *The Measurement and Evaluation of Library
Services*, 2nd edn, Information Resources Press, Arlington, VA.

Ballard, T. H. (1989) Planning and Output Measures, *Public Libraries*, **28**, 292–4.

Barbour, R. (2008) *Introducing Qualitative Research: a student guide to the craft of doing
qualitative research*, SAGE Publications, Thousand Oaks, CA.

Bartle, P. (2007) *Community Empowerment Collective: report writing. Different kinds of reports
for mobilizers: Part C, How to write reports*,
http://cec.vcn.bc.ca/cmp/modules/rep-how.htm.

Barzun, J. (2001) *Simple and Direct: a rhetoric for writers*, 4th edn, Quill, New York, NY.

Bazeley, P. and Jackson, K. (2013) *Qualitative Data Analysis with NVivo*, 2nd edn, SAGE
Publications, London.

Beck, S. E. and Manuel, K. (2008) *Practical Research Methods for Librarians and Information
Professionals*, Neal-Schuman Publishers, New York.

Belzile, J. A. and Oberg, G. (2012) Where to Begin? Grappling with how to use
participant interaction in focus group design, *Qualitative Research*, **12**, (4), 459–72.

Biblarz, D., Bosch, S. and Sugnet, C. (eds) (2001) *Guide to Library User Needs Assessment
for Integrated Information Resource Management and Collection Development*, Scarecrow
Press, Lanham, MD.

Bishop, K. (2007) *The Collection Program in Schools: concepts, practices and information sources*,
4th edn, Library and Information Science Text Series, Libraries Unlimited,
Westport, CT.

Blakely, R. (2009) *Understanding and Using Demographic Data*, Cornell University,
Community and Rural Development Institute. PowerPoint presentation,
http://cardi.cornell.edu/cals/devsoc/outreach/cardi/training/loader.cfm?csModul
e=security/getfile&PageID=552346.

Bogdan, R. and Biklen, S. K. (2003) *Qualitative Research for Education: an introduction to
theory and methods*, 4th edn, Allyn & Bacon, Boston, MA.

Booth, C. (2009) *Informing Innovation: tracking student interest in emerging library technologies at
Ohio University*, Association of College and Research Libraries, Chicago, IL,
www.ala.org/acrl/sites/ala.org.acrl/files/content/publications/booksanddigital

resources/digital/ii-booth.pdf.

Borrego, A. and Fry, J. (2012) Measuring Researchers' Use of Scholarly Information through Social Bookmarking Data: a case study of BibSonomy, *Journal of Information Science*, **38** (3), 297–308.

Bradshaw, J. (1972) The Concept of Social Need, *New Society*, 30 March, 640–3.

Broadus, R. N. (1981) *Selecting Materials for Libraries*, 2nd edn, H. W. Wilson, New York.

Brooks-Kieffer, J. (2010) Yielding to Persuasion: library data's hazardous surfaces. In Orcutt, D. (ed.), *Library Data: empowering practice and persuasion*, ABC-CLIO/Libraries Unlimited, Santa Barbara, CA.

Bryman, A. (2008) The End of the Paradigm Wars? In Alasuutari, P., Bickman, L. and Brannan, J. (eds), *The SAGE Handbook of Social Research Methods*, SAGE Publications, London, 13–25.

Bryman, A. (2012) *Social Research Methods*, 4th edn, Oxford University Press, Oxford. Companion website http://global.oup.com/uk/orc/sociology/brymansrm4e.

Bryman, A. and Bell, E. (2011) *Business Research Methods*, 3rd edn, Oxford University Press, Oxford.

Burchfield, R. W. (2004) *Fowler's Modern English Usage*, rev. 3rd edn, Oxford University Press, Oxford.

Burns, R. B. (1997) *Introduction to Research Methods*, 3rd edn, Addison Wesley Longman Australia, South Melbourne.

Burton, J. K. and Merrill, P. F. (1977) Needs Assessment: goals, needs, and priorities. In Briggs, L. J. (ed.), *Instructional Design*, Educational Technology Publications, Englewood Cliffs, NJ.

Calvert, P. and Pope, A. (2005) Telephone Survey Research for Library Managers. *Library Management*, **26** (3), 139–51.

Cayley, R. (2014) *Explorations of Style: a blog about academic writing*, http://explorationsofstyle.com.

Chambliss, D. F. and Schutt, R. K. (2013) *Making Sense of the Social World: methods of investigation*, 4th edn, SAGE Publications, Thousand Oaks, CA.

Chang, S-J. L. (2009) Information Research in Leisure: implications from an empirical study of backpackers, *Library Trends*, **57** (4), 711–68.

Charles, S. and Webb, A. (1986) *The Economic Approach to Social Policy*, Wheatsheaf Books, Brighton.

Chatman, E. A. (1990) Alienation Theory: application of a conceptual framework to a study of information among janitors, *RQ*, **29** (3), 355–68.

Chatman, E. A. (1992) *The Information World of Retired Women*, Greenwood Press, Westport, CT.

Chatman, E. A. and Pendleton, V. E. M. (1995) Knowledge Gap, Information-Seeking and the Poor, *Reference Librarian*, **49–50**, 135–45.

Choo, C. W. (2001) *Information Management for the Intelligent Organization: the art of scanning the environment*, 3rd edn, ASIST Monograph Series, Medford, NJ, Information Today.

Chowdhury, G. G. and Chowdhury S. (2011) *Information Users and Usability in the Digital Age*, Neal-Schuman Publishers, New York, NY.

Christensen, L. B., Johnson, R. B. and Turner, L. A. (2011) *Research Methods, Design and Analysis*, 11th edn, Allyn & Bacon, Boston, MA.

Clark, P. M. (1983) *New Approaches to the Measurement of Public Library Use by Individual Patrons*, University of Illinois, Graduate School of Library and Information Science, Urbana, IL.

Cohn, J. M., Kelsey, A. L. and Fiels, K. M. (2002) *Planning for Integrated Systems and Technologies: a how-to-do-it manual for librarians*, 2nd rev. edn, Facet Publishing, London.

Colmar Brunton Research (2009) *Financial Investors' Information Needs: final*, Retirement Commission, Wellington, NZ, http://ndhadeliver.natlib.govt.nz/delivery/DeliveryManagerServlet?dps_pid=IE53 06574&dps_custom_att_1=ilsdb.

Community Tool Box (2014) *Conducting Focus Groups*, http://ctb.ku.edu/en/table-of-contents/assessment/assessing-community-needs-and-resources/conduct-focus-gr oups/main.

Connaway, L. S. and Powell, R. R. (2010) *Basic Research Methods for Librarians*, 5th edn, Library and Information Science Text Series, ABC-CLIO/Libraries Unlimited, Santa Barbara, CA.

Content-analysis.de (2013) *Resources Related to Content Analysis and Text Analysis*, www.content-analysis.de.

Coote, H. and Batchelor, B. (1997) *How to Market Your Library Service Effectively*, 2nd edn, Aslib, London.

Corbin, J. and Strauss, A. (2008) *Basics of Qualitative Research: techniques and procedures for developing grounded theory*, 3rd edn, SAGE Publications, Thousand Oaks, CA.

Cornell University. Community and Regional Development Institute (CaRDI) (2014) http://cardi.cornell.edu/.

Cornell University. Cornell Office for Research on Evaluation (2014) https://core.human.cornell.edu/about.

COUNTER (2014) www.projectcounter.org.

Creative Research Systems (2014) *The Survey System*, www.surveysystem.com.

Creswell, J. W. (2014) *Research Design: qualitative, quantitative and mixed methods approaches*, 4th edn, SAGE Publications, Thousand Oaks, CA.

Cullen, R. and Calvert, P. J. (2004) Organisational Factors Affecting the Delivery of

Service Quality in Academic Libraries. In Parker, S. (ed.), *Library Measures to Fill the Void: addressing the outcomes*, Emerald, Bradford, 155–72.

Cutler, J. (2005) *The Cross-cultural Communication Trainer's Manual*, 2 vols, Gower Publishing, Aldershot.

DanielSoper.com (2014) *Statistics Calculators Version 3.0*, www.danielsoper.com/statcalc3/default.aspx.

Davies, K. (2009) Quantifying the Information Needs of Doctors in the U.K. Using Clinical Librarians, *Health Information and Libraries Journal*, **26** (4), 289–97.

Davies, K. (2011) Information Needs and Barriers to Accessing Electronic Information: hospital-based physicians compared to primary care physicians, *Journal of Hospital Librarianship*, **11** (3), 249–60.

De Saez, E. E. (2002) *Marketing Concepts for Libraries and Information Services*, Facet Publishing, London.

Digital Analytics Association (2014) *The Official DAA Definition of Web Analytics*, www.digitalanalyticsassociation.org/?page=aboutus.

Digital Methods Initiative (2013) *Qualitative Content Analysis*, www.digitalmethods.net/MoM/QualContentAnalysis.

Document Foundation (2013) *LibreOffice 4.1. Calc Guide: working with spreadsheets*, https://wiki.documentfoundation.org/images/4/47/CG41-CalcGuideLO.pdf.

Dowd, N., Evangeliste, M. and Silberman, J. (2010) *Bite-sized Marketing: realistic solutions for the overworked librarian*, American Library Association, Chicago, IL.

Economic and Social Research Council, the Researcher Development Initiative, and the Institute of Education at the University of London (n.d.). *The Research Ethics Guidebook: a resource for social scientists*, ESRC, London, www.ethicsguidebook.ac.uk.

Excel Easy (2014) *T-Test*, www.excel-easy.com/examples/t-test.html.

Fan, W. and Gordon, M. (2014) Unveiling the Power of Social Media Analytics, *Communications of the ACM*, **57** (6), 74–81, http://cacm.acm.org/magazines/2014/6/175163-the-power-of-social-media-analytics/abstract.

Fisher, C. B. and Anushka, A. E. (2008) Research Ethics in Social Science. In Alasuutari, P., Bickman, L. and Brannen, J. (eds), *The SAGE Handbook of Social Research Methods*, SAGE Publications, London, 95–109.

Forsyth, P. (2010). *How to Write Reports and Proposals*, rev. 2nd edn, Kogan Page, London.

Fourie, I. and Bothma, T. (2007) Information Seeking: an overview of web tracking and the criteria for tracking software, *Aslib Proceedings*, **59** (3), 264–84, http://137.215.9.22/bitstream/handle/2263/5834/Fourie_Information(2007).pdf?sequence=1.

Gerring, J. (2012) *Social Science Methodology: a united framework*, 2nd edn, Cambridge

University Press, Cambridge.

Gibbs, G. R. (2002) *Qualitative Data Analysis: explorations with NVivo*, Open University Press, Milton Keynes.

Gibbs, G. R. (2007) *Analyzing Qualitative Data*, SAGE Publications, London.

Glaser, J. and Laude, G. (2013) Life with and without Coding: two methods for early-stage data analysis in qualitative research aiming at causal explanations, *Forum Qualitative Sozialforschung/Forum: Qualitative Social Research*, **14** (2), Art. 5, www.qualitative-research.net/index.php/fqs/article/view/1886/3528.

Glesne, C. (2011) *Becoming Qualitative Researchers: an introduction*, 4th edn, Pearson, Boston, MA.

Glitz, B. (1998) *Focus Groups for Libraries and Librarians*, Forbes Custom Publications, New York, NY.

Gob, R., McCollin, C. and Ramalhoto, M. F. (2007) Ordinal Methodology in the Analysis of Likert Scales, *Quality & Quantity*, **41** (5), 601–26.

Gobo, G. (2008) *Doing Ethnography*, SAGE Publications, London. Companion website www.sagepub.co.uk/gobo.

Gomm, R. (2008) *Social Research Methodology: a critical introduction*, 2nd edn, Palgrave Macmillan, Basingstoke.

Gorman, G. E. and Clayton, P. R. (2005) *Qualitative Research for the Information Professional: a practical handbook*, 2nd edn, Facet Publishing, London.

Gowers, E. and Gowers, R. (2014) *Plain Words*, Penguin/Particular Books, London.

Greenbaum, T. L. (2000) *Moderating Focus Groups: a practical guide for group facilitation*, SAGE Publications, Thousand Oaks, CA.

Grefsheim, S. F. and Rankin, J. A. (2007) Information Needs and Information Seeking in a Biomedical Research Setting: a study of scientists and science administrators, *Journal of the Medical Library Association*, **95** (4), 426–34.

Grover, R. J., Greer, R. C., and Agada, J. (2010) *Assessing Information Needs: managing transformative library services*, ABC-CLIO/Libraries Unlimited, Santa Barbara, CA.

Gubriam, J. F., Holstein, J. A., Marvasti, A. B. and McKinney, K. D. (eds) (2012) *The SAGE Handbook of Interview Research: the complexity of the craft*, 2nd edn, SAGE Publications, Thousand Oaks, CA.

Guiltinan J. P., Paul, G. W. and Madden, T. J. (1997) *Marketing Management: strategies and programs*, 6th edn, McGraw-Hill, Boston, MA.

Gupta, K., Sleezer, C. M. and Russ-Eft, D. F. (2007) *A Practical Guide to Needs Assessment*, 2nd edn, John Wiley and Sons/Pfeiffer, San Francisco, CA.

Harris, L. K. (2008) *Library User Needs Analysis Report*, http://works.bepress.com/lindsay_harris/3.

Harris, N. (2003) *DELIVER: user needs analysis report*,

www.jisc.ac.uk/whatwedo/programmes/divle/finalreports.aspx.

Harvard University, Kennedy School, Library and Information Services (2014) *U.S. Government Information Sources*, http://guides.library.harvard.edu/hks/us_government_information.

Haughey, M. (2013) *An Introvert's Guide to Better Presentations: improving your public speaking despite hating crowds*, https://medium.com/@mathowie/an-introverts-guide-to-better-presentations-be7e772b2cb5.

Hayslett, M. M. and Wildemuth, B. M. (2004) Pixels or Pencils? The Relative Effectiveness of Web-based Versus Paper Surveys, *Library & Information Science Research*, **26** (1), 73–93.

Henczel, S. (2005) To Be Truly Accountable to Your Clients, Identify Their Needs, *Information Outlook*, **9** (2), 32–3.

Hennen, T. (2002) Great American Public Libraries: the 2002 HAPLR rankings: the eagerly awaited – if overdue – measure of the nation's public libraries, *American Libraries*, **33** (9), 64–8.

Hennink, M. M. (2007) *International Focus Group Research: a handbook for the health and social sciences*, Cambridge University Press, Cambridge.

Hepworth, M., Harrison, J. and James, N. (2003) Information Needs of People with Multiple Sclerosis and the Implications for Information Provision Based on a National UK Survey, *Aslib Proceedings*, **55** (5/6), 290–303.

Herman, E. and Nicholas, D. (2010) The Information Enfranchisement of the Digital Consumer, *Aslib Proceedings: new information perspectives*, **62** (3), 245–60.

Hilyer, L. A. (2008) *Presentations for Librarians: a complete guide to creating effective learner-centred presentations*, Chandos Publishing, Oxford.

Hofstede, G. and Hofstede, G. J. (2010) *Cultures and Organizations: software of the mind. Intercultural cooperation and its importance for survival*, 3rd edn, McGraw-Hill, New York, NY.

How Stuff Works (2014) *How Microsoft Bing Works*, http://computer.howstuffworks.com/internet/basics/microsoft-bing2.htm.

Huitt, W. (2007) Maslow's hierarchy of needs, *Educational Psychology Interactive*, Valdosta State University, Valdosta, GA, www.edpsycinteractive.org/topics/regsys/maslow.html.

IBM (2014) SPSS software: predictive analytics software and solutions, www-01.ibm.com.

International Standards Organization (2008) ISO 11620: *Information and Documentation – Library Performance Indicators*, Geneva.

Irving, R. and Smith, C. (1998) *No Sweat! the indispensable guide to reports and dissertations*, Institute of Management Foundation, London.

Jackson, N. M. (2011) *Questionnaire Design Issues in Longitudinal and Repeated Cross-sectional Surveys*, Duke University, Durham, NC, dism.ssri.duke.edu/pdfs/Full%20report%20final%203-7-12.pdf.

Jansen, B. J. (2009) *Understanding User-Web Interactions via Web Analytics*, Morgan & Claypool, San Rafael, CA.

Jay, A. (1993) *Effective Presentation*, Pitman and the Institute of Management, London.

Jegede, O. (1995) Collateral Learning and the Eco-cultural Paradigm in Science and Mathematics Education in Africa, *Studies in Science Education*, **25**, 97–137.

Joubert, D. J. and Lee, T. P. (2007) Empowering Your Institution Through Assessment, *Journal of the Medical Library Association*, **95** (1), 46–53.

Kahle, R. W. (2007) *Dominators, Cynics and Wallflowers: practical strategies for moderating meaningful focus groups*, Paramount Market Publishing, Ithaca, NY.

Kamberlis, G. and Dimitriadis, G. (2008) Focus Groups: strategic articulations of pedagogy, politics, and inquiry. In Dinzin, N. K. and Lincoln, Y. S. (eds), *Collecting and Interpreting Qualitative Materials*, 3rd edn, SAGE Publications, Thousand Oaks, CA.

Kaufman, R. and English, F. W. (1979) *Needs Assessment: concept and application*, Educational Technology Publications, Englewood Cliffs, NJ.

Kellehear, A. (1993) *The Unobtrusive Researcher: a guide to methods*, Allen & Unwin, St Leonards, NSW.

Kennedy, M. R. and LaGuardia, C. (2013) *Marketing Your Library's Electronic Resources: a how-to-do-it manual*, Facet Publishing, London.

Knepp, A., White, K. and McCormack, F. (2011) Leveraging a Needs Assessment to Enhance Service, *Information Outlook*, **15** (7) 19–21, 36.

Kopycinski, D. and Sandro, K. (2007) *User Surveys in College Libraries*, Association of College and Research Libraries, Chicago, IL.

Kramer, S. S., Martin, J. R., Schlimgen, J. B., Slack, M. K. and Martin, J. (2011) Effectiveness of a Liaison Program in Meeting Information Needs of College of Pharmacy Faculty, *Medical Reference Services Quarterly*, **30** (1), 31–41.

Krueger, R. A. and Casey, M. A. (2015) *Focus Groups: a practical guide to applied research*, 5th edn, SAGE Publications, Thousand Oaks, CA.

Leech, T. (2004) *How to Prepare, Stage, and Deliver Winning Presentations*, 3rd edn, American Management Association, New York, NY.

Leedy, P. D. and Ormrod, J. E. (2013) *Practical Research: planning and design*, 10th edn, Pearson, Boston, MA.

Lehmann, D. R. and Winer, R. S. (2002) *Analysis for Marketing Planning*, 5th edn, McGraw-Hill/Irwin, Boston, MA.

Leigh, D., Watkins, R., Platt, W. A. and Kaufman, R. (2000) Alternate Models of

Needs Assessment: selecting the right one for your organization, *Human Resource Development Quarterly*, **11** (1), 87–94.

Leland, E. (2011) *A Few Good Online Survey Tools*, www.idealware.org/articles/fgt_online_surveys.php.

Lewis, S. (2008) E-book Discovery and Use Behaviour Is Complex, *Evidence Based Library & Information Practice*, **3** (2), 38–41.

Li, H. and Rao, N. (2009) Multiple Literacies: beliefs and related practices among Chinese kindergarten teachers, *Knowledge Management & E-Learning: an international journal*, **1** (4), 269–84, www.kmel-journal.org/ojs/index.php/online-publication/article/viewFile/40/31.

Liamputtong, P. (2011) *Focus Group Methodology: principles and practice,* SAGE Publications, Los Angeles, CA.

Linstone, H. A. and Turoff, M. (1975) *The Delphi Method: techniques and applications*, AddisonWesley, Reading, MA.

The Listening Resource (2012) www.qualitative-researcher.com.

Luke, A. and Kapitzke, C. (1999) Literacies and Libraries: archives and cybraries, *Curriculum Studies* **7** (3), 467–91.

MacDonald, T. (1993) *Te Ara Tika: Maori and libraries: a research report*, New Zealand Library and Information Association, Wellington.

Maddock, M. N. (1981) Science Education: an anthropological viewpoint, *Studies in Science Education*, **8**, 1–26.

Makri, S. and Warwick, C. (2010) Information for Inspiration: understanding architects' information seeking and use behaviors to inform design, *Journal of the American Society for Information Science and Technology* **61** (9), 1745–70.

Malibu Community Library (2005) *Community Library Needs Assessment,* County of Los Angeles Public Library, Los Angeles, CA, www.malibucity.org/AgendaCenter/ViewFile/Agenda/10302013-324.

Mangione, T. W. (1995) *Mail Surveys: improving the quality*, SAGE Publications, Thousand Oaks, CA.

Manjarrez, C. and Shoembs, K. (2011) *Who's in the Queue? A Demographic Analysis of Public Access Computer Users and Uses in U.S. Public Libraries*, Institute of Museum and Library Services, Washington, DC.

Marcella, R. and Baxter, G. (1999) A National Survey of the Citizenship Information Needs of the General Public, *Aslib Proceedings,* **51** (4), 115–21.

Marcella, R. and Baxter, G. (2000) Citizenship Information Needs in the UK: results of a national survey of the general public by personal doorstep interview, *Aslib Proceedings*, **52** (3), 115–23.

Marchionini, G., Plaisant, C. and Komlodi, A. (1996) *Users' Needs Assessment for the*

Library of Congress' National Digital Library, Computer Science Technical Report Series, University of Maryland, Human-Computer Interaction Laboratory, Center for Automation Research, College Park, MD.

Maslow, A. (1954) *Motivation and Personality*, Harper & Row, New York, NY.

Matthews, J. R. (2002) *The Bottom Line: determining and communicating the value of the special library*, Libraries Unlimited, Westport, CT.

Matthews, J. R. (2004) *Measuring for Results: the dimensions of public library effectiveness*, Libraries Unlimited, Westport, CT.

May, C. B. and May, G. S. (2009) *Effective Writing: a handbook for accountants*, 8th edn, Prentice Hall, Upper Saddle River, NJ.

McClelland, S. (1994) Training Needs Assessment Data Gathering Methods: part 4, on-site observations, *Journal of European Industrial Training*, **18** (5), 4–7.

McKenzie, J. F., Neiger, B. L. and Thackeray, R. (2012) *Planning, Implementing and Evaluating Health Promotion Programs: a primer*, 6th edn, Pearson/Benjamin Cummings, San Francisco, CA.

McKillip, J. A. (1987) *Need Analysis: tools for the human services and education*, Applied Social Research Methods, 10, SAGE Publications, Newbury Park, CA.

McNabb, D. L. (2008) *Research Methods in Public Administration and Nonprofit Management: quantitative and qualitative approaches*, 2nd edn, M. E. Sharpe, Armonk, NY.

Metoyer-Duran, C. (1993) *Gatekeepers in Ethnolinguistic Communities*, Ablex Publishing, Norwood, NJ.

Millar, M. M. and Dillman, D. A. (2011) Improving Response to Web and Mixed-mode Surveys, *Public Opinion Quarterly*, **75** (2), 249–69.

Millward, L. J. (1995) Focus Groups. In Breakwell, G. M., Hammond, S. and Fife-Shaw, C. (eds), *Research Methods in Psychology*, SAGE Publications, London.

Monsour, M. (2012) Libraries Innovate with New Financial Education Programs, *Public Libraries* **51** (2), 36–43.

Mora, M. (2013) *Three Popular Online Survey Tools – What They Give For Free*, www.relevantinsights.com/free-online-survey-tools.

Nason, L. (2007) The Farmer in the Library: information needs of farmers and how the rural public library can fulfill them, *Rural Libraries*, **27** (2), 19–45.

Neuman, W. L. (2011) *Social Research Methods: qualitative and quantitative approaches*, 7th edn, Allyn & Bacon, Boston, MA.

New Zealand. Department of Statistics (1995) *A Guide to Good Survey Design*, 2nd edn, Wellington, New Zealand, www.stats.govt.nz/methods/survey-design-data-collection/guide-to-good-survey-design-2nd-edition.aspx.

NHS Bolton Library (2012) *Public Health Information Needs Analysis 2012*, Bolton, http://blogbhm.files.wordpress.com/2012/03/nhs-bolton-library-presents-public-health-information-needs-analysis-2012.pdf.

Nicholas, D. (1997) Understanding End-users. In Scammell, A. (ed.), *Handbook of Special Librarianship and Information Work*, 7th edn, Aslib, London, 113–44.

Nicholas, D. (2000) *Assessing Information Needs: tools, techniques and concepts for the internet age,* 2nd edn, The Association for Information Management and Information Management International, London.

Nicholas, D. and Herman, E. (2009) *Assessing Information Needs in the Age of the Digital Consumer,* 3rd edn, Routledge, London.

Norwood, G. (1999, rev. 2014) Maslow's hierarchy of needs, *Deepermind,* www.deepermind.com/20maslow.htm.

Oliver, P. (2012) *Succeeding with Your Literature Review: a handbook for students*, Open University Press, Maidenhead.

Online QDA (2012) http://onlineqda.hud.ac.uk/Intro_QDA/what_is_qda.php.

Open University (2014) *Conducting an Interview,* http://www2.open.ac.uk/students/skillsforstudy/conducting-an-interview.php.

Orna, E. (2004) *Information Strategy in Practice*, Gower, Aldershot.

Osborne, J. W. (2013) *Best Practices in Data Cleaning: a complete guide to everything you need to do before and after collecting your data*, SAGE Publications, Thousand Oaks, CA.

Oxford English Dictionary 3rd edn Online (2010) Oxford University Press, Oxford. [Access through institutional subscribers.]

Pavlichev, A. (2004) Population. In Lewis-Beck, M. S., Bryman, A. and Liao, T. F. (eds), *The SAGE Encyclopedia of Social Science Research Methods. Volume 2*, SAGE Publications, Thousand Oaks, CA, 835–6.

Penner, K. (2009) Information Needs and Behaviours of Theology Students at the International Baptist Theological Seminary, *Theological Librarianship*, **2** (2), 51–80.

Penzhorn, C. (2002) The Use of Participatory Research as an Alternative Approach for Information Needs Research, *Aslib Proceedings*, **54** (4), 240–50.

Percy-Smith, J. (1996) Introduction: assessing needs – theory and practice, in Percy-Smith, J. (ed.), *Needs Assessment in Public Policy*, Open University Press, Milton Keynes, 3–10.

Perryman, C. L. and Wildemuth, B. M. (2009) Studying Special Populations. In Wildemuth, B. M., *Applications of Social Research Methods to Questions in Information and Library Science*, Libraries Unlimited, Westport, CT, 138–44.

Pew Research Center (2014) *Questionnaire Design,* www.people-press.org/methodology/questionnaire-design.

Pickard, A. J. (2013) *Research Methods in Information,* 2nd edn, Facet Publishing, London.

Posavac, E. J. (2013) Program Evaluation. Pearson New International Edition: methods and case studies, 8th edn, Pearson, San Francisco, CA.

Potter, N. (2012) *The Library Marketing Toolkit*, Facet Publishing, London.

Powell, R. (2006) Evaluation Research: an overview, *Library Trends*, **55** (1), 102–20.

Project Management with an Interactive Online Gantt Chart (2014) Smartsheet.com, www.smartsheet.com/online-gantt-chart.

Punch, K. F. (2014) *Introduction to Social Research: quantitative & qualitative approaches*, 3rd edn, SAGE Publications, London. Companion website www.uk.sagepub.com/punch3e/main.htm.

Randell, R., Mitchell, N., Thompson, C., McCaughan, D. and Dowding, D. (2009) From Pull to Push: understanding nurses' information needs, *Health Informatics Journal*, **15** (2), 75–85.

Reviere, R., Carter, C. C., Berkowitz, S. and Ferguson, C. G. (1996) Preface, in Reviere, R. et al. (eds), *Needs Assessment: a creative and practical guide for social scientists*, Taylor & Francis, Basingstoke, xi–xiii.

Reviere, R., Carter, C. C., Berkowitz, S. and Ferguson, C. G. (eds) (1996) *Needs Assessment: a creative and practical guide for social scientists*, Taylor & Francis, Basingstoke.

Robertson, J. (2005) *Conducting Intranet Needs Assessment*, www.steptwo.com.au/papers/kmc_needsanalysis/index.html.

Roddy, K. (2005) Community Profiling, *Library + Information Update*, **4** (5), 40–1.

Ross, C. S. and Nilsen, K. (2013) *Communicating Professionally: a how-to-do-it manual for librarians*, 3rd edn, American Library Association/Neal-Schuman, Chicago, IL.

Rossi, P. H. and Freeman, H. E. (1985) *Evaluation: a systematic approach*, SAGE Publications, Beverley Hills, CA.

Rossiter, N. (2008) *Marketing the Best Deal in Town: your library: where is your purple owl?* Chandos Information Professional Series, Chandos Publishing, Witney.

Rouse, M. (2014) *Gantt Chart*, SearchSoftwareQuality.com, http://searchsoftwarequality.techtarget.com/definition/Gantt-chart.

Rowley, J. (2006) *Information Marketing*, 2nd edn, Ashgate Publishing, Aldershot.

Ryan, G. and Valverde, M. (2005) Waiting for Service on the Internet: defining the phenomenon and identifying the situations, *Internet Research*, **15** (2), 220–40.

Scacciaferro, J., Goode, S. and Frausto, D. (2009) Using Photovoice as Participatory Needs Assessment with Youth at a Latino Youth Action Center, *Undergraduate Research Journal for the Human Sciences*, **8**, www.kon.org/urc/v8/scacciaferro.html.

Scott, J. (2013) *Social Network Analysis*, 3rd edn, SAGE Publications, London.

Search Engine Watch (2014) http://searchenginewatch.com.

Secker, J. (2005) DELIVERing Library Resources to the Virtual Learning Environment, *Program: electronic library and information systems*, **39** (1), 39–49.

Seeholzer, J. and Salem, J. A. (2011) Library on the Go: a focus group study of the mobile web and the academic library, *College & Research Libraries*, **71** (1), 9–20.

Shenton, A. K. (2013) Analysis of Existing, Externally Created Material. In Pickard, A. J., *Research Methods in Information*, 2nd edn, Facet Publishing, London, 251–61.

Shep, S. (2005) Historical Investigation. In Gorman, G. E. and Clayton, P. R., *Qualitative Research for the Information Professional: a practical handbook*, 2nd edn, Facet Publishing, London, 160–81.

Shoaf, E. C. (2003) Using a Professional Moderator in Library Focus Group Research, *College & Research Libraries*, **53** (2), 124–32.

Smallwood, C., Gubnitskaia, V. and Harrod, K. (2012) *Marketing Your Library: tips and tools that work*, McFarland and Company, Jefferson, NC.

SmartDraw.com (2014) What Is Gantt? www.smartdraw.com/articles/gantt-chart/what-is-gantt-chart.htm.

Soriano, F. I. (1995) *Conducting Needs Assessments: a multidisciplinary approach*, SAGE Publications, Thousand Oaks, CA.

SRI Consulting (2005) *VALS Psychology of Markets*. Available at www.sric-bi.com/VAL.

Stanford Institute for Higher Education Research. National Center for Postsecondary Improvement (2003). *Tools for Qualitative Researchers: interviews*, http://web.stanford.edu/group/ncpi/unspecified/student_assess_toolkit/interviews.html.

Stat Trek (2014) *Teach Yourself Statistics*, http://stattrek.com.

Statistics New Zealand (2014) www.stats.govt.nz.

Stewart, D. W., Shamdasani, P. N. and Rook, D. W. (2007) *Focus Groups: theory and practice*, 2nd edn, SAGE Publications, Thousand Oaks, CA.

Stufflebeam, D. L., McCormick, C. H., Brinkerhoff, R. O. and Nelson, C. O. (1985) *Conducting Educational Needs Assessments*, Evaluation in Education and Human Services [Series], Kluwer-Nijhoff Publishing, Boston, MA.

SurveyMonkey (2014) Create Surveys, Get Answers, www.surveymonkey.com.

Sussams, J. E. (1998) *How to Write Effective Reports*, 3rd edn, Gower, Aldershot.

The Listening Resource (2012) www.qualitative-researcher.com.

Thomsett-Scott, B. C. (ed.) (2013) *Marketing with Social Media: a LITA guide*, Facet Publishing, London.

Tolich, M. and Davidson, C. (1999) *Starting Fieldwork: an introduction to qualitative research in New Zealand*, Oxford University Press, Melbourne.

Trochim, W. M. K. (2006a) Inferential Statistics. In *Research Methods Knowledge Base*, www.socialresearchmethods.net/kb/statinf.php.

Trochim, W. M. K. (2006b) *Research Methods Knowledge Base*, www.socialresearchmethods.net/kb.

Trochim, W. M. K. (2006c) Selecting Statistics. In *Research Methods Knowledge Base*, www.socialresearchmethods.net/selstat/ssstart.htm.

Troll Covey, D. (2002) Academic Library Assessment: new duties and dilemmas, *New*

Library World, **103** (1175/1176), 156–64.

UNESCO (2005) *EFA Global Monitoring Report 2006: education for all, literacy for life*, Paris, UNESCO, www.unesco.org/new/en/education/themes/leading-the-international-agenda/efareport/reports/2006-literacy.

United Kingdom National Statistics (2014) Publication Hub, www.statistics.gov.uk.

University of Canberra (2014) *Report Writing*, www.canberra.edu.au/studyskills/writing/reports.

University of the South Pacific. USP Library Survey Team (2013) *The University of the South Pacific Regional (Campus) Libraries User Satisfaction Survey Findings and Analysis*, University of the South Pacific Library, Suva.

Vaughan, L. (2001) *Statistical Methods for the Information Professional: a practical, painless approach to understanding, using and interpreting statistics*, ASIST Monograph Series, Information Today for the American Society for Information Science and Technology, Medford, NJ.

Verso Consulting (2007) *Information Needs Analysis: summation report: October, 2007*, Report to the Independent Living Centre of WA (Inc), Clifton Hill, Vic, http://ilc.com.au/wp-content/uploads/2013/08/verso_summation_report__f__061007.pdf.

Waldrip, B. G. and Taylor, P. C. (1999) Permeability of Students' World Views to Their School Views in a Non-Western Developing Country, *Journal of Research in Science Teaching*, **36** (3), 289–303.

Wallace, D. P. and Van Fleet, C. (2012) *Knowledge into Action: research and evaluation in library and information science*, ABC-CLIO/Libraries Unlimited, Santa Barbara, CA.

Watkins, R., Leigh, D., Platt, W. and Kaufman, R. (1998) Needs Assessment – a digest, review, and comparison of needs assessment literature, *Performance Improvement*, **37** (7), 40–53.

Watkins, R., West Meiers, M. and Visser, Y. L. (2012) *A Guide to Assessing Needs: essential tools for collecting information, making decisions and achieving development results*, The World Bank, Washington, DC, DOI: 10.1596/978-0-8213-8868-6.

Web Center for Social Research Methods, www.socialresearchmethods.net.

Westbrook, L. (2001) *Identifying and Analyzing User Needs: a complete handbook and ready-to-use assessment workbook with disk*, Neal-Schuman Publishers, New York.

Whiteman, N. (2013) *Undoing Ethics: rethinking practice in online research*, Springer, Heidelberg.

Whittaker, K. (1993) *The Basics of Library-Based User Services*, Library Association Publishing, London.

Wildemuth, B. M. (2009) *Applications of Social Research Methods to Questions in Information and Library Science*, Libraries Unlimited, Westport, CT.

Wildemuth, B. M. and Jordan M. W. (2009) Focus Groups. In Wildemuth, B. M. (ed.), *Applications of Social Science Research Methods to Questions in Information and Library Science*, Libraries Unlimited, Westport, CT.

Williams, R. C. (2003) *The Historian's Toolbox: a student's guide to the theory and craft of history*, M. E. Sharpe, Armonk, NY.

Wilmoth, W. S. (2007) The Effect of Smart Cards on Library Use: the Griffin Technical College case, *Georgia Library Quarterly*, **44** (2), Art. 5, 15–21.

Witkin, B. R. (1984) *Assessing Needs in Educational and Social Programs: using information to make decisions, set priorities and allocate resources*, Jossey-Bass, San Francisco, CA.

Witkin, B. R. and Altschuld, J. W. (1995) *Planning and Conducting Needs Assessments: a practical guide*, SAGE Publications, Thousand Oaks, CA.

Wolcott, H. F. (1990) *Writing up Qualitative Research*, Qualitative Research Methods [Series] 20, SAGE Publications, Newbury Park, CA.

Wolcott, H. F. (2009) *Writing Up Qualitative Research*, 3rd edn, SAGE Publications, Newbury Park, CA.

Yang, K. (2010) *Making Sense of Statistical Methods in Social Research*, SAGE Publications, London.

Yin, R. K. (2011) *Qualitative Research from Start to Finish*, Guilford Press, New York, NY.

Young, V. L. (1993) Focus on Focus Groups, *College & Research Libraries News*, **7**, July/Aug, 391–4.

Younger, P. (2010) Internet-based Information-seeking Behaviour amongst Doctors and Nurses: a short review of the literature, *Health Information and Libraries*, **27** (1), 2–10.

Zeng, D., Chen, H., Lusch, R. and Li, S.-H. (2010) Social Media Analytics and Intelligence, *IEEE Intelligent Systems*, **25** (6), 13–16, http://ieeexplore.ieee.org/stamp/stamp.jsp?tp=&arnumber=5678581.

Index